ELEMENTARY SCHOOL CURRICULUM

ELEMENTARY SCHOOL CURRICULUM
BETTER TEACHING NOW

Betty Atwell Wright / Louie T. Camp /
William K. Stosberg / Babette L. Fleming

THE MACMILLAN COMPANY, NEW YORK
COLLIER-MACMILLAN LIMITED, LONDON

The Macmillan Company
866 Third Avenue, New York, New York 10022

Collier-Macmillan Canada, Ltd., Toronto, Ontario

Library of Congress catalog card number: 74–123528

First Printing

PREFACE

This book is about elementary school curriculum for contemporary education that must give equal weight to the needs of children and the dictates of changing times—curriculum that brings children and knowledge together to form new blends of personal development and self-understanding, intellectual and aesthetic activities and appreciations, and advancing knowledge about the world of human affairs and concerns.

Curriculum is a global word that implies both the development of individuals and the learning experiences that contribute to this development. Curriculum viewed as diversified school–community situations for which teachers and parents have responsibility and through which they design with children tasks appropriate for each one's education is an awesome responsibility, but the unthinkable alternative is the development of "teacherproof" school programs and curriculum projects already being recommended by some school critics, with partial justification.

No curriculum has any meaning at all until teachers and students together, with new technology and information, bring it to life. The professional teacher uses all he is capable of learning to build bridges between theory and practice—between curriculum on paper and curriculum in fact—between the research of professional psychologists, sociologists, and philosophers and school practices that reflect these and the persistent factors and problems that characterize our times.

Psychologists, sociologists, and philosophers are engaged in academic exchanges regarding the nature of their disciplines—the goals, procedures, and appropriate places in intellectual inquiry. They rightfully expect educationists to be engaged in the business of *translating* and *applying* these disciplines into forces for curriculum development and improvement when research and concepts are appropriate for the school setting. We have made no attempt in this book to tell the reader "how much" or "what" curriculum content should be included at various age or grade levels, because to do so equates learning with the amount of time spent sitting in classrooms. Our major efforts are directed toward suggesting the *kind* and *quality* of learning experiences appropriate for children who will live more of their lives in the next century than in this one. They are also focused on applying presently available knowledge and research to elementary curriculum "lags" and illustrating gifted teaching and dynamic learning experiences in practical descriptions of curriculum development and adaptation.

The pressures for clearer and more precise curriculum designs make it imperative for the key member in curriculum, the teacher, to know the theory on which much modern teaching is based. The primary sources of knowledge which contribute to intelligent curriculum practices are psychology, sociology, and philosophy. Hence, this volume is divided into studies in these three foundation areas to introduce many concepts taken from the mass of theory which modern practices and research have determined as being the substantive base. Details on the presentations in each of the areas of psychology, sociology, and philosophy are outlined below.

Psychology as a Curriculum Force. Principles discussed in Section I pertain to such topics as innate ability, self-image, mental maturity, cognitive styles, creativity, socioeconomic environment, peers, sex differences, health, school environment, individuality, thinking processes, emotions, and assessment. Psychological theories and application of those theories in educational settings are presented to clarify these broad topics in psychological foundations.

A lack of understanding of theories of instruction, human growth and development, and evaluation of pupil growth definitely affects the teaching program. Often teachers perform their duties without understanding why. When this occurs, teaching is a routine, unproductive chore that reduces thinking and learning to a minimum, stifles creativity, and discourages the development of individuality.

Classroom scenes encompass all content areas in an effort to suggest the *kind* and *quality* of learning experience most desirable for children. These illustrations are examples from actual clinical instruction and are presented to reinforce the theories they support.

The professional teacher achieves better teaching now by knowing and using sound practices to design a curriculum that is scientific in nature rather than one that is static and stereotyped.

Sociology as a Curriculum Force. The community is society. Through interaction with the community, teachers can develop a social conscience. The emphasis, then, in Section II is on the community structure, agencies, problems, and social environment. The community is defined and discussed in terms of the functions of agencies, roles of individuals, and utilization of human and natural resources.

Section II helps teachers acquire a breadth of knowledge regarding the community in order to understand its impact on the classroom. Important social factors, including attitudes and values, mass communication, interpersonal relations, socioeconomic influences, family patterns, population, races and cultures, mobility, and narcotics are examined; instances of their influence in curriculum design are cited. Using these same topics, classroom illustrations are given which show how teachers can incorporate these social learnings into the daily life of the child.

Teachers usually reflect the social values common to their class and culture. Because of increased mobility and emphasis on desegregation, teachers are coming into contact with more and more children from differing social and economic backgrounds, and they must be able to accept, understand, and identify with all types of children. The more teachers know about the make-up of society and the structure of the community, the more effective they will be in assessing student behaviors and in establishing the dignity of each individual which can help to remedy social ills, to teach positive social values, and to bring harmonious interpersonal relations.

Philosophy as a Curriculum Force. Content regarding the various philosophies and their contributions to educational thought concludes the discussion on the three foundational studies for *Better Teaching Now*. This presentation is predicated on the assumption that teachers develop a personal teaching philosophy through knowledge and a background of experience.

Teachers must have the verbal ability to discuss educational philosophies and to support their viewpoints in guiding children, presenting instructional topics, grouping for learning, and promoting individuality. Without knowledge of the various philosophies, the teacher places his faith in teaching as he was taught or becomes a carbon copy of a model that he thinks is good. Such a teacher proves to be ineffective when confronted with unusual or new situations and feels insecure in deviating from regimented teaching. Even worse, he cannot structure learning which helps students to learn to think. And sadly, he misses the thrill of new accomplishments, of a job expertly done, and the enthusiastic feedback from students who know their teacher is outstanding.

Principles from traditionalism, pragmatism, and existentialism are cited insofar as they influence curriculum design. With these initial insights into philosophical thinking, the teacher can progress through further readings in the bibliography.

Use of the Book. As the teacher increases his knowledge in the areas which affect curriculum design and implementation of the program he becomes more secure and better able to make the decisions which result in better teaching and learning. The theoretical concepts with adaptations to the classroom are presented to stimulate thinking and to provoke discussion as to outcomes, variabilities, and alternatives in a given task or setting. As the reader develops new ideas or challenges those presented, it is recommended that a notebook be kept to provide a running account of opinions, information, problems, and ideas. Moreover, keeping ideas in a notebook will result in a permanent record of notes, readings, and class discussions.

This book is broad in scope. It introduces the reader to theory, research, and practice to stimulate his thinking and to help develop clear concepts about children and their educational programs. Whether one considers education as an art, a science, or a vocation, this book outlines, one by one, major principles that assist the teacher in developing the curriculum intelligently through personalized instruction for each boy and girl.

Freed from traditional dogmas and restrictions, the newly liberated and more professional teacher has enormous privileges and responsibilities in connection with being able to design, diagnose, prescribe, continue to learn, assess, change, and create. Teachers will be helped increasingly by other professionals and paraprofessionals, new media for content and skills acquisition, and new knowledge and conditions. Today's and tomorrow's teacher-designer-guide will use generalizations, concepts, and facts from among which they and their students will be able to select alternative units and sequences. As knowledge, facts, and conditions change, teachers must become more astute at making corresponding adjustments in children's learning experiences and judging the implications for local, national, and international education.

All of the authors are teachers who have served in varieties of situations and roles in education. They have seen the profession of teaching advance from the days of many time-consuming, nonprofessional teaching "duties" to the current new status and new hopes for personal fulfillment and social purpose. They believe that teaching is the most rewarding, challenging, and stimulating profession one can enter—and they believe, most of all, in the right of children to the best possible education that can be devised.

B. A. W.
L. T. C.
W. K. S.
B. L. F.

CONTENTS

SECTION III
Philosophy
AS A CURRICULUM FORCE

PROLOGUE

Dynamic New Roles for Teachers

As schools become more complex they require more of the professional teacher than traditional approaches to curriculum imply. As we round the corner of the twentieth century, schools must do much more than pass on accumulated knowledge and heritage. They have a responsibility to develop and use new knowledge about the human condition and to direct new knowledge and technology toward helping people enjoy effective citizenship and live better with one another.

These are not new goals for education; in fact, they have been around for some time. But they are more urgent now than ever before as bases for *affective curriculum.* A glance at some of the newer kinds of assessments for affective student behavior will confirm their validity for these times. Among these are alienation scales, attitude inventories, behavioral self-ratings, self-concept scales, emotional maturity measures, anxiety scales, interest inventories, interaction studies, intensity-of-involvement scales, personality ratings, situational tests of empathy, tests for creativity, scales for student assessment of teachers' qualities, and varieties of new kinds of achievement tests. These indicate clearly the scope of educational concerns today.

The sections of this book which follow concentrate heavily on modern concepts of curriculum that stress skills of functioning as the result of what children and their teachers learn together. This is the main difference between *curriculum static* and *curriculum developing.* The ability to apply research and theory from the fields of psychology, sociology, and philosophy makes the difference between a teacher who is just a place-holder and one who is truly effective with the now generation. For this reason, we direct this prologue to the prime force, the teacher, in dynamic curriculum development and in relation to the new roles teachers will need to assume.

1

The more familiar qualities of good teachers are friendliness, empathy, personal maturity and security, good mental and physical health, among others. These will be illustrated many times throughout this book, and are assumed. But teaching today most assuredly calls for the performance of new and generally unfamiliar functions, for the better performance of familiar functions, and for curriculum that is relevant to the lives of children who will live a larger part of their lives in the next century than in this one. These will also be illustrated often.

A professional teacher today is more than a person with new responsibilities; he is a person with new *understandings*. To understand implies a process that is never finished and the possessor of understanding will be able to function in different times and places equally well. We have selected four teaching roles we consider to be especially significant for these times. There are others we could have chosen for teachers who are going to be capable of implementing new ideas and who will not be stymied by traditional school systems that have always been inclined to look more favorably upon those who ask few questions, make no changes, and help them maintain the status quo.

As you think about the roles that are discussed here, note others that occur to you. When you are teaching, refer back to these ideas occasionally. In years to come, the notes you make now and the high hopes you have for your career as a teacher may help you maintain the courage of your convictions and revive flagging resolutions when you are tempted to conform, move on, or give up teaching entirely.

Teachers as Learners

Gone are the days when a teaching certificate guaranteed the inalienable right to "teach all common branch subjects" into infinity. Today's rapidly changing, dynamically intensified social, cultural, and intellectual revolutions have left this concept of teaching and curriculum far behind to gather dust with gaslights and horse-and-buggy whips. Teaching today requires people who are "with it," who are in step with the times and with children's needs in changing times.

Curriculum for modern living results from the teacher's ability to bring students into contact with educational research, new knowledge and technology, and changing social and cultural milieus. Teachers need not only to master what is required of them during their preservice preparation, but more importantly, to have an unusual thirst for continuous learning. Consider for a moment the following statements which are admittedly overdrawn but which do illustrate the need for continuous learning.

1. A teacher enters teaching with neophyte abilities and techniques because specialized backgrounds and field training are minimal and incomplete at college graduation.

2. School districts make contracts with professionally immature teachers whose preparation, initially minimal, is already outdated.
3. When tenure is granted after three, four, or five years, the teacher is less well prepared than when he was originally hired—especially if he has been denied stimulating opportunities for further education and innovative experimentation in the school setting.
4. By the time a teacher is considered a career teacher, his training in both curriculum content and behavioral sciences may already have reached the point of obsolescence.

In the days when teachers had only to teach reading lessons already designed around moralistic themes and when major qualifications for teaching included the ability to teach the subject matter deemed important by the employing group, a continuous learner would have been neither sought nor appreciated. Additionally, education for all the children of all the people was not a common goal for education. Thus, "the onward march of education and the systematic development of the teaching profession were painfully slow" (1). One must also wonder how much the teaching profession was retarded by the aristocracy versus common-man theme which still exists in some places today and which holds that educational practices and curriculum content are to be used "to protect the rest of society from a working class that might otherwise become vagabond and prove dangerous to life and property" (2). Historically, teachers' backgrounds and training have been cloistered, sheltered, and conditioned by attitudes and functions that limited incentives to continue learning.

As attention is directed to the vastness of already accumulated knowledge, new knowledge continues to accrue at an ever-increasing rate, and as one focuses on ways to understand and use what is already known, the new and untried beckon invitingly. The continuous learner makes certain that part of his mind is left free to focus on the implications of newly emerging knowledge and to envision the effects of new developments upon what is now being done and what is already known. Teacher-learners who would be catalysts for other lifelong learners realize that there is literally no aspect of social, political, or economic life today that remains static from one day to the next. Other professions must also cope with what is known and what is being discovered, but they do not need the same scope that teachers do. Each specialist—be he a doctor, lawyer, engineer, scientist, or other professional—copes with the known and the unknown in relation to his particular specialty. But there is no other person (other than a child's parents) who daily affects *every aspect* of a child's social, emotional, physical, and intellectual well-being more than the teacher.

Realizing that the more rapid the accumulation of knowledge the greater the problems of obsolescence, the professional teacher as a continuous learner cannot depend upon textbooks alone—they may already be obsolete by the time they are received. Even they never really arrived in schools as a result of valid educational recommendations, but rather they "started as a new kind of rite that has continued into present-day courses of study, and one can at least raise the question of the extent to which [textbooks] perpetuated" (3) various studies in public schools. Yet another deterrent to continuous learning for teachers may be schools' administrative pigeonholing of children combined with the idea that certain bodies of knowledge and certain teaching materials were for certain children. Surely these practices have affected curriculum development because "the work considered appropriate for a given level determined the content of the textbook, and then the content of the textbook came to be regarded as appropriate for the grade. In time more fundamental procedures for determining the curriculum were scarcely considered" (4).

Even as new knowledge to counteract these practices has come from the disciplines that affect education—from the fields of psychology, sociology, and philosophy—teaching–learning practices have not changed rapidly enough and schools remain in cultural and intellectual lag. The teaching profession, at the preservice and in-service levels, has often fallen into the traps of conformity sprung by administrative gimmicks in schools that concentrated on organizing children and subject matter rather than on the needs of children. Various curricula in schools and colleges have historically existed "in response to the needs created by developments in the school system" (5) rather than in response to changing social and cultural patterns and the application of new knowledge and techniques.

College students today know that social and cultural patterns not only are different, but are becoming more different at an ever-increasing rate. Any lag in recognizing and dealing with them when and as they occur puts the teacher and his students out of touch with reality and renders the school and teacher impotent. Chroniclers of change describe in detail what these changes must mean for national legislative programs, for living satisfying and meaningful lives, and for new educational programs. They usually mention the explosion of knowledge, population explosions and relocations, and technological advances. As new kinds of living accommodations and arrangements, relocations of population with attendant problems, variations of employment and retirement patterns, changing composition of populations, and long overdue demands of civil rights groups highlight the necessity for changing institutions, teacher preparation centers and school systems must take leadership in cooperative experiences for neophyte teachers as they begin their internships and as they continue in-service. If this can be accomplished, the creative, able, well-prepared teacher who is willing to continue to learn and to innovate will not find that "the school climate is often such that these abilities are forced to lie fallow" (6).

The main goal of teaching is to be able to produce students who will want to go on learning long after school is over and who will re-educate themselves many times during their lives. Lifelong learning populations do not evolve in schools that have thought in terms of "the mind as a storehouse to be filled when we should be thinking of it as an instrument to be used" (7). Positive attitudes toward personal continued learning make the difference between a professional career teacher and one who is just "marking time"—lacking stimulation, ambitions, sensitivity, and motivation. The former will motivate students in the direction of "growing their own plants instead of giving them cut flowers" (7); the latter will stultify and blight any student who has the misfortune to be associated with him.

There are even publishing companies who advertise teacherproof materials—in other words, materials with which the child can learn *in spite of the teacher!* Some scholars who have developed and experimented with new elementary school curriculum have even observed that they find "children perfectly receptive to the course but teachers wholly unprepared to handle it" (8). Not only do teachers need to be the kinds of people who are willing to handle what children can understand, but they also need to be well versed enough to make on-the-spot changes for more relevant curricular experiences when they find themselves and their students faced with obsolete materials.

If teachers are to bridge the gap between the cultures and curricula which schools have traditionally represented and those that will characterize the majority of the country's populations, they will need "curricula, teaching materials, and forms of pedagogical practice which most of our schools have scarcely dreamed of, much less developed" (9). Professional teachers know that neither they nor their students can possibly know, or need to know, all the facts—these are readily available if one learns where and how to locate them. The important abilities become *how to use knowledge, how to think critically, how to form and test hypotheses, how to envision new possibilities,* and *how to make the best choices from among many possibilities.* It is probably in these areas that the real failures of traditional curriculum exist—in the areas of human development and redevelopment—and because schools were not organized to change when the times changed. They were "turning children off when they should have been turning them on" (10).

Increasingly, curriculum is concerned with global concepts of teaching and learning, with the human aspects that impinge upon academic achievement. As people who intend to continue learning, teachers can reverse the processes of personal and academic alienation. This will involve systematic, deliberate, and immediate action using all that is known and can be learned about the behavioral and social sciences, the professional specialties of education, and allied fields of study and experience. Given today's interacting forces and their implications for the future, curriculum may be "people of all ages and in all states of being and becoming; people teaching and people being taught. The raw material of curriculum, of teaching, and of learning is at our command every day in the *people* who live, learn, teach, work, and function together" (11).

The rate of development of new knowledge about the human condition brings a new "sense of urgency to an old dilemma—how much *must* a teacher know and how much *can* a teacher know?" (12). Remembering that the significance of knowledge is not its mere acquisition and possession but, more importantly, how it is applied, let us think about the various levels of knowledge. In so doing, we see not only the boundaries and limitations of knowledge, but are also able to anticipate some of the consequences of applying knowledge.

1. There is the usual, but now rapidly accelerating, "explosion" of knowledge. This idea is familiar as the *extension of knowledge* and has the over-all effect of adding to what we already know. But with growing efficiency in processes and procedures for producing new knowledge, more effort is required of each person in order to extend his own personal knowledge and scholarship.
2. Then there is the idea of the *displacement of knowledge*. This occurs when explanations that have long been accepted are replaced by new proofs and explanations and means that some of what we think we already know must be discarded—as in, for example, scientific discoveries.
3. Finally, and of great importance to teachers, there is a growing body of dependable knowledge in relation to *areas of human activity*. As dependable knowledge replaces "hunches" and intuition, it must be used to justify educational practices and as the measure of validity of human affairs.

Fortunate is the prospective teacher who catches a feeling for the nature of applied scholarship and a thirst for continuing self-education during preservice days, because this person will continue to learn on the job. This teacher is assured the constant possibility of dynamic new experiences, the potential for being able to initiate innovative school curricula, openness to new kinds of experiences, and the continuing hope of self-fulfillment and leadership opportunities. The added power and inner strength that scholarship brings individuals will be its own reward.

Finally, the learning teacher, who is secure in his own scholarship and abilities, is mindful of children's needs to be intimately involved in their own ever-changing and ongoing learning experiences. He accepts the responsibility to involve children in curricular experiences from which they, and he, will learn continuously. He considers this privilege so important a responsibility that he will not allow it to become lost in organizational structures that reflect ways to organize children, knowledge, and skills rather than ways to help children learn and apply skills and knowledge. The ultimate goal, of course, is that the knowledge and skills be applied creatively to the daily tasks of learning from and with children, extending knowledge, accepting and applying new knowledge and techniques, and cooperating in the development of new knowledge about curriculum and learning. Then teacherproof materials can never become a reality.

Teachers as Open Individuals (13)

To be able to continue learning, teachers need to be open individuals, the kinds of people of whom Erich Fromm (14) spoke when he wrote, "The whole of life of the individual is nothing but the process of giving birth to himself."

Being "open" implies the ability to receive and profit from new knowledge, new experiences and encounters, and innovative ideas. Openness, by itself, is not enough, however. One must also react, because response to things familiar and unfamiliar is what propels individuals ahead or drives them backward. If teachers can learn to respond to new knowledge and new encounters in constructive and affective ways, students will learn to respond similarly. In tandem, teachers and students can cooperate in curricular experiences that are contemporary and continuous.

We know that learning and behavioral environments have structures and meaning—in the formal school setting and in the home–community setting. We also know that transfer of learning and innovative behavior depend upon the climate and the rewards implicit in the environment. Small children are receptive to stimuli in their environments and learn through a multisensory approach because all of their senses are at a peak. Shortly after they enter school this openness to experience—the interest in everything about them, spontaneity, questioning, and sensitivity to everything—begins to disappear. And it is a rare adult who makes it through traditional education systems with any degree of openness left. The greatest gift adults can give children is to show them that learning is a continuing process and that open individuals are valued in this changing world.

All people are receptive to stimuli in their environments and individual responses to new situations are characteristically complex, variable, and patterned by these environments. Individuals learn those responses and attitudes which are relevant to their own goals and purposes as well as to the goals and purposes of the power structure and the motivations existent in the learning and behavioral environments. People are more conditioned by traditional cultures and education to fear the unknown and untried than to welcome them.

Being open to and unafraid of newness and wonder of things is a quality that is very important for teachers if they intend to demonstrate to children that learning is a continuous process and not simply a body of knowledge and morals to be listened to, read, digested, and regurgitated. To be open and unafraid of newness does not negate all that has gone before; on the contrary, what has previously occurred constitutes the base from which every human being progresses or regresses throughout his lifetime. Schachtel (15) believes that men are capable of continued growth and development throughout their lives if they can succeed in remaining open to the world and train themselves to be capable of allocentric interests. This concept of openness, he says, is the basis of progress and creative achievement in individual life as well as in the history of mankind.

As opposed to openness, embeddedness is what happens when individuals become overly conditioned by their cultures or when they retreat from the implications of new encounters and ideas. The act of emerging from embeddedness to have direct encounter with the world implies that an individual needs first to be open to the impact of the world and, second, to respond to the impact. If one imagines a continuum of life with *embeddedness* in the far left and *openness* on the far right, and considers the encounters every individual has as he travels through life, it may be possible to plan the kinds of encounters which can be studied for their effectiveness in keeping children, young people, and adults open to learning from them.

The ability to re-examine ideas may be one of the criteria to be used in evaluating responses to new situations and degrees of openness. Adults, on the whole, are not remarkable in their ability to re-examine ideas and "if children now in school do no better than their elders in this respect, they, even more than we, will be closed off from understanding an increasingly large part of the world" (16). Adults who are incapable of re-examining ideas will affect adversely the lives of children; they will teach by example that it is safer to leave things just as they are.

The capacity for self-renewal is another behavior related to openness and is a necessary adjunct to being able to cope with rapid changes. *The Annual Report of the Carnegie Corporation* (17) notes that no one knows why some individuals seem capable of self-renewal while others seem incapable of it. It suggests that it is time to turn "to the thing that is really blocking self-development—the individual's own intricately designed, self-constructed prison; or, to put it another way, the individual's *incapacity for self-renewal*." Children do not build their own prisons. One has but to watch a child or a group of children playing informally to realize their endless sense of wonder and imagination. This is natural self-renewal which adults in children's lives should protect as a priceless natural resource. Adults in children's lives can make the difference in developing and keeping alive their own and children's capacity for self-renewal.

Gardner speaks of the necessity for building a vigorous and creative culture capable of adapting to change and getting itself out of its own rut when he says that we must have "education that fosters versatility—habits of mind that will be useful in new situations—curiosity, open-mindedness, and respect for evidence" (18). The person who retreats from new encounters and new evidence never has a chance to develop these habits of mind that will be useful in new situations; in teachers this is catastrophic.

Until teachers develop more openness, we will continue to have under-educated students. Studies show that traditional education, for example, has not caused stereotypes to be rejected and there is a great deal of additional evidence to show that the educated are no less ethnocentric or prejudiced than the uneducated. In fact, one analysis of data from national surveys and opinion groups concluded that, "on many issues the educated show as much prejudice as the less educated, and on some issues they show more" (19).

Looking closely at the antecedents of current educational practices, it is not difficult to understand why teachers for traditional schools have not needed to be open kinds of people. Teachers generally grew up, were educated, and taught in the same geographic area. Curriculum was dictated by the local culture or sect, and teachers were selected and judged according to their abilities to please the employing group. Young people today are less likely to stay in their original neighborhoods, will travel more widely and live in many diverse kinds of communites, and are more likely to have wider cross-cultural experiences. Many young people entering the teaching profession will have been involved in studying abroad, student exchange programs, or people-to-people programs in this country or another part of the world. All of these are opening up kinds of experiences and will be of great benefit in developing less embedded teachers.

Imaginative teacher preparation programs are deliberately exposing prospective teachers to a variety of situations and cultures during their undergraduate years. As for more experienced teachers, there are many who would benefit by transfer to different schools—those who have deliberately sought new teaching assignments in areas unfamiliar to them have found that the new situation or encounter itself becomes a catalyst for self-renewal, for new enthusiasms and ideas, for innovative practices, and for what Schachtel calls "intercourse with the world." This is in direct contrast to teachers who teach in the same grade level, in the same classroom, in the same school and neighborhood year after year for as long as anyone can remember. Protected by community and colleagues, they are apt to become more closed, provincial, and rigid as the years wear on.

Each individual should give thought to the kinds of diverse experiences and new encounters that are most likely to help him move along the continuum from embeddedness in his own cultural milieu to openness to the world. And individually and collectively educators should devote a great deal of thought to planning curricular experiences that will keep children's natural openness alive. If the main job of teachers is to help students discover the infinite and inexhaustible mysteries of the world in which we live, they must also seek them out. As you read this book you will find many illustrations of the ways creative teachers have found to help themselves and their students emerge from the known to the unknown and from secular to cosmopolitan understandings. Both circumstances and choice enable men to look beyond the horizon of the cultures and social groups into which they were born and to transcend them to seek the humanity of other men. Within the world into "which man is born, he can remain tied to the past, trying to fit in and thus retain the security of embeddedness, or he can try to be born more fully, to emerge from such embeddedness, and to become capable of interest in and love for the larger and richer world in which he lives" (15).

We have said that to emerge from embeddedness requires being involved in and reacting to new confrontations and encounters. To be able to do so will be a measure of our humanity and teaching professionalism; it will determine whether those teaching and those being taught will become citizens of the new world or members of lost civilizations. Open teachers will take the lead in recommending changes in curriculum content, will show active interest in new methodologies and technologies, will apply and help gather new knowledge about the human condition, will show active interest in fields of specialty other than their own, and will recognize and use constructively the social and cultural revolutions occurring today. They will trust their own judgment and abilities which will be based upon evidence they collect and analyze. They will be able to make decisions and carry them out, cooperatively and individually, and to accept successes and failures.

Knowing full well that some risk taking and trial and error are always involved in newness and openness, their continuing openness compels them to move beyond "pat answers" and easy recipes. They are energizers, catalysts who affect environment rather than just letting things happen. Their positive views of human potentiality enable them to see the relevance of new situations and people to those with which they are already familiar. They are able to bring controversial issues into classrooms for discussion without attempts at rancor or indoctrination. They have a broad interest in the entire spectrum of education, in contrast to closed teachers who care little about what colleagues are doing, interrelationships among experiences and studies their students share, what happens to students outside of the immediate classroom and the school itself, and what new learning experiences might replace better those that interest students least even though they are most familiar to the teacher. The influence of open teachers will be seen and felt in the curricular experiences they devise and recommend.

Teachers as Creators

Today's teachers find themselves in a profession that is complicated and rapidly changing in knowledge, base, functions, and tools. Teachers who are open individuals and continuous learners have new kinds of opportunities and privileges to cooperate in the creation of relevant and imaginative curriculum.

It has been said that we are "truly the products of our times, but our times are also the product of our actions" (20). The nature of traditional teaching has been such that they have not been expected to participate in curriculum construction or policy making; in fact, studies show that a great deal of the work done by teachers could be done by clerks and paraprofessionals. This is changing and many of the traditional, routinized, and unprofessional tasks once performed by teachers are being taken over by paraprofessionals and machines. Freed of old restrictions and concepts about teaching, the modern teacher can now pay more attention to the creative teaching act and to innovative school programs.

There are some noteworthy examples of innovative, "model" schools in the country today, but by and large, it is true that:

1. Curriculum in most school systems is a patchwork of cut-ups and paste-ups arranged by curriculum "committees" in curriculum "guides" that mainly collect dust until someone gathers them up for the next "revision."
2. Learning environments have not really changed much in the past century and individual differences are still largely ignored in most schools.
3. Isolation and stereotyping of minority group youngsters is still occurring after many years of effort on the part of our courts, civil rights groups, and concerned parents to desegregate schools and faculties.
4. Standardized testing and rote memorization still prevail and validated educational research has not permeated general school practices.
5. Creativity is still stifled by conformity and rigid curricula and teaching.
6. What teachers are supposed to teach and children are supposed to learn are still prescribed and diagnosed by persons other than teachers and children.
7. The arts and humanities still take a back seat in school programs; in fact, there are many educators and laymen who still call them "frills."
8. Teacher welfare programs often ignore the improvement of teaching professionalism and the best interests of children.
9. Pupil and parental involvement in selecting learning experiences is largely resented and ignored.
10. There is still more concern for administrative gimmicks that pigeonhole children than for the learning experiences they should be having.

There is great need for teachers who can design and create new kinds of learning experiences with their students and with their colleagues. Manolakes (21) calls teachers major creators and says that the elementary school we need is not an unattainable goal or ideal to be contemplated for some distant, future date, nor is it a seedling that must await the nurture of yet-undiscovered techniques or resources. Its major creators are professional people and others well prepared, knowledgeable, and willing, whose actions are consistent with their "commitments to children . . . and to sound ways of learning and growth. Each child travels this road but once" (21).

Many people will say that they are not creative, but those who have studied creativity say that it is a characteristic possessed in different and unique degrees by all human beings, and that what creativity really means is the ability to produce something new, unique, original, or nonexistent before in the experience of that individual (22). A creative act helps individuals find new unities and see new relationships or similarities not understood before. Isn't this, after all, what teaching is all about?

Scholars have identified more than fifty factors of the intellect that seem to have a bearing on creativity (23). These will be discussed in more detail in relation to psychology as a curriculum force. Other scholars have studied the neurotogenic forces that hinder creative, intellectual development and one of these believes that as a result of "our failure to face up to the neurotogenic forces in the educational process, erudition and creativity are often at war with one another. *To put it more precisely*, creativity rarely survives the educational rat race . . ." (24). Teachers and students who let their imagination and creativity work for them are more fully functioning individuals, but Torrance states that "a student who lets his imagination have free rein, as in creative writing or painting, takes a calculated risk" (25). He and his associates, who have developed the Torrance–Minnesota Test of Creative Thinking, conclude that this is true in most classrooms for children who express unusual ideas or offer unusual productions, and that in such settings it takes a great deal of courage for a child to press for presentation of his unique ideas because they "are frequently hooted at and deprecated as silly or screwy" and subjected to teacher–peer disapproval.

Children react this way because teachers have been subjected to the same treatment and have reacted this way; they are simply passing on what they have learned to approve or disapprove. Children learn to read teachers rather quickly and they react in ways that will be approved by the teacher. Implicitly or explicitly, teachers let it be known that deviation will not be tolerated and will be put down with the techniques most devastating to a child—derision and sarcasm. Or they let it be known that original ideas and diverse opinions will be welcomed and reward them with the techniques most desired by a child—approval and praise.

In sharp contrast to the days when teachers shut their classroom doors and jealously guarded their own teaching "secrets," the teacher–creator needed in today's schools welcomes brainstorming with colleagues about curriculum, techniques, and other problems requiring concentrated attention. Newer, more innovative school settings find teachers participating in team efforts, planning together for common groups of children, sharing their talents and insights, observing and constructively criticizing one another, and sharing and building upon one another's ideas. There are a number of ways teachers can think about their own abilities to create, and there are vast studies that will help them to be more creative personally and with their students. The following research briefs could be used by an undergraduate class of prospective teachers or by a group of teachers in the field to get them started:

1. With the discovery of 50 or more dimensions of the mind, only a handful are currently included in our I.Q. tests (26).
2. What we are really saying is that those people who cannot learn *our* way cannot learn (27).
3. A child tends to produce in his behavior anything that the culture demands if it is in his repertory of possible responses (28).
4. It is urgent to encourage those who can think creatively. By encouraging unorthodox approaches to problems, we can benefit from the talents of imaginative persons, and nurture the attitude of initiative characteristic of a contributing life beyond school (29).

Or suppose creative thinking were to be encouraged among teachers by having them brainstorm around these research findings rather than being handed preset groupings and schedules:

1. Grouping of some kind can hardly be avoided. But we also recognize the learning gains that result from a number of different kinds of grouping procedures (30).
2. It seems probable that this [putting children in ability groups for reading or arithmetic] type of thinking persists because schools have historically been dominated by the data of curriculum construction and teaching methods rather than by evidence of growth (31).
3. The uneven growth patterns of individual children make grouping hazardous. One is never certain that a given child will long retain the personal and academic attributes governing his placement in a group (32).
4. There are those who say that homogeneous grouping offers more chance for success and happiness, eliminates snobbishness and conceit of bright pupils, and that slow children do not experience the discouragement of daily failures. These ideas are based on the assumption that homogeneous grouping provides for better attitudes of pupils (33).
5. Although other races, other nationalities, other generations have a great deal to teach, there is little in their [suburban children's] education to familiarize them with the rich diversities of American life. In this sense, despite many enviable features in their environment, the children of suburbia are being short-changed (34).

These are just some of the concepts around which teachers should be developing their ability to create and to innovate. Teachers who have an important part in designing learning experiences for their students will never discuss curriculum in the old, narrow sense of subject matter alone. A modern concept of curriculum includes all of the experiences boys and girls have under the guidance of, or in connection with, the school. Of these, the longest remembered and the most useful in later life may be the recognition by teachers that they and their students have creative and innovative abilities that were never called into play in traditional concepts of curriculum. "When conditions are at their best, the atmosphere in the American classroom fosters and encourages a free, creative interplay of intellect and spirit between pupils and teachers and between pupil and pupil. The curriculum, ultimately, is what happens to pupils and teacher under such circumstances" (35).

Teachers as Risk Takers

Today there is much more that is unknown than is known. To be true voyagers on the uncharted sea of learning, teachers must not only be continuous learners, open individuals, and creators but they must also be risk takers. The unknown has always been frightening and teaching for the unknown is an awesome responsibility.

The teaching profession has already had to take some courageous stands that pose threats to long-held ideas, attitudes, and values. In the summer of 1969 the largest teachers' group, the NEA, which has over a million members, even rebuked the President of the United States when he relaxed school desegregation deadlines for some states that had not yet complied with Supreme Court orders. They demanded at their annual conference that there be *no deviation from full compliance* with desegregation orders. They stated emphatically that "we must be realistic, we must be loyal, we must walk tall, and stick to our desegregation timetable" (36).

Society around the world has placed an inordinate value upon the questionable virtue of avoiding innovation and conforming to the group. Teachers from grade school through graduate school have not been expected to take stands that represent personal commitments or to have personal convictions that disagree with their establishments. Local and world conditions are among the most cogent reasons why teachers can no longer afford to be neutral when everyone else can, and does, express personal convictions. Resistance to change has been characterized by some critics of educational lag as the teaching profession's disease. The people of the world are moving—emerging from centuries of isolation and embeddedness; human life spans are increasing and people "are awakening to the hopes of a full stomach, a bit of leisure, and an equal opportunity for schooling" (37) as well as their share of the other good things of life.

Who among us knows what the dimensions of life in the twenty-first century will be? As teachers assume more important roles and leadership in education, they will have to participate in developments that threaten established notions. They are the ones who will be working with young people who live more of their lives in the next century than in this one and they will be expected to participate in societal changes that will cause them to encounter strong feelings of dissension and conflict. To be able to function effectively during changing times, people must feel challenged and attracted by the changes and must be able to operate in the midst of strong feelings because they understand their own grounds for conviction and action.

If new teachers are to bridge the curriculum gaps successfully between validated research in the fields of psychology, sociology, and philosophy and what educational practice in the schools they go to actually *is,* they are going to have to take calculated risks. Lane (37) believes that self-awareness, knowing one's grounds for belief, and a sense of wonder are prerequisites in teacher preparation for the unknown. Haubrich (38) thinks that teachers must develop tolerance for ambiguity, which he describes as tolerance for things which do not match, for arguments which are not quite logical, and the ability to face the doubtful and uncertain. And Maslow (39) has written eloquently about the place that taking risks and learning to enjoy them, even when they mean hardship and pain, has in the lives of self-actualizing people. Many authorities writing about the current disruptive qualities of youth analyze them not only in terms of alienation but also in relation to the lack of any need for risk taking in legitimate, productive ways.

Fromm (14), too, reminds us that life in its mental and spiritual aspects is by necessity insecure and uncertain, and that there is certainty only in birth and death. The psychic task which a person can and must set for himself, he says, is "not to feel secure, but to be able to tolerate insecurity without panic and undue fear . . . there is complete security only in an equally complete submission to powers which are supposed to be strong and enduring, and which relieve man from the necessity of making decisions, taking risks, and having responsibilities. Free man is by necessity insecure; thinking man by necessity uncertain."

As teachers help young people translate their natural risk taking desires into constructive and beneficial behaviors that make sense to them, they must be willing to use new insights gained from phenomenological psychologists, humanists, and sociologists which are of greater value in understanding human learning than nineteenth-century principles of psychology that equated human learning with animal learning. Considerable risk taking is going to be involved in finding better ways to measure human growth, develop more relevant curriculum, devise more defensible ways to group and regroup for modern curriculum, and investigate new uses for automated devices and paraprofessional assistance.

It is going to take courage to buck the tides that block individualization of instruction in the majority of the nation's schools, perpetuate antiquated grading and marking systems, institutionalize level concepts of teaching and learning, and equate actual learning with the amount of time spent sitting in classrooms. There is risk in holding each student responsible for his own progress in learning, because risk taking conflicts with bureaucratic systemization. Those who are not prepared to deal with these forces, to run the risk of engagement and contribute to the solution of the problems of school and society, would be wise to choose a profession other than teaching. There is nothing they can contribute to education if they are unprepared to face a world that is becoming more dangerous and ambiguous and dare to deal with it for the sake of the young people they hope to lead into it.

The coming together of teachers and young people can be the most challenging, exciting, and potentially rewarding experience either will ever have. When planning for the optimum benefits of the association, education will be responding not only to the national concern for the maximum use of everyone's talents, but will also be contributing to the risky, unfinished business of the democratic process.

Discussion Questions

1. Hold a mock staff meeting in which any one of the following are topics of discussion:

grouping	teaching scholarship
individualization	research vs. practice
creativity	teaching for the unknown
curriculum relevancy	student unrest
self-understanding	automation and teaching
personal convictions	risk taking

2. What *direct experiences* do you think are necessary or desirable for prospective teachers? How can these be made feasible?
3. Choose one of the new roles for teachers discussed here or one that you would like to develop yourself. Describe *why* you think it is needed and why it might be difficult to put into practice.
4. Discuss this statement: Man is always on the road from embeddedness to openness.
5. Discuss this statement: Man's ability to emerge from embeddedness constitutes the measure of his humanity.
6. What policies do you think school districts should develop in order to help teachers keep abreast of new knowledge?
7. Select one current social reality and describe what you think it means for teachers and for what happens in classrooms.
8. How do you think teachers can be sensitized to have better interpersonal relations? Do you think this is important for teachers, for children, and for curriculum development?

References

1. Elsbree, W. S., *The American Teacher*. New York: The American Book Company, 1939, pp. 135–136.
2. Atkinson, Carroll, and Eugene T. Maleska, *The Story of Education*. Philadelphia and New York: Chilton Company, 1962.
3. Elsbree, op. cit., pp. 137–138.
4. Goodlad, John, and Robert H. Anderson, *The Nongraded Elementary School*. New York: Harcourt, Brace & World, Inc., 1959, pp. 44–49.

5. Pangborn, Jessie M., *The Evolution of the American Teachers College.* New York: Teachers College, Columbia University, 1932.

6. Griffiths, Dan E., "The Elementary School Principal and Change in the School System," *Theory into Practice,* Vol. II. Washington, D.C.: National Education Association, December, 1963, pp. 278–284.

7. Gardner, John W., *Self-renewal: The Individual and the Innovating Society.* New York: Harper & Row, 1964.

8. Bendiner, R., "Can American Teachers Teach?" *Redbook,* October, 1964.

9. Fischer, John H., "The Inclusive School," *Teachers College Record,* Columbia University, October, 1964.

10. Wright, Betty Atwell, *Teacher Aides to the Rescue.* New York: The John Day Company, Inc., 1969, p. 86.

11. Wright, Betty Atwell, *Educating for Diversity.* New York: The John Day Company, Inc., 1965, p. 40.

12. Sowards, G. Wesley, "The Explosion of Knowledge and Continuity in Teacher Education." An unpublished paper prepared for the Task Force on Continuity in Teacher Education, ASCD, Washington, D.C., 1965.

13. Wright, Betty Atwell, "Premium on Openness for Continuing Education." An unpublished paper prepared for the Task Force on Continuity in Teacher Education, ASCD, Washington, D.C., 1965.

14. Fromm, Erich, *The Sane Society.* New York: Holt, Rinehart and Winston, Inc., 1955.

15. Schachtel, Ernest G., *Metamorphosis.* London: Routledge and Kegan Paul Ltd., 1963.

16. Henle, Mary, "On Understanding," *The New Elementary School.* Edited by Alexander Frazier. Washington, D.C.: National Education Association, 1968.

17. *Annual Report of the Carnegie Foundation.* New York: The Carnegie Foundation, 1962.

18. Gardner, John W., *Self-renewal: The Individual and the Innovative Society.* New York: Harper & Row, 1964.

19. Stember, Charles H., *Education for Attitude Change.* New York: Institute for Human Relations Press, 1961.

20. Shores, Harlan J., Preface in *Curriculum Decisions: Social Realities.* Washington, D.C.: Association for Supervision and Curriculum Development, 1968.

21. Manolakes, George, *The Elementary School We Need.* Washington, D.C.: Association for Supervision and Curriculum Development, 1965.

22. Michaelis, John, "We Look at Our Goals," *California Journal of Education,* California State Department of Education, May, 1962.

23. Getzels, Jacob, and Philip Jackson, *Creativity and Intelligence.* New York: John Wiley & Sons, Inc., 1962.

24. Kubie, Lawrence, "Research in Protecting Preconscious Functions in Education," *Nurturing Individual Potential.* Washington, D.C.: Association for Supervision and Curriculum Development, 1964.

25. Torrance, Ellis P., *Guiding Creative Talent.* Englewood Cliffs, N.J.: Prentice-Hall, Inc., 1962.

26. Wilhelms, F. T., and D. Westby-Gibson, "Grouping Research Offers Leads," *Educational Leadership,* Vol. 18, No. 7, April, 1961.

27. Gladwyn, Thomas, "The Need: Better Ways of Teaching Children to Think," *Freeing Capacity to Learn.* Washington, D.C.: Association for Supervision and Curriculum Development, 1960.

28. Olson, Willard C., *Child Development.* Boston: D. C. Heath and Company, 1959.

29. Drucker, Peter, *Landmarks of Tomorrow.* New York: Harper & Row, 1959, p. 263.

30. Franseth, Jane, "Does Grouping Make a Difference in Pupil Learning?" *Toward Effective Grouping.* Washington, D.C.: Association for Supervision and Curriculum Development, 1962–63.

31. Strauss, Samuel, "Looking Backward on Future Scientists," *The Science Teacher,* December, 1957.

32. Shane, Harold G., "Grouping in the Elementary School," *Phi Delta Kappan,* Vol. XII, No. 7, April, 1960.

33. Hammond, Sarah Lou, *Homogeneous Grouping and Educational Results.* Middletown, Conn.: Wesleyan University, 1967.

34. Meil, Alice, and Edwin Kiester, Jr., *The Shortchanged Children of Suburbia.* New York: Institute of Human Relations Press of the American Jewish Committee, 1967.

35. Leighbody, Gerald B., and Ernest F. Weinrich, "Balancing the Roles in Curriculum Decision Making," *Balance in the Curriculum.* The 1961 Yearbook of the Association for Supervision and Curriculum Development. Washington, D.C.: The Association, 1961.

36. Reece, Charles, President of the Indiana State Teachers Association, at NEA's 107th Annual Conference, Philadelphia, July, 1969.

37. Lane, Mary B., "Educating for the Unknown." An unpublished paper prepared for the Task Force on Continuity in Teacher Education, ASCD, Washington, D.C., 1965.

38. Haubrich, Vernon F., "Tolerance for Ambiguity." An unpublished paper prepared for the Task Force on Continuity in Teacher Education, ASCD, Washington, D.C., 1965.

39. Maslow, Abe, *Towards a Psychology of Being.* Princeton, N.J.: D. Van Nostrand Insight Books, 1964.

SECTION I
Psychology
AS A CURRICULUM FORCE

CHAPTER 1

Teachers Examine Children's Natural Styles

Responsibility for Total Well-being

In no other profession is one less apt to see immediate results than in the teaching profession, but in no other profession is the practitioner called upon to know so much about the principles and practices that affect the total behaviors of human beings. The cumulative results of the influence of teachers upon all aspects of children's growth may be years in the making and in making themselves known. The end product depends upon the efforts of not just one teacher but many, and the greatest achievements of each may never be pinpointed.

Teachers need not only a sense of the mission of education and new insights about their roles, but also "a restless enthusiasm to create new responsibilities for students through experience and further study to expand their effectiveness throughout their professional lives" (1) so that they can hope to ensure that the development of children's interests and talents is in tandem with their other developing characteristics.

Human beings are fragile, and the human condition is easily mutilated or destroyed by human institutions in which it is possible for individuals to become lost or forgotten. More knowledge about the human condition brings new power to help individuals develop effectively and calls for insights and actions far beyond inherited and conventional dogmas. If the dual job of teachers is to enhance common humanity and actualize the potentials of each individual, then the experiences they design for and with children must include all that is known and all that can be learned about innate and creative abilities, health and physical development, mental health and personality development, social and scientific understandings, skills, attitudes, values, and individuality.

We know that there are some developmental tasks common to every one, and that these can be roughly divided into three overlapping groups. These have been defined and generally agreed upon by Havighurst (2) and others:

- *Group I includes infancy and early childhood.* Among its characteristics are walking, taking solid foods, talking, learning to control bodily eliminations, learning about sex differences and other physiological functions, beginning to form ideas about social and physical realities, relating emotionally to family and others, acquiring independence and beginning to make moral judgments, and the beginning of self-understanding and self-imagery.
- *Group II includes the middle childhood and preadolescent years.* These years witness developing physical skills necessary for ordinary games, the building of healthy attitudes about one's body and oneself as a growing person, learning to get along with peers, developing concepts of masculine and feminine roles, growth in academic skills of reading, writing, and computing, growing understanding about everyday living, evolving values and attitudes, increasing interest in making moral judgments, decreasing dependence on adults and increasing dependence on peers, increasing personal independence, growing understanding of social groups and institutions, and the building of positive or negative self-image and self-concepts.

These two groups represent the span of time during which children are in primary and elementary schools. They lead to the adolescent years during which young people achieve more mature intersexual relationships with their peers, understand more about masculine and feminine roles, learn to accept their physical limitations and to use physical abilities effectively, develop independence from adults, seek economic independence, investigate and prepare for vocations, prepare for marriage and family life, develop skills and concepts necessary for effective civil participation, work for socially acceptable and responsible behavior in the framework of changing conditions or become alienated from society, and firm up values, mores, and self-confidence to guide their behaviors.

When the developmental tasks of growing up are grouped in these ways, we see not only the overlapping of the tasks themselves but also how they are related to education's responsibilities for total well-being. Children in schools do not go to one teacher-specialist in mental health and personality development, a second in social and scientific understandings, and a third to help them with their innate and creative abilities. These are part of the curriculum content which every teacher teaches and they are part of curriculum development for every single child. Curriculum development that ignores them is doomed to failure and irrelevance. The word *developmental* implies not only changing, but also *merging* of the characteristics of children's growth and the changes that result from the combined influences of growing and learning.

The transition from dependence to independence takes many years of trial and error and of wise counsel and guidance. Children need a structure that will guide them without restricting the growing processes and adults who will encourage them while helping them to set appropriate limits. The adults who will be able to structure teaching and learning for and with them must have a great deal of sensitivity to both biological and intellectual needs in relation to young people's changing social needs.

Growing is an individual and unique affair for each person and teachers cannot expect children to interpret situations or subject matter content in the same way. Similarly, individuals do not develop the same concepts from the same situation or environment—what may be one child's picnic may be another child's pap, and each one takes in and puts out in his own way and in his own time. Consequently, although we can learn from the developmental tasks that are generally similar among children and youth, we must keep these in mind as we design curriculum that is concerned with developing the uniqueness of individuals.

Innate and Creative Abilities

Egos and Self-images

The assumption that individuals react in consonance with the way they view themselves, others, and the world around them is an underlying tenet of perceptual psychology. Education should help children and adults "to know themselves and to develop healthy attitudes of self-acceptance" (3) and self-understanding. We have already suggested that teachers must examine personal meanings in relation to themselves—who they are, what they are, and why they are the way they are—and that, having done this and continuing to grow in self-understanding, they will help children do so.

By *self-image* we mean the perceptions that an individual has of himself. A constellation of factors appears to influence people's self-images or self-concepts, and these interweave and operate within individuals in different ways. Studies of self-concept have spread into many areas of psychology and, "psychologists have sought to make sense out of human action by positing a self or ego in order that they might understand the coherence and unity which they have thought that they have seen in human behavior" (4). Psychologists have differing and emerging views of the concept of ego. G. W. Allport claims that the concept of ego is made necessary by certain shortcomings in *associationism* and lists different uses for the concept of ego. During the 1940's, publications such as the *Psychological Review* were filled with articles that attempted to explain human behavior through discussions of individual concepts of self; among the psychologist-writers are names such as Allport, Bertocci, Chein, and Lundholm, but according to more recent reviews of the work done during those years, the studies reported "failed to make a lasting distinction between *the self as a subjective knower* and the *self as the object of knowledge* (4). So the *self as essence* continued to defy definition.

There were parallel attempts during the same period to construct useful concepts of self for both experimental and applied psychology, but teachers in training during those years were more involved in studying psychology's application to rats and mice than to humans. The psychologists were wrestling with human applications, but in theoretical frameworks. After all, even if they had known about it when it was happening, what would it have meant to teachers that Rogers was working on the problem of the *client-centered approach to psychotherapy* and that one of his students (Raimy) developed a construct that put *self* in a *perceptual frame of reference.*

What is significant about this period is that the groundwork was being laid for what we know today, and that Raimy defined the *self-concept* for the first time as both *a learned perceptual system* and *a complicated organizing principle for schematizing ongoing experiences.* The concept of self soon formed the basis for new approaches to the study of human behavior. By 1949, Snygg and Combs had developed these concepts of self further and reported in their book, *Individual Behavior,* that self could best be understood as *growing out of the individual subject's frame of reference.* In other words, behavior could be interpreted better through each person's unique phenomenal field than by the various analytical categories which could be set up by observers.

This development was a long way from Darwin's conceptions that brain functions were static, something like a telephone switchboard, and expressions of emotions in men could be roughly compared to those of animals. All one needed to do was to plug in the right connecting stimulus, set up common categories, and apply the results to everyone. Even though he later provided the stimulus for what came to be called *comparative psychology,* showing that there probably was a gradual transition from the lower animals to man in various faculties of the mind, we were still a long way from phenomenology.

Still later, in the early 1900's, stimulus–response methodology in psychology implied the notion of the *empty organism* and came very slowly to the realization that there must be some symbolic processes intervening between stimulus and response because animals could delay their responses to certain stimuli. The notion that memories and hidden experiences changed responses in animals began to be explored, but it took psychology a long time to graduate to the idea that early experiences, particularly preverbal experiences, were important to human beings. Early childhood was felt to be relatively unimportant to personality development or to intellectual development and was thought to have no effect whatever upon adulthood.

But time marched on, and by 1950, the idea that individuals had learned perceptual systems made phenomenological "views of self" the touchstone of a new movement in psychology. When Hilgard postulated in his American Psychological Association presidential address that there was "the need for a self to understand psycho-analytic defense mechanisms," and called for research on the self, psychology and its scholars listened. The theory of self, self-centered therapy, and the practices related to therapeutic change in a phenomenological frame of reference became actual theories for the first time.

Whether the self is an objective reality or whether it is more of a nebulous abstraction has been the crux of research and discussions dominating psychological literature for the past decade or more. There are now many attempts to validate self-concept measures.

It is the opinion of the authors that, even though more exact knowledge is needed about the self concept, teachers can grow in understanding themselves and individual children and will benefit by what we now know and can learn. We can *begin* by considering the following statements.

1. The very act of concentrating on the individual child develops a deeper appreciation of each child as an individual "self."
2. Teachers can explore ways to help each child develop a positive image of self which will have positive effects on what he learns and how he learns.
3. Self-understanding, among teachers and children, is the beginning of personal fulfillment and self-motivation.
4. By studying the individual and trying to divine inner selfness, teachers become convinced that there are no "pat" answers in dealing with individuals and with groups of children.
5. Teachers discover clues to techniques that will trigger individual and group learning experiences as they learn more about each individual.
6. Teachers will learn to lean more on their own strengths and insights and to understand their own behaviors better as they study behavioral patterns of individual children; they will understand their "teaching selves" better.

Perceptual and phenomenological psychology are providing teachers with insights that help them to deal with children who are noisy, disorderly, fidgety, withdrawn, boastful, sadistic, dreamy, lazy, tardy, and whiny. All of these are indications that a child is not happy with himself. Children who feel adequate and who have positive self-images will:

- Try to function logically and intelligently.
- Be more inclined to engage in creative acts.
- Communicate more effectively with peers and adults.
- Interact more wholesomely with others.
- Deal more analytically and competently with problems.

- Be better able to tolerate stress and pressures.
- Understand self and others better.
- Be more sensitive and perceptive to the world around him.
- Have more empathy for the innermost feelings of others.
- Be more sensitive to and accepting of differences in others.
- Be more open to constructive criticisms.
- Attempt experimentation and innovations.
- Accept new ways of thinking about and doing things.
- Give and receive affection.
- Share possessions and ideas.
- Participate in activities requiring new physical and mental skills.

As teachers gain confidence in studying individuals and using the knowledge they gain, they learn to infer from children's perceptions and to construct learning environments that will take into account both individuals and groups. In a secure, familiar setting some individuals may depreciate their own worth; conversely, in a new setting the same individuals may be stimulated to great effort and may regard themselves as highly competent when challenged. Let us consider a boy called John and the factors which affect his self-image.

John

John was an eight-year-old whose personality collided head on with his teacher's personality. Day after day he was banished to the corridor outside of his classroom by his teacher, whose growing resentment of him was expressed thus: "He's impudent and fresh; he's his mother's spoiled darling. She thinks he's so bright! He's at the bottom of the class and getting worse!" Each day, a note listing his misdemeanors accompanied him home. It became obvious to everyone that John's opinion of himself was sinking lower daily and efforts were made to create common bonds of understanding among the teacher, the child, and the mother through conferences with the school psychologist and the principal.

Finally it was mutually decided to put John in a new environment, in another classroom, with a new group of classmates and a different teacher. The teacher was herself a mother with a strong empathy for "problem" boys. The new teacher set the tone with the class before John's arrival by discussing with them John's need to "feel better about himself"; in fact, she used the occasion to have a group discussion about what makes people feel unhappy with themselves and how they feel inside when they are not satisfied with themselves. The other side of the coin is, of course, what makes people feel happy about themselves and how they feel inside when they are better satisfied with themselves.

The welcoming committee was to be responsible for John's "feeling better about himself" for the first two days. It was headed by a boy relatively new to the school who was assigned the additional duty of keeping track of John's special interests and competencies in the classroom and on the playground. Naturally, the teacher was also using every opportunity to observe and to praise, as well. At the end of the second day, John had not once been assigned to his wailing wall in the hall, and he carried home, proudly, a note which the teacher had written and shared with him before sealing it in its envelope.

It said, in part, that "John's friends and teacher wish to say how happy they are that John has come to our class. He's a great first baseman! And you should hear him sing! He knows a lot about science, too."

The combination of approval and encouragement at school and the joy that was created at home when notes like these accompanied John at the end of the school day began to work wonders. If this were fiction, there could be no happier incidents than those that were duly and truthfully reported. When John sang a solo at school assembly, when he was the Master of Ceremonies for a class science exhibit, and when he was elected by his classmates to the school council, his classmates shared with him "good feelings inside."

The events that continued to unfold included reading achievement that showed a gain of over three years at the end of the year, which placed John near the top of all of the readers in his age group. The behavioral manifestations of John's improved self-image were legion. They even included fine new relationships with his former classmates and after-school talks with his former teacher, who reported one day that John had confided to her that he had had "bad feelings inside about himself sometimes."

Unquestionably, John's superior innate abilities had not been observable as long as his opinion of himself worsened. The new setting stimulated him to greater effort and the new environment challenged his competencies. It may not always be advisable to change children from one teacher to another, but it would seem that part of pupil assignment should include intense consideration about matching teachers and students. This is almost virgin territory for research and experimentation, but John's story is illustrative of the potential for changed behavior that results from efficient pupil–teacher matching.

Research does show, however, that definite relationships exist between ego function and scholastic performance. Bhatnagar (5) explores this, especially in terms of *self-acceptance* and *self-rejection*. He concluded that a sense of responsibility, goodness, conscience, and self-assurance are important factors contributing to over-all academic success.

Factors Influencing Self-image

Accepting the belief that many aspects of the "self" and the environment affect a child's opinion of self, teachers gather information and analyze it in order to help clarify their own thinking. The data and clues are gathered from standardized tests and from personal observations. Items on which teachers need to gather information are

1. Innate abilities.
2. Social peer relationships.
3. Mental maturity.
4. Parental and family backgrounds and understanding.
5. Physical maturity, health, and nutrition.
6. In-school achievements and interests.
7. Out-of-school achievements and interests.
8. Ability to understand and accept self.
9. Acceptance of self and others.
10. Emotional stability and equilibrium.

Mental Maturity

Despite the efforts of psychologists, there are no tests which are capable always of measuring innate ability or IQ. Yet false assumptions are often made when test scores are received, which in turn affect and precondition both child and teacher. The illusion of limitations imposed by the test score may in reality be accepted by the teacher, and thus by the child, as true. In fact, Sigel (6) discusses the ways that *intelligence tests may limit understanding of intelligence and innate abilities.*

He develops two hypotheses: (1) past and present use of intelligence tests continues to restrict our understanding of intellectual function, and (2) proposals for alternatives to current practices of test analyses are necessary. He cites examples of the different ways minds function when faced with choices on the Wechsler Intelligence Scale for Children (WISC), and says that a correct answer to an analogies item, for example, "may be a function of *particular learning, perceptual discrimination, syllogistic reasoning,* or *any combination of these.* There is no way to judge, from the response itself, which of these processes was operating at the time the response was made."

Obviously, only one response is expected and one response only will be considered correct; but each person being tested has a repertoire of possible responses. Here are two examples of the kinds of thinking that can underlie final choices:

Example 1
> In a WISC similarities item (a verbal test for analogies), the question is asked, "How are a scissors and a copper pan alike?" Answers and their scores include: "They are both household items." (Score *One*); "Both are metal." (Score *Two*). Both responses require making class concepts, but how does one decide which class to use?

Example 2
> Guilford used certain items to determine ability to categorize and assess class units. He asked one to "pick one that does not belong" from among the following: *clam, tree, oven,* and *rose.* Fortunate was the child who selected *oven* for, although Guilford did not give the answer, assuming

that the tester *of course* knew what it was, it was probably the correct answer inasmuch as it was the only *nonliving* thing in the sequence. But Sigel points out that the same items could also be classified on the basis of *function*, since clam, tree, and oven are also related to the *preparation of food* and, thus, *rose* would not belong. And, he adds, "on the basis of *location*, the *clam* may be picked as not belonging because it lives in water and the other things belong on land. These would probably be wrong answers" (6).

These examples illustrate the hidden fallacies behind judgments made on the basis of standardized tests. Those being tested may have no common ground for shared classifying systems because of different social and cultural backgrounds. But, in addition, responses may also reflect *originality, uniqueness,* and a *novel approach to thinking and classifying.* Sigel suggests that there are uses for intelligence tests and that among these could be (1) studying different cognitive styles in relation to performance on intelligence tests; (2) studying the quality of verbal content; and (3) determining what can be learned from an analysis of errors on IQ tests.

Cognitive Styles

Any consideration of innate ability must give high priority to *cognitive styles.* What is meant by this term *cognitive style?* It is really an umbrella term covering the many ways an individual uses to perceive, organize, classify, or label various environmental factors. Operationally, in everyday life, each person has many alternatives from among a wide variety of stimuli to use as bases for selecting, organizing, classifying, and labeling.

The following situation illustrates how one teacher of a group of nine-year-olds planned to encourage thinking about possibilities for using the same words. At the same time, he was learning something about the cognitive styles of his students. These words were put on the chalkboard: *train, run, battery, shift.* Asked to use the words in sentences, boys and girls in the class contributed these:

The *train* takes you places.
I can *run* fast.
The *battery* went dead.
My daddy can *shift* gears in the truck.

Accepting these and indicating that they were possible and correct responses, he asked the students to think of other sentences in which the same words would have different meanings. This time he wrote these sentences beside the first ones:

A bride wears a *train.*
He made a home *run* in the ball game.
Girls get *runs* in their stockings.

He will *train* for the swimming team.
The *battery* is the pitcher and the catcher.
There was a *battery* of photographers.
I have a pink *shift*.
He lost his *train* of thought.
He had to *shift* around in his seat.

One possible way to study cognitive styles in very young children is to give them objects such as blocks, cardboard shapes, buttons, or seeds and ask them to see how many ways they can find to sort them. Even three- and four-year-olds will begin to group and regroup by size, color, shape, different properties, quality, and quantity.

Language, as illustrated in the first example, is the dimension of cognitive style that enables an individual to communicate about his environment, his understandings, and his "reasons why." The acquisition of the labels for describing and classifying is one of the chief functions of the school, and of the individual's total cultural, social, and economic environment.

No discussion of cognitive styles would be complete without some discussion of the work that has been done in the areas of *logical development of the thinking process, the nature and development of creativity,* and *the importance of peer associations.*

Thinking Processes

Inhelder and Piaget (7) suggest these key factors that lead to logical development in thinking processes: *maturation, experience, social transmission,* and *equilibrium.*

First, let us consider *maturation.* Once this was seen to be a natural process unaffected by environment. It was thought to occur naturally and independently and was the same for everyone. The modern view of maturation is that it is affected by environmental variables and that stimulation is essential to the development of the senses and the nervous system.

For example, children will learn to use scissors effectively if they have an opportunity to use them. The same is true of pencils, crayons, blocks, and books. They will learn to be at ease with peer groups only if they have an opportunity to be with them. They will communicate in a communicating environment where others around are trying to communicate. They will learn to classify in divergent ways if opportunities are provided and efforts approved and encouraged.

Now consider *experience,* a word that is rather loosely used in educational literature. Experience is necessary for concept development, but experience by itself is not enough. The mind must be actively engaged in the experience; as Piaget points out, knowledge is not drawn from objects, it is acquired from the actions effected by, or in conjunction with, objects.

Although there are many benefits for the child who is "just playing" with blocks, steps in the thinking process are encouraged when he is asked to think of ways to sort or group them. Given two containers of water differing in shape but containing the same amount of water, a child will quickly surmise that there is more water in the taller and thinner of the two containers. He will have an experience if he simply pours the water back in the sink. But he will be engaged in the experience if he is encouraged to test his observation, find some way to measure the amount in each container, and arrive at the logical conclusion that there is actually the same amount of water in each.

Social transmission, the third of Piaget's key factors, occurs when information derived from reading, listening, or observing is internalized. Again, just passing on the information is not enough, because the child who does not have some means of internalizing it may arrive at a false understanding or concept or "deform the knowledge in some way." The task for the child is to be able to "operate upon the information—to digest it mentally—to change previous mental pictures, and to come to some real applicable understanding" (7). Failure to provide experiences that help children internalize explains why children often do not know what teachers think they have taught. Again, the child has to be *engaged* in some way in order to take unto himself and apply information, to change attitudes, or to adopt values.

Inhelder and Piaget consider *equilibrium* to be the most fundamental and crucial of all developmental factors. When children are confronted with a cognitive conflict, they will react in order to compensate for the disturbance the conflict creates. Reactions take the form of logical, or illogical, operations to resolve the conflict. In resolving a conflict logically, one is helped to develop equilibrium. Again, we see the importance of helping children to develop logical thinking processes in order to have personal equilibrium.

Piaget uses logico-mathematical models to describe the properties of systems of actions that children use during the stage of *concrete operations,* or, those times when mental activity is oriented toward concrete objects, events, and data, rather than abstractions. There are four of these models:

Additive Composition. An example: The whole is the sum of its parts. Therefore, we put the parts together to form a class or group.
Reversibility. An example: Every cognitive action can be reversed. Various shapes can be divided into subclasses, then regrouped in various ways. The process can be reversed by putting them back into their original groups or classifications. Animals can be classed in subclasses, supraclasses, and so on and then the process can be reversed by putting them back in their original subclasses.
Associativity. An example: Trying to solve a problem in several dif-

ferent ways and finding that certain associations always work even though they are in different configurations. The example is given that the child is given one long stick and several shorter ones which taken together will be the same as the long one. He learns that it does not matter in what fashion the small sticks are laid out (zigzag, scattered), for when laid end to end they will still equal the length of the longer stick. In other words, there are different ways to put parts of things together or to think about the same problem.

Identity. An example: In order to compare events or objects, a one-to-one correspondence can be made between the various elements of each class. In identifying whether something is animal, vegetable, or mineral, a pupil thinks of whether the properties are identical to any one of these, whether all of the elements are used, and whether the two sets —the one given for classification and the elements of the classification— match. When the two sets are determined to be identical and criteria the same, the identity operation has been used.

It should be pointed out here that cognitive actions are often the results of all four properties. In the example just cited, the student may have used additive composition, reversibility, associativity, and identity, and any cognitive action may use one or more of the properties.

Creativity

Creativity is probably the most talked about and the least understood dimension of innate ability; within the past few years this ability has been opened to scientific examination and stands as one of the most exciting and significant fields related to educational psychology. Research on creativity is still in its infancy but there has been startling interest in it since about 1950.

Undoubtedly, in the past, fine teachers have applied many principles of creativity to teaching, providing opportunities for the release and development of creative talent in learners and establishing creative climates in classrooms through design or through an intuitive sense of what constitutes good teaching. In the light of research and findings in industry, in the armed forces, and in universities which have probed the complexities of creativity to identify, measure, redefine, and seek practical applications for development and release of creative talent, it behooves us to reflect upon the need to relate what is becoming known about creativity to school practices.

Studies cluster around definition, tangibility, testing, the creative process, whether creativity can be objectively measured, and the psychological study of creativity as a phenomena. The reader should review the section of the prologue devoted to teachers as creators, inasmuch as references and philosophy cited there are also applicable here.

...nge Hardison, noted sculptress and creator of the Negro Giants of History series, tells students and teachers with whom she works that everyone is creative. "Abilities are like seeds in a garden . . . they must have good soil, water, sunshine, and regular care to make them grow," she says as she works with clay, wax, plaster of paris, sand, excelsior, and other materials with which she creates and encourages young people to create. "Mental discipline is a matter of programming your thinking and the key to successful living."

She has also written poetry for young people and worked with boys and girls in creative dramatics. One of the poems that she and a friend, Margaret McCaden, have written is chanted with youngsters as they work together:

"I change my thoughts for the better, I change MYSELF.
I change myself for the better, I change my FAMILY.
I change my family for the better, I change my NEIGHBORHOOD.
I change my neighborhood for the better, I change my CITY.
I change my city for the better, I change my COUNTRY.
I change my country for the better, I change my WORLD."

Photo by Mr. Mazon, New Haven, Connecticut, Public Schools
Published with permission of Miss Hardison and Mr. Mazon

As this is being written, Guilford and others are continuing to study the psychometric approach to creativity as well as some operational definitions of it; for example, scores on tests of divergent thinking. There is much discussion and considerable confusion around the issue of whether divergent thinking and creativity are synonymous. Some psychologists are concentrating on the differences between and among characteristics of creative persons and less creative persons.

Still others are searching for ways to train children in creativity (8), and one group believes that the investigation of various personality factors will yield the best information for studying the creative processes. From past and indicated future studies of creativity, it seems that teachers should be concerned about how to use personal characteristics and different learning styles in relation to developing creativity at various levels. This seems to hold the most promise for a developmental approach to creativity. We need functional, behavioral ways to observe and stimulate boys and girls toward creative efforts.

Critics have charged specifically that schools ignore creativity, that in fact they stifle and suppress it. It may be that the traditional school's overemphasis on conformity and lock-step curriculum have allowed little room for experimentation and divergent thinking. But newer instructional programs are beginning to recognize the importance of the discovery method of teaching and learning, while newer concepts of curriculum and school organization provide environment and scheduling to encourage more pupil engagement in learning experiences and time for the incubation and development of ideas.

Some Factors in Creative Development

It is well known that a small child has an extraordinarily free and creative imagination which he demonstrates in his use of words, images, color, design and tones, and in his general attitude toward the world around him. Under the impact of growing up and the many forces that begin to press in on a child in early life, we know that this freely creative imagination begins to disappear or, at the very least, go underground. We know the nature of some of the destructive forces, and we can recognize that some of them arise as distortions in the child's development at home and at school.

We also know that children's spontaneous inhibitory processes are reinforced by cultural attitudes of parents and neighborhood, by the conspiracy of silence that surrounds the problems most important to children, by their own struggles with lustful and destructive impulses, through their curiosity about forbidden things having to do with their bodies and their bodies' apertures, products, functions, feelings, and sensations. Later on, these inhibitory forces and processes are definitely reinforced by certain ingredients in our educational system—specifically by a fetishlike emphasis on what someone has called "drill and grill."

In the learning process, people divide into at least three groups, possibly more, according to Dr. Azenath Petrie (9). There are those whom he would call "stimulus-bound"; these take in and give out promptly in response to percepts, but with little penetration into their own innermost psychological selves. These are the students who listen to a lecture and produce the most precise and perfect notes while little goes on inside of them.

There are others who take in and reproduce equally automatically, but then industriously and dutifully take their notes home and study them, drilling and grilling themselves as they learn in time-honored pedestrian and uncreative fashion. There are still others who may "take in" without even knowing that they are doing so, and who then proceed to process data with enormous speed and freedom, using analogic methods, and for the most part without interposing the delays that are inherent in the process of "conscious sampling." This is the so-called imageless thinking of the Wurzburg school—what we would call free association or *preconscious* processing.

We are beginning to realize that not many of even the most gifted and potentially creative students survive the impact of drill and grill. We really do not know how many survive and how many fail, but we do know that a heavy toll is paid by those who do survive. Those who are wasted or destroyed represent a potential reservoir of creative manpower. This destruction is not due to educational processes alone, but many methods of education certainly do destroy the freedom of preconscious functioning.

In defense of even the most traditional schools, there is an earlier process of destruction that comes from deep wells of unrecognized and superimposed guilt and fear that hamper the free play of human imagination and creativity. These are called neurotogenic forces and they are universal but variable. They are intensified, but not necessarily created by, the impact of wrongly oriented educational procedures.

One of the confusions that has muddled thinking about creativity is the argument about whether or not there must be a tangible product such as a poem, a composition, an innovation, an artistic creation, or a scientific invention as a result of creativity. Psychologists argue that there can be creative thinking and creativity even where there is no tangible product. Guilford (10) says that, "there are always some products of thought, and it does not matter whether they are expressed or not. They can still be detected in a number of ways."

We also have some general descriptions of the complete act of creative production to guide us. As far back as 1945 four familiar stages were defined: (1) preparation, (2) incubation, (3) illumination, and (4) verification.

Rossman (12) studied over 700 productive inventors and proposed that there are seven stages:

1. Observation of a need or difficulty.
2. Analysis of the need.
3. Survey of all available information.
4. Formulation of objective solutions.
5. Critical analysis of the solutions.
6. The birth of a new invention, or the "idea proper."
7. Experimentation to test out the idea.

The list is very similar to Wallas' list, except for the reference to the incubation period.

The most striking thing about both lists is their similarity to John Dewey's (13) hypothetical descriptive stages proposed for the rough description of problem solving. Dewey recognized five stages:

1. Recognition of the problem.
2. Analysis of the problem.
3. Suggestion of possible solutions.
4. Testing of the consequences.
5. Judgment of the selected solution.

Guilford says that he thinks it is safe to say that, "all problem solving that is genuinely problem solving is creative. It is not so clear that all creative thinking is problem solving, although a very high percentage of it can be so interpreted."

More recently, Maslow (14) and Rogers (15) speak of a drive or motivation called *self-actualization*. This comes closer, it seems to us, to expressing what the object of all intellectual achievement should be. Although it is a vague term, it does conjure up a mental picture of activity to satisfy and motivate one's *self*. And best of all, we welcome the belief that children and adults can be motivated toward personal accomplishments and intellectual achievements by something other than the standard needs of hunger, thirst, shelter, and bodily functions.

For practical purposes in observing children and for creating opportunities for self-actualizing among students, let us use some workable combination of the steps included in self-actualizing processes to plan learning experiences for children. For each child, there must be

1. A need or a motivation.
2. Supportive climate, environment, and materials.
3. Time to organize and prepare.
4. Incubation and assimilation periods.
5. Encouragement to experiment, compare, and verify.

How does this work in actual classroom practice? Let us look at examples selected to illustrate two different age groups:

EXAMPLE 1: A GROUP OF FIVE-YEAR-OLDS

A Need or a Motivation: The school newspaper is delivered to the classroom
by an upper classman. Teacher and children share some of the information it contains, and one child comments, "There's no news about us in
there!" This is followed by, "You have to tell people what's happening
to us"; "We do lots of things, too"; "Let's make our own newspaper";
"We can't write much yet"; "Nor read either."

The teacher suggests that there are other ways to let people know what
you are doing or thinking, and asks the children to think of some of them.
Responses included, "Sure, we can take pictures with my Dad's camera";
"Or draw pictures"; "Or make up a play about what we do"; "Or a song
maybe"; "The teacher can write what we say like she does sometimes."

Supportive Climate, Environment, and Materials: The teacher sets the tone
or climate with a comment such as, "Those are all good ideas, but which
of those things could you actually put in a newspaper? Suppose we
divide up and talk about it. Maybe you can try some of your ideas and
then show us what you mean."

The classroom has tables grouped together and group consultation
has been encouraged before. There are also centers where children are
used to painting and drawing, working with sand or blocks, or devising
with clay. There are areas where magazines can be perused and cut up.
There is a news bulletin board. There are places where colored paper,
scissors, paste, and string invite creation. There are puppets and a puppet
stage, dolls and blocks, toys and games, and picture books.

Time to Organize and Prepare: The children go eagerly back to their seats
and are soon involved in lively discussions. The teacher rotates and con-
sults with groups as needed, supporting ideas and suggesting possibilities. Knowing the children, the teacher suggests particular mediums or
projects based on children's already demonstrated interests and talents.

The children themselves begin to rule out some ideas as not appropriate for putting in a class newspaper. These, they say, would be better
for people to come and see—things such as a play, bulletin board, photograph, or puppet show. Other ideas are considered feasible and jotted
down by the teacher, who lists them on the chalkboard.

Incubation and Assimilation Periods: The teacher realizes that this may be
just temporary—that interest may be high now but that it may not be
sustained. If nothing concrete comes of the planning, the idea and the
process are good groundwork for future accomplishments, anyway. But
ideas are taking shape and individuals are selecting one or two from
among many to develop. They work with a chosen media to see whether
their idea can be shown. They ask one another for opinions and sometimes change or modify their idea according to criticisms.

Partially completed ideas are discussed in the entire group just before
dismissal for the day, and children are urged to think some more about
them at home. Some come back with more ideas the next day and these

are added to the chalkboard list. Some rush to their project to add something, and others, less motivated independently, are caught up in the group fervor.

The teacher does not push for a quick product as a result of the project. Teachers know that time to assimilate, act, and let an idea incubate is necessary.

Encouragement to Experiment, Compare, and Verify: The teacher praises ingenuity and effort. The chalkboard list is labeled with names of people taking various responsibilities. The finished product grows, aided and abetted by "author's conferences" to share ideas and reactions. Effort is sustained and interest remains high. Competition remains at a minimum because children are working in different areas of their choice. The newspaper, which will eventually be mimeographed and circulated, grows. It has shadowbox cut-outs showing playground activities, line drawings with labels to show a typical day's activities, a dictated account of a class visit to the grocery store, a labeled picture of the class hamster and the aquarium, and a play acted out by the children and dictated to the teacher.

In this case there was a product of the children's creativity—a product which represented their planning and their ideas—a product representing each child's individuality and originality.

EXAMPLE 2: A GROUP OF EIGHT-YEAR-OLDS

A Need or Motivation: Twenty-eight eight-year-olds were having difficulty imagining an island as other than a flat shape surrounded by blue paper water on a map. Pictures, models, and books did not bring "islandness" to life for most of them—they helped, but they were not enough. The actual concepts related to depth, size, contours, ability to support life, civilizations, and so on, eluded them, as indicated in their discussions. So often children learn the definition of an island and it is left at that. But the teacher felt that there were many understandings that apply to humans and to other water and land masses that could be derived from an in-depth kind of study of one island. Manhattan Island was within driving distance of the school, and teacher and children began to plan ways to see and experience "islandness."

Supportive Climate, Environment, and Materials: Thinking of possible ways to do this, children made these suggestions: "We could fly over it"; "Or take a subway under it"; ". . . take a bus or train through it"; "look at it from the elevated railway"; "go up on top of a high building"; and "We could sail around it." How to experience both its landness and its waterness inspired quite a bit of discussion, and it was finally decided that it would be best to sail around it. The teacher agreed and told the children that there was a special boat that took people on excursions around the island every day. Brochures about the boat trip were sent for, various Port and other authorities were written to for information, and other sources of information were solicited. Among these were fathers who worked in the city of New York on the island of Manhattan.

Time to Organize and Prepare: In addition to the activities listed above, the class subdivided into groups upon which they had mutually decided. There were teams of students to investigate history, geography, people, geology, relationship to New York City, goods and services, harbors, transportation, and problems. Books, art, music, models, films, slides, and even tapes were used. Newscasts were watched and reported upon. A team was selected to serve as guides on the day of the actual trip so that information gathered by the class could be shared with mothers accompanying the class. They now knew a great deal more about Manhattan Island, but the experience itself was still to be a catalyst for deeper and more creative efforts.

Incubation and Assimilation: Although a great deal of both of these had been occurring, each child was encouraged to keep a diary of his actual impressions—the sense, and feel, and touch, as it were—in an especially prepared trip diary. Following the trip, time was allowed for each child to share his own *impressions.* A list of impressions was written on the chalkboard and it grew rapidly because the children's discussion increased recall. The growing list of impressions included:

> The Statue of Liberty shrouded in a fog
> The sounds of fog horns and other harbor sounds
> Soaring sea gulls following ships' wakes
> Going under the George Washington and other bridges
> Feeling the salt spray in one's face
> The width of the Hudson River
> The size of the ocean-going liners
> The various tugs and barges with their crews
> The vastness and height of the skyline
> The variety of landmarks and signs
> The magnitude and beauty of the Palisades
> The variety of languages, dress, and color of shipmates
> The facilities and personnel of a small cruise ship
> The sensations of walking and riding on shipboard
> Phenomena such as whirlpools and eddies and tides
> The canyon feeling of being on the East River
> The lives of apartment dwellers from slums to penthouses.

Encouragement to Experiment, Compare, Verify: The ways that were found to explain and demonstrate impressions were of tremendous variety and creativity. They set the pace for many creative learning experiences throughout the remainder of the year that this teacher and these children were to spend together. Among these were imaginary stories and diaries, some involving experiences and impressions that early explorers may have had; poems; paintings and murals; three-dimensional models and dioramas; a musical history and some original music with words; an original play about Henry Hudson's discovery.

The teacher who shared this incident is sure that none of these would ever have been forthcoming in this particular project or in many that followed without attention to each of the steps he included in planning.

The experience, regardless of its stated purpose, encouraged deeper impressions and sensations than are ordinarily expected, facts and information coupled with experience led to new understandings and new concepts, and learning became a self-involving, self-actualizing process for each child.

Socioeconomic Status

Innate abilities are affected by socioeconomic status in a number of ways. As we shall see, cognitive styles, developing thinking processes, self-images, peer relationships, teacher–pupil relationships, and opportunities for creative and opening-up experiences are all deeply affected by a child's accident of birth in certain of society's classes. Consider these premises:

1. The social class into which a child is born influences his learning.
2. The ethnic background of a child affects the way he learns.
3. The place where a child lives and the people who surround him affect learning.
4. Family values and mores affect what a child learns and how he learns.
5. The kind of life his family leads affects a child's learning (16).

The *social class into which a child is born* influences his learning in a number of ways. For example, until very recently, when huge efforts have been made to encourage more educationally disadvantaged children to attend high school and college, the majority of students who finished high school and attended college came from middle- and upper-class homes. This is not to say that they were any more capable, but rather that they were expected by their families and friends to continue their education and their families were financially better able to allow them to continue.

In the past, the lower classes have tended to be less interested in formal education and society has tended to assume that they will drop out of formal school classes earlier. Many were expected to become unskilled or semiskilled manual laborers like their parents and their parents' friends. In addition, many underprivileged families live in either very crowded or very isolated communities and the best schools have not been available to them. Children from many undereducated families have had available to them only racially segregated schools where they met only similar children with similar aspirations.

The *ethnic or national background* has an effect on the way a child learns not because the child is different from others in innate ability and talent, but because of the social expectations of certain groups and because of the attitude of majority cultures toward minority groups. The Indian

American, the Negro American, the Mexican American, and the Puerto Rican American often have seen that certain occupations were not open to their culture groups and have not aspired to these occupations or professions because they believe they are closed to them (and often, they have been closed to them).

Many specific groups have selected certain occupations and their children are motivated toward these same occupations and expected to follow them in their adulthood. The patterns they have seen around them have strong directional tendencies to steer young people in a certain way. Thus they think that fewer choices are open to them. We see this in the stereotypes connected with thinking about certain groups who have entered farming, merchandising, science, teaching, factory work, and so on.

A child's home, neighborhood, and the kinds of people who surround him affect his learning. Such things as whether a child lives in an urban, suburban, or rural area can limit or extend learning opportunities. The stimulation and services provided or not provided by the neighborhood, its people, and its agencies affect what children learn and how they learn. Whether fathers are farmers, bankers, pilots, or engineers has an effect on the kinds of people with whom the family associates and thus on children's experiences that are basic to all learning. Oft repeated, but true, is the saying that a child "learns what he lives and lives what he learns."

Family values and mores affect what children learn and how they learn. If Jane and Bill grow up in a home where good music and literature abound and where there is interest and conversation about new ideas and discoveries, they are more apt to be propelled toward such things than are Sue and Tom whose home has either pulp magazines or none, and where there is a minimum of good music, conversation, or interest in current affairs.

Sometimes family influence affects children in subtle ways by causing them to reject family values and mores. Noneducated parents may create in their children a desire to be unlike them through their contempt for learning and their lack of economic success and social status. Generally, however, the children of well-educated parents will probably be more interested in academic success.

The kind of life his family leads affects a child's learning. For example, a child who has traveled with his family to many parts of the world is more apt to be interested in social studies, geography, and history than is the child whose travel experiences are limited or nonexistent.

In the first study of its kind, Sexton (17) pointed out the relationships between education and income and the inequities that occur in homes and thus in public schools. She was able to show graphically and conclusively that as income levels go up, achievement scores tend to go up, and that income of families is directly related to educational levels.

In another study, Milner (18) found that all children in the lower-upper and upper-middle classes were high scorers on reading-readiness tests, whereas all children in the lower-lower classes were low scorers. And in still another study, Hollingshead (19) says that upper-class students did better on IQ tests, because of greater motivation and different approaches to test taking. On the other hand, the lowest-class "adolescent has been subjected to a family and class culture in which failure, worry, and frustration are common. He has not been trained at home to do his best in school. His parents have not ingrained in him the idea that he must make good grades if he is to be a success in life. Moreover, the class system as it functions in the school does not help him to overcome the poor training he has received at home and in the neighborhood."

Davis (20) believes that, "half the ability in this country goes down the drain because of the failure of intelligence tests to measure the real mental ability of children from the lower socioeconomic groups, and because of the failure of the schools to recognize and train this ability."

Havighurst (21) talks about failures, problem children, and delinquents. They are the children, he says, whose "fathers are seldom or never at home and pay little attention to them when they are." These are the children who "come to school in the morning unwashed and in dirty clothes, sometimes without breakfast, often needing a doctor's care. They have trouble learning to read, the first thing in a long series of school difficulties. Their second disadvantage is verbal intelligence below average—a serious handicap in a society that places more and more reliance on verbal agility." Finally, the school fails this group. "When they are very young the teacher too often passes over their problems. She is so busy with those who get along passably well that she may allow these three or four children in her class to drift. Eventually, at thirteen or fourteen, they are reading at the level of third or fourth graders . . . and at about this point they become troublesome problems to the school."

In the next section of this book, there will be intensive discussion of sociology as a curriculum force, but the important thing to realize here is that the *effect* of sociological information about each child explains a great deal about what he learns and how he learns. Although we do not yet know all of the ways that intelligence is correlated with socioeconomic status, Nim (22) states that tests given to high school boys in low and high income groups indicate "that intelligence is positively correlated with socio-economic status."

Most certainly, socioeconomic status has a close relationship to social peer associations.

Social Peer Relationships

It is difficult for educators to admit that children may learn more from one another than they do from adults. Remember that among their developmental characteristics are decreasing dependence on adults, increasing dependence on peers, and increasing personal independence. The quality of their relations with others during these transitions is of utmost importance.

Tommy

Tommy, age ten, could easily have been voted the most unpopular boy in the class early in the term. He presented the classic picture of antisocial behavior—deliberately, it seemed, taunting and annoying classmates in school and out of school. His aggressiveness also showed itself in interrupting teachers, correcting them, and adding unrelated information to class discussions.

The teacher and student teacher reviewed Tommy's background, using cumulative school records and discussions with his mother. They learned that Tommy had been separated from his older brother and his father as a result of divorce that occurred shortly after his birth. As a boy living alone with his mother, he had been overprotected from associations with age mates, had spent a great deal of time with adults, and had not started school until he was nearly seven. Tommy's mother and teachers realized that his overbearing mannerisms made him unpopular with classmates and that these were a manifestation of his need for approval. Tommy had never learned to see himself in relation to others, nor had he learned how to gain attention and approval in a manner acceptable to either adults or peers.

It was agreed that, if one or two major interests or special talents could be determined, these could serve in the dual capacity of helping Tommy to gain real approval and admiration from his peers as well as from adults. The student teacher had noted his keen interest in plant life during a visit to a nearby greenhouse to see the orchids of an elderly botanist. He had also noted that shortly thereafter Tommy had ordered some atomic-energized seeds with which to experiment independently. There were two other boys in the class with similar interests. Here was the clue to helping Tommy have his first really constructive peer relationship.

Consultation with the owner of the greenhouse revealed that he would welcome visits from students with special interests and that he would be glad to spend as much time as they would like helping them with their plant experiments. As the time went on, the relationship among the boys became a strong and supportive one under the mutual guidance of teacher, student teacher, and the boys' greenhouse mentor. Tommy's attitude changed and he made efforts to gain other friends in the class. At midterm he was elected president of the science club—an office he had very much wanted. He displayed great leadership potential in directing the activities of the club and in helping to plan programs for it.

Tommy's problems were not magically solved, nor were all of his peer relationships yet completely successful, but he was headed in the right direction and realized increasingly the importance of peer support in his growing self-esteem.

Carlotta

What teachers often characterize as behavior so unusual that it is called problem behavior is often the child's reaction to his own feelings that he is not accepted by his peers. Children need to have group experiences that help them to uncover common feelings such as anxieties, personal doubts, difficulties in human relations, and guilt.

Carlotta overcame anxiety caused by her inability to speak English through the specialized understanding and help of her teachers and classmates. Not only was Carlotta a Cuban refugee living in the United States alone with her mother, but both were concerned about the safety of her father, who had remained in Cuba. Carlotta was an excessively shy child and her acquaintance with the English language was slight because Spanish was spoken exclusively at home.

A two-pronged program was designed for Carlotta by her teachers. First, she was provided an individually programmed reading and English project so that she would be competing only with herself in gaining English skills; she was given tapes and a tape recorder to record her new vocabulary and linguistic abilities, and special Spanish–English books so that she could maintain her proficiency in both languages. Second, the class started participating in Spanish lessons conducted daily on television, and Carlotta was invited to be the "assistant teacher" for these lessons.

Carlotta was able to help classmates with their Spanish pronunciation at the same time she was gaining proficiency in English. She gained confidence as she discovered that English-speaking children sound strange, too, when they are learning another language. Overcoming her anxieties, she began to participate in other group activities with the support and admiration of her classmates. Changes were slow, but teachers and peers grew in understanding Carlotta's needs for resolving her anxieties and improving her self-image. And, in time, Carlotta became a much beloved and fully participating group member.

Jimmy

For many children school is the only place they have a chance to belong to an organization or a social club. The class itself can serve as the sole organization for these. Sexton (23) says that lower-income children are "much less likely than upper-income children to belong to organizations." In one of her studies she reports that 37 per cent of upper-middle-class boys of age fourteen to sixteen, and only 17 per cent of working-class boys, belonged to any "organization" at all. "This means," she states, "that more than twice as many working-class boys were non-joiners with any organizational ties." At the same time, more than half of the upper-middle-class boys (52 per cent) belonged to more than one organization, as compared with 31 per cent of working-class boys.

School-sponsored group activities during and after school hours are necessary in order to give lower-income youths some of the confidence and social poise that their more affluent peers possess. Jimmy was one of these children who had been denied these experiences in almost inverse proportion to his needs. Meeting these kinds of needs in lower-income areas calls for extra effort and an expanded concept of the school day on the part of every teacher.

Jimmy was fortunate enough to have a teacher who encouraged him to join a YMCA program, where he became proficient at swimming and archery. His teacher also sponsored him in the Cub Scout den which he held after school hours. In both activities Jimmy had a chance to meet boys from other parts of town, from other socioeconomic groups, and from other ethnic groups. As a Negro American he had been brought up with negative attitudes about his blackness, but acceptance by peers of different color and cultures helped enormously. Learning that he had talents that he had not known about, and with new interests to widen his own horizons, Jimmy changed from a resentful, troublesome, and troubled boy into a charming and thoroughly delightful person. His group mates were the first to go to his defense one day when another boy called him "Nigger." "O.K. So you're white and he's black," one of them said, "but that don't make him no nigger!" Jimmy's equilibrium and sense of humor were equal to the competition, too. One day, he was heard to say, "Hey, throw that white ball to this black boy!"

Sex Differences in Learning

It is interesting to ask why sex differences in learning have been acted upon so little in educational practice. Some of the newest curriculum and teaching manuals do not even mention this as a factor for consideration. Yet sexual conflicts and anxieties as well as sex differentiation of interests, mental abilities, motor development, personality, and rate of growth should have a great deal of importance in any consideration of how children learn and what kinds of curriculum experiences will best help them learn.

Among sensory drives, sex is probably most closely related to one's developing sense of *selfhood*. When anxieties and fears arise in connection with sex impulses which are a normal and natural part of growing up, tradition has dictated rigidly prudish attitudes about this basic human need. Although early schools separated boys and girls for learning experiences, we can surmise that this was done more on the basis of moral persuasions that spilled over from the rest of society than on the school's desire to assess the separation's effect on children's learning.

When, as educators, we claim that we are dealing with basic human needs and then studiously avoid any attention to the fears, perplexities, and anxieties that arise from sex drives and sex roles, how can we be believed? We claim that we are vitally concerned about the physical maturity and health of children, but know little about the implications of sex differences in growth and development. We know that more boys than girls eventually drop out of school and that there are more boys than girls in remedial reading groups, but we spend little time trying to find out whether schools may be more girl-geared than boy-geared. And we know that there are male and female needs in connection with sexuality, but we do not recognize them in instructional programs.

Boys and Girls Grow and Develop Differently

The growth patterns for boys and girls differ. Their hearts follow different growth patterns and there are differences in blood pressure. Marsh (24) reports that "during most of childhood, boys' hearts are a little larger than girls'," but from the age of "nine or ten to thirteen or fourteen girls' hearts are usually larger than boys'. After the age of thirteen boys' hearts continue to grow at a rapid pace, whereas girls' hearts grow very slowly." He also says that there is little difference between the blood pressures of boys and girls during early childhood, but "between the ages of ten and thirteen blood pressure is higher in boys than in girls. After the age of thirteen the blood pressure of boys exceeds that of girls, the difference increasing with age."

If you have ever watched a group of preadolescent boys and girls at a boy–girl party, you realize the difference in the heights of boys and girls just previous to puberty. There is biological research to explain why girls are often so much taller than boys at this stage of their development. Boynton (25) retested anthropometric characteristics of boys and girls from the time his sample groups of boys and girls were five and one half years old to the time they were sixteen and one half. He used thirteen measurements of growth increment and his data show that although the five-and-one-half-year-old boy is 65 per cent as tall as he will be at seventeen, the five-and-one-half-year-old girl is already 75 per cent as tall as she will ever be. The boy at this age has about 18 per cent of his adult grip but a girl of the same age already has approximately one third of the grip she will have as an adult.

Think about the implications of children's ability to grip things in relation to what the school requires of them as soon as they start formal education in kindergarten or first grade. Crayons and pencils are part of the special phenomena that begin to trap and frustrate boys from the beginning, for writing activities are among the first "lessons." Observation of any preschool, kindergarten, or first grade will convince the unconvinced that girls have less difficulty than boys in pleasing the teacher and getting better grades when it comes to their written work. Boys struggle heroically, but the results are often understandably illegible because their coordination does not yet match that of their female peers.

This female advantage of more advanced physical development holds throughout the elementary school years. Sex differences in motor development have also been documented by Garrison (26), who discusses the striking sex difference observed in the chronological age at which boys and girls reach the period of maximum growth which is known as the preadolescent growth spurt. He says that "girls reach this stage of their physical development and ultimate physical maturity considerably earlier than boys. When the growth rates of different parts of the body are compared, we note that boys are larger than girls in thoracic circumference and girth of forearm, whereas girls have a larger thigh."

Basal metabolism, or oxygen consumption, is different between the sexes. Garn and Clark (27) reported studies of about 160 boys and girls under morning fasting conditions and concluded that "the pattern of sex difference in oxygen consumption was found to be consistently higher for boys than for girls, with the differences becoming more pronounced after the age of eleven years." Certainly these statistics should help us to account for and to provide the needs that boys have for greater activity than girls. Yet most schools require the same tasks of boys as of girls and the majority of schools still value quietness and inactivity over purposeful noise and activity. Although both boys and girls need a balanced program of quiet and more active experiences, boys are forced to conform to programs which do not provide a natural outlet for their different energies and activity needs.

Need we say that boys and girls develop differently in total sexuality? Even this everyday fact is generally ignored in elementary school programs. The sexual revolution is only one part, although it is a very important part, of the changing world in the latter part of this century; but along with other real-life problems and concerns, schools have contrived to avoid teaching about sexuality. We can never assume that boys and girls will get the information and guidance they need at home, but we can always assume that the home and the school have at least an equal responsibility to help children understand their sexuality right from their earliest school experiences.

The place of family life and sex education in curriculum design will be illustrated in more detail later, but here it does seem important to stress how sexuality results in diverse treatment, and thus in diverse learning opportunities, for boys and girls.

Society Treats the Sexes Differently

From the day they are born, boys and girls are treated differently by parents, peers, teachers, and society in general. Different cultures and different social classes within cultures vary in their treatment of positions and responsibilities for males and females. But although many sex distinctions are sharply reduced in modern America and in other countries, society still has certain expectations for boys and girls and for men and women. For example, a boy is told early in his life that he must be "like a man . . . courageous and manly." He must not cry since this is supposed to be a female characteristic and prerogative, and he is not supposed to show his emotions. Girls, on the other hand, are supposed to be more refined and ladylike. They are inadvertently trained in the subtleties and nuances of what a "lady" is supposed to be like, how she is supposed to behave, and even what life vocations and avocations will probably be expected of her.

Generally speaking, parents expect more conformity from their daughters than they do from their sons. Parents have been known to brag a little about the difficulties their sons get into, but seldom do you hear them speak with pride of their daughters' discrepancies. Boys are often allowed more freedom at an earlier age than are girls, in the belief that they need unsupervised experiences in order to achieve manhood. But generally it is assumed that girls need carefully supervised experiences in order to "practice for" womanhood.

To the degree that girls do conform more fully to the requirements set by teachers, and to the degree that these teachers still prefer conformity to rebelliousness, girls may get a shade of advantage in their school marks (28). How far such inclinations, derived from customary attitudes persisting in our culture, modify the treatment by teachers of girl and boy personalities and thereby affect the personal development of each sex is worthy of consideration by any teacher—man or woman (29).

The standards, or criteria, that male and female teachers use to judge the personality of learners further complicates the development of boys and girls. Even though there is considerable agreement among teachers about criteria they use to distinguish the best and most poorly adjusted youngsters, there are differences enough to warn both men and women of sex-oriented culture biases of which they may not be aware. Quoting from the conclusions of a study completed by Beilin and Werner (30), criteria used most often by male teachers include, "maturity, good judgment, dependability, trustworthiness, lack of self-consciousness, and being secure as a person." The criteria that female teachers mention most often are "humility" and "modesty." Female teachers also place greater stress, when talking about poor adjustment, on "negativism, hostility to authority, discipline problems, and getting into trouble in school."

In this same study, items listed under character-control were more often favored by female teachers, but items classified under emotional-personality were more often preferred by male teachers. What this all adds up to is that boys and girls can be judged very differently depending upon whether they have a man for a teacher or a woman. And what is implied for all teachers is that they need to pay more attention to their own sexuality and sex biases in working with young people.

Growing awareness of the cultural origins of masculinity and femininity provides a wonderful opportunity to use educative processes for reducing biases and for providing learning environments that will emphasize sex identification and sexual understanding. Activity drives that can be directly traced to sexuality include physical urges that become especially noticeable during and just prior to puberty, and that have really been present as far back as infancy. These desires and drives can range all the way from desires for physical activities to erotic impulses all along the continuum of life. They are part of each person's desire to be treated as a loving, attractive, desirable, and acceptable individual. They are deeply involved in concepts of selfhood and definitely affect learning responses.

Boys and Girls Have Different Interests Because of Their Sexuality

Finally, boys and girls have different interests and talents. This is due partly to the ways that society and schools have trained them and partly to innate characteristics of growth and personality. Conflicts in modern life and tasks to be considered by schools revolve around many of the misconceptions that have grown up about the roles of males and females.

Bott (31) studied the play interests of children in nursery school and discovered that, although all children are interested in locomotor toys between the ages of two to five years, after age four interest in movement seems to increase with age for boys and to decrease with age for girls. By kindergarten and first grade, sex roles can be observed as having been adopted by children, and are already strongly influencing children's likes and dislikes.

Tyler (32) found significant differences between the kinds of activities selected by five- and six-year-old boys and girls among the following kinds of interests: (1) active play outdoors, (2) playing with toys indoors, (3) paper-and-pencil activities, and (4) helping adults with work. Boys most often chose interests in categories 1 and 4 and girls most often chose those classified under 2 and 3. In a later study using boys and girls of nine and ten years of age, she found more definite repudiation of things that children thought to be characteristic of the opposite sex. Boys rejected as inappropriate anything that they connected with "being a sissy," and any kind of work that they considered "girl's work." Girls, in turn, were already rejecting physical activities, aggressive behavior, and most often things that they had been taught were unladylike.

We know that children's interests change as they mature and as they have many opportunities to participate in a greater range of activities. There is evidence that maturity is a more reliable index than socioeconomic status or race in determining interests, and that organized games and biological concerns hold higher interests for both boys and girls as they grow older. But Kaufman (33) also found that boys and girls in grades four through eight (ages nine and ten to thirteen or so) had increasingly different interests. Among 2,234 children he found that boys' interests were already turned in the direction of professional services, service, and technical occupations, whereas girls were interested in office and entertainment services. Curricular interest of boys showed growing preferences for science and mathematics while girls were skewed toward the language arts and social studies.

One can at least wonder whether these findings represent innate talents and abilities or whether they represent the preconditioning influences of our society in relation to the occupations appropriate for males and for females. One final idea before you are invited to think about some suppositions: as things stand now, the close supervision that girls generally experience in our society has caused them to need close personal relationships and to imitate rather than to innovate or to reconstruct and abstract pertinent ideas to form new hypotheses.

With less supervision and less immediate reward for the "manlike" lessons learned, boys probably develop different learning styles which involve defining their goals, restructuring the field of evidence, and abstracting ideas that have worked to combine with new ideas and to form new principles of behavior and accomplishment.

A number of studies support the following hypotheses. Can you substantiate or deny them on the basis of your own personal observations and other evidence you have?

Discussion Questions

1. Females will tend to demonstrate greater needs for relationships and affiliations than will males. Do you agree or disagree and why?
2. Females tend to be more dependent upon other people than males do. Do you agree or disagree and why?
3. In any given situation, females seem to depend on *external* context clues and hesitate to deviate from the given of perceptual situations.
4. Males have better problem-solving skills than do females.
5. Females are more receptive to standards set by others than males are.
6. Males are more concerned with internalized moral standards than females are. Can you substantiate or deny? Give your reasons.
7. Females are less active and more submissive than males. Can you agree?
8. Males have more sexual drive than females. Do you agree or disagree?
9. Certain professions are more suited to males than to females. Do you agree or disagree and why?
10. Both male and female teachers exercise sex biases in dealing with students. Can you substantiate or deny? Give your reasons.

Additional Suggested Reading

Gessell, A., et al., *The First Five Years of Life.* New York: Harper & Row, 1940.

Gessell, V., F. L. Ilg, et al., *Infant and Child in the Culture of Today.* New York: Harper & Row, 1943.

Sarason, S. B., K. S. Davidson, et al., *Anxiety in Elementary School Children.* New York: John Wiley & Sons, Inc., 1960.

Seward, G. H., *Sex and the Social Order.* New York: McGraw-Hill Book Company, 1946.

Sweeney, E. J., *Sex Differences in Problem Solving.* Stanford, Calif.: Stanford University Department of Psychology, Tech. Rep. 1, 1953.

Terman, L. M., and C. C. Miles, *Sex and Personality.* New York: McGraw-Hill Book Company, 1936.

Thorpe, L. P., *Child Psychology and Development.* 2nd ed. New York: The Ronald Press Company, 1955.

Watson, E. H., and G. H. Lowrey, *Growth and Development of Children.* 2nd ed. Chicago: Yearbook Publishers, 1954.

Health and Physical Development

Mental Health and Personal Development

Physical and mental health go hand in hand and the physical state of being has a decided effect upon one's personality development and upon the ability to learn from one another. A child's state of health causes him to be happy or unhappy, energetic or apathetic, mentally alert or lethargic, emotionally stable or unstable, and socially adjusted or maladjusted. Such things as height or lack of it, obesity or scrawniness, energy levels, and various physical handicaps have a decided effect upon peer perception, self-perception, and adult perceptions of children.

Nature, nurture, home background, and environment have a great deal to do with a child's physical appearance and his state of health, but there is also a great deal that schools can do to educate children in regard to health and physical development and to help them live effectively with nature's endowments.

Remember that among the developmental tasks listed earlier are: knowledge of physical realities, developing physical skills, accepting physical limitations and using physical abilities effectively, irregular growth patterns for different individuals, and building healthy attitudes about one's body and oneself as a growing person. Remember, too, that there are definite differences between boys and girls, not only biologically but also in relation to coordination at different ages, height and bodily development, heart growth and respiration, strength and aptitudes, and mental and emotional outlooks.

Susan will illustrate what we mean when we say that physical characteristics can distort children's mental and social equilibrium, their state of self-satisfaction and well-being, and their total personalities.

Susan

At ten years of age Susan annoyed her classmates and caused them to reject her by seemingly constant concern for her own appearance, comfort, importance, and abilities. She was obese and called attention to herself by demanding that classmates admire a new article of clothing, a new possession, or a new hairdo. She bragged about her abilities, which were not obvious to her peers, and would make comments like, "Don't you think I'm the best artist in the class?" or, "My story is better than anybody's."

She needed the largest chair in the classroom and invariably pushed it between another child and the teacher even though her lethargy often caused her to be the last one to join the group. On the playground, she never participated in games, but declared loudly that, "I could beat everybody if I wanted to." At lunch and recess times, she gorged herself with snacks brought from home and ate considerably more than the other children.

When not bragging or eating, she often sought a lonely corner of the classroom or playground and moped. At an age when other girls were beginning to notice and try to attract the opposite sex and when boy and girl parties were beginning, Susan was excluded from social invitations to her classmates' homes. At the same time, conferences with her parents revealed that they felt that Susan's obesity had little to do with her personality difficulties and that she would "outgrow" her "baby fat." As an only child, she was adored and indulged by doting parents.

The approach taken by the teacher, the school nurse, the school guidance counselor, and the physical education teacher included educating the parents to the dimensions of Susan's problems of physical health and mental well-being, initiating special dietary studies in the classroom, prescribing special physical education activities, and recommending that Susan be put under a doctor's care. When the parents, who were intelligent and well-educated people, realized the seriousness of Susan's problems and possibly disastrous consequences of allowing them to become ingrained, they cooperated fully.

They were interested in and receptive to information regarding obesity and its effect on personality development. They accepted the implications in one research study verified by Werkman and Greenberg (34) in which it was found that obesity "appears to be accompanied by consistent personality difficulties of a serious nature." Obese girls in their studies showed unusual narcissism, had difficulty with impulse control, had considerable social anxiety, and demonstrated behavioral immaturity and depression. Obesity was also shown to restrict their social and occupational horizons and to cause faulty perception of significant self-concepts. Psychoanalytically, narcissism is an arrest or a regression of the first stage of sexual development in which the self is an object of sexual pleasure, and often manifests itself in the ways described in Susan's case.

Susan's problems were not miraculously solved, naturally. But as she approaches the age of twelve, she diets, eats more conservative and healthier foods, is better coordinated, joins in group games and activities, and develops new interests. Most importantly, she shows more interest in her classmates and their activities. She is able to praise them for accomplishments and they, in turn, can honestly praise hers. Although Susan is a girl, there are many boys to whom the same criteria can be applied. The girls and boys in our schools need the help and support of the home, the school, and the community to help them build knowledge and attitudes about healthful living.

Effects of Labeling

Consider the effects of the labels that are attached to various children or groups of children, especially in relation to those variously lumped as exceptional children. Clinical labels have an effect on children and on teachers. Combs and Harper (35), for example, found that labels affect teachers' perceptions of children. This seemed to be true regardless of whether teachers were experienced or inexperienced. Further, they found that teachers were not only conditioned by various labels to think and perceive in certain ways, but that experiences with children did not seem to affect the original perceptions and impressions. Obviously it is necessary to ensure that experience with "different" children (and each child is unique), will change teachers' perceptions and will help encourage children to understand their own assets and limitations.

In our society, as in most societies, there are certain premiums placed upon one type of physique as compared with another. For example, the prowess of the football hero, the svelteness of female models, the good looks of movie idols—these customarily conjure up certain images and models. Thus the tall girl, the short boy, the masculine-looking girl, the feminine-looking boy, the fat boy or girl, or the skinny child find themselves with added complications brought about by the real or imagined perceptions of others.

Teachers have a responsibility to understand the roles that have been assigned and to help children make constructive use of their bodies. For example, it is easy to ask the tallest boy to wash the chalkboards, the strongest boy to carry a stack of books, or the most attractive girl to act as room hostess when guests are expected. But these experiences may be more needed by other children.

Returning to the idea of labels, children with various irregularities or deformities need special understanding, support, and help to learn to respect themselves and others in spite of shortcomings. In addition to the children who are too weak, too sickly, too fat, too uncoordinated, or too awkward, there are those with actual physical deformities—crossed eyes, a withered hand, a limp, a twisted spine, a mongoloid appearance, or overly large ears—who need special attention, affection, and understanding. If teachers like and respect them, this affects the way children feel about themselves and the way others will feel about them. This is the beginning of self-esteem and self-understanding which helps a child put his best foot forward.

Grouping will be discussed in more detail later, but here it seems important to mention that grouping has a serious consequence as far as labeling is concerned. There is considerable evidence to show that children grouped according to academic problems, intellectual achievement, and special physical problems tend to elicit negative or positive labels from teachers and to lend one another negative rather than positive support. A group labeled in a negative way causes teachers to expect less of children and to demand less of them.

Bowman (36), studying the effects of grouping underachievers together, concludes that "the experimenters seemed to agree that it was not wise to group underachievers together in the same class because they tend to give each other negative support rather than positive." And Olson (37) says that, "A child tends to produce in his behavior anything that the culture demands, if it is in his repertory of possible responses. Groups thus supply goals toward which children aspire and grow."

School-Sponsored Environments

Children and teachers do interact with their surroundings. In our uptight world, it is essential that the mind and the body have opportunities to unwind—to be more fully conscious of sights, sounds, colors, and subconscious thoughts.

Today, 70 per cent of our population lives in cities and it is projected that soon at least 90 per cent of our people will be living in cities. In almost every city in America today there are legitimate complaints of overcrowded, cheerless schools with inadequate recreational and sanitary facilities. Some schools have no playgrounds at all, and many are without health suites, teachers' rest rooms, health personnel and services, or inside play areas. Bathrooms are poorly located and are often without soap and tissue. Sometimes they even require unlocking, and woe unto the hapless child who cannot wait until they are unlocked.

These school "learning environments" are more common than we would like to think or to admit. They limit abilities to have proper play and rest, adequate health care, and even proper elimination and cleanliness. Often the children who go to these schools have an equally bad home environment. A dirty apartment in a crowded part of town and a dreary, outdated, and inadequate school are not only physically unhealthy but they reinforce negative ideas of self-worth.

Especially for more disadvantaged children, but also for every child, school buildings should be planned for health, safety, beauty, and cleanliness; and appropriate personnel and services should reinforce the school plant. That there is a relationship between the school plant and the services it provides and its occupants should be common knowledge by this time. But because this knowledge has been acted upon so little, the top educational organizations of the country continue to recommend sharply escalated efforts to accomplish these objectives.

The American Association of School Administrators (38) has consistently said that children's "fullest potential cannot be achieved unless every aspect of the physical environment is so controlled that it contributes to the comfort and health of the pupils and the professional staff." And the United States Office of Education (39) has said that, "Mental, physical, social, and emotional well being is fostered when the leadership is understanding and qualified, the program challenging and suitable, and the environment right," in discussing good programs of health and physical education.

Beyond the Actual School Plant

While we are talking about learning environments, let us not limit our thinking to the actual school building and its surroundings. With astounding figures about population growth and concentration of increasing numbers of people in cities, we must turn our attention to the needs of city-dwelling children, the lack of available space for good schools and recreation facilities, and the possibilities for using areas other than the traditional school site for learning opportunities.

Biologists are receiving alarming implications from experiments conducted with mammals such as mice, rats, deer, and rabbits forced to live in overcrowded living conditions. It has been determined that mammals require certain amounts of living space or they begin to exhibit the most destructive tendencies in biological and emotional behavior. Among these destructive forces are disrupted reproductive cycles, loss of male–female sexuality, genocide, suicide, and death from shock or apathy. Professor Ross Wilhelm of the University of Michigan, writing for the *Bell Telephone Magazine*, feels that human beings may also have the same needs for required amounts of living space, and that riots are caused by people hating their living space rather than their fellow man.

Relief from noise pollution was a topic discussed by Stainbrook (40) in a recent symposium on "Man and Nature in the City." He suggests that a city dweller's ears are "constantly bombarded. In self-defense, he learns to let in only a tiny proportion of the sounds, sights, and smells of the city—the portion his mind can manage . . . the effort to hold back that ever-pressing flood arouses anxiety and anger. . . ."

Scientists tell us that our bodies have certain, predictable biological rhythms that include daily, weekly, lunar, seasonal, and annual cycles. Dr. Stainbrook suggests that the city's noise, dirt, impersonality, and crowding may produce fatigue, inefficiency, and "more subtle impairments that can lead to an early evolved *locking in* of our biological processes to events in the natural environment."

Access to open, natural, clean surroundings away from noise, dirt, crowded living, and excessive traffic can, according to anthropologist Edward T. Hall, also writing for the *Bell Telephone Magazine*, reverse the deadly process of "a series of destructive behavioral sinks more lethal than the hydrogen bomb." He speaks of the anonymity of city life and the rare opportunities that city dwellers have for interrelationships in unhurried, uncrowded, face-to-face living and communicating.

Impetus to plan for *different learning environments* comes both from the devastating facts that biologists, anthropologists, social scientists, and psychologists are verifying, and from our own experiences with unwinding tense emotions. Walk through a lovely park or woods, sail in a boat on the open water, sit by a lake at sunrise or sunset, or climb a mountain, and you have feelings of mind and sense expansion. Your mind starts to unwind and allows the intrusion of new sights, sounds, colors, and thoughts. Perhaps this is why mystics and poets use metaphors from nature to explain the depths of human emotion—of human minds and souls.

Can Schools Use Parks and Camps to Better Advantage?

Think of the possibilities for teachers and for children if part of every school year could be spent in a national forest, at a national park, near a seashore or a lake or a river, or even in public parks or nature centers. School-sponsored camp programs and outdoor education offer exciting possibilities for teachers and for children; those who have participated in them come back feeling that they are not only better human beings—healthier and more vital—but they also return with increased respect for one another.

In one experiment, emotionally disturbed children were shown to benefit remarkably from a two-week camp experience. Methods, materials, and organization used in program planning were studied in relation to the interpretation of their behavior in the traditional school building and at the camp. The camp experience was found to have resulted in greatly improved home and school behavior (41).

Admittedly, it is difficult for one school or one school system to maintain and staff a camp site, but there are many possibilities for combining resources among schools and school systems to cooperate with a national forest, for example. These camp sites are often located in national forests and maintained by city–county camp commissions. The commission provides a well-qualified staff of counselors who work closely with the schools that use the camp. The camp can be used for both camping and for outdoor education and can be shared by different schools at the same time, giving children from different schools a chance to become acquainted.

Pilot projects in school camping have included children as young as six for a few days at a time. Others take very young children for day camp programs.

Outdoor education needs to be considered as a vital and integral part of the curriculum at all age levels. Preparation by teachers and students planning experiences in outdoor living begins in September. Objectives for personal, social, and educational growth are developed by the participating students recognizing needs, interests, and differences of the class members. Children maintain enthusiasm while considering exciting adventures in outdoor living. Unit topics focusing on wildlife, soil, water, and the galaxy come alive in an outdoor setting. Daily contacts with the

School-sponsored programs of camping and outdoor education offer exciting curriculum possibilities. Furthermore, teachers and children who have participated in such programs return feeling that they are better human beings; they have increased respect for, and knowledge of, one another.

forest ranger, soil conservationist, ornithologist, marine biologist, geologist, and entomologist help students to become acquainted with the world around them.

Students have the opportunity to identify with groups in cabin living, special interests, and work.

Important factors in outdoor education are the democratic procedures students demonstrate while living together in a community setting. From experiences in outdoor education children can discover that nature and living things are interdependent.

Often, camping programs are included within a health and physical education framework because the physical education teacher and the school nurse are the coordinators of programs. But the classroom teacher should also be very much involved for a number of reasons. Among these are camp learnings which affect peer relationships, teacher–pupil relationships, many areas of the curriculum, and health and physical–mental well-being of children. There are a host of possible science learnings and certainly many possibilities for social learnings. Nature study, rock collection, cooking, and planning and working together are some of the other ingredients of camping experiences. Not least among all of these is the aesthetic aspect of being out of doors.

When teachers, parents, and children plan for outdoor education and camping experiences, they will want to fit the program to the age levels of the children, plan for definite educational experiences, and consider potential and existing sites. Professional educators are in an excellent position to lead communities in making such opportunities available to children.

Additional Suggested Reading

Van Til, William, "Schools and Camping," *Toward a New Curriculum*. Washington, D.C.: National Education Association, 1944.
Montgomery, B. A., "Experiments in School Camping," *Instructor*, June, 1950.
Smith, Julian W., "Planning for School Community Camping," *Education*, Vol. 73, September, 1952. (Entire issue is devoted to school camping.)

Physical Growth as Program Planning Base

Our *physical growth* constitutes almost one third of our normal life span. Garrison (26) has studied the exact measurement of physical growth and tells us that genetic studies of the development of children have not only furnished valuable information about the nature of both physical growth and motor development at different ages, but that "these can be measured objectively." Writers like Garrison have designed their studies so that the student of educational psychology will understand physical growth and motor development and "view these aspects of growth as integral parts of the total growth and development of the individual."

Through the studies of geneticists and physical anthropologists, we now know more, and continue to learn more, about

1. *Growth, variability, and sex differences in motor development, height, and weight.* Yet conventional schools tend to hold to traditional ideas about what boys and girls should or should not do.
2. *Normal and abnormal weights for bone structures.* But schools continue to weigh and measure children, record and send these home for parental signatures, and do nothing more about problems pertaining to overweight and underweight.
3. *Development of sensory organs such as ears and eyes.* Even so, schools have embarked on programs to force children to read earlier and earlier in spite of the fact that we know that binocular vision is closely related to reading readiness and that there is grave danger in forcing young children to use their eyes for close vision before their eye muscles have developed sufficiently.
4. *Anatomical development and its relationship to self and peer perceptions.* Yet we fail to use this knowledge to help children understand themselves and others better.
5. *Circulatory and respiratory systems.* We know that boys have special needs for more activity than girls at the elementary school level, but we still put both through the same lock-step curriculum and judge both on their ability to tolerate it.
6. *Motor development, growth in general bodily control, and specialized motor abilities.* We know the fallacy of the same set of experiences for all children of the same age level and yet we use our knowledge little in individualizing programs for elementary school-children.

The real question for schools and for teachers is whether they can, and will, use new information as an intelligent basis for changing programs and practices that are now failing to serve the best interests of elementary school boys and girls. We must not only know about the new knowledge that is available in relation to physical growth and motor development, but also be able to apply it in planning for the social, mental, and personal growth of each child.

Generally speaking, good schools include the following objectives in their school health programs. These take into account the knowledge we are gaining about the total growth and development of individuals and are intended to educate so that children will

1. Be increasingly able to plan well-balanced lives for themselves including work and play, activity and rest, and social and individual activities.

2. Understand that their health is important to them not only now but also throughout their lives.
3. Know and practice good dietary and physical exercise programs.
4. Understand safety measures, basic first aid, the importance of medical and dental care, and drug use and abuse.
5. Have better understanding of the importance of community health improvement programs, including communicable diseases, elimination of slum areas, problems of air and water pollution, and conservation of human and natural resources.
6. Have better understanding of personal strengths and weaknesses in relation to personal development and good mental health.
7. Have congruity in developing attitudes and knowledge about physical fitness, appropriate clothing, personal hygiene, developing sexuality, and preparation for family and community living.

School–Community-Sponsored Health Services

We have long passed the time when schools can be expected to accomplish all of these objectives alone. We are at last coming to the realization that there are many well-staffed and well-equipped community agencies which can be encouraged to share the responsibilities. The enormous expense of comprehensive programs is one factor that forces schools to look beyond their own resources. Another is the variety of talent available in community agencies and not generally available in schools.

Schools and communities can work together to provide pediatricians, dentists, nurses, psychologists, psychiatrists, and nutrition experts for schoolchildren. Public health department staffs and school staffs can share facilities, personnel, and funds for better health and physical education programs. Community, city, county, and state can cooperate in the use of open space for school camping and outdoor education. Together, parents, civic groups, public health and recreation groups, and school staffs can channel the efforts and the facilities of many to help educate parents and children, to examine and treat those in need, to share appropriate information, and to develop preventive and compensatory programs.

The need for these services and programs is urgent. Study after study shows that even though children come to school with no noticeable health problems or physical defects, health problems develop in direct proportion to the length of time they have been in school. Increasing numbers of children are requiring glasses, have hearing and speech defects, have correctable physical defects associated with bone growth, have psychosomatic ailments, and develop cardiac and digestive ailments. We do not suggest that schools create these defects, but we cannot question their responsibilities, along with other community agencies and parents, to take action and to reverse the trend. Inasmuch as it is impossible to cover each facet of a good health and physical education program here, the following references are provided:

Health in the Elementary School. Washington, D.C.: National Department of Elementary School Principals, 1950.

Holsey, Elizabeth, and Lorene Porter, *Physical Education for Children.* New York: The Dryden Press, 1958. Also see *Physical Education for Children.* New York: Holt, Rinehart and Winston, Inc., 1963.

Knapp, Clyde, and E. Patricia Hagman, *Teaching Methods for Physical Education.* New York: McGraw-Hill Book Company, 1953.

Miller, Arthur G., and Virginia Whitcomb, *Physical Education in the Elementary School Curriculum.* Englewood Cliffs, N.J.: Prentice-Hall, Inc., 1957.

McNeeley, Simon A., and Elsie Schneider, *Physical Education in the Child's School Day.* Washington, D.C.: U.S. Department of Health, Education and Welfare, Bulletin No. 14, 1950.

Olson, Edward G., *School and Community Programs.* Englewood Cliffs, N.J.: Prentice-Hall, Inc., 1949.

Salt, E. B., et al., *Teaching Physical Education in the Elementary School.* Albany, N.Y.: State Department of Education, 1962.

Van Hagen, W., G. Dexter, and J. F. Williams, *Physical Education in the Elementary School.* Sacramento, Calif.: State Department of Education, 1951.

Walker, Herbert, *Health in the Elementary School.* New York: The Ronald Press Company, 1955.

Wheatley, George M., and Grace T. Hallock, *Health Observation of School Children.* New York: McGraw-Hill Book Company, 1956.

Willgoose, Carl E., *Evaluation of Health Education and Physical Education.* New York: McGraw-Hill Book Company, 1962.

In-School Achievements and Interests

In Relation to Individuality

To illustrate his belief in the talents and interests each child brings to school, each teacher regards the *understanding of individual difference* as being a prime principle of learning psychology. In recognizing his responsibility to understand and use these individual differences to the best advantage for each student, the teacher practices

1. *Being less rigid and more flexible in daily program and lesson planning.* This does not imply less planning. In fact, it implies quite the opposite. Teachers should plan individually with children so carefully that they feel perfectly secure in deviating from rigid curricula and preset plans. Long-range goals can still be adhered to—only the road to be taken is changed.

2. *Emphasizing the worth of each individual in an instructional setting.*
   When real belief in the worth of every individual permeates the
   philosophy of the teacher, less emphasis will be given to mass planning for the purpose of keeping children busy, and more time will be
   allotted to individual and small group teaching and probing particular interests and problems of individual learners.

3. *Helping to design or remodel school plants.* As teachers are brought
   into the planning of new school buildings, we can expect to see
   changes implemented in relation to the individual and personalized
   needs of children. For example, there will be individual study carrels,
   outdoor patios for social and academic learning, more attractive and
   healthful facilities, provision for parent and community meetings
   and activities, and so on.

4. *Innovating teaching techniques.* Realizing that new approaches to
   personalizing instruction are needed, learning environments will be
   designed around individualized curriculum that allows the student
   to participate in a variety of activities and teachers to serve as individual and small group consultants. No longer will we erect egg-
   crate units and expect teaching programs to "fit in." Rather, programs
   will be more flexible, learning inspired and designed. Keeping in
   step with newer teaching techniques and better ways to use pupil
   and teacher talents will require flexibility in space arrangement and
   equipment.

5. *Using released time for programming instruction.* Time will have to
   be provided for each teacher every day so that more effective learning conditions, facilities, and programs become reality.

6. *Learning about the potentials for using teacher aides for clerical
   help, tutorial help, and teaching assistance.* If teachers are to have
   time to teach they must be released from many of the duties that can
   just as well be done by paraprofessionals.

7. *Changing philosophies about the roles of teachers.* Tomorrow's teachers will be in tune with philosophy that casts the teacher as a counselor and guide rather than a purveyor of facts. The teacher will be
   a part of a teaching team that guides and helps children with
   mutually decided learning interests and goals.

8. *Prescribing for individual children on the basis of observation and
   the gathering of all available information about each one.* Just as
   physicians, judges, ministers, sociologists, and socal workers study
   the history of each individual and spend a great deal of time conferring individually with patients and clients, so must teachers prescribe on the basis of individuals. Large-scale group assignments
   obliterate the qualities that distinguish one individual from another.
   Unfortunately, overemphasis on well-organized lessons and courses
   of study has conditioned many teachers to overlook unique individual needs.

Grouping to Individualize

In the past, factors considered in planning for the grouping of elementary schoolchildren have been primarily those of age, reading ability, and achievement in other academic areas. Although these areas are partially relevant to plans for grouping children and although sheer numbers of children force schools to group, any recommendations for grouping should take into consideration the *individualization of instruction* and the *best ways to relate subject matter to each child's interests, talents, social development, special needs, and personal goals.*

Grouping on the basis of subject matter or academic achievement alone denies one of education's chief goals—that of facilitating different levels of learning so that changed behavior will result. Groups, seen in this context, supply the organizational framework in which we hope to identify common interests and problems of children and to supply goals mutually rewarding to individuals who comprise groups.

Other reasons why groups are created include creating situations in which children can experience critical thinking stimulated by peers; stimulating children to independent action; helping children develop individual talents and abilities; fostering social development; and encouraging creative group and individual thinking.

Thus it can be seen that groups, which so often become static and sterile when children remain in the same ones as time goes on, can also supply the antithesis of those opportunities we want for children. Regrouping frequently on the basis of new interests and purposes of instruction can help children make individual discoveries and can help open up new possibilities for personal development. The element of pupil choice should always be considered even though a general topic has been decided upon. For example, the topic may be "Brazil Today," but teachers of eleven-year-olds can plan with students to set up committees to study various aspects of geography, history, culture, government, language, and family life. Small groups can work together to gather and present information with help from teachers in regard to general outlines and possible resources. Children can select the group that interests them most, but they will also benefit from the work that is being done by other groups.

We say that some children are eye-minded or ear-minded. What we really mean is that our observation of them leads us to believe that they learn best through visualizing or through hearing. The same can be said of tasting, and feeling. All children need tactile experiences with objects and artifacts or various media, but some children learn better in these ways than in others. Individualization occurs when we take advantage of children's own unique learning styles in helping them to acquire others.

Homework is one means of individualizing instruction if it is used to reinforce classroom learning and to extend personal interests that will contribute to group learning at school. Of secondary importance, it provides opportunities to involve parents in knowing about school activities. The same homework assignment for an entire class can seldom be justified and is, more often than not, repetitious "busywork." Teachers feel that the same assignment for all children simplifies lesson planning and is less time consuming. And they are right. But this is teacher-oriented and not individual-student-oriented planning.

Children are capable of self-selected homework assignments and can be led to define areas in which they need more work, more time, or facilities and materials not available at school. Some time should be spent each day to help children plan out-of-school learning activities such as:

1. Making and bringing articles for class bulletin boards, exhibits, or displays.
2. Reading independent books or reports of their own choice.
3. Developing collections of stones, shells, stamps, shapes, colors, sizes, or other classifications.
4. Developing an individual research project in an area of special interest.
5. Making hand puppets or dioramas to illustrate stories or reports.
6. Interviewing neighborhood residents or community officials.
7. Comparing a radio and a TV newscast.
8. Writing stories or poems for personal diaries.
9. Comparing newspaper accounts of the same incident.

When one starts to consider assignments such as these, and when one grows in knowledge of individual children in a group, the possibilities for individualizing assignments are almost endless. One teacher has a personal comment for each child as she bids them good night at the school. The comment includes something they have planned for homework and may go something like this:

John, remember that you are going to ask your father to tell you more about what it was like where his family used to live so that you can tell us some more about Switzerland tomorrow.

Susan, don't forget to bring that costume you told us about. See what your mother knows about it, all right?

Tammy, you promised to bring your rock collection and tell us about it tomorrow. We'll see what books we can find about rock collecting when we go to the library tomorrow.

Billy, you are going to see how many words you can find that begin with "sub" tonight, isn't that right?

Jane, you and Sandra are in charge of the news board this week and you remember we thought there may be some good news clippings about the space flight in tonight's paper.

Joan, you are going to work on your subtraction facts tonight, isn't that what we agreed?

Lewis, please try to finish that wonderful story you started today. I know your parents are going to like it, too.

Joe, be ready to give your oral report on the book you've just finished tomorrow. I like your idea of making believe it is a newscast to tell people about this new book.

This teacher is not only showing personal interest and individualizing homework assignments, but she is also providing a way that parents can be cued to what's going on at school. Not the least of the dividends is the purposeful and happy manner in which each child leaves the school day's learning environment, and the enthusiasm with which he returns the next day.

Pacing Individual Learning

The small group structure does not guarantee successful involvement of each child in the group's work, but it does provide an opportunity for teachers to try different ways of keeping imagination and curiosity alive while personalizing learning experiences. One important benefit of grouping and regrouping as needs and interests change is the increased possibility of pacing learning.

Being able to *pace learning* relieves children of pressures they experience when they are lumped together in large groups where some children work faster and some work more slowly than they do. Pacing gives each child the opportunity to proceed to the next level of learning when he is ready and to select new data and techniques as he is ready. Steps for teachers to consider in planning paced instruction are the following:

1. *The identification of objectives in terms of pupil behavior.* When teacher and pupil have objectives to be pursued clearly in mind, both are apt to feel more confident and relaxed in working toward these objectives.
2. *The selection of independent study materials and media.* These include programmed texts, sets of prepared materials, video tapes, teaching machines, children's trade books, varieties of textbooks, periodicals, records, and so on. With materials and media selections decided upon, the child can work individually and can check himself on various proficiencies for restudy, teacher guidance and consultation, or advancement to another level.
3. *The development of checklists* that help teachers trace quickly whether students are using logical problem-solving approaches, using past knowledge to form new associations, and seeking new ways of finding out.

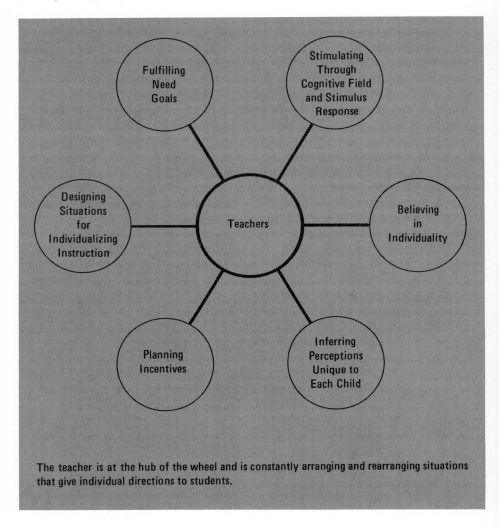

The teacher is at the hub of the wheel and is constantly arranging and rearranging situations that give individual directions to students.

4. *The development of both situational and paper-and-pencil tests* for observing and recording children's special interests and competencies. Records, which teacher aides can assist in developing and keeping, will include anecdotal notes, examples of special interests and talents, records of parent conferences, and notes about strengths and weaknesses observed by each teacher in addition to standardized academic, IQ, and psychological tests.

Pacing learning means that the teacher is at the hub of a constantly rotating wheel that allows teachers and children to arrange and rearrange learning situations so that each child has opportunities to participate in a variety of individual and group situations. With increasing knowledge about each child, the teacher is better equipped to fulfill need goals, stimulate through cognitive field and stimulus response, shore up belief in individuals and individuality, plan special and unique incentives for individuals and groups, decide what his own perceptions infer for designing individual learning situations, and design these situations.

Needed Experimentation

Let us return briefly to the idea of experimentation needed in schools. Traditionally, educators as a group have been inclined to say, "Find some place where this has been successfully tried, and we may consider it here." If everyone adopts this attitude, no one can progress at all—and there won't be any demonstrations of success or failure. Remember that one new role for teachers is risk taking and that the reason we include this role and give it such emphasis is because we are not only teaching for the unknown, but so much is still unknown about how children learn best.

We must dare to try new ways to learn more about individuals and how they learn, and we must expect some partial failures. Science has made enormous progress through some colossal failures; in fact, scientists expect failures so that they learn what not to do and so that they can recombine successful elements. So we welcome failures that give us an opportunity to study and learn more about new possibilities. If you try something that does not seem to work at first, but that does have merit for valid changes, study the failing elements carefully. Was the new plan tried long enough? Did you involve students and their parents in the new plan? Did failure have anything to do with the attitudes of parents, students, or other educators? Can the parts that were successful be used in some different way?

We must find new ways to evaluate, value, and use human diversities. Doing so has not been the long suit of traditional education, but to fail to do so now is unthinkable. Modern teachers must no longer face classes and see featureless throngs. They must see individuals, each one different in different ways. Teachers may not know exactly how, or even what, to teach each new class, but the individuals in it can make it clear if time is taken to listen and learn from them. For a beginning, the teacher who really respects and cares about individual differences will

- Avoid giving uniform assignments.
- Not expect uniform behavior.
- Not look for uniform effort.
- Reject teaching to a "grade level."
- Not hope for uniform achievement.
- Never make lesson plans that ignore differences.
- Not assign seats by number or alphabet.

- Rarely have classes sitting in straight rows.
- Not confine his efforts to the classroom alone.

Instead, he will

- Give individualized assignments.
- Study and act in terms of deviant behaviors.
- Expect effort to be congenial with motivation.
- Realize that there are many levels in every group.
- Know that children achieve differently.
- Use special interests and talents.
- Experiment with different classroom seating arrangements.
- Consider community-wide learning environments.
- Provide a wide range of choice in learning materials.

The wise teacher's interest inventories, observations, and personal interviews give him plenty of clues to personalizing learning. He knows that varied assignments will result in varied results, and he expects that achievement rates and marks will vary accordingly. He not only accepts this, but he actually experiments with different approaches to encourage it. He manipulates situations so that different kinds of growth and ways of expression are the rule rather than the exception. The more skillful he becomes in dealing with individual differences, the greater the differences will become. He has reached the heart of education when he knows beyond a reasonable doubt that the real job of education is to encourage versatility and diversity, to value differences more than conformity, and to use individual differences to design creative, innovative learning–teaching environments.

Every teacher who ever walks into a classroom is personally responsible for the actualization or the alienation of the future citizens with whom he lives and works daily. His love, understanding, and actions based on knowledge and empathy will lead to actualizing; the lack of these can lead only to alienating. The following are suggested reading references on individual differences:

Bruner, Jerome S., *The Process of Education*. Cambridge, Mass.: Harvard University Press, 1967.

Gardner, John W., *The Pursuit of Excellence*. Garden City, N.Y.: Doubleday & Company, Inc., 1961.

Human Variability and Learning. A collection of conference reports with current ideas about learning theories as they relate to individual differences. Association for Supervision and Curriculum Development, 1961.

Mouly, George J., "Individual Differences," *Psychology for Effective Teaching*. New York: Holt, Rinehart and Winston, Inc., 1960.

Providing for Individual Differences in the Elementary School. Edited by Norma

Cutts and Nicholas Mosely. Englewood Cliffs, N.J.: Prentice-Hall, Inc., 1960.

Raths, Louis E., and Anna P. Burrell, *Understanding the Problem Child.* West Orange, N.J.: The Economic Press, 1963.

Robbins, Maxine H., "It's Good That Children Differ," *The Clearing House.* Teaneck, N.J.: Fairleigh Dickinson University Press, 1960.

Wiles, Kimball, *Teaching for Better Schools.* Englewood Cliffs, N.J.: Prentice-Hall, Inc., 1952.

References

1. Educational Policies Commission, *An Essay on Public Education.* Washington, D.C.: National Education Association, 1959, pp. 13–22.
2. Havighurst, Robert J., *Developmental Tasks and Education.* 2nd ed. New York: David McKay Co., Inc., 1966.
3. Jersild, Arthur T., *When Teachers Face Themselves.* New York: Teachers College, Columbia University, 1955.
4. Lowe, C. Marshall, "The Self-Concept: Fact or Artifact?" *Children: Readings in Behavior and Development.* New York: Holt, Rinehart and Winston, Inc., 1968.
5. Bhatnagar, K. P., "Academic Achievement as a Function of Ovis Self-Concepts and Ego Functions," *Education and Psychology Review,* Vol. 6, No. 4, 1966, pp. 178–182.
6. Sigel, Irving E., "How Intelligence Tests Limit Understanding of Intelligence," *Children: Readings in Behavior and Development.* New York: Holt, Rinehart and Winston, Inc., 1968, pp. 317–334.
7. Inhelder, Bartel, and Jean Piaget, *The Growth of Logical Thinking from Childhood to Adolescence.* New York: Basic Books, 1958. Jean Piaget is also noted for his pioneering work in the study of mental development. His *Language and Thought of the Child* (1922) is now classic in its field.
8. Torrance, E. P., *Rewarding Creative Behavior: Experiments in Classroom Creativity.* Englewood Cliffs, N.J.: Prentice-Hall, Inc., 1965.
9. Petrie, Azenath, *Annals of New York Academy of Sciences,* 1960 Yearbook.
10. Guilford, J. P., "Intellectual Factors in Productive Thinking," *Productive Thinking in Education.* Washington, D.C.: The National Education Association and the Carnegie Corporation of New York, 1965.
11. Wallas, G., *The Art of Thought.* London: C. A. Watts and Company, 1945.
12. Rossman, J., *The Psychology of the Inventor.* Washington, D.C.: Inventors Publishing Company, 1931.
13. Dewey, John, *How We Think.* Boston: D. C. Heath and Company, 1933.
14. Maslow, A. H., "Emotional Blocks to Creativity," *Humanist,* 1958 Yearbook.
15. Rogers, C. R., "Toward a Theory of Creativity," *A Source Book for Creative Thinking.* New York: Charles Scribner's Sons, 1962.
16. Richardson, Sybil, and W. Ritter, "The Learner," *Learning and the Teacher.* Washington, D.C.: Association for Supervision and Curriculum Development, 1959.

17. Sexton, Patricia C., *Education and Income: Inequities in Our Public Schools.* New York: The Viking Press, Inc., 1964.
18. Milner, Esther, "A Study of the Relationship Between Reading Readiness in Grade I School Children and Patterns of Parent-Child Interaction," *Child Development,* June, 1951.
19. Hollingshead, August B., *Elmtown's Youth.* New York: John Wiley & Sons, Inc., 1949.
20. Davis, Allison, "Socio-Economic Influences upon Children's Learning." A speech delivered at the Midcentury White House Conference on Children and Youth, Washington, D.C., December 5, 1950.
21. Havighurst, Robert J., "Knowledge of Class Status Can Make a Difference," *Progressive Education,* Vol. 27, No. 4, February, 1950.
22. Nim, O. P., "Intelligence and Socio-Economic Status," *Psychology Annual,* Vol. 1, No. 1, 1966–1967.
23. Sexton, Patricia C., *Education and Income: Inequities in Our Public Schools.* New York: The Viking Press, Inc., 1964, p. 147.
24. Marsh, M. M., "Growth of the Heart Related to Bodily Growth During Childhood and Adolescence," *Journal of Pediatrics,* Vol. II, 1953, pp. 382–402.
25. Boynton, P., and J. Boynton, *Psychology of Child Development.* Minneapolis: Educational Publishers, Inc., 1938, p. 114.
26. Garrison, Karl C., "Physical Growth and Motor Development," *Educational Psychology.* Edited by Charles E. Skinner. Englewood Cliffs, N.J.: Prentice-Hall, Inc., 1961.
27. Garn, S. M., and L. C. Clark, "The Sex Difference in the Basal Metabolic Rates," *Child Development,* Vol. XXIV, 1952, pp. 215–224.
28. Hadley, S. T., "A School Mark—Fact or Fancy," *Educational Administration and Supervision,* Vol. XL, No. 5, 1954, pp. 305–312.
29. Bruce, William F., "A Teacher's Theory of Personality: Development, Dynamics, Ideal," *Educational Psychology,* 4th ed. Edited by Charles E. Skinner. Englewood Cliffs, N.J.: Prentice-Hall, Inc., 1961, pp. 90–91.
30. Beilin, H., and E. Werner, "Sex Differences among Teachers in the Use of the Criteria of Adjustment," *Journal of Educational Psychology,* Vol. XLVIII, No. 7, November, 1957, pp. 426–436.
31. Bott, H., "Observation of Play Activities in a Nursery School," *Genetic Psychology Monograph,* Vol. IV, 1928, p. 75.
32. Tyler, L. E., "The Relationship of Interests to Abilities and Reputation among First-grade Children," *Educational and Psychological Measurement,* Vol. XI, 1951, pp. 255–264. Also see this author's "The Development of Vocational Interest: The Organization of Likes and Dislikes in Ten-year-old Children," *Journal of Genetic Psychology,* Vol. LXXXVI, 1955, pp. 33–34.
33. Kaufman, M. M., "Expressed Interests of Children in Relation to a Maturity-Age Index in Grades Four Through Eight." Unpublished Doctoral Dissertation, Northwestern University, 1955.
34. Werkman, S. L., and Elsa Greenberg, "Personality and Interest Patterns of Obese Adolescent Girls," *Psychosomatic Medicine,* Vol. 29, No. 1, 1967, pp. 72–79.
35. Combs, R. H., and J. L. Harper, "Effects of Labels on Attitudes of Educa-

tors Toward Handicapped Children," *Exceptional Children*, Vol. 33, No. 6, 1967, pp. 399–403.

36. Bowman, Paul H., "Personality and Scholastic Underachievement," *Freeing Capacity to Learn*. Washington, D.C.: Association for Supervision and Curriculum Development, 1960.

37. Olson, Willard C., *Child Development*. Boston: D. C. Heath and Company, 1959.

38. American Association of School Administrators, *Health in Schools*. Washington, D.C.: National Education Association, 1951, p. 89.

39. U.S. Office of Education, *Educating Children in Grades Four, Five, and Six*, 1960, p. 111.

40. Stainbrook, Edward, Professor and Chairman of the Department of Psychiatry at the University of Southern California School of Medicine in Los Angeles in a symposium on "Man and Nature in the City," 1968.

41. McCreary-Juhasz, Anne, and S. E. Jensen, "Benefits of a School Camp Experience to Emotionally Disturbed Children in a Regular Classroom," *Exceptional Children*, Vol. 34, No. 5, 1968, pp. 353–354.

CHAPTER 2

Teachers Study Children's Thinking and Emotions

Thinking Processes

Intimately related to new curricular emphases appropriate for today's children is the shifting from dependence upon memorization for grades and report cards to concern for the quality of their thinking. If the goal of good teachers is to have children initiate thinking—to have them reach the point where they independently observe, classify, compare, formulate problems, imagine, state and defend positions, recognize assumptions, and analyze their own accomplishments and behaviors—then curriculum planned with and for them should demonstrate this focus and evaluation should recognize the purposes of the curriculum.

Approaches to teaching children how to think lead children toward skills that will serve them throughout a lifetime, and their learning will go on and on. Teaching children how to think is an important part of every content area and is the concern of every teacher because it permeates every area of human affairs. It also lends itself to numerous ways of organizing subject matter, the use of a variety of learning media and teaching techniques, and many activities that help children uncover new meanings, relationships, and concepts.

Liking and Disliking Oneself

Study these incidents to see how teachers helped children think about themselves positively or negatively:

INCIDENT 1: A HAPPENING IN A CROWDED SCHOOL CAFETERIA
What Happened: Simon, age six, reached across the table for the salt. He tipped over his glass of milk while retrieving the salt. There were quick

Helping children learn how to think is an important part of every curriculum content area and is the concern of every teacher because it permeates all areas of human affairs. It lends itself to numerous ways of organizing subject matter, varieties of media and techniques, and many kinds of innovative activities.

Photo by Mr. Mazon, New Haven Public Schools.

tears and a murmured, frightened, "Oh, oh! I've been bad again!" The nearby monitoring teacher snapped, *"Bad* isn't the word for it! That's the second time this week! Won't you ever learn? You're so *clumsy!"*

Analysis: The milk cost five cents, but the price for the loss of the child's self-esteem is inestimable. The loss was considerably escalated by the teacher's reaction. It would have been so much better, in spite of the frustration of the moment, to respond kindly and constructively, "You're not *bad* because you spilled your milk again. It was an accident. Here's the sponge so you can clean it up. We'll get some more milk, but let's try to remember how to get the salt without spilling the milk next time." From a relatively minor mishap, a teacher could have demonstrated mature ways of handling mishaps, and Simon would have learned a positive lesson about himself, his teachers, and possible ways of coping with minor and major catastrophes. Adults in children's lives need to learn the disastrous effects of insults and sarcasm on a child's self-liking structure. Snide remarks ("How clumsy can you get?" "You are a walking disaster!" "What a slob!" "Well, you did it again!") destroy the bone marrow of a child's personality—his self-esteem. He usually believes adults and accepts their assessment of him and the roles in which they cast him, unfortunately.

INCIDENT 2: A HAPPENING IN AN ART CLASS
What Happened: A group of ten-year-olds had been working on scenery for a class play. The clean-up job had been neglected and the teacher let the children know how she felt about it. She expressed her annoyance, irritation, and displeasure clearly and effectively: "I cannot stand this mess you've left. It looks like the aftermath of a cyclone. This room needs to be cleaned up for the next class. I get angry when I see a mess like this!" The children responded cheerfully, "O.K. We'll clean it up. We forgot how late it was getting." And they did, while the teacher went about her own preparations for the next class.

Analysis: The teacher deliberately said nothing negative about the *children* and consciously avoided invectives and epithets ("*You* left this room like a pigsty." "*You* have no sense of responsibility at all!" "*You* don't deserve the privilege of painting!" "I'm not going to be *your* slave and clean up after *you!*") Instead, she intentionally stated what she saw and how she felt about what she saw. She also stated what needed to be done. She was authentic, real, and honest—and she expressed her feelings without humiliating herself or demeaning the children. The children knew that there was no personal vindictiveness and that they had neglected a responsibility. Both teacher and children were able to maintain their self-esteem and coexisted effectively while the mess was being cleaned up. The teacher cast a role for children that helped them realize that *they were not rejected* but the mess was!

INCIDENT 3: A HAPPENING IN A SCHOOL LIBRARY
What Happened: George, age twelve, voluntarily gathered up the books from his group's table and put them back in their proper places on the shelves. As the class was lined up and ready to leave the library, the teacher said:

"The library looks nice—your library teacher and I are very pleased. Every book is back where the next class can find it. That helps everyone. George, thank you for helping all of us." George just smiled, but he seemed to stand a little taller.

Analysis: This teacher praised when praise was due and recognized in his statement to the class the effort that one member had contributed. He did not vilify those who had not taken the responsibility for the books they had used, but rather emphasized the significance of the accomplishment George had voluntarily contributed to his group and to the class. The teacher concentrated his statement of approval on the appearance and order of the library, and on his own pleasure in an individual's behavior for the benefit of everyone. In the final analysis, a child does not need to be told, "You're wonderful, just great, better than all of the others!" A child can put two and two together and draw positive conclusions about himself. So can his peers. A child's self-esteem and his other-people-esteem depend upon what he says to himself in response to a teacher's words, actions, and implications. When teachers make positive and specific statements, the child's inferences will be positive and specific.

INCIDENT 4: A HAPPENING ON A SCHOOL PLAYGROUND

What Happened: Kim, age eight, was not playing with the other girls and boys. Instead, she clung to her young male teacher, and was overheard to say, "My daddy says I'm a homely little mutt. You don't think I'm pretty either, do you?"

Teacher: You're not happy with yourself, are you?
    Kim: No! I hate myself!
Teacher: Would you like to be different?
    Kim: Yes, I'd like to be pretty and smart.
Teacher: I've known that you are smart for a long time. And lately I've noticed how much neater and cleaner you look with your hair combed nicely and your fingernails cleaned. You're becoming a much nicer person to know, too, and that makes us all happy. That's how I see you, but apparently you don't see yourself as others see you.
    Kim: Do you *really* think those things you said?
Teacher: I surely do!
    Kim: (*Skipping off*) I've got to think about that!

Analysis: This is a helpful and positive teacher–pupil dialogue. Children often make statements to get someone to contradict their stated views or to receive a compliment. The teacher did not fall into these traps ("Of course I think you're pretty!"), nor did he ridicule ("Oh, you say the same thing every day! So what else is new?"), nor did he moralize ("Looks aren't everything, you know. Pretty is as pretty does!"). He neither agreed nor disagreed, but instead he acknowledged Kim's opinion sympathetically and stated his own opinion succinctly. When children berate themselves, adults' denials do little to help them; in fact, denials reinforce negative convictions. The best help teachers can give is to acknowledge respectfully the child's expressed opinion and offer his own opinions. It is hoped that the child will conclude that if the teacher respects him, he *deserves* respect, if the teacher loves him, he must deserve to be loved, and if the teacher likes him as he is, he must be a desirable person.

In these kinds of ways, teachers help children think about themselves in positive and productive ways. Does helping a child think about liking or disliking himself have anything to do with reading, writing, and arithmetic? Of course it does! No matter what the content area of the moment is, a child can be led to like himself for trying even if he is only partially succeeding at the moment. But if he is given the impression that he is a complete flop at reading, for example, then he concludes that not only is he himself an unworthy person but that reading, also, is for the birds.

Small children do not yet differentiate between the self and the nonself. They believe that the world appears the same to everybody and that it is and remains what it appears to be to them at each particular moment. To them, the fragmentary and temporary perceptions of others are absolute, and they do not yet know that they are dependent upon time, space, and other experiences. They do not yet know that a mountain seen from one position looks different when seen from another position and cannot yet understand that someone else might perceive them differently in the same situation.

Perceptual and phenomenological psychology have advanced our understanding of the effects of cumulative experiences on adulthood and helped explain memory processes that intervene in the learning process. Surely negative ideas about oneself and one's abilities have a distorting effect upon everything one attempts. So, too, do unrealistic appraisals of one's abilities, as when great praise is lavished for mediocre functioning when individuals are capable of doing better.

Observing and Classifying

Helping children learn how to observe, and to draw inferences from close observation of everyday things, calls for teacher skill and imagination. Being able to infer from observation is an essential component of the concept-centered curriculum and observation activities cut across all subject areas. The illustrations which follow will suggest many other kinds of learning experiences that help children *infer from their observations*.

Fours and Fives
ACTIVITY 1. OBSERVED AND DISCUSSED A FROZEN NEWSPAPER

1. Saw newspaper left outside in cold weather.
2. Discussed how it looked and felt.

3. Wondered what made it freeze.
4. Took it inside to see what warmth would do.
5. Watched and discussed what happened.
6. Discussed the ways that water, cold, and heat affected the newspaper.

ACTIVITY 2: LOOKED FOR THINGS MISSING IN PICTURES

1. Decided what was missing such as an arm or leg.
2. Decided what was missing such as a roof or window.
3. Decided what was missing such as a wheel, and so forth.
4. Tried to draw it in its proper place.
5. Observed and discussed one another's completed pictures.

ACTIVITY 3: GIVEN ASSORTED OBJECTS TO ARRANGE AS THEY LIKED

1. Some arranged them by color.
2. Some arranged them by size.
3. Some arranged them by shape.
4. Some arranged them by weight.
5. Some arranged them by class—seeds, dominoes, and so on.
6. Some arranged them by utility—buttons, pins, and so on.
7. Some arranged them by texture—rough, smooth, and so on.
8. Some simply made designs of them.
9. Some put them in even and uneven piles.
10. Each was helped to understand the others' arrangements.

Fives and Sixes
ACTIVITY 1: WATCHED FOR SIGNS OF SPRING
1. Planted bulbs outside in the fall and inside in spring.
2. Brought forsythia and pussy willow branches inside.
3. Watched what happened to all three outside and inside.
4. Observed a maple tree daily.
5. Watched birds and animals.
6. Checked the weather daily.
7. Made daily notes and drawings about observations.
8. Shared observations with one another.

ACTIVITY 2: WATCHED A FLOCK OF BIRDS ON THE SCHOOL LAWN

1. Observed what attracted them (seeds on a plant).
2. Watched their bills and tongues as they ate.
3. Watched how they shared (or failed to share).
4. Discussed what made them fight.
5. Compared color in sun and shade.
6. Observed the way they walked and flew.
7. Discussed why they all flew away.

ACTIVITY 3: LISTED OR DREW THE THINGS THEY SAW IN A CIRCLE DRAWN WITH CHALK ON THE CLASSROOM FLOOR. COUNTED DIFFERENT WAYS

1. *Top half* (two blue circles, one red circle, three green squares, one orange shape. Or three circles, three squares, and one other shape. Total number, 7).
2. *Bottom half* (two red shapes, one black triangle, three white circles. Or one triangle, three circles, and two other shapes. Total number, 6).
3. Same activity, but this time using quarters; the top right quarter, the top left quarter, the bottom left quarter, and the bottom right quarter.
4. Observed and classified using shape, size, color, and number of objects of each classification and together.
5. Agreed that number of objects was the same regardless of how they were organized or classified.

Sixes and Sevens
ACTIVITY 1: WERE SHOWN A PICTURE OF A VARIETY OF FOODS IN A SUPERMARKET

1. Looked briefly.
2. Listed or drew what they had seen (how many foods?).
3. Were shown the picture again.
4. Discussed what they had remembered and not remembered.

ACTIVITY 2: OBSERVED A LIGHTED CANDLE

1. Watched flame changes—height, color, direction.
2. Discussed why there were changes.
3. Experimented to see what made it burn or go out.
4. Observed and recorded time of decreasing length.

ACITIVITY 1: WERE SHOWN A PICTURE OF A VARIETY OF FOODS IN SUPERMARKET

1. They took them out and inspected them.
2. They returned them to their envelopes.
3. They listed or drew as many as they could remember.
4. They exchanged envelopes and tried other items.
5. They worked in pairs to list objects for one another.

Sevens and Eights
ACTIVITY 1: WALKED ACROSS THE PLAYGROUND IN A HIGH WIND

1. Discussed how the wind felt to them.
2. Discussed sounds they heard.
3. Observed what happened to others' clothing.
4. Observed what happened to trees, leaves, dust, and so on.
5. Discussed difference going across and coming back.

ACTIVITY 2: VISITED A NEARBY SCHOOL FOR DEAF CHILDREN

1. Observed how deaf children communicated.
2. Observed their games and learning activities.
3. Observed and compared school buildings and equipment.
4. Discussed similarities (appearance, play, needs, and so on).

ACTIVITY 3: OBSERVED LENGTH AND CHANGE IN DAYS AT FALL EQUINOX

1. Recorded time it got dark for several weeks.
2. Noted changes in family habits including mealtime, study time, bedtime, and other activities.
3. Observed changes in necessary artificial lighting.
4. Checked temperature differences.
5. Observed changing habits of animals and birds.

Eights and Nines

ACTIVITY 1: OBSERVED EGGS IN INCUBATORS AT HATCHERY. OWNER OPENED SOME

1. Saw tiny heart and veins at end of first week.
2. Saw partially formed baby chick at end of second week.
3. Saw fully formed chicks peck out of shells at the end of the third week.
4. Observed work-rest cycles during emergence from shells.
5. Observed first efforts to hold heads and to walk.
6. Compared with chicks after first week of life.
7. Observed and discussed artificial life-giving simulations at the hatchery—light, heat, and so on.

ACTIVITY 2: OBSERVED DEVELOPING FROG'S EGGS

1. In the sun and not in the sun.
2. With covers and without covers.
3. With other fish in jar and without other fish in jar.
4. Studied and recorded size of growing embryos.
5. Observed tadpole forming and beginning to move.
6. Noted emergence from jelly masses.
7. Observed behavior immediately afterward.
8. Observed behavior and looks after a few days.
9. Compared behavior of those removed and those retained there.
10. Watched what happened with food and without food.
11. Observed growth and development of those who lived.

ACTIVITY 3: OBSERVED FOR A HALF HOUR IN ANOTHER CLASSROOM

1. Recorded observations and impressions.
2. Compared notes with observation team.
3. Discussed differences in what they observed.

Nines, Tens, and Elevens

ACTIVITY 1: TWO TEACHERS STAGED A MOCK BATTLE FOR THE CHILDREN

1. Children discussed what they saw.
2. They discussed what they heard.
3. They were surprised that they did not see and hear the same things.
4. They discussed some of the reasons why this happens.

ACTIVITY 2: CHILDREN TOOK A BOAT RIDE AROUND MANHATTAN ISLAND (They kept diaries of what they saw and did from beginning to end.)

1. Some noted more time schedules than other things.
2. Some concentrated more on rules and regulations.
3. Some made more notes about the things they saw.
4. Others were fascinated with new sounds.
5. A few noted smells and impressions.
6. One was more interested in the varieties of shipmates.
7. One concentrated on dining facilities and food.
8. One was interested in the different shipboard jobs.

ACTIVITY 3: OBSERVED DIFFERENT MATERIALS WHEN HEATED

1. Noted materials that expanded or contracted.
2. Observed qualities of materials that expanded.
3. Compared time it took to contract after heating.

ACTIVITY 4: REMEMBERING WHAT WAS SEEN ON THE WAY TO SCHOOL

1. Noted usual things they passed.
2. Noted people they saw.
3. Noted anything unusual or different.

ACTIVITY 5: OBSERVED A NEW HOUSE BEING BUILT

1. Kept a diary of observed procedures from ground breaking to completion and occupation.
2. Noted variety of workmen and skills needed.
3. Noted variety of sources of materials.
4. Observed finishing details.
5. Talked with contractor and others.
6. Observed family moving in to occupy house.
7. Noted family activities to complete lawn, shrubbery, and so on.

Classifying and Ordering

Although the basic emphasis in the previous illustrations is on training children's observational abilities and developing their abilities to infer from observation, note also that a great deal of classifying is taking place. For example, children given objects will immediately begin to sort them in different ways or to pattern them in some way. In counting activities, they are apt to count circles, squares, triangles, and other shapes as separate units.

Being able to classify groups and sets of things is part of concept formation because it involves going from a single item to a group of items that have some commonality. It involves going from specifics to generalizations, in other words. Grouping can be accomplished in a variety of ways unless one category is obvious; but regrouping occurs when the rules change, as we have seen in several of the illustrations.

The following illustrations of catalysts for classifying activities are not arranged by age inasmuch as they, and the previous illustrations as well, are adaptable to many different ages. These, and any of the previous illustrations, are appropriate if the teacher has determined that the activity will help a child because he does not really observe or he cannot seem to classify. Building upon a child's present understanding, whether he is five, ten, or more years of age, illustrates the *spiral curriculum*. Some children need more experience with some steps than with others, and some seem to skip some steps in arriving at appropriate generalizations. The following activities in classifying experiences allow every child to begin where he is and proceed to another level, developing concepts step by step.

Possible classifying and ordering activities include

1. Sorting pictures, toys, or objects into these categories:

numbers	animals	tools	plants	activities
colors	occupations	clothes	air	sports
shapes	vegetables	seasons	water	books
sizes	fruit	toys	transportation	textures
utility	foods	flowers	time	weather

2. Selecting words that can be applied to a category; for example, one teacher put a list of words on the blackboard. The list included words that pertained more to boys, words that pertained more to girls, and some that pertained to neither. Children were asked to list words that pertained to their own sex and then to list words that pertained to the opposite sex. All other words were to go in a third column.
3. Class excursions offer many opportunities for classifying. Children can be asked to keep track of one kind of thing such as: occupations, performers, trainers, animals, machines, equipment, sounds, literature.
4. A class newspaper provides many opportunities for classifying ma-

terials to be included. Among these are social news, sports news, current events, jokes, cartoons, advertisements, illustrations, weather, local news, state news, national news, international news, puzzles. Newspapers and magazines provide study guides for possible categories.

5. Books are classified in various ways and classroom libraries can be reclassified in a variety of ways. Seven- and eight-year-olds begin to learn standard library classifications beyond picture-story books as they use the library. Children learn to classify different types of stories and poems, reference books, and various audio-visual aids.

6. A building construction project offers children opportunities to classify metals, plastics, glass, stones, and bricks.

7. Road and street signs offer opportunities to classify by shape, number, name, and meanings.

8. Number process symbols are methods of classifying, and the way we use certain words helps us classify them grammatically.

9. Listening to various types of music provides experiences in classifying by melody and rhythm. For example, folk music, pop music, rock-and-roll music, various instrumental categories, or more advanced categories such as tempo, rhythm, legato, or marcato.

10. Bulletin boards offer many possibilities for classifying and arranging, as do exhibits of such items as coins, stamps, or ships.

11. Children are classifying when they are alphabetizing, when they keep track of weather conditions, when they work with time and calendar ideas, or when they try to group people and events by historical time.

12. People, places, and events can be classified by urban, suburban, or rural implications, or by continent, country, state, town, or city.

13. Animals can be classified by different characteristics and by utilitarian uses, or by self-protection methods.

14. Boys particularly like to classify cars, license plates, and machinery of various kinds.

15. Rocks, shells, and plants offer many possibilities for categorizing from simple to complex ways. Size, shape, characteristics, seasonal implications and use are just a few of the possibilities.

16. Older children can classify art works, architecture, periods of furniture, constellations, and even preferred and common stocks.

17. Foods can be classified by nutritional values, balance in meals, source (animal, vegetable, mineral), native or import, calories, and by color, taste, or smell.

18. Basic human needs can be classified, as can more subtle things such as luxuries.

19. Early experience can be given in devising statements that tell who, what, why, when, and where. Oral and simple written work or drawings are ways to have children illustrate their thinking at first.

As time goes on, they can write lead paragraphs for an imaginary newspaper article and include all five elements of concise explanation.
20. Cell structures, germs and bacteria, and chemical elements all become categories of classification as time goes on.

Constructing

Logical thinking processes are necessary for concept formation because they are built on logical progressions and associations that lead to views of the whole. Being able to construct is more than being able to classify in that it implies *longitudinal thinking* as well as latitudinal categorizing. Teachers ask questions like these to help children construct and reconstruct:

What is missing?
What else do we need to know?
What do you think follows this?
Shouldn't something happen before that?

Experiences teachers have provided to help children construct or reconstruct include these examples:

Early Primary: Story sequence and ideation
1. *What the Teacher Does:* Tells a story using a flannelboard and flannel cut-outs for various objects and characters. Retells the story, and distributes cut-outs to various children for flannelboard placement during story sequence.

What the Children Do: Volunteer to tell story and place cut-outs themselves or distribute them to classmates and have them place them at proper cue from storyteller.

2. *What the Teacher Does:* Reads a story that will lend itself to dramatization. Provides some simple props for children.

What the Children Do: Reconstruct the story by acting it out. Puppets can also be used for reconstructing story sequence.

3. *What the Teacher Does:* Takes children's dictation and asks leading questions to help them decide what may come "next."

What the Children Do: Think of a good story idea or plot, decide about characters and action, develop the story as a group with each adding ideas, and plan a group resolution and ending.

It is not difficult to see that there are extensions of these illustrations that build toward more complex reconstruction exercises at upper primary and intermediate school levels. As soon as children can write sufficiently well, they can write their own stories or accounts using group or individually developed outlines for sequence, plot, characterization, and lead paragraphs. They can construct their own creations from the beginning, or they can reconstruct stories or experiences the group or individuals have had. They may illustrate using pantomime, puppets, or drawings from the earliest to the most advanced levels.

Early Primary: Numbers and numerals

1. *What the Teacher Does:* Sets up a number line (on chalk tray, on the floor, with clothesline and pins, on playground) using large cards with a sequence of numerals and a corresponding number of pictures of objects on each. Deliberately mixes up the number sequence for first experiences, and gradually leaves out different numbers such as even numbers, odd numbers, and multiples of two or three.

2. *What the Children Do:* Put the numbers back in proper sequence. Put the even numbers or odd numbers back in proper place. Replace the missing multiples. Children begin to do this first by number of pictures of objects, and eventually by looking only at the numeral that represents the number of objects.

Later Extensions: Numeration

Children and teacher construct adding machines, subtraction machines, multiplication machines, or division machines. Using their knowledge of subtraction and addition as inverse numerical operations, and of multiplication and divison as inverse numerical operations, they discover that one machine can do many operations, simply by changing the rule under which it operates.

EXAMPLE

What's the secret rule? Fill the other blocks in each square when you know.

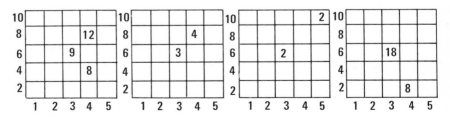

Students are not given the rule, but rather are to study the illustration and thus discover what rule is operating and reconstruct the numerals that fill the other blocks. Try this yourself and you will see that patterns begin to emerge which make it unnecessary to complete the individual operation each time. There are patterns that develop horizontally, ver-

tically, and diagonally. To construct them, you need only to discover the
rule and the pattern. You reconstruct what is missing, and if you change
the rule, you can reconstruct a whole new machine.

The strands of mathematics that ran from the simplest to the most advanced mathematics study are invaluable for children's logical thinking
growth in constructing and reconstructing sequences in any situation.
Whether we use number concepts (sets, number and numeration, enu-
meration systems, geometry, properties and techniques of operations,
equalities and inequalities, measurement, or statistics), or social science
concepts, it is possible to design with children experiences appropriate for
next levels of logical and sequential thinking. The unifying ideas and the
patterns of sequence and operation waiting to be discovered help them to
be more proficient in all learning situations because developing logic in
mathematics has applications to developing logic in problem solving of
other kinds.

There is no "new" mathematics in "new math" teaching; rather the new
approaches that are used lead children to question, discover, create, think,
test ideas, formulate problems, and learn in ways that help them develop
and apply real understanding and self-direction.

The spiral, concept-centered curriculum recognizes the validity of "big
ideas," starting early with refinement and sophistication being the sequential and ongoing growing edges of knowledge. The professionally alert
teacher knows that mathematics, or any other subject content area, is not
a series of increasingly difficult flash cards with answers to be rote-
memorized and repeated in shorter and shorter lengths of time. He knows
that it is not just memorizing rules and never understanding how and why
they operate. And he knows that it is not a tell-test-forget part of curriculum. His main concern is not that all children become bookkeepers or
accountants, but rather that they experience the joy of thinking and of
discovering, and of lifelong learning.

Recognizing Assumptions

Children need help to distinguish between opinions and facts, between
fact and fancy, and between assumptions and truth. Here are some of the
ways sensitive teachers have found to help them do so:

> (Miss Blake's class was made up of children from many cul-
> turally different and educationally disadvantaged homes. On
> the first day of school, she listened to the children's conversa-
> tions. One of the first conversations was about boats, and sur-
> prisingly the children were discussing the number of wheels
> on a boat. At the first opportunity, she asked the class, "How
> many wheels are there on a car?" Most children knew that
> there were four.)

Teacher: How many wheels are there on a boat?
Clay: Two.
John: Two!
Sue: Two!
Teacher: Suppose you draw a picture of the boat you are thinking of. (*Everyone was eager to illustrate his boat version, and when each child had completed his picture, every boat had two wheels under it.*)
Teacher: Here is a picture of a boat on the ocean. Do you see any wheels on it?
Clay: No, but they're under the water.
Teacher: Have any of you seen a boat on the water?
Bill: (*Only child responding*) Yes, I have.
Teacher: Did you see any wheels?
Bill: No, they were in the water.

Throughout the conversation, Miss Blake was thinking of their urban backgrounds and their distance from a body of water. Knowing that the children did not have boats at home, she took a chance and drew a boat mounted on a two-wheel trailer on the chalkboard.

Bill: That's a boat like Uncle's.

The next day during a neighborhood walk, they came to the house of a man the children called "Uncle." Sure enough, in his yard was the only boat that these children had ever seen. And it was parked on a trailer. "Uncle" was invited to tell the children about his boat, and how he trailed it to the place where he could put it on a river.

At school the next day, the children found that Miss Blake had brought pictures of boats for the bulletin board and had borrowed models of several boats, trucks, cars, buses, and trailers.

Miss Blake, having visited the children's homes and neighborhoods, and being aware of the cultural deprivations in these children's lives, planned many kinds of similar learning adventures with these children. Their educational journey included trips, not to completely unfamiliar places, but to areas where some familiar things helped them to build confidence, experiment with ideas, and gradually build new associations and concepts. She knew that concept development is a continuous process of understanding familiar and new relationships and that concept formation moves from the concrete to the abstract.

Like other fine teachers who realize that children's problems, needs, and interests are the basis for changing the instructional program, Miss Blake got inside the children to learn what their thinking was and whether they had assumptions and misconceptions that needed attention before going on to new learning experiences. Here are other ways that have helped children to understand the differences between assumptions and proofs:

1. When a bird's nest was brought to class, a group of six-year-olds immediately called it a robin's nest. But when they studied pictures

of birds' nests and the teacher read to them from the text explaining how and why various birds build their nests as they do, they learned that it was a red-winged blackbird's nest.

2. Children read and discussed fairy tales. They chose certain parts to discuss in terms of "this could be true if . . ." and "this could never be true because. . . ."

3. Compositions were checked to see whether children tend to make assumptions not based on facts. Individual conferences and special resources helped them to see why their remarks were only assumptions, and to help them distinguish between fact and fancy.

4. Children challenged one another when giving oral reports. They helped each other think about checking facts before presenting material as accurate and defensible.

5. Simple word problems were used to help children think about what might change an obvious fact. For example, if two loaves of bread cost 60 cents, how much does each one cost? The expected answer is 30 cents and most children said this before they were asked to think about possible reasons why this might not be so: the bread may be of different kinds, of different quality, and we may be talking about two loaves of different size.

6. Older children studied political speeches for assumptions that politicians make in preparing speeches for certain audiences.

7. Games like Gossip or activities like the Rumor Clinic helped children understand the assumptions that are made in trying to repeat what has been heard or seen without rechecking original sources of information.

Comparing and Evaluating

Some children have lived with parents and teachers who did not recognize a child's right to compare and analyze things and events. Their thinking seems to have stagnated because they have not had to use their own thinking abilities; things have been decided for them and they have been told what to do and what to think. Drill-and-grill curriculum was strictly an exercise in "we'll tell you what to learn and you had better learn it." Under that system children "learned" teachers quite well by the time they finished high school, if they did not drop out altogether. They learned that the safest thing to do, and the way to get the best marks, was to regurgitate the teacher's exact facts and statements, even though they might not agree or might legitimately question them.

"Modern man is aware of the quicksand of fact; he confronts it in all aspects of life, scientific and common. So long as each day overturns another verity, the schools ill serve the student if they are entirely fact- or solution-oriented. Education in *how* one arrives at 'solutions' is increasingly recognized to be indispensable. Periodically deprived of his working truths, the modern human being requires a mastery of the processes of clear thought, of how to go about making decisions when not only is tradition no guide, but yesterday's scientific terra firma is turning soft" (42).

We have always needed minds that search for and discern interconnections and relationships, but the instability of modern life with its fluid and rapid changes makes abilities to associate, compare, and evaluate a necessity.

When we speak of being able to compare and evaluate, we speak in terms of helping individuals become more open and flexible rather than closed, argumentative, and judgmental. We concentrate on the ways that children can be helped to make comparisons to counteract dogmatism, prejudice, and rigidity. And we expect that, as a result of learning experiences that help children compare and evaluate, they will have more self-assurance and self-confidence.

The following topics are intended to be suggestive only. They can be intrasubject and adaptable to many levels. Compare the following:

1. Objects for size, shape, color, function, class, rank order, texture, weight, and temperature.
2. Photographs of the same scene at different times of day.
3. Time-lapse photography of a flower opening, a chick emerging from an egg, or a tree through the seasons.
4. Charts and graphs of all kinds and on many subjects—simple graphic to complex graphic and concepts.
5. Paintings on the same subject by different artists, for example, fruits by Cézanne and Picasso, or people by El Greco, Manet, Toulouse-Lautrec, and Renoir.
6. Contrasting newspaper versions of the same event.
7. Periods of architecture and building functions, including changes in design and purposes of schools.
8. Painting, sculpture, music, and dance as ways of creating and expressing oneself.
9. Two or three versions of the same playground incident.
10. The same character in two or three versions of the same story, such as Cinderella in original and modified storybook form and in Walt Disney's movie.
11. Various ways of measuring and locating things. Ways of describing locations of streets, waterways, or ship locations.
12. Man's changing dependence on geography and nature.
13. The "cardboard" or stereotyped characters in stories.
14. Different ways poets handle the same theme.
15. Different ways dramatists, speech writers, and storytellers handle the same themes.
16. Fictional characters and oneself, oneself and the "spoiled Prince," for example, or "Penrod and Sam."
17. Contrasting governmental structures and philosophies.

18. Historical and modern events such as Magellan's and an astronaut's trip around the world.
19. Political party platforms.
20. Various patterns of culture and family life.
21. Advertising gimmicks.
22. Different number systems such as decimal, duodecimal, and binary.
23. Machines replacing work people used to do by hand.
24. Handmade and machinemade articles.
25. Different neighborhoods in the same city.
26. Similarities of all human beings.
27. Effects of different environments on animals and humans.
28. Chemical changes produced by different elements.
29. Two paintings by the same artist in different periods of his life or two musical compositions by the same composer at different times during his career.
30. Examples of individual courage or cowardice.

There are other categories that can be used to develop similar suggested curricular experiences for planned thinking experiences. You may use categories such as developing the ability to criticize constructively, test hypotheses, decide upon alternatives, or think imaginatively. Try it yourself and see what categories you think are important and what kinds of curriculum experiences you think would further that type of thinking.

For over thirty years, child psychologists at the Institute of Educational Sciences in Geneva, Switzerland, have been studying not only how children think at various ages but also why they think as they do. Using the technique of interviewing each child individually and basing each new question on the child's response to the previous question, they have been able to understand some of the thought processes children use. Many of the findings, particularly those of Jean Piaget and Barbel Inhelder, are extremely significant to elementary school teachers because of the implications they have for curriculum planning and for teaching methods.

For example, Piaget has discovered that young schoolchildren up to the age of about eight are still egocentric—not in the customary meaning of the word, but in relation to their ability to distinguish fully between themselves and the rest of the world. Because of this, people continue to be the prototype of objects to which children assign human characteristics and which they conceive as being alive. A hill changes shape when a child looks at it not because he has moved but because it has moved. Clouds have personalities and can change these personalities from human to animal or bird and back again because, in the child's mind, they move themselves, they can change themselves into various characters, and they follow the child as he walks or skips along. The wind is also alive; it has a personality, too. Otherwise it could not blow.

Today, Piaget and his staff associates believe that modern children may outgrow egocentric thought earlier than in the past because they are exposed to more sophisticated experiences earlier—at school and through movies and TV. But we can discern children's egocentric imaginations in a conversation like this one which started when one six-year-old said that his uncle was working on the moon:

Second child: That's nothing. My Dad works there, too.
Third child: There's no food there, but it's got grape-flavored dirt so you don't get hungry.
Fourth child: It's not grape. It's cold orange ice.
Fifth child: It's not either orange ice—Jesus painted it yellow.
Sixth child: The moon watches over us. It can laugh, too.
Seventh child: There's a lot of craters just like my freckles.
Sixth child: Ha, ha, ha! The moon's got freckles!
Second child: My Dad takes a bus there.
First child: My uncle's got his own space ship.
Third child: Mr. Moon covers his face when he doesn't want to see us.

Sometimes teachers can simply let children's imaginations be sparked by children's conversation that kindles the imagination of others. This is not the time to help them distinguish reality from imagination, because to do so may stop the flow of thought and creativity. At times, teachers provide experiences to encourage this free flow so that they can study their students' thought processes and their abilities to differentiate between people and things. Children gradually learn to distinguish between themselves and the world and between people and things, and eventually develop the ability to serialize on a more formal level and search for real cause-and-effect relationships. In the primary school years, young children do not understand physical causality for movements of the earth, wind, rain, and the like. Nor do they understand the constancy of quantity, of size, weight, or volume. Concepts of time and space, geographical relations, past and present and future develop gradually at different ages and they are grasped differently at different ages. Yet school programs and teaching techniques are not closely related to *thinking growth* in most schools throughout the country and the world today.

Studies like those of Piaget help us to realize the complexity of evolving thinking processes and intellectual growth, and teachers need to be able to recognize the kind of thinking of which children of certain ages are capable.

Jot down your own ideas for extending children's abilities and for studying the kind of thinking processes they have. We do not pretend to begin to suggest here all of the thinking skills and levels that enter into and facilitate children's abilities to think. What we do want to emphasize is the importance of understanding that the object of being able to think for themselves is to make children increasingly independent of teachers and other adults. Developmentally, this is going to happen, anyway. But as it happens we can be more confident that children will advance to thinking adulthood if they have been taught *how to think*. Those who have been taught only *what to think* will not possess the tools and skills they need to deal with changing times.

Emotional Equilibrium

As Psychological Organisms

"Sometimes it's just like you had a puzzle inside your head and then all of a sudden all of the pieces begin to go together like!" This statement was made by a seven-year-old boy who was fortunate enough to have a teacher who recognized that his emotional equilibrium was out of sorts and, being convinced that emotional development is an essential component of intellectual development and curriculum construction for individuals, tried to help him bring his emotional equilibrium into balance.

Teachers must consider emotional factors in personality development if they really want to give children's intellects a chance to function freely and fully. But some schools and many parents have not wanted teachers to be actively concerned with understanding emotions as an integral part of learning and of school curriculum. Actually, *the quality of the relationships that children have with peers and with teachers may be the most important single indicator of success in academic and intellectual pursuits.*

Children Need Help to Resolve Conflicts

Richard, the seven-year-old who likened his emotional problems to a puzzle inside his head, represents millions of boys and girls in elementary schools who need special understanding in order to utilize their real potential fully. By the end of their elementary school years, understanding teachers can mean the difference between happy, well-adjusted lives or emotionally crippled ones filled with fears, failures, anxieties, and misunderstandings (43).

Richard went to kindergarten, where most of the children received praise and enjoyed satisfaction in playing, building things, painting, singing, making new friends, helping one another, and learning other kinds of things. But the school's confidential report at the end of the year was disparaging as far as Richard was concerned. It read, in part:

> Richard does not join in group activities, has temper tantrums, is aggressive and unpopular with his peers, is often moody, and daydreams excessively. Parents and neighbors report similar difficulties at home.

During first grade, when an added year of age caused his family and the school to expect even more of him, he showed intensified signs of the maladjustments noted in kindergarten; his temper tantrums, playground fights, and general unhappiness intensified. Academically, he fared no better than he did socially or emotionally.

Testing results showed that Richard probably had superior abilities, but emotional upheavals continued to stymie his achievement. Early in his seventh year of age, any attempt to define limits of behavior or force attention to reading or writing would send him into a fierce tantrum. He was already threatening adults—teacher and parents included—as well as other children. His temper tantrums were so severe that he often had to be isolated for his own and others' safety. Psychological tests showed intense fear of darkness, of punishment, of animals, and of "big boys."

One of the few things Richard really liked to do was talk. He talked volubly and easily and, like most seven-year-olds, expressed himself dramatically and grandly. This was something his sensitive new teacher could use to help him verbalize and understand some of his conflicts. She made time for the private conversations that Richard loved and came to request often. And she planned group conversations in which Richard could participate and excel.

One day when the class was discussing family responsibilities and privileges, Richard volunteered a bit of information: "My kid brother doesn't help at home at all. He gets away with everything. He's a nuisance, too. And I'll be glad when my grandmother goes to heaven." This was noted by his teacher and put aside for thought.

In conference with his mother a short time later, she shared the comment and learned that the coming of Richard's grandmother to live in their home had made it necessary for him to give up his own room and share his younger brother's room. He resented the move and bullied and teased his younger brother, causing his parents to scold him repeatedly and to be protective of their younger son. Realizing that the difficulty was more serious than they had imagined, his parents decided to remodel another unused area and make a room Richard could call his own to see whether one cause of deviant behaviors could be modified.

Things began to improve at home and at school, but there were still some rough times ahead. Most young children go through various stages of storytelling, pilfering, and sex play, and Richard was no exception. But his home was very disciplined and morally strict, and his parents needed help to understand that, while these were not unusual behaviors of alarming dimensions, children do have needs for the appropriate answers to their questions and responses to help them understand and control "misbehavior."

It was agreed that the teacher should feel free to answer Richard's questions about sex at school and the parents would try to do the same at home. Parents and teacher would meet often to discuss information given and shared. The child began to accept his physical development as a natural and discussable phenomenon and to acquire honest respect for others—the most reliable bases for real respect for authority and for self-directed personal responsibility.

Richard soon began to reap the rewards that come from being able to make responsible decisions about his own behavior. When some money was missing from a desk, the teacher told the class that her faith in them made her sure that the child who had taken it had only borrowed it, and would be willing to tell her about it and return it. She suggested a game in which each would whisper anything he wished to her with the sure knowledge that no one else would know what each had whispered.

One by one they whispered such things as, "I didn't take it, honest," or, "I love you," or "When can you come to my house for supper?" Each received a hug and a whispered reply from the teacher. When Richard's turn came, it was obvious that he had had some tussles with his conscience while waiting. It took him some time to whisper, "I took it and I'm sorry. I'll wait after school and give it to you." He got a hug like all of the rest, and his teacher whispered back, "I'm so proud of you, Richard!"

By the end of that school year, Richard was beginning to make full use of his superior abilities. His achievement test scores showed it, and his true and delightful personality was beginning to emerge. Gone were the perpetual scowls and in their place were frequent smiles. His peers recognized and rewarded the new Richard by including him in their in-school and out-of-school activities. Naturally his family was elated.

Had Richard not had a gifted teacher, wise in helping children emotionally so that they can grow intellectually, Richard's story might have been far different. Sensitive teachers like this one accept children as they are, start where they are, share and understand their hopes and fears, and guide them to emotional and intellectual health and growth in regular classrooms.

Psychological Selfhood

Who am I? In one way or another, every child and every adult asks himself this question. Our emotions vacillate from depression to elation and our psychological, emotional selves are constantly aware of changing moods as they affect our mental and intellectual outlooks. Mental health, personality, and achievement are so closely related that feelings of acceptance or rejection, accomplishments, attitudes toward ourselves and others, and of liking and disliking are deeply involved in what we learn, how we learn, and whether what is learned is of any value in demonstrated behavior changes.

Broadly speaking, we human beings differ as psychological selves from physical selves in that our physical selves try simply to survive—to maintain life and to seek creature comforts. These psychological selves push us relentlessly to become all that we are capable of being. Jersild (44) says that man has a need "not just to survive, but also to use his powers, to perform, to produce, to experiment, to venture into the unknown and untried. The individual has to spend energy, not just to save it. Associated with the possession and the development of a capacity or power is an impulse to use that capacity or power."

Other psychologists speak of these drives in terms of the human organism's tendency to "actualize itself" (45) and in terms of the processes of self-actualization. Still others speak of the role that emotions play in helping us to become fully functioning persons.

We can observe early self-actualizing efforts when a baby first attempts to communicate something other than his basic physical wants and needs. We see him begin to react differently to different people, to show love and displeasure, and to experiment with his newly developing locomotive powers. His family and his home are the first influences upon his emotional development during these beginning self-actualization efforts. The degree of approval and encouragement, acceptance or rejection, or overpermissiveness and overprotection he experiences in his home conditions his responses and his efforts.

If he is constantly reminded through words and deeds that he is "a baby," "awkward," "stupid," or "slower than Susan was," his psychological self is conditioned to low self-esteem and mental apathy. On the other hand, if overprotectiveness is one of the child-rearing patterns in his home, he is not allowed opportunities that other children have to exercise his growing energies and powers and to become a productive, capable little person.

Children with home patterns of rejection, disapproval, and overprotectiveness arrive at school with retarded psychological growth compared to children who have spent their infancies and early childhoods in accepting and encouraging atmospheres. The latter are farther along in mental and emotional development when they enter school; the former enter school with somewhat of a handicap in both. Each group needs opportunities to understand and develop healthy emotional attitudes, but the former needs special help from teachers who are able to understand, communicate, and demonstrate the importance of self-understanding and self-esteem.

Teachers need to be especially alert to children as growing psychological organisms. Realizing that children come to school with patterns of behavior established in the home, they know that children's efforts from infancy to entry in school have been the source of either good feelings about themselves or frustration, depending on rewards or criticism they have experienced. However, failure or lack of approval at home did not preclude generally another chance to try; and it never involved some of the emotionally damaging practices that traditional schools have meted out such as nonpromotion, isolation from peer groups, or worse under the influence of incompetent teachers and administrators.

Some schools have not only damaged the emotions and the egos of children, but have also not expected teachers to be actively concerned with understanding and dealing with emotions as an integral part of curriculum and of learning.

Schmuck (47) talks about a classroom "liking structure" and states that among students who are highly involved with, and *liked by*, their teachers and peer groups, "significant relationships exist between actual liking status on the one hand and the utilization of abilities, attitude toward self, and attitude toward school on the other hand."

In classroom climates where students tend to feel liked by peers and teachers, is school achievement actually higher? Aspy (48) collected evidence that would seem to prove that it is. He worked in six third-grade classes in which teachers taped two full weeks of interaction with students during reading periods. The recordings were made two months apart to get a broad sampling of teacher–pupil interaction and four-minute segments of the recordings were randomly selected for rating by three raters who worked independently. The rating criteria included the degree of congruence or genuineness shown by the teacher, the degree of "prizing" or unconditional positive regard, and the degree of empathic understanding. When standardized Stanford Achievement Reading Tests were given, the children in the classes taught by teachers with the highest degrees of these attitudes rated significantly greater gains in reading achievement than did the children in the three classes rated with lesser degrees of these teaching qualities.

Analyzing the gains made by the children helped to justify the need for teachers to serve as facilitators, designers, and creators. Because a child's entry into the formal school situation involves many new interpersonal relationships and is especially designed to include experiences that cannot be duplicated in the home setting, the teacher's influence can be inestimable in helping children to become more independent, more responsible for their own learning, more creative, and more capable of developing their potential.

The school's past errors are compounded when the teacher believes that subject matter is generally considered to be more important than interpersonal relationships in the human learning processes. Schools may actually be hindering learning rather than facilitating intellectual development. Rogers (49) thinks that teachers who are "facilitators of learning" show themselves to their students as real people rather than as the stereotypes they think pupils expect to meet. He says that most teachers do not show themselves to their students as real people, but rather, "simply as *roles*. It is quite customary for teachers rather consciously to put on the mask, the role, the façade, of being a teacher, and to wear this façade all day removing it only when they have left the school."

Teacher Self-understanding

Rogers also suggests that teachers who can allow their real personalities and their real emotions to show through can be exciting facilitators of social and academic achievement. Adults who are real people and who are able to be honest about their own feelings and emotions encourage children to be honest and introspective about feelings and emotions.

The following is an example of how one teacher received help from students in analyzing her own emotions.

> The teacher had been provoked to tell one of her nine-year-olds who had misbehaved repeatedly that day, "Well, you certainly are in a bad mood today, aren't you?" His retort, which had a lot of truth in it when the teacher thought it over, was, "Yeah. But so are you!"

> "You know, you're right. I have good days and bad days, too, and today just wasn't one of my good ones," she told him. "Aw, that's O.K. It wasn't one of mine, either," he replied. "Why don't we just tell each other when these days are coming on," he said, "so's we won't expect so much!"

> From that day on, a miniature flag-holder was always present on this teacher's desk. It had three flags variously displayed to represent the mood the teacher thought she was in that day. The white flag meant she thought she was in a *very* good mood, the blue one meant a *fairly* good mood, and the red one meant, "Warning! I'm in a bad mood today." The agreement she had with her students included their right to change the flag if they thought she had misjudged her own mood.

> The flags, she reported, initiated a lot of discussions about how and why people feel the way they do, how emotions affect their friends and their work, and what can be done about emotions.

This teacher was able to share thinking about her emotions with her students and to demonstrate behaviors affected by one's emotions and feelings. Her students learned at firsthand that it is important to recognize emotions and to develop satisfying methods of release or control. The teacher learned that the practice of discussing her emotions was a technique to introduce opportunities for students to interchange ideas about their own emotions.

Sylvia Ashton-Warner is an example of a teacher who is neither ashamed nor afraid to let the real personality of the teacher show through. When an editor questioned her about her creative teaching methods, which included allowing her Maori primary schoolchildren to decide what words they wanted to study each day, she responded: "A few cool facts you asked me for. I don't know that there's a cool fact in me, or anything else cool for that matter, on this particular subject. I've got only hot long facts on the matter of Creative Teaching, scorching both the page and me!" (50).

Teachers' negative or positive attitudes about children's potential are also factors that must be scrutinized carefully. Emmerling (51) was able to group teachers into two general groups after asking them to indicate what they regarded as their most urgent problems in teaching.

The first group, which he characterized as the "open" or "positively oriented" group listed the following problems:

1. Helping children think for themselves.
2. Helping children be independent.
3. Getting children to participate.
4. Learning new ways of helping students develop maximum potential.

When Barrett-Lennard's Relationship Inventory was administered to the students of these teachers, their students saw them as more real, more acceptant, and more empathic than the students in the second group perceived their teachers to be.

The second group tended to see their most urgent problems in teaching in negative terms and in terms of student deficiencies and inabilities. Here are their top priorities:

1. Teaching children who lack a desire to learn.
2. Trying to teach children who lack ability to follow directions.
3. Teaching students who are below grade level.
4. Getting children to listen.

Not unsurprisingly, these students saw their teachers as rather insincere, ungenuine people lacking in acceptance, trust, and understanding.

The harm that a person with negative attitudes about boys' and girls' potentials can do in classrooms is difficult to document, but it seems safe to say that the teaching profession, more than any other profession, needs people emotionally secure enough to help others build positive attitudes about themselves. In defense of some of the neurotic teachers now working in schools, Bower (52) of the National Institute of Mental Health says that "When you walk into a school, it's almost impossible to separate it from a prison. Bells ring, inmates march. A teacher is locked all day in her cubicle . . . anyone who wants to get into that institution needs a pass. Quiet is the order of the day—but quiet and order are not what this institution is supposed to be all about."

If this is an accurate description of most schools today, let us change them! They most certainly will undermine any sensitive, open, creative teacher. Other writers suggest that traditional schools have "infantilized" teachers and that they are designed to depress teachers' mental health. There is undoubtedly a strong correlation between the way teachers are treated by their superiors and the way that teachers in turn treat their students. When teachers are graded by superficial standards such as loyalty, dress, deportment, punctuality, attendance, discipline, and plan books, they may unconsciously retaliate by judging children that way. Certainly sweatshop conditions such as punching time clocks and having no time to go to the toilet are not conducive to mental health of teachers;

nor are supervisory ratings based on criteria like these conducive to fostering dynamic teaching–learning environments.

Bard (53) has studied reports of teacher instability and says that some
teachers may be mentally unfit to begin with. He interviewed teachers,
parents, mental-health specialists, education professors, leaders of
teacher organizations, and parent groups to find out what actual evidence
of teacher unfitness exists, what is being done about it, what should be
done, and how children can be protected from disturbed teachers whose
emotions negatively affect children's lives.

Although the majority of the nation's teachers maintain amazing emotional health under the conditions that exist in many schools, Bard says,
he cites and documents innumerable instances of the cruelty that mentally
sick teachers daily inflict on schoolchildren. Many of these cruelties are
overt and shocking and others are much more subtle. One piece of sub-
stantiating evidence was a comprehensive study of teacher instability
made in 1959 by Louis Kaplan (53) who was then a professor of education at the University of California. Applying the minimum percentages
of teacher maladjustment to the number of teachers in the nation's
schools, he concluded that there were nearly 120,000 teachers who were
seriously maladjusted and that these daily affected the lives of more than
3 million children in their classes. Dr. Kaplan estimated that the odds are
"7 to 1 that a child will be under the influence of at least two unstable,
neurotic, or psychopathic teachers during the course of his 12 years in
school."

Supervisory treatment of teachers also came under Bard's scrutiny. He
quoted Ruth Newman, codirector of the Institute of Education Services
in the School of Psychiatry in Washington, D.C., as likening teachers'
situations "to that of being in a concentration camp," after she talked with
teachers and watched how supervisors treated them during tours of schools
around the country.

Sylvia Ashton-Warner (54) speaks about supervisors, too, when she
describes the visit of one of the "Inspectors" and his reaction to her planning notes for her reading schemes. Even though he noted that it was re-
freshing to find someone really thinking, she reports, he came back after
she thought he had left to say, "The workbook. We'll have to make a special case of you. But be so kind as to not mention it to other teachers.
Imagine what would happen in the Board if all the teachers turned irre-
ducible." Then the author says:

> Once more he's gone. I don't relax so smartly this time. Matawhero checks
> up on his car leaving. But I'm excused from the curse of my teaching life.
> True, he said nothing about my Maori books, but I'm used to that. I pick up
> the child again and stare at him until I see him. He laughs, and his sister
> Waiwini . . . laughs, too, and in no time a few more nearby catch it, like
> singing or crying, not knowing why, and Lo! here is the fantastic situation of

an Inspector just gone, the teacher and children laughing behind him, with no flicker of bitterness whatever.

Again we see how Miss Ashton-Warner is able to tolerate inspections by sharing her honest reactions and emotions with her students. Her students are not judged the way she is judged mainly because her own convictions are matched by her emotional equilibrium. She does not take it out on the children, but reflects equilibrium in the classroom.

Concern for Children's Psychological Needs

Jersild (55), in a study of two thousand students ranging from fourth grade through college, found that emotional characteristics and social relationships were mentioned much more often than academic achievements when considering "What I like about myself," and "What I dislike about myself." When experiences at school were mentioned, they were named more often as a source of self-reproach than as a source of pride or self-confidence.

If, as many studies indicate, most students feel that emotional and academic worlds are so far apart, modern schools and new teachers must search relentlessly for ways to bring them closer together. Otherwise, some children will continue to fail in their school work even though their innate abilities could lead them to success. Others will function reasonably well academically, but not as well as they might if they did not carry emotional burdens that schools often ignore.

Teachers who are concerned and understand children's psychological needs *demonstrate* these concerns in the classroom, in the school setting, and in the community setting. They know that in each of these settings, every child has basic needs that include

1. *Having self-respect.* Teachers help build self-respect by providing children with many opportunities for success.
2. *Being valued.* Teachers help by seeing that peers and adults know about the valuable contributions each child has to offer.
3. *Having faith and trust in people.* Teachers help children develop healthy faith, trust, and respect that are not to be confused with obedience secured through fear.
4. *Being given freedom to make plans.* The teacher helps by encouraging children to make plans, to make choices, and by allowing them to analyze the rewards, good and bad.
5. *Accepting responsibility for oneself.* Teachers help children learn that accepting responsibility for one's behavior and accomplishments brings freedom and freedom's responsibilities.
6. *Having fun.* Teachers help when they themselves have a good sense of humor and when they deliberately encourage laughter and fun.

7. *Living creatively.* Teachers help when they recognize and encourage children's abilities, talents, and innate creativities.

One Teacher's Experiment

Here, in a teacher's own words, is an account of a technique tried with a group of eight-year-olds. This teacher consistently demonstrated concern for children's emotional needs and sought new ways to help them understand themselves better (56).

I keep wondering if I am making just as sure that my students grow up with good mental health as I do that they know how to read and write. I think it is important to make sure that we take time and create the special opportunities to help children find out what they're really like and how they *feel* about the people and the world around them. A fascinating thing happened in my third grade classroom this year.

Michael's father is a psychiatrist, and he volunteered, with some urging by guess who, to try some group "talking" sessions about feelings. The responses he got from this group gave me insights into the individuals in it that I could not have gained in any other way. From now on, I'm going to be more conscious of knowing what my children are *thinking* and *feeling*, thanks to this father who works mainly with adults as a regular thing and wasn't sure he would know how to talk to children other than his own.

Dr. Feder and I planned these group discussions about feelings after a classroom visit from a pediatrician who had emphasized that healthy bodies and healthy minds frequently go hand-in-hand. In our pre-planning, my main contribution was to acquaint Dr. Feder with some of the characteristics of the group members—things I'd noted on anecdotal records I kept and things I'd learned from the school's permanent records and from parent conferences.

This group had two fatherless children, a child who had been apprehended for vandalizing the school, halves of two sets of twins, one adopted child, the usual variety of only-middle-oldest-youngest children, and several children with emotional problems severe enough to warrant the family's involvement in professional family service counseling.

I especially liked the way Dr. Feder started his first group discussion. "How do you feel on a sunny day like today, compared with a rainy day like yesterday?" he asked. The children immediately responded with happy words like: good, happier, swell, "no recesses yesterday but we will today," etc.

"Some of the things you've just mentioned are *feelings*—and that's what we're going to talk about today—*feelings* and how we develop *thinking* along with *feelings* as we grow up. As babies, our wants are taken care of by adults who change, feed, bathe, and cuddle us without any effort on our part at all. All we have to do is cry and sometimes not even that!"

He explained that as we learn to walk, talk, and think, we are expected to make our wants known. We don't really understand why the "giants" don't automatically come running anymore but, instead, seem to expect us to understand and communicate our needs and wants. Then a younger brother or sister arrives (groans from the class!) and the "giants" give him the same attention we once got. We wonder if they love us as much as they used to.

"As we grow up," he said, "we all have these and many other kinds of feelings. They are there all of the time and everyone has them. They are natural feelings to have, but we're puzzled by them. By learning to recognize and accept them, we will have a better outlook on life and we can *help ourselves* to have good healthy minds."

As I listened to Dr. Feder, I, too, was aware of "feelings"—certainties that we can't start too young to help children understand and cope with their feelings. Feelings aren't automatically turned off when these children and I enter this classroom door. They are here all the time—when the children and I are studying, playing, meeting other teachers and parents, and sharing all of the experiences that make up a school day and a whole bunch of days that, strung together, make up a whole school year. I thought how we have a responsibility to teach things about feelings just like we have a responsibility to teach the three R's!

If you are an only child, do you ever wish you had brothers and sisters, Dr. Feder wanted to know. Three "onlies" in the class replied that they did. Then he asked those who had brothers and sisters how they felt about having them. Responses ranged all the way from "nuisances," "pests," "mean," "Baby," "tattle-tale," "not fair," and "bossy" to "all right sometimes" and "fun." These, they were told, were honest feelings that he knew his own son and daughter had. His son, Michael, joined in with, "You said it, Dad."

You could tell that the "only" children in the class had never thought about the disadvantages of having siblings, and that those who had them had never really thought what it would be like not to have them. "Did you ever think that your brothers and sisters feel the same way about you?" he asked the brothered and sistered group. You could tell that it was thought-provoking to look at things from the other fellow's point of view.

Here's the kind of question he asked the twins in the class: "How do you think it would feel to be just one?" John said he'd like to know for a change, because "people always ask which one is which and I feel like saying I'm *me—John*—that's which!" Janie, half of another twin set, said that she just couldn't imagine what it would be like, because "everybody is so used to *both* of us. Like they say 'how are the twins?' They never say 'how is Janie and how is Janet!' "

After Michael's father asked him if he could tell the others how he felt when the new baby arrived at their house, the others wanted to talk about how they felt when new babies arrived at their houses. Here's how they said they felt: "a little jealous," "I envied him," "I thought my parents loved him better than me," "He was always crying," "He was my enemy," and "I couldn't play so much with the kids anymore."

In another session, Dr. Feder decided to try to get the children to talk about different kinds of feelings. He asked them whether they had ever felt guilty when someone in the family got sick. One girl thought her mother was in the hospital at that moment because she had had an automobile accident while returning with her daughter from Sunday School. "I wished I'd never gone to Sunday School, then Mommy wouldn't be hurt," she said. One boy said he thought his baby sister had been very sick because he didn't like her and hit her. And still another boy (Robert, who had vandalized the school a few weeks ago) said that his mother had been in the hospital a lot this year, and it "was probably to get away from me." Robert's mother is an alcoholic, and I hadn't imagined that he was carrying around such a load of guilt about her frequent hospitalizations and her irrational behavior when she was home.

You see, I wouldn't have dared to ask some of these questions because I wouldn't have known what to say after the children said what they did. But Dr. Feder simply replied that "people sometimes *think* their inside wishes make people sick, and then they *feel guilty*. They feel this way because their wishes did have magic power when they were very small, but later this is no longer true. No matter what happens, your wishes have no power and wishes can't do things."

He asked other feeling-provoking kinds of questions, too, such as: How many girls have a favorite boy in the class? And, how many boys have a favorite girl in this class? This was a touchy subject, and yet the girls were giggly and responsive and readily admitted that they already had favorite boys. The boys were embarrassed and silent. Dr. Feder carried these typical reactions into the area of adult feelings, and told the children that all boys and girls and men and women like one another—that these are *natural* feelings to have.

This was followed by an inquiry about whether the children had ever seen their mothers cry. He and his son discussed for the class how they had both *felt* like crying when Mrs. Feder had been very ill. All of the children agreed that they had seen their mothers cry, but had never seen their fathers cry. "You see, men are trained to control their feelings more, but they feel the same inside," Dr. Feder told them. "They feel sad, happy, worried, afraid, guilty, responsible, etc."; I could tell that the children had never yet given much thought to the feelings that adults have and I resolved to myself that I would share my real feelings about things with them more often.

One boy asked whether nightmares have anything to do with what happens during the day. Dr. Feder thought this was a very good question and said so. He told the children that "we have dreams to get over our fright. Dreams, he said, are *homework for feelings*. They help relieve pressures, something like the air going slowly out of a balloon."

In the final classroom session, we summarized together the kinds of feelings we had been able to talk about. The list included love and liking, hate and dislike, jealousy, anger, guilt, happiness, sorrow, understanding, sympathy, shame, courage, resentment, and fear. And we agreed that by learning more about how to recognize and accept them as feelings that everyone has, we can grow up with healthier minds and bodies.

This year I know that my children were much more conscious of their own and other's feelings and opinions, and I found living with and teaching them infinitely more rewarding because of this. I found myself asking questions like: "How do *you* feel about that?" or "What do *you* think we should do?" or "How do you think *he* felt? How would you feel if *you* were in *his* place?" I guess you could say that the classroom climate was changed and that it was entirely possible to have good *group* discussions about almost anything that came up. The children approached problems in human relationships with a depth of understanding that I would not believe possible. And I've got a long list of comments and actions to show that the children benefitted enormously. Just incidentally, I'm proud of their achievement on those *dreaded* yearly achievement tests, too!

The children's thank you notes to Dr. Feder were as revealing as their subsequent actions have been. Robert, the boy who thought he was responsible for his mother being sick so much and the one who was able to talk about how and why he got involved with a group of older boys who vandalized the school, said it better than I could ever say it. Here's what he wrote:

Dear Mr. Feder:

Thank you for coming to our classroom to talk to us about our feelings. I've been in a lot of trouble lately, and you helped me and my friends to understand me better. Please come some more.

Love,
Robert

This teacher was a learner and saw the job of a teacher as involving a great deal of effort to learn from the children so that their educational opportunities could be improved. Anything that a child says or does that reveals something about his feelings is an obvious effort either to reveal or to hide something about his feelings. The second thing about this teacher is that she was alert to her own feelings. What teachers can understand about the feelings of children is influenced by their own feelings and by the interplay of feelings between and among students and teachers. The importance of good mental health for teachers so that their own anxieties and neurosis do not stand in the way of understanding children cannot be overemphasized. This is not to criticize teachers, but it is to say that they, more than other adults, must seek to understand themselves if they hope to understand children.

As Social Organisms

Emotions arise from each child's and each adult's activity drives—from *muscular activity drives*, from *sensory activity drives*, and from *intellectual activity drives;* and each of these involves *social drives.*

There are needs associated with a growing person's social drives. These are generally connected with a person's ability to respond socially, and include most of the needs already discussed: being loved, showing affection, seeking to belong to a group or to a family, gaining approval or recognition, and seeking to be accepted. There is definite overlapping among emotional and social needs because, for example, if one takes the idea of being loved, there is also implied the capacity to love in return.

Love is of such vital necessity to human beings that infants have been suspected of dying when it was withheld. The word *love* is rare in educational literature, but it is an important word for teachers. Basically, teachers should have great capacity for loving and for being loved if they are to respond to the social and intellectual needs of children. So, too, every child has these needs.

Gates (57) mentions the importance of social functioning as a corresponding function of physical, intellectual, and emotional behavior: "The widening of a child's range of social activities parallels and is interwoven with other features of his growth. Many of the early signs of intellectual growth, for example, appear in connection with a child's response to other people. . . . The interrelation of mental and social behavior is seen especially in the development of language, which involves intellectual symbols and also operates as a means of communicating with others. Even the mental processes involved in private thinking have a social orientation, for frequently in his thoughts a person is trying to formulate answers in such a manner that he can communicate them to others."

Gates also says that an individual's social and emotional behavior are interwoven in complex ways so that it is difficult to treat separately such phenomena as jealousy, shyness, stage fright, affection, sympathy, and other forms of reaction to situations and to people.

Kluckhohn and Murray (58) talk about the socialization process as one that starts in infancy and continues throughout life. A child, having learned in infancy various "moderations" of his expressions, methods, manners, and emotional needs will be assumed to be capable of establishing satisfactory "interpersonal relations within the legal and conventional framework of society. When the child begins to behave in a predictable, expected manner it is well on the road to begin socialized."

The Process of Socialization

The drive to become a social being is expressed in many ways, but one can assume that a child or an adult behaves differently under different circumstances and that the term *social growth* is a result of these drives, activities, and circumstances. This is the general consensus around which many psychologists have built their definitions. For example, McGuire and Havighurst (59) propose this definition of socialization:

> *Socialization* is the process of presenting alternate channels for individual behavior together with positive and negative sanctions which lead to acceptance of some and rejection of others. It emphasizes the influence of social groups, formal and informal, upon the personality of the individual.

Social growth, then, is the result of individual functioning in a particular environment under a set of particular set of circumstances.

Within the process of social growth is also our concept of the importance of becoming more open if there is to be progress in growth. In order for progress to occur, there must be increasing levels through which a person passes. Tryon and Henry (60) talk about these levels:

Two essential aspects of living organisms are the need to change, to grow and differentiate toward greater complexity, and the need to integrate and maintain equilibrium and wholeness, to consolidate our gains. But the latter never means static "adjustment" to the well-oiled functioning of the machine in good working order. Rather we must think of the individual's adjustment as a process in which, through interacting with his environment, he deals with his adjustment needs continually. He behaves in certain ways in order to maintain equilibrium or to relieve the tensions that come from imbalance.

Doll (61) is one of the scholars who has done intensive work with the formulation of the characteristics of social growth and functioning from ages one to thirty years. The progressive nature of social growth assumes the activity drives of growing individuals, but it also indicates to educators the possible environments and learning situations that will give direction to social growth. We have come to give words like *character* to the social habits that individuals develop, to the practice and training of inner and outer processes of socialization.

In Doll's *Vineland Social Maturity Scale* (62) items are arranged categorically so that among the behaviors variously designated as occupation, communication, locomotion, and socialization one can see where these characteristically (but not always, of course) develop at various chronological ages. Of those behaviors, the following are typically ascending *social behaviors* from birth onward:

- Reaching for familiar persons.
- Demanding personal attention.
- Playing with other children.
- Playing cooperatively with other children.
- "Performing" for others.
- Playing simple, then more complicated, games.
- Engaging in group activities and competitions.
- Assuming responsibilities beyond own needs.
- Contributing to social welfare.
- Inspiring confidence.
- Promoting civic progress.
- Sharing community responsibility.
- Advancing general welfare.

From the first social advances seen in the baby's desire to reach toward those familiar to him to the highest levels of advancing general welfare of others, we can observe the growing human being as a person in the process of social growth.

It is especially revealing to compare *communication behaviors* with social behaviors to see how, and whether, language does indeed develop more in relation to social needs than to other needs. See what you think about these typically ascending communication behaviors:

- · "Crowing" and laughing.
- · Imitating sounds and eventually words.
- · Following simple instructions.
- · Using names of familiar objects and persons.
- · Talking in short sentences.
- · Printing simple words.
- · Reading on own initiative.
- · Writing short letters.
- · Making telephone calls.
- · Enjoying books, newspapers, and magazines.
- · Communicating by letter.
- · Participating in group discussions.
- · Following and discussing current events.
- · Speaking up for causes and for justice.

Influences upon Socialization

Obviously, homes, churches, cultural and civic groups, various other community and governmental institutions, and the school are the agencies and institutions that influence both social growth and communicating behaviors. Among these, the responsibility of the school is of utmost importance. Even though schools work in partnership with the others, they should be the leaders among them and are in the best possible position to bring about a congruence among all of the influences upon a child's total growth.

Hightower (63) speaks of the school's social responsibility when he says:

> . . . it is my firm belief that education should take the lead. And we may take the lead by focusing our attention on the points common to all people in the culture. I do not assume that it is the school's responsibility to directly build a new social order, but I do assume that it is the job of education to build the kind of persons who will continuously remake society in the light of the needs of all mankind.

Most writers agree that there are physical factors, physique and glandular development, for example, that influence social development. All agree that physical environment has a strong influence upon social growth, and that social status within economic groups also affects it. Today a great deal of attention is being given to poverty and to the effects of poverty on the socialization of individuals.

Concern for Children's Social Needs

The effects of poverty or affluence, class status and its implications, and environment for social learning must be understood by teachers. It is essential for teachers to know *how* pupils think, feel, express thoughts and emotions, respond to different individuals and groups, and *why* they behave and feel as they do. In order to do so, teachers must have ways of knowing a great deal more about children's cultural environments. We will discuss this in greater detail later, but here we want to share with you some conversations that teachers have had with children when using photographs to determine some of children's apperceptions. As you think about each of these, see whether you think language and children's ways of communicating verbally are, in fact, an index to their social growth. Think what the implications would be for you, as a teacher, if you were to have these kinds of revelations about your students' social insights.

The Fives

Photograph Used (64): A multiethnic group of children playing in a city park on jungle gyms and merry-go-rounds.

General Socioeconomic Status of Students: This group of kindergarten children lived in a depressed area of a medium-sized city. Most had moved often; many were on welfare or had parents who had menial, migrant-type jobs; many had single parents; and all were from the newest culture groups to arrive in the city.

Synopsis of Preceding Teacher–Pupil Discussion: The teacher had asked questions about what the children thought was happening in the picture, and how the people in the picture felt about what was happening. These five-year-olds knew about parks and slides, and associated easily with activities shown in the photograph. The teacher then asked them, since they had said that the children looked happy, to tell what it meant to be happy. These responses were noted:

Children: Happy is when you feel like swell.
Happy is when you get a place to live.
Hapy is when you feel like hugging yourself.
Happy is when Mommy get some money.
Happy is for new shoes.
Happy is when you want to jump up and touch the sky.
Happy is when your heart is beeping nice and well.
Teacher: Now, what does it mean to be unhappy or sad?
Children: Sad is like you don't have no friends.
Sad is when you mother leaves you.
Sad is when momma don't got no money.
Sad is when you ain't got no shoes.
Sad is when you have to move again.
Sad is when it's night and there ain't nothin' to eat.
Sad is somebody got kilt.
Sad is if you feel like going away.
Sad is if your heart been breaking down.
Sad is when a new baby comes to our house.

The Sixes
Photograph Used (65): Movers transferring furniture either to or from a truck in a rather dilapidated neighborhood. People are watching from nearby porches, stairways, and windows.

CONVERSATION 1:

General Socioeconomic Status of Students: These six-year-olds lived in an affluent section of a medium-sized city. Some had always lived there and others had moved there so that their fathers could accept occupational promotions. Most parents were highly educated and their fathers were professional or semiprofessional workers.

Teacher: What do you think about when you look at this picture?
Children: Those men probably bought some old furniture.
I think somebody's moving out of a bad neighborhood.
They could be moving in but I don't think so.
Nobody would move there! It looks like they'd move away.
I guess that's where niggers live.
Maybe it's niggers moving there.

CONVERSATION 2 (same photograph):

General Socioeconomic Status of Students: Six-year-olds in the same city, but in a depressed area much like the one shown in the photograph.

Teacher: What does this picture make you think about? What do you think is happening here?
Children: Them's gotta move someplace else.
Mebbe they's movin' to this place.
That man takin' their stuff away.
They gotta move 'cuz they can't pay the rent.
Folks don't move in the day—they move at night!
Ma says we need a chair like that.
That ain't no chair—it's a settee.
They wonder where they gonna move.

The Sevens
Photograph Used (66): A large complex of bridges, roads, and traffic.

General Socioeconomic Status of Students: Children of migrant worker parents attending classes in a church annex.

Synopsis of Preceding Teacher–Pupil Discussion: Children had discussed the implications of roads and the kinds of vehicles in the photograph. They had also discussed various ways of crossing waterways.

Teacher: Now let's see how many different ways we can think of that help people and things travel.
Children: In addition to the standard ways of travel, these children named "carts," "wagons," "swamp buggies," "bean wagons,"

"chow carts," "police cars," "bunk trucks," and "shanks' horses."

The Eights

Photographs Used (67): Two contrasting pictures taken in a city—one taken in a disadvantaged area and one taken in an advantaged area.

General Socioeconomic Status of Students: Students in two different neighborhoods in a large city; one neighborhood was disadvantaged, and the other very advantaged.

Synopsis of Preceding Teacher–Pupil Discussion: The photographs were used to encourage comparative critical thinking. The homes, general character of the neighborhoods, width of streets, size of lawns, amount of shrubbery, and the appearance of children and adults living in each neighborhood had been compared. Both groups used the words "poor" and "rich" and each teacher considered these significant enough to see what children mean by these terms.

Teacher: What other words tell something about being rich or poor?

Children:	Inner City Children		Outer City Children	
	Rich	Poor	Rich	Poor
	money	no money	travel	shacks
	food	hungry	money	slums
	houses	rents	cars	black people
	parks	no parks	furs	dirty
	nice schools	old schools	jewels	lazy
	parks	no shoes	clean	stupid
	tennis	hiding	work	unhappy
	happy	sad	mansions	drunk
	well	sick	stocks	dope
	good teeth	sorry	bonds	no work
	fur coats	bad teeth	happy	on drugs
	warm	cold	lawyers	bad
	lazy	work hard	doctors	dirty
	hire people	out of work	bands	rats
	jewels	shabby	employers	mice
	bathtubs	no bathtubs	bosses	bugs
	shoes	dirty	free	sick
	nice clothes	tired	more fun	servants
	big cars	lonely	friends	skinny
	clean	crowded	healthy	hungry
	easy	hard	nice	afraid

The Nines

Photograph Used (68): A postman handing an envelope to a child sitting on a dilapidated doorstep.

General Socioeconomic Status of Students: Children lived in a very depressed area of a large city and consisted of largely Negro, Cuban, and Puerto Rican children. Their area was scheduled for demolition as part of a redevelopment plan for the city.

Teacher: What do you think is happening in this picture?
Children: He gettin' a summons.
  Kids don' git no summons . . . folks do.
  Mebbe he the lanlor' for the money.
  They gonna haf ta move some more again.
  That ain't a lanlor'—he look too happy.
  The man dress like a cop in hot times.
  It ain't no fuzz—he ain't got no gun.
  He passin' out somethin'.
  Mailmens wears stuff like that.
  He don't come on our street—remember?
  He do, too. He brings bills.
  My aunt got a letter onct.
  We don' git no letters.
  You gotta write somebody you want a letter, stupid!

The Tens and Elevens

Photograph Used (69): A girl is shown in an air hostess uniform with wings pinned on one lapel and flowers on the other shoulder. She is smiling at a man who is handing her a diploma, since she is just graduating from training. The girl is a very attractive Negro American.

General Socioeconomic Status of Students: A poverty-stricken area in a large city. Children were from impoverished black and white homes.

Teacher: What do you think is being given to the girl in this picture?
Children: A scholarship.
  Her picture.
  Orders to go someplace.
  A bill.
  A letter or a telegram.
  Money for something.
  Good news.
  A summons.
  Some paper for something.
  A map.
  Directions for going someplace.
  Something nice because she is smiling.
  Her marks.
  A license.
  A permission card.
Teacher: Can we decide what she is getting if we look at her clothes?
Children: She got a flower.
  She got a pin too.
  That a uniform?

She work for somebody?
She won't smile that a bill.
The man, he smile, too.
Mus' be good news in that.

Commentary: Continuation here included helping children eliminate most of
the words that had been given before through deductive thinking. Reconstruction helped them think of the kind of uniform, the significance
of the wings and the corsage, and the expressions on both faces. The
words *graduation* and *certificate* or *diploma* were finally elicited. The
children had to be told that this was an airline hostess who had completed her training and was graduating and getting her diploma. The
teacher helped students to observe, think aloud, compare, choose among
possibilities, rule out illogical conclusions, and agree on the most logical
of the possibilities. The problem was that neither black nor white children thought of a black airline hostess or any black person in terms of
"graduating."

Objectives for Teachers Who Are Concerned About Social Growth

Teachers who are concerned about children's social needs will demonstrate these concerns as a result of understanding and applying the preceding discussions. They will

1. Consider the community as an extended classroom.
2. Visit children's homes and neighborhoods.
3. Learn more about children's cultural mores.
4. Help families understand school goals and purposes.
5. Value children as they find them.
6. Plan diversified activities to counteract environment.
7. Differentiate and personalize curriculum experiences.
8. Plan interpersonal and intergroup learning opportunities.
9. Counteract prejudices and stereotypes with facts.
10. Keep anecdotal records to note cognitive learning styles, behavior
    patterns, and social use of language by students.
11. Provide opportunities for growth in social behaviors.
12. Share community responsibility for advancing social progress.

Children whose teachers are concerned about social growth as an essential ingredient of intellectual functioning will

1. Trust and respect peers and adults.
2. Feel accepted and valued.
3. Contribute to group plans and activities.
4. Share responsibility with others.
5. Express themselves verbally regardless of colloquialisms.
6. Learn to communicate more effectively.

7. Compete in healthy and socially approved ways.
8. Reject prejudices and stereotyping of themselves and others.
9. Reject "pat" answers and seek new evidence.
10. Follow and discuss current events.
11. Assume responsibilities beyond their own needs.
12. Be flexible and comfortable in new situations.
13. Be unafraid to experiment.
14. Promote civic progress and improvements.
15. Speak up for causes and for justice.

Observant teachers will keep anecdotal records of conduct and language and they will note anxieties, rejections, withdrawals, motivations, new insights, and other pertinent data that will allow corrective and supportive social measures while there is still time in elementary schools. They know that the child himself and, whenever possible, his parents need to share in the development of social understandings, standards, and goals. Especially important is planning for *mutual appraisal of progress*. Realistically, teachers know that they cannot change all the factors that impinge upon a child's social growth, but sensitive empathy helps them to know when, how, and how much to help so that children are led to perform within their power to succeed.

Education for social growth and social responsibility should begin with earliest school attendance. Curriculum planning from preschool onward must include activities that demonstrate concern for social understanding and functioning.

Social growth is not an isolated development and cannot be left to happenstance. The main goal in facilitating social growth is to be able to use all that is known and available in the way of supportive services and facilities to habilitate individuals to constructive participation in society. Without rewarding experiences in constructive participation, they cannot make positive personal associations nor will they contribute to the general welfare through reasonable and productive conduct. Certainly their intellects will be partially blocked from full potential functioning unless they do have rewarding experiences and constructive guidance.

As Intellectual Organisms

Emerging Views of Intelligence
Emerging views of intelligence as something more than what intelligence tests test have exciting implications for the future education of elementary school boys and girls. Old definitions of intelligence assumed that intelligence was rather fixed or set. Newer concepts of intelligence include *the varieties of ways that individuals have available for processing and organizing incoming information and impressions.*

Almy (70) talks about the contrast of the older and newer versions:

"intelligence, rather than being fixed by genetic factors at birth, emerges as it is nurtured. Each stage of development carries with it possibilities for the acquisition of new abilities, new ways of processing information."

To the extent that teaching is based on understanding the developing child—physically, emotionally, socially, and intellectually—his capacity to learn will not only be freed but it can also be nurtured through provisions that teachers make for learning experiences. The amount and kind of intellectual nurturing that children's developing intelligence receives is dependent upon teachers' abilities to infer from children's comments and other behaviors not only the level of their understanding but also their present ways of organizing and processing information.

Before we take a closer look at the kinds of thinking children do, let us think about these examples that illustrate ways teachers have found to learn more about the *levels* of their thinking:

How It Began: A group of six-year-olds had been discussing the kinds of people who can be in immediate and extended families. The discussions had been recurring over a period of time and the group was now familiar with the word *relatives* for the various people who can be classed as "family."

What Happened: A new student arrived from Appalachia, and the teacher forgot that she might not know the words *relatives* or *family* and did not notice her bewilderment when they were discussed. A classmate noticed, though. He interrupted to say, "Wait a minute, Teach. She don't understand." Turning to the newcomer, he said, "Relative—family—that means your folks or your kin."

How It Began: Some five-year-olds had painted pictures which most of them anxiously carried home for parental approval as usual. One child did not take his picture home that day or the next, in spite of his teacher's reminders.

What Happened: Finally, his teacher reminded him on the third day that all of the other children had taken their pictures home to put up on their walls. Didn't he want to take his picture home for his wall, she wondered? He began to sob loudly, to her surprise, and finally blurted out between wails, "I don't have no wall." The teacher learned that he shared one room with four other families and that his family, being the last to arrive, had inherited the middle of the room.

How It Began: A group of seven-year-olds had taken an intelligence test. During recess, they apparently compared notes to see what answers others had given. One item was the cause of a great deal of argument and unhappiness. It showed pictures of a barn, a basement, a kennel, and a pasture, and the task was to circle the place where people kept their dogs.

What Happened: One little girl cried at home that night and told her mother that she had failed in school that day. "All of the other children put a circle around something they call a kennel or a dog house. Our dog lives in the barn, so I put a circle around barn!"

How It Began: In a program for preschool educationally disadvantaged children, a teacher was making suggestions for block construction and said, "How about building a wall?" She discovered that the word *wall* had no meaning to them.

What Happened: She moved from the blocks to the wall of the room and asked them to tell her what it was. They gave her words such as *paint, blue,* and *wood,* but not *wall.* In similar ways, she learned that they did not know the word for horse, much less that it is classed as an animal; or the word for banana, much less that it is a fruit.

Teachers learn in these ways that a child does not necessarily have a concept just because he has been exposed to it. They learn that there are ways to help him demonstrate his level of understanding so that they will be able to determine the next step with him. They learn to use open-ended questions to determine what kind of thinking a child does. The open-ended question invites teacher–pupil interaction, and does not require a right or wrong answer. Rather, teachers who learn how to use the technique of asking open-ended questions are looking for *degree of response* so that they can design the next step, or level, of learning.

Following are examples of *open-ended questions:*

· What do you think is happening in this picture?
· What would be a good name for this picture?
· Why do you suppose the boy in the story acted that way?
· Would you have ended the story differently? How?
· Would you rather visit the city or the country? Why?
· What are some of the advantages or disadvantages of living in the city? The country? The suburbs?
· Why do you think this is true? Or untrue?

As you work with children, you will find other kinds of questions that help you understand more about children's thinking, that keep communication between teacher and pupils open, and that lead teachers and students toward the level where both can assume that children do understand. It is at this level that reinforcement for *right* responses has the most significance.

Types of Thinking and Cognition

As one gains experience in studying children's comments and other behaviors to determine levels of thinking, it is possible to categorize responses as to *types of thinking.* Be familiar with these descriptions of various types of thinking because they are essential to curriculum planning, to understanding cognitive learning and concept formation, and providing meaningful learning experiences. They are not to be practiced in separate periods through separate drills. Rather, they are necessary and basic to learning to behave in ascending levels of achievement, and they deserve a great deal of attention and time for development during elementary school years.

- *Perceptual thinking* involves responses to the *immediate environment*. It is a highly individual matter, and involves an individual's immediate abilities to see, hear, and sense. Test this by discussing with your colleagues a film that you have seen together, or a lecture that you have all attended. You will be surprised at the things that others saw and heard that you did not see or hear, and vice versa.
- *Associative thinking* includes the learning that is sometimes called conditioning, as well as much of what is traditionally taught in schools in the realm of facts and skills. It involves stimulus and response and is indicated through the ways we learn to associate two or more things. The "correct" response is then rewarded with some sort of approval.
- *Conceptual thinking* eventually characterizes most learning. This kind of thinking, often referred to as "concept formation" is often the result of perception and association. It involves being able to make a generalization that covers a class or a group or a set. It also helps people to distinguish and to discriminate between and among different classes, groups, and sets. The important thing to remember is that although it sometimes results from immediate discovery, it sometimes develops gradually through added layers of meaning and experience.
- *Problem-solving thinking* involves at least five steps: the problem must be understood, relevant data must be collected, several possibilities (hypotheses) may be formed, the hypotheses need to be tested, and some possible conclusions need to be drawn. From among these, the most logical one is generally selected. One or more of these steps is sometimes avoided, depending upon individual abilities to perceive relationships, to associate elements into logical sequences, and to understand the concept involved.
- *Critical thinking* is not always classed separately by psychologists, but it is involved in curriculum planning and in teaching. According to most psychologists, critical thinking involves at least three factors: experience and knowledge in the area of concern, attitudes of suspended judgment or further questioning, and the ability to measure an idea against some kinds of agreements or norms. At the very least, it is important to being able to distinguish between fact and fancy, and it is essential to thinking about cause-and-effect relationships.
- *Creative thinking* may possibly involve all of the other kinds of thinking, but again it is a more personal, idiosyncratic kind of thinking in both its nature and its influence. The problem in other kinds of thinking is more apt to be posed by outside circumstances or other persons.

In creative thinking, it may be posed through outside circumstances or may evolve as a result of a personal need of one's own for expression or fulfillment. The result, or product, is truly one's own even though others have independently created or expressed themselves in the same way. There can also be *creative group thinking* in which the conditions that foster creativity in individuals are present and in which group members reinforce one another's creativity.

Traditionally, schools have not taken advantage of inquiry methods of learning and of thinking. The open mind and the autonomous learner are both central values to the process of inquiry. A child who is perceptually open to the world about him is challenged by the uniqueness of a problem, and the wonder of a problem or situation. So we need to think about types of thinking in relation to divergent and convergent thinking.

In *convergent thinking*, the students' responses and thought processes are directed by the teacher or by the text to a correct, acceptable, or conventional answer. But in *divergent thinking*, the situation presents many opportunities for learners to become searchers. The searcher is one who seeks different directions, more flexible ideas and approaches to problems or new situations, and envisions varieties of responses. By encouraging more divergent thinking, teachers will be much more able to learn more about how and why children think as they do. They must also learn to expect and to accept more unusual and diverse ideas and responses.

Attitudes, Interests, and Values

Attitudes, interests, and values evolve, as part of intellectual functioning, from the social and emotional experiences children have. These determine how individuals operate within different learning environments.

WHAT IS AN ATTITUDE? Allport (72) defines an *attitude* as "a mental and neutral state of readiness, organized through experience, exerting a directive or dynamic influence upon the individual's response to all objects with which it is related." Dictionaries define attitudes as ideas with emotional impact and content, important beliefs, prejudices, biases, predispositions, states of readiness or "set," and appreciations.

Creating and shaping attitudes is one of the most important functions of schools. Most of us would agree to this. And if we agree to this, then we must also feel that *attitudes can be changed*. The school has available influences that hope to change and to influence attitudes, and attitudes have been changed through the influence of one special teacher, peer associations, events and experiences, curriculum materials, extracurricular activities, or combinations of these. The school has the potential for improving attitudes, but it has also been known to head them in the opposite of the desired direction. Here are some of the ways traditional schools contradict themselves:

- Children are taught that ours is a democratic society and that all people were created equal, but they are arbitrarily placed in groups that limit their horizons.
- Children are taught the importance of cooperation, but are often placed in situations so competitive that they are forced to withdraw, cheat, or just plain give up.
- Children are taught that they are unique individuals, different from any other. Then they are labeled on the basis of a few narrow characteristics, pigeonholed, numbered, and assigned in ways that deny personal identity.
- Children are taught that it is important to succeed, but are placed in situations where graded materials and prepackaged curriculum are too easy, too hard, or too irrelevant.
- Children are taught to like school and the importance of participation in school activities. But they often find themselves static recipients rather then active participators.

How Attitudes Begin: Attitudes toward authority figures begin in the home with a child's efforts either to please his parents and receive praise, or to displease his parents and receive their attention by being punished, scolded, or disapproved.

What Happens: The child comes to school with either negative or positive attitudes about authority figures. Teachers are authority figures. The child then transfers either his efforts to please or to displease, depending upon what he has been conditioned to think got him the most attention at home. If he has received more attention by displeasing adults at home, he will respond in the same ways at school by doing something that is forbidden or to which teachers will respond with disapproval and displeasure.

What to Do: Obviously, this attitude needs to be changed if the child is to learn to live happily and safely with peers and teachers. He must learn that his old attitudes and behaviors for getting attenion will not earn attention at school. The problem for a teacher is to ignore as much as possible his present attention-getting attitudes and gradually help him to learn to get attention in acceptable ways. The average child soon learns what *will* direct attention at him in the new situation, and changes his attitudes and behaviors accordingly.

Russell (73) describes attitudes as having qualities of intensity, direction, extensity, and duration. By using these to think about the problem of the child who has come to school with negative attitudes toward those in authority, we can decide possible courses of action for helping the child gain attention in ways that we can accept.

· *Intensity* concerns the extent to which the attitude motivates a child's behavior. This is observable in the amount and kind of behavior, and the inhibiting factors it takes to change or to redirect behavior. Does the behavior *always* occur in just one kind of situation, or does it occur in several kinds of situations? How intense is it? Is it a safe kind of behavior to tolerate or ignore while it is being redirected?

· *Direction* of attitudes and behavior can be observed by noting those situations that repel, attract, motivate, or fail to motivate a child. In order to change direction, teachers study these situations so that they can provide new conditions that may reverse the attitude or behavior.

· *Extensity* is both a matter of whether the attitude has broad or limited applications and whether redirection requires broad or limited powers. If the attitude has broad applications to the child's functioning, then more global stimuli will be needed to get changed responses. But if the attitude has limited applications as the teacher observes the child, then the teacher will use specific stimuli that direct behavior to the desired response in that particular situation.

· *Duration* is important to teachers, because it is difficult to realize that annoying attitudes and behaviors will last only as long as they promote the goals of the individual. If he does not get attention through the use of the behaviors that have formerly earned attention, his negative attitudes may last only a short time because they are not now being reinforced by experience. New experiences can completely reverse the attitude.

In the chapters that follow, we will discuss curriculum planning for changing attitudes. Among these are *psychodrama, play therapy,* and *puppetry,* which require the teacher to have understanding of the genesis, nature, and qualities of children's attitudes.

WHAT ARE INTERESTS? Interests help teachers find more ways to specialize and personalize intellectual experiences for children. Ideally, instruction begins at a point of interest for a child and teachers cannot begin at this point unless they know what the child's interests are.

William James (74) talked to teachers about *interests* in the late nineteenth century. He discussed interests as a form of "selective awareness or attention that produces meaning out of the mass of one's experiences." Later on, Berdie (75) saw interests as "factors that attract an individual to, or repel him from, objects, persons, and activities." Strong (76) sees interests in two dimensions. He calls interests "likes" and aversions "dislikes." Others refer to interests as attraction to particular things because they are "stirred" or their sensory systems are "teased."

Some children come to school with special interests, and most have special aptitudes when we look for them. But the school as a learning laboratory is in an ideal position to help children *create interests,* for most of the definitions we have just studied imply the existence of stimulators and the process of selection.

Just as some people dislike certain kinds of food and may never learn to like them, children reject the same diet in school environments. If few or no choices are given, and the child cannot develop an interest in what is offered, he is doomed to failure or at least to tolerating what is available or going without. The modern elementary school has available to it an infinite variety of materials, many possibilities for creating stimulating learning environments, and numerous ways to broaden children's interests.

Interests relate to our earlier discussions of self-image and self-concept, also, because students' growing understandings should contribute to clear impressions of special interests that lead to potential achievements. These eventually dictate lifelong vocations and avocations, depending upon whether they are short-term or long-term interests.

How can teachers learn about and use special interests?

Teachers observe children in varieties of situations.
Teachers provide a variety of possibilities in learning environments.
Teachers confer with individual pupils.
Teachers confer with parents and with other teachers.
Teachers note preferences and special learning styles.
Teachers find ways to use children's interests.
Teachers experiment with new ways to broaden their interests.
Teachers design curriculum to help a child use his interests.
Teachers look beyond the classroom and the school for catalysts.
Teachers use the community to develop new interests.
Teachers invite other adults with special interests to share them.
Teachers develop ideas that stimulate and motivate.

As each child grows in the ability to appraise himself realistically, his special interests and aptitudes will become more observable if he is given the opportunity to follow and develop them. They will lie fallow if his school experiences are identical to those with whom he is grouped for learning. The first concept of educational possibilism is dynamic; the second is static, unchallenging, and deadly.

WHAT IS A VALUE? Values evolve from the social and intellectual experiences that children and adults have and could just as easily have been listed and discussed in connection with the child as a growing social organism. Some writers class values as social concepts. In classifying them this way they say, as for example Russell (77) does, that "as social concepts, they are involved in the educative process because they are basic to the society of which the child and the school are parts."

Since we are including values in these discussions of intellectual development and functioning, we feel that, although they evolve from the society of which the child and the school are parts, they have a great deal of importance in relation to how a person functions intellectually. Values affect behavior and behavior affects intellectual development.

Values relate to the worth or weight given to specific kinds of things including objects, acts, and conditions. Pseudovalues are those that people adopt by conforming to given situations for the rewards implicit in the situation. The difference between values and pseudovalues is that values are internalized; pseudovalues are not. Many values that we can observe are conforming, or pseudo, values adopted for the purpose of receiving approval from certain groups or individuals.

Discussing a classroom approach to values, Wright (78) includes these important points:

1. Values to be discussed should be related to the interests, needs, and experiences of the group.
2. Basic knowledge that pertains to the value under consideration should be made available to pupils.
3. Learning should be organized around a particular situation as realistic and as close to pupil needs as possible.
4. The problem that is presented should involve conflicting values.
5. Free expression of present and future consequences of values should be encouraged.

Stendler (79) points out that school experiences affect the development of responsibility and honesty more than they seem to affect loyalty, moral courage, and friendliness. He thinks that values such as responsibility and honesty have less deep emotional content, and are easier to put into practice. They are also easier to observe in behavior.

In attempts to prescribe what values should be the concern of schools, criticism is bound to result. For if one says that certain ones are important, others are sure to disagree and will want to substitute those they consider to be more important. It is here that we often see the effects of long-inculcated values at work in adults. For example, we say that it is important to present problems that involve conflicting values, yet few teachers are willing to tackle controversial issues. Do you remember that we said that one of the qualities needed among new teachers is the willingness to take risks in teaching for the unkown? Teaching for the unknown (and that is really what we are all doing) involves, as we previously emphasized, being able to bring controversial issues into classrooms and discuss them without rancor or attempts at indoctrination.

CHANGING ATTITUDES AND VALUES Probably one of the most emotionally charged issues of our times is the matter of race relations and civil rights. If schools intend to build the kinds of people who will continuously remake society in the light of mankind's needs, surely they will recognize and teach about the importance of intercultural appreciation and intercultural relationships. Intellectually, most people agree that traditional education has not changed class and race biases and hatreds. Research confirms the existence and effects of these, yet schools find it difficult to take the steps that will be necessary to change these attitudes and values.

Racial and class biases are prevalent in life generally, and so they exist in classrooms. Here's an incident that occurred in a classroom of seven-year-olds:

How It Began: Jean was a first-year teacher when she faced her first class of all-Negro second-graders. She learned very quickly that not only did her young charges have low self-esteem, but that they also had deeply entrenched class biases. When they were angry or upset, they called one another names—"black," "nigger," "son of a nigger," and worse. When they were not in her presence, they called her black, too, as she learned when the class tattler reported, "Jimmy called you an awful name outside. He called you black!" When Jean wore new brown lace stockings to school one day, the children disliked them intensely and told her so. Trying to understand why, she talked with the children about what could make them so unhappy about her stockings. Finally one child spoke for the rest when she said, "Because they make you look *black* like us!"

What Happened: Jean knew that she was in uncharted territory and that these children were awfully young. But she decided that if these values and attitudes were already so deep, she must try to do something to help them change them. She brought news clippings about the city's school population shifts and plans to balance schools racially. She read parts of the clippings to the children and then asked them how they would like to have some other children from different parts of the city come to their school. The responses were intensely negative! Reasons given included "Because they're all Wops and Jews," "They hate us," and "We don't like them."

Discussion disclosed that none of the reactions was based on really knowing one white child, that these were words and impressions they had heard their parents and other adults use.

Jean had a social conscience and she was an unusually intelligent and gifted young teacher. She voluntarily attended the school system's intergroup education in-service training program even though the school system could not afford either extra money or released time for this. She spent a great deal of time in the library and in the film center locating books and films with intergroup themes. And she scoured magazines and newspapers for pictures showing interracial friendliness and cooperation. She started a "Junior Peace Corps at Home" by arranging for interschool visits with another second grade in another part of the city.

Jean worked intensively with the children's parents after school and on weekends. She considered this just as important as what she was trying to do in the classroom, because without parents' support and understanding, she could not have planned the kinds of classroom curriculum experiences that she hoped would help change attitudes and values. Jean's ongoing anecdotal records contained comments like these, indicating some attitude and value changes:

> The children are doing less name-calling, but forget sometimes.
> Some children from both schools are seeing one another out of school now.
> John went to Joe's for lunch and a birthday party on Saturday.
> Susan spent a weekend with Jane's family at their country camp.
> Tom is going to stay at Stan's house tonight.
> Jack asked whether I can get him "another black-and-white book."
> Tammy said she never saw any children like herself in books before.
> Happy Day! Selma told me that, "Some white folks ain't all that bad!"

There should be more teachers like Jean. She not only finds out about what the intergroup and intercultural problems are, but she tries to do something about them. Unless other teachers who follow her help too the effects may be lost, because there has to be continuing reinforcement in order to change group animosities and individual attitudes and values.

Above everything else, values and attitudes cannot be isolated from other aspects of intellectual development; they are part of it. Certainly there must be planned curricular activities to help teach them and to help boys and girls develop life skills concerned with man's common humanity, and with the nature of democracies.

References

42. Fischer, John H., "The Inclusive School," *Teachers College Record*, Columbia University, October, 1964.
43. Atwell, Betty, and Betty Warner, "Helping Primary School Children Understand Themselves," *Childhood Education*. This incident was the basis of this article published by the Association for Childhood Education International, Washington, D.C., 1951.
44. Jersild, A. T., "Emotional Development," *Educational Psychology*. Edited by C. E. Skinner. Englewood Cliffs, N.J.: Prentice-Hall, Inc., 1961.
45. Goldstein, K., *Human Nature in the Light of Psychopathology*. Cambridge, Mass.: Harvard University Press, 1947.
46. Maslow, A. H., "A Theory of Human Motivation," *Psychological Review*, 1943, APGA Yearbook.
47. Schmuck, R., "Some Aspects of Classroom Social Climate," *Psychology in the Schools*. Washington, D.C.: Association for Supervision and Curriculum Development, 1966.

48. Aspy, D. N., "A Study of Three Facilitative Conditions and Their Relationship to the Achievement of Third Grade Students." An unpublished Ed.D. dissertation, University of Kentucky, 1965.

49. Rogers, Carl R., "The Interpersonal Relationship in the Facilitation of Learning," *Humanizing Education: The Person in the Process*. Washington, D.C.: Association for Supervision and Curriculum Development, 1967.

50. Ashton-Warner, Sylvia, *Teacher*. New York: Simon and Schuster, Inc., 1963.

51. Emmerling, F. C., "A Study of the Relationships Between Personality Characteristics of Classroom Teachers and Pupil Perceptions." An unpublished Ph.D. dissertation, Auburn University, Alabama, 1961.

52. Bower, John, Reported in, "Mentally Unfit Teachers," *Ladies Home Journal*, February, 1969, p. 80.

53. Bard, Bernard, "Mentally Unfit Teachers," *Ladies Home Journal*, February, 1969.

54. Ashton-Warner, Sylvia, *Spinster*. New York: Bantam Books, 1958.

55. Jersild, A. T., *In Search of Self*. New York: Teachers College, Columbia University, 1952.

56. Wright, Betty Atwell. This classroom experiment later became the basis for an article called, "Helping Children Understand Why They Feel as They Do," and was published in the *NEA Journal*, September, 1960.

57. Gates, A. I. et al. *Educational Psychology*. 3rd ed. New York: The Macmillan Company, 1948.

58. Kluckhohn, Clyde, and Henry Murray (Eds.), *Personality in Nature, Society, and Culture*. New York: Alfred A. Knopf, Inc., 1949.

59. McGuire, and Havighurst, "Social Development," *Review of Educational Research*, Vol. XVII, December, 1947, p. 345.

60. National Society for the Study of Education, *Learning and Instruction*. Forty-ninth Yearbook, Part I. Chicago: University of Chicago Press, 1950.

61. Doll, E. A., "The Relation of Social Competence to Social Adjustment," *Educational Record*, Vol. XXIX, January, 1948, p. 81.

62. Doll, E. A., *Vineland Social Maturity Scale* (Manual of Directions). Minneapolis: Educational Test Bureau, 1947, pp. 3–8.

63. Hightower, H. W., "The School—Its Social Role," *Progressive Education*, Vol. XXV, January, 1948.

64–69. Wright, Betty Atwell, *Urban Education Studies*. Photographs used in Album D, "A City Is . . ."; Album G, "Recreation Is . . ."; Album C, "A Neighbor Is . . ."; Album A, "Growing Is . . .". Special City Albums, "New York Is . . ." and "Detroit Is . . .". New York: The John Day Company, Inc., published from 1965–1968.

70. Almy, Millie, "New Views on Intellectual Development in Early Childhood Education," *Intellectual Development: Another Look*. Washington, D.C.: Association for Supervision and Curriculum Development, 1964.

71. Wright, Betty Atwell, *Rural Education Studies* and *Urban Education Studies*. New York: The John Day Company, Inc., 1965–1968. (See *Teachers' Guides*.)

72. Allport, G. W., "Attitudes," *Handbook of Social Psychology*. Edited by Murchison. Worchester, Mass.: Clark University Press, 1935, p. 810.

73. Russell, I. L., "Development of Attitudes, Interests, and Values," *Educa-*

tional Psychology. Edited by C. E. Skinner, Englewood Cliffs, N.J.: Prentice-Hall, Inc., 1961, p. 325.

74. James, William, *The Principles of Psychology*, Vol. I. New York: Holt, Rinehart and Winston, Inc., 1890, p. 402.
75. Berdie, R. F., "Interests," *Encyclopedia of Psychology*. New York: Philosophical Library, 1946, p. 305.
76. Strong, E. K., *Vocational Interests of Men and Women*. Stanford, Calif.: Stanford University Press, 1943, p. 6.
77. Russell, I. L., "Development of Attitudes, Interests, and Values," *Educational Psychology*. Edited by C. E. Skinner. Englewood Cliffs, N.J.: Prentice-Hall, Inc., 1961.
78. Wright, M. A., *Education and Morals*. New York: Appleton-Century-Crofts, 1950.
79. Stendler, C. B., "Class Biases in Teaching Values," *Progressive Education*, 1950.

CHAPTER 3

Teachers Investigate Life Management Curriculum

Children Live in a Series of Learning Environments

An Overview of Various Environments

A child lives simultaneously in a series of learning environments, and each one has its own operating system that affects human learning capacities and cognitive developments. The emotional atmosphere and psychological climate engendered by each one limits or extends horizons, closes off or opens up the world, conditions self-concepts and other-people-concepts, and affects attitudes, interests, and values. Even though the teacher has primary responsibility for the school-sponsored environment, he must also know about and understand the others if he hopes to understand and teach each child effectively.

First, there is each person's own internal environment. This changes and develops with evolving thinking and feeling processes of individuals. Individual internal environments are intimately related to each person's abilities to rationalize, understand, and cope with internal and external forces. The operation of internal environments can be observed through the methods children use to resolve their conflict situations, their ways of relating to others, and various other personality manifestations discussed in the preceding chapters.

Second, there is the environment created by family units. This includes child-rearing practices in homes, punishments and rewards to which children have been accustomed, attitudes toward education, moral and ethical values, and parental attitudes toward the larger society. These will be discussed in greater detail in Section II, as will the third environment. Third, is the environment that is created by the community microcosm, which is generally closely related to family unit environments.

Fourth, there is the environment created by the school. Fifth, there is the larger environment created by forces and elements in the national and international cultures and concerns.

A Closer Look at School Environment

The school environment is of utmost importance to both individual and social psychology. If the school takes seriously the implications of the study of the science of human behavior, the school environment must take into consideration the nature of child growth and development, the appraisal of personality characteristics, the assessment of individual differences in various behavioral aspects, and the understanding and discovery of patterns of influences that produce deviant behaviors such as aggression, withdrawal, delinquency, and the like.

Both the psychology of individuals and social psychology, which is the bridge between psychology and sociology, are operating in school environments. Thus, it is as important to consider the psychology of group structures the school creates and sponsors as it is to consider other aspects of the school learning environment. In the early twentieth century John Dewey and other psychologists were concerned with school environments, and Dewey said that the business of school environment is "excellence"— whether we permit chance environments to do the work or whether we "design environments for the purpose makes a great deal of difference."

Professional teachers design school learning environments with the imagination and skill of stage directors. They know that comfort and beauty are important, that a wide variety of up-to-the-minute materials and equipment are necessary, and that it is essential to provide for a student's individual learning styles, special interests, and personalized needs. But even more importantly, they are convinced that the emotional *atmosphere* they create will set the pace for learnings whose behaviors are observable. They know that this is a mandate of professional practice.

Guiding Psychological Principles for School Environment

· Physical and social environments promote or limit realization of one's purposes, goals, needs, and potential.
· Biological organisms have certain needs, but as they grow and develop, their methods of satisfying them are socially determined.
· Behavior is caused and is not its own cause. This is a very complex and interrelated process, but discovering causes leads to *understanding behaviors*.
· Human behaviors have purposes and goals. Individuals may not understand their own purposes and goals, or the factors that influence them, but the study and application of psychology helps others

understand them so that they can be helped to understand themselves.

- Patterns of personality characteristics evolve through interaction among genetic, social, and physical factors. The patterns we can observe and prescribe for include motives for behavior and actions, how one organizes and develops one's self, values and attitudes, and interrelationships with others.
- Even though individuals differ from one another in personal values, attitudes, personalities, and roles, members of a group must possess some common characteristics and agree upon some common values.
- Social groupings are ways and means of developing group cooperation and provide vehicles for working together toward satisfaction of common needs. Each social group to which an individual belongs helps shape his behaviors and perceptions.
- Differences are valued among individuals because modern culture needs a variety of vocations and avocations. Differences also help to furnish the flexibility and creativity that are needed in order to bring about social change and development.
- Personality structure and individual behaviors are largely influenced by the socialization processes of different groups, cultures, social classes, and societies. Value standards developed reflect themselves in new group situations, but new patterns of behavior are related also to the structure and organization of the new groups in which they are placed. An individual exhibits different qualities in different groups—qualities such as leadership, followership, aggression, submission. The group relationships and the need-satisfying qualities of different groups cause different kinds of behavior in the same individual.
- Individuals who remain in static, unchanging groups resist change. Groups and institutions stagnate because of reluctance to change the purpose for which they were originally created. Thus groups are often oriented to negative or obsolete goals simply to preserve identity.

The Physical Setting

Modern schools are much more concerned about the use of space, lighting, ventilation, appropriate seating, sanitary and health facilities, and the physical surroundings of the educational setting than schools of the past. Every good teacher is conscious of the importance of beauty, color, comfort, and convenience. The classroom will invite, it will entice, and it will embrace learning.

Concurrently, good teachers know that it is necessary to provide materials and equipment tailored to the interest, needs, and abilities of individuals. The picture concerning educational materials and equipment is changing so rapidly today that no longer can standard classroom equipment be confined to chalkboards, maps, globes, and play equipment.

Equipment and materials available to help children gather facts and to reinforce learning now include:

- Varieties of charts, maps, and projections.
- Records and record players.
- Television and radios.
- Tapes and tape recorders.
- Transparencies and overhead projectors.
- Models and kits.
- New sensory and manipulative materials.
- Encyclopedias, dictionaries, and other references.
- Programmed texts and workbooks.
- Teaching machines and programs for them.
- Microscopes and other science equipment.
- Multiple text and trade books.
- Films, filmstrips, slides, screens, and projectors.
- Individual audio-visual equipment and programs.

All of these materials are either part of permanent classroom equipment or are made easily accessible and available to teachers and children. Some of it is designed into individual learning carrels; some of it is conveniently nearby so that pupils master the skills of operating and using equipment for independent and small group work; and some of it is in decentralized learning resource libraries convenient to clusters of teachers and children.

There are imaginative new ways to use school space and teacher–pupil time. Clusters of open space classrooms are gaining favor and have the advantage of encouraging more pupil–pupil, pupil–teacher, and teacher–teacher communication and cooperation; additionally, they invite interage and multi-interest grouping. Whether we enter a well-equipped single self-contained classroom or a multiclass learning environment, we know there is a professional teacher in charge as we look around.

There are books, books, and more books. The classroom library includes varieties of paperbacks and hard-cover trade and textbooks. Up-to-date reference works, supplementary textbooks and workbooks, and periodicals are easily available to students. The teacher has his own personal, professional books and well-organized files conveniently at hand. There are well-understood and simple procedures for children to use and account for materials they borrow.

There are bulletin boards, pictures, and other visuals. Bulletin boards have themes and are learning areas. They are student prepared, organized, and maintained. There are maps, graphs, charts, and diagrams on walls and chalkboards. Student work is in evidence, as are pictures that pertain to units of study. Visually the room invites learning and it says, unmistakably, that learning is going on here.

There are teaching–learning aids of other kinds. The filing cabinets are

The picture concerning educational materials and equipment is changing rapidly. There are accompanying changes in the roles of teachers.

Photos courtesy of Florida Atlantic University.

well organized and enticing with areas for individual pupil folders, teacher-made tests, drawings, pictures, transparencies, special stencils, and project ideas. Shelves have tapes, slides, and records organized by subject and titles. One of the various projectors may be in place ready for film, filmstrip, slide, or transparency use.

There are boys and girls involved in real learning adventures. Some may be working alone on independent study projects at various interest centers around the room. Many are working in small groups with their desks drawn together in a circle, or with their chairs grouped together in a corner, or with their heads bent over a mural and paint jars. They are talking quietly, and purposefully. The teacher moves among individuals and small groups. His role is to give help and counsel when needed, to note special needs and interests, and to provide support and reinforcement.

There is a teacher or a team of teachers. Their guidelines for ordering and purchasing classroom materials include:

- *Manipulative materials* such as blocks, games, puzzles, disks, crayons, models, toys, dolls, puppets, and so on.
- *Materials to help pace individual learning,* including programmed lessons for individual skill development, syllabi for independent study, audio-visual teaching machines for use in learning carrels or by small groups, varieties of text and trade books for individual reading and literary growth, and kits of related, special-interest materials.
- *Materials to stimulate the senses,* for example, hearing (tapes, records, radio), sight (slides, films, exhibits, pictures, maps, charts), smell (foods, nature, science laboratory), touch (models, sculpture, woods, metals, glass, animals), taste (national and international foods).

Professional teachers know that there are now available many new teaching–learning aids such as computer-assisted instruction, and that there are more on the horizon. They understand the psychological principles of logic and order built into independent study materials to help children progress at their own rate and pace their intake of factual information. Understanding the importance and purpose of pacing individual learning of facts and study skills, they know that their own primary functions will be in areas of helping children to gain insights about the *meaning and relationships of facts* to improved relationships and behaviors.

The Psychological and Emotional Setting

Remembering that the quality of the interpersonal relationships a child has at school may be the most important facilitator of learning, a professional teacher has examined the role education should play in his own and his students' lives, and he is prepared from the very first day of each term to work constantly and consistently to establish good psychological climate. He plans carefully for the ways he will welcome students and parents on the first day, and he continues to find ways of welcoming, orienting, planning, and guiding so that positive teacher–parent–pupil relationships will set the tone for mutual trust and cooperation.

Initial parent–pupil impressions are important because they create a lasting impression. Knowing the excitement of the first day, the teacher capitalizes on fresh enthusiasms and new beginnings by greeting parents and children warmly, inviting them to see the new classroom, being familiar with the class roster so that he can introduce pupils to pupils and parents to parents, and allowing time for individual browsing and short, pleasant conversations. Sincere greetings and interest take only minutes, but may save hours of effort to establish rapport later in the year. The teacher realizes that there may be some parents who will not or cannot come to the classroom or to school-sponsored activities, so he makes a special effort to set up appointments and visit parents at home early in the year.

Parents should also be encouraged to visit the classroom informally, and when they do come they should be introduced to the class and drawn into the activity or discussion of the moment. Specific use of parents as resource persons, and of parents and others as volunteers will be discussed in greater detail later. Here we want to emphasize the importance of the relationships and partnerships that will be established by positive first encounters.

Teacher–Pupil Planning

How quickly good psychological climate and harmony can be achieved when classroom management is tackled by both teachers and pupils! Discipline problems and traditional systems of reward and punishment are nonexistent when teacher-pupil planning and evaluation are the keynotes of classroom learning environments. The implementation of these partnerships between teachers and children comes from teachers' personal security and from their faith in each individual's ability and capacity for accepting responsibility.

Above and beyond *physiological, safety,* and *security* needs, Abraham Maslow (80) suggests categories of needs that are also basic motivating factors of human behavior:

- *Love and belonging* include helping to establish rules and regulations for the general good of all, as well as being the basis for pupil–pupil, teacher–pupil, and other relationships at school.
- *Esteem needs* are important not only to ideas of self-worth, but also to other-people-worth interactions.
- *Self-actualization* needs mandate opportunities for independent and group progress since both are necessary bases for forming values and attitudes.

- *Needs to know and understand* can be satisfied in the physical and psychological climate that the school establishes.
- *Aesthetic needs* related to beauty and creativity are obvious, but frequently neglected, concerns of school environment.

The teacher is, of course, the leader in helping boys and girls organize, initiate, and direct the activities of the class. Children look to the teacher for guidance and for clarification as well as for help in the values that are to be realized from classroom activities. But children need to help create the activities and values that will guide school living and learning. Student riots around the country today are centered about student exclusion from helping to determine their own learning activities and needs. They are telling us in unmistakable terms that this is *their* life and that they insist upon helping to plan it.

Involving students in planning is in sharp contrast to authoritarian leadership that sometimes characterizes schools and group work. Teachers learn how to plan by planning with school administration, and children learn how to plan by planning with teachers. Both kinds of cooperative planning include helping to set up the objectives and the possible ways to achieve mutual objectives. When boys and girls share in planning objectives and ways to achieve objectives, they identify with one another, with teachers, and with the school. They have a vested interest in learning.

What teachers need to learn is when to give direction or not to give it, when to support and praise and not overpraise, or when to move out of the picture and let individual initiative take over. In every group there are children with many kinds of needs, interests, and abilities. Even if it were possible to group children exactly using these as matching criteria, the teacher's main job would be to make them as different as possible as fast as possible. It is only through the differences among individuals that teachers learn to prescribe for individuals rather than for the stereotype of an assumed group.

These individual differences are considered desirable and valuable by professional teachers, because they enable teachers and children to plan different activities so that all can know the satisfaction of accomplishment and achievement. The teacher does not then assume that every child will achieve the same end product at the same rate or by the same route. The teacher adopts, instead, the goals of having all children experience success and worthiness and of allowing flexibility for varieties of children who will learn in a variety of ways.

Within classroom groups, successes and failures become public knowledge at once. Failure increases personal threat to children's personalities, so teachers analyze and prepare carefully so that fear of failure is minimized and hope of success is maximized. Professional teachers never use classroom situations to cause any child to be ridiculed or embarrassed. The wise teacher never uses sarcasm or threats to keep children in line, threats that sometimes include angry telephone calls or letters to a child's home, failure of promotion, being kept from a special activity, or being sent to the principal's office. Any of these makes a child a lesser person in his own and in others' eyes. Any one child's subjection to these weakens the group spirit, a power that goes beyond the individuals who make up groups.

In groups where spirit is high and morale is good, weak individuals are spurred on to higher achievements and better behaviors. In groups where morale has broken down, children who would otherwise achieve become indifferent and ineffectual.

How does a teacher begin to involve children in planning? Planning together means that a problem or a project is being considered cooperatively; that some objectives have been set, jobs to be done have been decided upon, and that different tasks have been assigned. Planning together and working together means that everyone understands the goals and that everyone will work to accomplish them. Establishing small groups for specific purposes is the method of accomplishing basic routine responsibilities as well as the basis for educational, social, and governmental operations in a classroom.

Children and teachers can first plan co-responsibilities that will eliminate many of the routine, time-consuming things teachers sometimes concern themselves with so that there will be more time for flexibility and for real teacher–pupil planning of more important things. Students can check their group or the seating chart to report absences, set up housekeeping committees on a rotating basis to clean chalkboards or water plants, serve as hosts and hostesses for room visitors, serve as stock and supplies clerks, and help other students who have been absent by briefing them on what they have missed during their absence. They can return papers, check borrowed materials in and out, and collect lunch and bank money. With involvement in classroom management routines, they also help make the rules for health and safety of the group inside of the building and on the playground. They take turns organizing games, leading groups to playground and special classes, and are involved in understanding and planning routines for fire and other emergency drills, as well as for class trips.

At the same time as they plan and accept these kinds of responsibilities, they are also being involved in other kinds of planning. Every curricular area offers possibilities for teaming up children, for establishing groups temporarily, for disbanding and establishing new groups, and for having some learning "buddies." Whether a "science team" works at a microscope, a "film team" operates the audio-visual equipment, "buddies" study their spelling lists together, or a "reading group" works on a play, a puppet show, or sharing reading interests, the group process is at work.

The teacher makes sure that every group is balanced—that no one group has all of the lowest achievers or the greatest number of "problem" children. Suppose we apply this idea to a block of time we shall call the *language arts* and see what can happen. We enter a classroom with twenty-eight students in it to see:

1. One group of children reading a play. They have decided who is to take each of the five parts and are working with some props such as a crown for the king and queen. Each awaits his turn anxiously, but also listens to what the others are reading. Sometimes they interrupt their reading to suggest action or to improvise dialogue.
2. Another group is busy at the author's research center. One is looking for a word in the dictionary, another is copying his finished and corrected original story in his own picture-story book, a third is illustrating his story, and a fourth is looking through his personal "Idea File" to see whether he has started something he wants to finish today.
3. The teacher is sitting with a small group of children who are having an "author's conference." They have partially completed original stories which they read aloud to one another for the group's plot, characterization, or resolution suggestions. We are amazed at the maturity with which these nine-year-olds consider each of these and the way each child seems able to handle positive and negative criticisms given and received.
4. Two children are testing one another on their knowledge of word endings using family word flash cards, and two others are working together on some spelling words that one of them missed while he was absent.
5. One child is adding the name of a book he has just finished to his card file of books read so far this year, and three children are working on a bulletin board about authors.
6. Some children are reading independently in the library corner. Each has a different book, but occasionally we see one ask another to help him with a word or one show an interesting picture to another.

These children could just as well be preparing radio or TV scripts, preparing a news broadcast, giving oral book reports, writing and producing an original play, or working on a class newspaper. The important thing is that no child is failing, all are involved and interested in what they are doing, and that their activities are so well planned that they can proceed without the constant guidance of the teacher. We learn that all of the activities we observe are part of ongoing, mutually planned projects, and we know that these are representative of classrooms where teachers are neither autocrats nor complete permissivists. This teacher has control of the situation, but it is the kind of control in which children have a planned and planning part and for which they accept co-responsibility.

Time for Learning and Teaching

In this example of a block of time that is used for language arts instruction, we see the value and interrelatedness of different activities to accommodate different needs, abilities, and interests. Inheriting as teachers do the responsibility of helping children learn, they must perfect techniques that will identify the needs of individuals and, at the same time, carry over into other areas of school and out-of-school life.

For years curriculum groups have written guidelines covering scope and sequence, but in practice teachers have felt frustration in omitting what they consider to be more valuable materials and activities than those covered in the curriculum guide. They have felt that there was insufficient time to cover the required material, and so they have by-passed teacher–pupil planning of individual and group projects that would hold more interest and motivation for students in favor of a specific number of problems to solve, pages to read, or questions to answer in an allotted time, on a specific day, and in a specific way.

With our present understanding of children and of curriculum, we need to take a fresh look at apportionments of time that will improve the performance of both students and teachers. Through new teaching–learning patterns and through new allotments of time and space to fulfill modern educational objectives, better use of time and talents of children and teachers can be used to improve achievements and lift morale, as well.

Team teaching, provision for special resource teaching, the use of paraprofessional volunteers, and paid teacher aides all give promise of helping to alleviate some of the problems connected with lack of time and wise use of talents. Before advocating the use of any of these, however, a school faculty or an individual teacher should look at basic principles with high priority for governing the wise use of time and talents.

Large blocks of time are necessary to study any subject in depth, and time units must be flexible and planned in terms of children and teachers working together in the following areas:

1. Acquiring knowledge and direct experience.
2. Developing concepts, understanding and association.
3. Providing for interest and need fulfillment.
4. Evaluating goals and progress toward them.
5. Creating new situations and materials.

In the process of integrating pupil goals and needs with subject content, students have opportunities to explore cross sections of curriculum concerns as well as longitudinal studies. *Blocks of time* provide both the time and opportunity for cross-fertilization to take place, and give teachers and students time to plan together and individually. The advantages of planning blocks of time over quick changes in schedule can be readily observed as students become more fully absorbed in projects that interest them. When at the end of a block of time the teacher finds it necessary to end one kind of learning activity and proceed to another, groups or individuals concentrating on self-selected and cooperatively planned goals and skills are more likely to carry on independently at a later time or out of school. Under cooperative planning and independent progress, children take more responsibility for their own accomplishments. Behaviors that demonstrate the value of the learning activity will carry over into other areas of living and learning.

Team teaching, the use of paraprofessionals, and special resource people may be some of the ways to provide more released time for teachers to prepare for better class instruction. A teacher's contribution to the child, school, home, and community is so important that all school personnel must continue to find improved techniques that will use teachers' professional skills in

1. Selecting and programming materials of high interest level for students of varying abilities.
2. Studying and contributing to individual cumulative record files.
3. Visiting homes and conferring with parents at school.
4. Sharing information and ideas with other teachers.
5. Previewing new books and other publications for children, as well as being familiar with educational toys and games, films, tapes, filmstrips, records, slides, and audio-visual equipment and programs.
6. Attending professional conferences and study groups.
7. Organizing and integrating instructional materials and activities to take into account the principles of human behavior and to ensure pupil self-activation.
8. Becoming familiar with and using new media such as programmed instructional materials, instructional television, teaching machines, tapes, and so on.
9. Devising teacher-made tests appropriate for individual and group learnings.
10. Participating in other kinds of in-service education for personal and professional growth.

Understanding Anxiety, Fear, and Threat

Children who feel *threatened* in classroom situations cannot concentrate, nor are they eager to approach new problems. Some students may not volunteer information because they are afraid they will be wrong. It is not uncommon for a child to play dumb because of his desire to escape criticisms of his peers and teachers. It is easy to overlook the child who is docile and quiet, but it is essential for teachers to examine carefully the reasons why children withdraw and do not contribute. When the threatening causes have been discovered, it is incumbent upon the teacher to design with the child situations that are more free of threat for that individual. This will have been accomplished when teachers note that children seem happier, contribute more often, volunteer information, respond more readily, and join in group activities more easily.

Related to the concept of fear and threat is the presence of some degree of *anxiety* in all learning. The anxieties connected with learning can be positive forces if they are kept at the level where a child seems to function at his best. Anxiety occurs because the learning task confronting the child is accepted as a challenge which he hopes to conquer. Children create their own anxieties which eliminate the need for externally imposed threats when teachers understand how to motivate and sustain children's learning abilities.

Watch a group of children when they are giving a class play or program for parents or schoolmates. Tension increases in the group as each individual's anxiety mounts. Each wants to do his best and to receive praise for effort expended. The anxieties mount as each person sustains himself to function adequately.

Concomitantly, children's unnatural and unnecessary anxieties can be alleviated if teachers plan and suggest learning tasks with them; otherwise excess anxieties create the kind of frustration that drains children's emotions and blocks motivation. This is what happens when children are arbitrarily given assignments that are too difficult or too general. It is the schools' role to help children experience more success than failure. Some failures are to be expected, but they need not be devastating if there is an understanding and supportive adult on hand to help redirect efforts and if peers view some failures as steppingstones to greater accomplishments.

For example, we know that communication abilities are closely related to social success and to achievement in school. Therefore, teachers help children develop communication skills of speaking, writing, and reading by providing many individualized opportunities to select, to participate, and to experiment. Teachers see that children have the specialized help in skill development that they need at the time that they need it. But they do not put all children through the same unnecessarily repetitious drill. Instead, they provide opportunities for flexible and changing groups, and for self selection and personalized planning with each child. Thus the learning experience is not only tailor-made, but it is also more prone to success because the goals and methods are by student choice. Among the choices children have are

1. Participating in group planning and discussion.
2. Time for browsing among varieties of books.
3. Opportunities to select books of high personal interest.
4. Time for individual and small group counseling with the teacher.
5. A chance to progress at their own speed and in their own way.

6. Shared reading and talking experiences.
7. Programmed materials for independent skill and fact gathering.
8. Encouragement to clarify concepts and expand knowledge through participating in varieties of experiences with different groups of children. For example, children of differing reading abilities can participate in the same dramatization, pantomime, mock TV or radio program, group discussion, puppet show, or class newspaper production. In these kinds of activities, varieties of needs, interests, and talents are an asset and lead to individual and group feelings of success.
9. Developing understanding and assurance that there is no one sure method or road to success; there are many choices available.
10. Self selection and group volunteer participation based on greatest needs and interests at each stage of development.

More About Assessment

In earlier discussions of innate ability and intelligence testing, we warned teachers about accepting intelligence test scores and achievement test scores at face value. We also discussed the serious side effects of labeling that occur for teachers and for children as the result of accepting IQ scores at face value and grouping children accordingly. Children and teachers suffer many misconceptions when children are labeled as low achievers, average achievers, or high achievers. The students labeled and assigned to low-achieving groups suffer from low self-esteem and from low teacher expectations. Paradoxically, the student who achieves high scores and builds a reputation for himself may suffer also. Sometimes the teacher excuses the "superior" student when, for the same behavior, he chastises the "poor" student. David's story illustrates this.

David

On the basis of David's recorded intelligence test score of 130, David's teacher demonstrated discerning teaching behavior when he noted discrepancies between David's *demonstrated performance* and his IQ scores.

David *seemed* to be a very bright, articulate student. But he tended to monopolize classroom discussions, sometimes correcting other children after interrupting their explanations and idea trends. This often resulted in pupil-to-pupil arguments in which David would never concede that he might be wrong, even though questioning revealed that he did not have all of the supporting facts.

Investigation showed that David was the youngest and only boy in a family of five girls whose parents were middle-aged. At home he was given special attention as a boy and as a younger brother. Additionally, parents, sisters, and former teachers often praised him for work that was superficial. David's teacher did not think he showed the depth of study and thinking of which he might be capable. He wanted to help him take better advantage of superior abilities, if indicated capabilities were accurate, but he also realized that David's superficiality deterred both learning and peer acceptance.

In class planning for a series of lectures that students in David's group had volunteered to give in other classes throughout the school, David decided to lecture on the subject of dinosaurs. In order to give a "lecture" each student must become "expert" in his chosen subject and, before giving the lecture, it was decided that a committee of upper classmen in the adjoining classroom would serve as interviewers of prospective lecturers. The purpose of the interviewing committee would be to ensure accurate and stimulating information before the lecture was actually given in other classrooms.

The committee asked David some preliminary questions and found that some of his information about dinosaurs was shallow. They told him that he would have to do additional research before he could lecture. This turned out to be a valuable lesson for David because he was able to accept the criticism from a committee set up for the purpose in a different class where he had been unable, or unwilling, to be corrected by individuals in his own class. He returned to the topic determined, for the first time, to balance ego with hard work. When the lecture was rechecked and approved by the committee, David delivered it to his own classmates and to other classes. He was congratulated by the chairman of the committee, his peers, and his teacher—and he deserved the praise he received.

As the year progressed, David applied what he had learned to research on other subjects. With sure knowledge, and praise only when praise was due, both David and his teacher were able to agree that he was taking a more responsible and mature outlook toward the development of his own intellectual growth and innate abilities.

Life Skills Curriculum

In order to study curriculum in the context of children's learning environments and to see how teachers use the information they gather to diagnose children's needs and plan with children for these needs, we need to think about what the word curriculum really means and to arrive at some workable definition of what we are actually talking about.

Curriculum is a global word that encompasses the development of individuals and the learning experiences they have. Curriculum, as we will be discussing it here and as we have previously discussed it, is composed of the diversified learning situations for which teachers have responsibility and through which teachers design with children, tasks appropriate for each child's learning. Thus, to be able to design suitable learning experiences for and with children, teachers must be able simultaneously and successfully to diagnose factors that impinge upon both the learner and his learning processes.

At one time teachers emphasized memorization of facts in the various disciplines because the theory of faculty psychology advocated rote memorization. Time passed, and field theorists proved rather conclusively that memorization of a variety of facts did not increase memory ability and that there was no assurance that specific facts and skills were either transferred to new situations or resulted in changed behaviors.

The Diagnostic Curriculum

Today we have quite different conceptions. We view classrooms as centers of discovery, as laboratories where children's responses are encouraged to be both unique and logical. We encourage different approaches to learning so that all children, from the very creative to the highly structured, can explore and discover free from excessive regimentation. And we care whether curriculum experiences transfer meanings to new situations.

It is not enough to say glibly, "It is important to start where the child is." How are we to *know* where he is? Educational psychology has given us a number of ways to try to find out, and the diagnostic curriculum includes knowing the possibilities of understanding "students' capacity, receptivity, and difficulties; interests, attitudes, and values; and present knowledge and skills" (81).

With diagnostic information, teachers can personalize instruction, devise leading questions, adapt instructions, and design activities for individuals. As teachers diagnose and prescribe curriculum experiences they

1. Show acceptance and understand that children's realities are subjective.
2. Give approval and guidance as children identify with tasks.
3. Reinforce desirable behaviors with praise and recognition.
4. Plan jointly with children concerning need-goals and self-enhancement.
5. Use both nationally validated testing techniques and techniques which permit the child to participate in self-evaluation.

Levels of Diagnosis

The wonderful thing about using schoolrooms as learning laboratories for teachers and for children is that all during the day a teacher has many opportunities to gather information about individual students and, most often, he can immediately use this information to build on-the-spot learning experiences. "Teachable moments" happen when there are acceptance, approval, guidance, reinforcement, joint planning, and mutual evaluation.

Life-skills curriculum designs opportunity for children to acquire symbolic skills

- For personal exploration, inquiry, experimentation, and creativity.
- For systematic exploration of organized disciplines.
- For cooperative inquiry and problem solving.
- For experiences in managing an environment, giving service, and governing.
- For enjoying literature, the arts, and physical recreation.

. . . we cannot be satisfied with continuous progress on simple learning skills alone. The direction in which we must work is the development of persons with feelings, the social and conceptual skills, and the values that will help them play a noble part in a world moving from the twentieth to the twenty-first century.

Alice Miel, "Elements and Structure: a Design for Continuous Progress," A Curriculum for Children, ASCD, 1969.

Strang (82) suggests seven levels of diagnosis to determine where a child is in reading, for example:

1. *"Obtaining information on the student's reading performance."* This includes observing strengths and weaknesses in vocabulary, word recognition, sentence and paragraph comprehension, etc. This, she says, does not go far enough. At this level, we do not know how students actually read different kinds of material under different kinds of conditions.

2. *"Observing student behavior while reading different kinds of material under different sets of conditions."* Examples of behavior to observe might be general passivity, low energy levels, meager speaking vocabulary, limited sentence structure, or other "verbal communication disorders." Anxiety and work habits are also factors to note.

3. *"Attempting to analyze the pupil's reading process rather than merely describing his reading performance."* This can be done systematically with the Illinois Test of Psycholinguistic Abilities in which reading skills are broken down into components of visual reception, visual and auditory perception and discrimination, and conceptualization. By using a variety of test results and teacher observation, strengths and weaknesses can be detected and specific instruction and practice provided.

4. *"Determining whether there are other mental abilities involved in, and underlying, success in reading abilities."* These might be suggested by some of the subtests of the Wechsler Intelligence Scale for Children or by the Wechsler Adult Intelligence Scale. Some of these subtests involve more subtle aspects of memory, reasoning, and spatial relationships.

5. *"Analyzing clinically the personality traits and values of each child."* Teachers, with the help of clinicians, can learn to use techniques such as figure drawing, sentence completion, thematic apperception tests, and other projective techniques. These may supplement, confirm, or contradict unstandardized, more informal observations.

6. *"Examining neurological data,"* including possible brain damage, neurological disorganization, hemispheric dominance, and other pathological conditions. Here, again, even though a neurologist has been involved in diagnosing difficulties, Kleffner (4) says that in the present state of "lack of definite correlations of brain pathology with inability to learn readily, to retain the meaning of what has been learned, and to recall that which is stored," remediation is largely dependent upon the teacher's observation of behavior and the counteracting learning experiences designed for the child.

7. *"Having readers describe their own reading processes."* This is an as yet little explored area of diagnosis, but has the potential for revealing significant insights. "Teachers," says Strang, "may merely ask

children how they managed to pronounce an unfamiliar word or knew the meaning of a word they had not been taught, or arrived at the meaning of a sentence or paragraph." Teachers can gather this kind of information informally as they teach and will be able to understand better, for example, the impact of modern mass communication on children's vocabulary and concept development.

These levels, or modifications of them, may help teachers diagnose and prescribe in many areas of human learning, since language and communication are so basic to all intellectual and social functioning. Observing and using behaviors as a basis for creating learning experiences for children in classrooms brings into play both their in-school and out-of-school experiences because a variety of factors influence children's ways of *receiving and storing information,* and of *thinking and perceiving.* Studying children in these ways, diagnosing through a combination of formal and informal techniques, and creating learning experiences suited to each child underscores the importance of the individual. Teachers have available to them up-to-date ways to learn about a child's attitudes toward home, school, and self; and also about how these and other influences affect what he learns, what he fails to learn, how he learns, why he learns, what he remembers, and what he forgets (83).

The teacher can apply, with variations, the various techniques described in levels of diagnosis to the clusters of curriculum concern grouped generally as social sciences, natural sciences, and humanities.

Behaviors of Diagnostic Teachers

The mark of a teacher who uses professional knowledge for diagnosis includes the following behaviors:

- The teacher observes students and gathers information on performance.
- The teacher studies the same child in different settings.
- The teacher analyzes learning processes of individuals.
- The teacher uses formal and informal tests to help diagnose.
- The teacher uses clinical analysis techniques to determine values.
- The teacher examines neurological data.
- The teacher has children describe how they think they learn.
- The teacher works with children to personalize instruction.
- The teacher accepts children where they are and as they are.
- The teacher gives approval and guidance as children identify with tasks.
- The teacher reinforces desirable behaviors with praise.
- The teacher designs classroom learning laboratories.
- The teacher adapts instruction and designs activities for and with children.

The Concept-Centered Curriculum

We admit that we are stunned by the rapidity with which facts become obsolete in today's world. We have looked at the role that pertinent facts play in forming generalizations useful in changing times. We know that schools have a mandate and an ultimatum to educate *all* children, and that they can no longer afford the luxury (or the snobbery) of saying that children must "fit" the curriculum or leave school. The curriculum, on the contrary, must fit the children. It must have immediate and long-term utility and it must demonstrate concern for social understanding and functioning.

Five Life Skills

It should be quite clear by now that the authors feel that errors of the past are compounded in schools that consider subject content and courses of study more important than learning environments and human inter-relationships in facilitating learning. Passing on information is still important and so are the recent reforms that involve scholars of the various disciplines in updating curriculum content, and the automated systems that enable students to learn how to learn. But if schools are to build the kinds of people who "will continuously remake society in the light of mankind's needs," new kinds of skills for living will be needed. Meade (84) says that five life skills are especially adaptable to the modern situation:

> Yet it seems that curriculum reforms which modify and modernize content and improve instruction will not be sufficient to the challenges we face. We have underestimated the obsolescence of "facts." What now seems indicated is an emphasis upon . . . *powers of analysis, characterological flexibility, self-starting creativity in the use of off-job time, a built-in preference and facility for democratic interpersonal relations, and an ability to remain an individual in a mass society.*

With new techniques for programming facts and fact-gathering skills, we can turn our attention to helping children understand, synthesize, or generalize information and apply it. Emphasis can finally be placed on improving the human condition, our own and others. New learning apparatus and automated systems, properly used, make teachers more important than ever before.

As an infant is constantly interacting with his environment, he is not conscious of concepts that are being developed while seeing, hearing, tasting, feeling, and smelling. But it is through these experiences that he begins to develop concepts, to put together the essential attributes of associated ideas and to arrive at a universal notion.

With increased insight into the importance of concepts, or all that is characteristically associated with a general or an abstract idea, classroom teachers are examining possible ways to help children develop concepts. What are concepts? How important are they? How do you teach them? Are concepts and factual knowledge mutually beneficial to children, are they the same or different, and does one have priority over the other?

One way to begin thinking about concepts is to examine one's own attitudes about a course in which one was recently registered as a student. Think about these questions:

- Do you recall emphasis being placed on concepts?
- Were you encouraged to form concepts by going from concrete facts to associated ideas and universal notions?
- Were you helped to make newly acquired generalizations, to abstract generic mental images, to see logical relationships and interrelationships?
- Are newly acquired concepts improving your classroom teaching?
- Are concepts helping you to help children through generalizing thought operations?

In evaluating the effect of the course, it is possible that you cannot immediately assess its worth. It may be much later before you realize its impact. It should be no surprise to you that you cannot identify many of your conceptual learnings with any one particular course, since concepts are learned slowly and their acquisition is dependent upon more than a fact, a course, or an instructor. The process of *synthesizing ideas* occurs through general mental operation over long periods of time.

Contrasting Classrooms

In examining the following illustrations, the teachers' efforts to show children relationships between facts and concepts can be appreciated.

CLASSROOM 1: NINE- AND TEN-YEAR-OLDS

A class of twenty-eight children is studying the historic contribution that the Mayflower Compact made to the establishment of self-rule in America. The students have read, as a large group assignment, a chapter about Plymouth Colony. They have now broken up into smaller groups to work on various aspects of the historical incident in relation to democratic ideals of self-determination and self-rule:

1. Three children are using three different resources to identify the kinds of transportation (ships) that played such an important role in the discovery and development of this country. Their list includes the *Niña*, the *Pinta*, the *Santa Maria*, the *Mayflower*, and the *Constitution*, also known as *Old Ironsides*.

2. Three other children are sketching pictures of the ships preparatory to making a mural.
3. Two children are organizing and labeling an exhibit of model ships which include sailing vessels, steamships, and the first atomic submarine.
4. Four children are engaged in discovering problems encountered by the Pilgrims in a new and primitive country.
5. Four more are locating and finding out about other new settlements in North America.
6. Another pair of boys is working on an historical time line.
7. Six children are making charts to show present-day branches of the federal government.
8. Others are busily engaged in trying to generalize, in chart or story form, ideas about democracy, our heritage, citizenship responsibility, differences between then and now, and possible future self-rule needs. Children, working independently and together, are learning a great deal from one another. The teacher circulates to spend time consulting with children where, and as, needed.

CONTRASTING CLASSROOM 2: CHILDREN OF SAME AGES AS CLASSROOM 1

This group is studying Lincoln's election to the Presidency. There is a teacher-prepared list of names of persons, places, dates, and events which the class is told they must memorize for a forthcoming test. Each child has a mimeographed list and each takes a turn reading one item from the list and giving the fact the teacher expects in connection with it.

Ronnie interrupts to ask whether Lincoln's election caused the Civil War and slavery. The teacher comments that there is not time for that now because "we have to get ready for the test." He adheres to his original goal for the lesson, the fact regurgitation continues, and Ronnie and others doodle or pretend interest until their turn comes again.

Visitors in these two classrooms perceive two quite different philosophies of education and of teacher–pupil behavior. The teacher in the first classroom has mastered the principles of relating subject matter to concept formation using children's special needs, interests, and talents. The teacher in the second classroom is teaching subject matter from one text as a means to one end, the TEST. In the first classroom, *understanding* and *associating* historical events with modern times is stressed. In the second illustration, the teacher is not concerned with helping children to understand and associate persons, places, dates, and events. Providing situations to help children find relationships among ideas influences teaching—learning practices and *extends thinking* in classroom 1, whereas in 2 the use of a single text, a single list, and a single objective *limit learning* possibilities.

Classroom 1 has a teacher who is practicing sound principles of psychology. Replacing the timeworn practice of drill and grill, the teacher uses specific facts including persons, places, dates, and events, and direct experiences to help children develop new ideas and insights. These become the raw material for new concepts that have meaning for children and that push them to become involved in the learning process by thinking and by doing. The teacher's objectives in classroom 1 are in sharp contrast to those demonstrated by teacher 2; they include the following:

1. To introduce new concepts relating to those already known.
2. To show underlying relationships among a variety of ideas.
3. To involve students in activities that help give meaning and purpose to abstract ideas and faraway times and events.

We see, too, the role that can be played by drill and memorization. They are sometimes necessary, and they are valuable as long as there are varieties of classroom experiences to help children understand and reinforce what has been learned. Children will participate in drills they understand as necessary to fulfilling their own need goals, just as a tennis player will practice to improve his serve or his backhand stroke when he understands that he must perfect it to improve his game. When drill and practice are seen as a means to an end, children and adults will take it upon themselves to master the necessary skills and techniques.

Why Children Fail

Despite teachers' dedication to helping children learn, they fail for a variety of reasons. Among the reasons children fail are these:

1. Their needs for status, approval, self-esteem, and love are overlooked.
2. The content of texts is often artificial and dull and not relevant to the lives and needs of children.
3. Children have no role in planning and selecting learning experiences.
4. Facts change and books become obsolete; what is learned is not practical.
5. The single, basic texts chosen do not allow for flexibility.
6. Textbook assignments are used so extensively that there is no opportunity for manipulative, sensory, and participation activities.
7. Pressures are exerted to complete a text or a program and time is not allowed for group discussion, problem solving, self selection among varieties of research materials, or pupil–teacher planning and evaluation.
8. Little time is devoted to diagnosing children's own learning styles in order to personalize their instruction.
9. Pacing is standardized so that those who need to go slower or faster are frustrated.
10. Application of knowledge to problem solving is often ignored.

Children soon forget facts that are not reinforced in practical situations and that have no application to living.

11. Identical rather than individualized standards of achievement and evaluation are used, encouraging conformity rather than unique ability development.
12. Students' and teachers' interests in behavioral change is overshadowed by grades and percentiles.
13. Students are grouped with others whose self-esteem is low. They are not given the chance to function in a variety of groups but are pigeonholed according to a few narrow traits.
14. Teachers do not change when the times change and there is dichotomy of teacher–pupil points of view.

"Failure in a success-oriented culture is hard to take," states Fromme (85). Children cannot fail unless their teachers are also failing, because it is the job of teachers to see that children succeed. Even children who receive good grades and are "promoted" are failing to learn a great deal that schools should hope to teach them—abstraction, curiosity, and especially appreciations. The subject matter of a course is really only a vehicle for teaching these most important intellectual abilities. But all too often, subject matter becomes an end in itself.

John Holt is a teacher who started to teach feeling that if a teacher just keeps explaining what children do not know and keeps steady pressure on them to learn, they will of course achieve. After a while, he questioned the results he was getting because the "good students stayed good and some may have got better; but the bad students stayed bad and some of them seemed to get worse. If they were failing in November they were still failing in June" (86).

Being a teacher–learner from and with children, he decided that there must be better answers than the assumptions on which he had been operating, and decided that he should turn his attention to preventing children from becoming chronic failures in the first place. He observed his students and kept a journal of his observations; and he noted the strategies children use to meet or dodge the demands teachers and parents make on them, the effect of fear and failure on children, the distinctions he observed between real and apparent learnings, and the ways he thought schools fail to meet the needs of children. As time went on, he noted that the teacher can learn these kinds of things only as he is able to "get inside the mind" of his pupils. When he read over the observations he made in the process of trying to get inside of his students, he came to the conclusion that it is a very curious and unsettling process for a teacher to change his mind on a subject about which he has very positive convictions. Being so firmly convinced that children need to be kept under pressure, he found himself coming to realize that what hampers children's thinking, what drives them into narrow and defensive strategies, and what causes them to actually fail "is a feeling that they must please the grownups at all costs."

He found that the really able thinkers in his class were children who did not feel so strongly the need to please grown-ups. The able thinkers were not necessarily all good students, either. Some of them were very good students, some good, and some not so good; but their distinguishing characteristic was the ability to please themselves rather than to please teachers.

In a book based on the ways this teacher found to help children succeed, he speaks of his discovery of children's *natural styles* of learning which he feels sure are warped or destroyed entirely by later training. He observes that a child "has no stronger desire than to make sense of the world and to move freely in it . . . to do the things that he sees bigger people doing" (87). He also came to the conclusion that "many thousands of children teach themselves to read every year" and that "teachers might do well to find out how many such children there are and how they managed to teach themselves." And on the subject of tangible and practical results, Holt believes now that "to be able to do something well, to get visible results, gives him [the child] a sense of his own being and worth which he can never get from regular school-work, from teacher-pleasing, no matter how good he is at it."

The goal of this teacher and other good teachers is to have children reach a point where *they initiate thinking*—where they independently observe, classify, compare, formulate problems, imagine, state and defend positions, recognize assumptions, distinguish between what is real and what is unreal, and analyze their own thinking and behaviors. In the process of learning to do these kinds of things, children develop self-esteem, they feel good about themselves, and they become the self-propelled learners we hope for. Even more importantly, they learn life skills that will serve them well throughout their lifetimes. Having learned these human kinds of skills that not only carry over from subject content area to subject content area but are also applied in their day-by-day living, they have within themselves the necessary skills to deal with continuing social change and to adapt to new sets of conditions.

Teachers select various combinations of curriculum approaches as they organize learning experiences for concept-centered, life skills curricula. In so doing, they strive for healthy equilibrium in skills that are immediately practical and skills that will have long-range applicability. As there are accelerating rates of research and discovery with correspondingly rapid obsolescence of knowledge, and in view of "the relatively small amount of time available for formal education, we consider the task of the schools as increasingly one of teaching students to continue their education. The learner must be given increasing responsibility for his education, made a partner in the enterprise of teaching" (88). The combinations of curriculum approaches for concept formation and life skills include these:

1. *Problem situations in everyday living in local, national, and international affairs.* The problems can be identified and analyzed in various

ways—some at firsthand and others vicariously in these days when starving children in Biafra or an American Indian Reservation are as near as the nearest city's ghetto via television, or one's immediate neighborhood. In these ways, the situations are provided in which hypotheses can be proposed, questioned, and validated. Evidence can be sifted and synthesized to help children make associations and form generalizations in relation to what is already known and what has been added.

2. *The use of varieties of learning resources and experiences.* The professional teacher now has available a wide array of multitexts and trade books, neighborhood and community resources, programmed instruction, instructional television, individual and group audio-visual teaching machines and other audio-visual materials, newspapers and periodicals, and new technologists and other professional and paraprofessional specialists. In effect, the teacher becomes the director of a fine symphony seeking to bring each of these resources into consonance with learning and the learner so that creative ideation and concept formation for continued learning are the ongoing outcomes. Individual needs, interests, and talents determine the kinds of learning experiences from which children will benefit and the possible materials and resources to use singly or in groups.

3. *Contacting children "where they are" to extend their immediate worlds so that they will gradually be interrelated with larger portions of understanding and operating in the world around them.* Fantini and Weinstein (89) discuss this idea in connection with a *contact curriculum*, and have detailed a series of learning continua from established curricular approaches that avoid contact with the learner to those which offer better possibilities for contacting him. These learning continua (89) include curriculum development that ranges

FROM	TO
A curriculum that is prepackaged, rigidly scheduled, and uniform throughout a school system.	One that is flexible and geared to the unique needs of individual schools within the system.
A curriculum that is primarily symbol based.	One that is primarily experience based.
A horizontally programmed disjointed sequence of skills.	A vertically programmed small-step sequence of skills.
A curriculum that is past and future oriented.	One that is immediate oriented.
A what curriculum.	A why curriculum.
A completely academic curriculum.	One geared to social participation (doing).
An antiseptic curriculum.	One that attempts to explore reality.
Emphasis solely on cognitive, extrinsic content.	An equal emphasis on effective, inner content.

We agree with these authors' conclusion that most schools have made the mistake of not meeting the child "in his home territory and then to take him for the ride. Until now we have been asking the child to meet us in our territory and to begin the ride from there. Possibly this is why we have been losing so many passengers psychologically and physically" (89).

Teaching for Global Understandings

From Egocentric to Allocentric Interests

A logical and necessary extension of the contact curriculum, if we would practice democracy as well as praise it, is continuing education to help children become responsive to new demands and urgent needs of the ever-changing world in the international arena. As children are given opportunities to grapple with the principles of self-rule, cooperative planning, individual responsibility, freedom of inquiry, and majority decisions with minority opinions, it is not always possible to have direct experience with the problems of other peoples in other places in the world. But a really good elementary school curriculum will reflect the persistent factors and problems that characterize our times here and abroad.

Today's children, worldwide, receive so many messages from so many media; they have more knowledge and more to contribute as they communicate with the world through languages, war, peace efforts, rebellions, poetry, biology, visual arts, dance, and the like. Television brings the war in Vietnam, starving Biafrans, Arab-Israeli conflicts, the investitures of royalty in new times amid old pomp and circumstance, and moon landings with earth receding in the distance. While there are strong reactionary and isolationist forces in every country, including America, the thinking individual of today knows that no nation in a world grown so small can continue to develop and prosper without cooperation and understanding from the others. America has developed, and can hope to continue to develop as a strong, diversified nation precisely because of the strength that comes from ideas and people of many cultures and subcultures from other parts of the world.

As long as poverty, ignorance, and disease are still the way of life for millions of the world's people, no child can be assured of a life in which he himself can seek self-fulfillment and self-satisfaction. As long as nearly half of the world's children receive no education at all, those who are literate will have a staggering and impossible responsibility for the illiterate. These and other world problems are here today. They need to be discussed and investigated today, and intensive remedial, compensatory, and humanitarian efforts are needed today and into future times. Starting with our youngest schoolchildren, educators in the most privileged country in the world have a responsibility to build into curriculum development the concepts of *world interdependence,* and to develop the skills of compassion and social responsibility which will help future citizens respond to and affect world conditions.

For almost a century there have been international telecommunications among the neighborhoods of the world. The International Telecommunication Union (ITU) has survived two major world wars and many smaller ones, and now emerges as one of our strongest instruments of world peace. Man's efforts to build other world organizations to coordinate international concerns met frustration and disillusionment in the League of Nations, and the United Nations is floundering and imperfect—in fact, it may yet be replaced by other efforts to achieve a better world for all people. Institutions, by their very nature susceptible to being molded in a certain image, should be able to change, reorganize, set new goals and methods, and enter into new relationships and memberships. The needs and concerns of the present United Nations are vast and staggering, and these and others yet to be defined are of great and continuing interest to young people.

Dag Hammerskjöld spoke eloquently of the continuing need for a climate of rational discussion and constructive, peaceful processes among the world's peoples when he said: "For all who believe in the future, in life itself, now is the time to speak for their beliefs. These are the voices we need to create the calm and steady climate of public opinion in which governments could deal constructively, by patient discussion, by all the peaceful processes of conciliation and negotiation set out in the [United Nations] Charter, with the difficult problems which challenge us" (90).

Technology has created nuclear weapons, machines capable of doing much of the work formerly done by men and women, conquered many formerly fatal diseases, and sent men to the moon. "It is now technically possible, morally desirable and absolutely necessary to wipe mass poverty, chronic ill-health and resulting personal and national frustration off the face of the earth. . . . We had better heed the cry for help before it is ours. For our own peace and prosperity depend upon our knowing these close neighbors, upon our comprehending their legitimate aspiration, and upon our recognizing how we can and must speedily help them to achieve in decades what we and our ancestors took centuries to accomplish" (91).

Contact and Content

As we move from the *what* curriculum to the *why* curriculum and from the known to the unknown and back again, surely man's efforts to create a peaceful, cooperative world and to secure mutual benefits for all of mankind come under scrutiny often. One group of eight-year-olds and their teachers (special and team teachers) planned related learning around the generalized theme of *Three Historical Units for Peace and Human Advancement.* They used the following formalized peace-keeping groups to find commonalities, types of problems faced, successes and failures, and restructuring abilities and needs:

1. *The Iroquois League of Six Indian Nations,* which had made some remarkable progress toward mutual protection and cultural advancement before white men came to America.
2. *The League of Nations,* which was set up following World War I with the purposes of studying and removing the causes of war. Included were the organizations and agencies that came into being to work out international financial, trade, health, and other shared international problems. Set up in 1920, it began to fail in the 1930's and was completely ended by World War II, but some of its agencies continued to exist.
3. *The United Nations,* which came into formal being with the signing of its Charter in San Francisco on June 26, 1945, and incorporated existing international agenices with new concerns.

Naturally, children of this age are not able to understand all of the ramifications and forces of history that are rooted in the beginnings of these efforts, but they can begin to develop concepts basic to understanding past and present while looking toward the future and they can relate to the generalizations in regard to men's continuing need to understand and cooperate with one another. They are quite capable of making astute observations about the problems rampant in today's world in relation to the ways our present United Nations provides for arbitration and alleviation. As time goes on, the groundwork will have been laid for understanding needs that will continue whether the United Nations, or a successor to it, is in existence, because men and nations will continue to need:

1. A place and means for talking over problems bothering them.
2. Methods by which nations may work together to solve these problems.
3. Plans for peaceful settlements of disputes by international laws.
4. Means for stopping nations planning harm to world neighbors.
5. Ways to help nations improve their economic and social welfare.
6. Ways to increase the rights of all peoples.
7. Methods to develop better relations among nations through the sharing of knowledge, improvement in education, sharing of commodities and natural resources, and better communication among world neighborhoods.

Even very young children can begin to understand that most of peoples' and nations' disputes grow out of *economic* and *social,* rather than political and military, problems. Helping the people of India or South America grow more food and produce fewer children may seem less exciting than the latest war news, but fewer people with fuller stomachs will do a great deal to keep the world more peaceful and cooperative.

In today's world, the absence of a world forum can be catastrophic, especially in view of the fact that the world's problems are chiefly economic and social. In the present United Nations, children can be impressed with the importance of an ongoing Economic and Social Council (ECOSOC) when given continuing experiences in comparing living conditions around the world and suggesting and planning steps by which the living conditions of others here and abroad can be improved. The central ideas behind the establishment of ECOSOC provide the nucleus for a variety of firsthand and vicarious studies related to helping to improve living conditions, solve international social and economic problems, and increase respect for human rights and freedoms. A list of the ECOSOC commissions provides the basis for thinking about the kinds of problems this organ deals with. Among these are: International Commodity Trade; Transport and Communications; Population, Social, Human Rights; Status of Women; Narcotic Drugs, and others.

Other groups of study and investigation are suggested by specialized agencies which have working agreements with the United Nations but which have their own separate constitutions, budgets, organizations, and memberships. All of these have grown out of the international needs of people in today's world and others will be needed:

1. *International Labor Organization* (ILO)—to help improve working conditions in all countries, and to send experts to various lands or to arrange exchanges of workers between nations.
2. *Food and Agriculture Organization* (FAO)—to improve the supply and distribution of food and other products from farms, forests, and fisheries and to raise standards of nutrition.
3. *U.N. Educational, Scientific and Cultural Organization* (UNESCO) —to promote intercultural and intergroup cooperation and understanding, education, and scientific development among nations.
4. *International Civil Aviation Organization* (ICAO)—to aid in the development of civil aviation and increase air safety over the world.
5. *World Health Organization* (WHO)—to improve the health of all people.
6. *International Bank for Reconstruction and Development* (BANK)—to make loans for the purpose of productive reconstruction and development projects.
7. *International Monetary Fund* (FUND)—to help stabilize world currencies.
8. *Universal Postal Union* (UPO)—to aid the international exchange of mail.
9. *International Telecommunication Union* (ITU)—to improve international cable, telephone, radio, and television communications.
10. *World Meteorological Organization* (WMO)—to increase knowledge about world weather conditions and to promote exchange of information.
11. *Inter-Governmental Maritime Consultative Organization* (IMCO) —to provide for cooperation between nations on shipping questions.

12. *International Trade Organization* (ITO)—to improve trade relations among nations.

Just think of the new possibilities—international atomic energy commission, international moon control mission, international space exploration commission—and who knows what other international and interplanetary needs such as interplanetary germ control, space traffic pattern commissions, or international pollution control.

Furthermore, existing and possible new international commission purposes suggest an infinite variety of human resources—professionals and laymen who will work with educators and children in many ways to develop international and intercultural understandings.

To help his students think graphically about the world's characteristics in relation to life in the United States, one teacher used the idea of an imaginary town made up of world people and reduced in exact proportion to a community of 1,000 people (92). In this imaginary town, there would be only sixty Americans and the rest of the world would be represented by 940 persons.

The investigations and discussions that centered around this imaginary world town were legion and lasted the entire school year among the eleven-year-olds in a class whose learning and doing had just begun, it is hoped. Think about the proportions represented by the facts, and think what kinds of curriculum experiences could accrue if you were to use these, or similar, statistics (which would now have to be revised in an even more shocking comparison).

In the imaginary town with the world reduced in exact proportion to a community of 1,000 in the year of 1960, the sixty Americans received half of the income of the entire town and the other 940 inhabitants had to divide up the other half. White people totaled 303 persons and 697 were nonwhite. The sixty Americans had an average life expectancy of seventy years, but the other 940 could expect to live less than forty years on an average. The sixty Americans had fifteen times as many possessions per person as all the rest of the people. They produced 16 per cent of the town's total food supply, but they ate seventy-two per cent above the maximum food requirements and they either ate most of what they grew or stored it for their own future use at enormous cost. The Americans also enjoyed a disproportionate share of electric power, coal, fuel, steel, and general equipment. Even the lowest income group among the sixty Americans was much better off than the average of the rest of the town. About 330 people in the town were classified as Christians and, of these, fewer than 100 were Protestants while some 230 were Roman Catholics. Because the 940 non-Americans were hungry, the disparity in the food supply understandably led to some ill feeling among the townspeople, as did the disparity of income, health, possessions, electric power, coal, fuel, steel, and general equipment.

The point we have been trying to make is that the need to consider the

world's needs has existed all along, but it exists now in greatly intensified and dangerous proportions because mankind is still giving only lip
service to fulfilling old needs while new ones crowd in. Should some
other kind of world organization eventually replace what we now know
as the United Nations, the needs would still go on and on. Unless the
youngsters growing up today are helped to understand this, the earth-
shaking revolutions that will influence and dominate the rest of their
lives will make life for almost everyone almost untenable—if not nonexistent.

Children's international education will also include these specific skills:

1. Better knowledge of global geography with emphasis on particular
   regions and areas of the world, and including understanding the
   world's natural resources (including food) and their distribution.
2. Increased intergroup and intercultural understanding of our own
   and the world's people, including knowledge basic to race, religion,
   culture, economic circumstances, and educational opportunities.
3. More use of current events as reported by the press, radio, television, and other mass news media.
4. Wider use of other professionals and paraprofessionals who have
   special skills and knowledge in relation to developing world understanding.
5. More use of information gathering through research, correspondence, personal and group interviews, trips, films, pamphlets, and the
   like.
6. Abilities to relate local community, area, and national problems to
   world problems and concerns.

There are many excellent resources for teachers and for children. They
are so extensive that it is impossible here to suggest more than one or two
that are comprehensive and provide a great deal of thought for curriculum development and action, as well as exhaustive lists of films, books,
pamphlets, charts, models, artifacts, resource people, and pictures. Two
excellent books are *Workshops for the World* (91) and *Read for World
Understanding* (93).

It is interesting to read a forward-looking curriculum book written as
recently as 1951 in which it was said that "a most important frontier of
curriculum improvement in these critical times is that of education for
international understanding and for the defense of freedom. A whole
generation of young people may grow up in a world beset by tensions,
mobilization, and military preparations" (94). Well, a whole generation
has grown up since that time and they have been beset by all of the tensions mentioned and others. Why? Because international understanding
has never yet become the heart of curriculum improvement and, late as
it is, we remind our readers that there is no time to dilly-dally. It must
become the frontier of curriculum development now.

Children's international education includes:

- Better knowledge of global geography, with emphasis on regions and areas of the world, including the world's great natural resources (including food) and their distribution.

- Increased intergroup and intercultural understanding.

- More and better use of current events.

- Wider use of other professionals and paraprofessionals.

- More diverse information-gathering techniques.

- Improved techniques for relating to people here and elsewhere in the world.

(Photo courtesy of Florida Atlantic University.)

As John Gardner (95) has pointed out, our society is still a very primitive problem solver and it need not be so. "Our capacity to create new problems as rapidly as we solve the old has implications for the kind of society we shall have to design. We shall need a society that is sufficiently honest and open-minded to recognize its problems, sufficiently creative to conceive new solutions, and sufficiently purposeful to put those solutions into effect. It should be, in short, a self-renewing society, ready to improve solutions to problems it won't recognize until tomorrow."

References

80. Maslow, Abraham, "Emotional Blocks to Creativity," *Humanist,* 18, 325–332, 1958.
81. Strang, Ruth, "Levels of Reading Diagnosis," *The Educational Forum,* Vol. XXXIII, No. 2, January, 1969.
82. Ibid. pp. 188–189.
83. Kleffner, F. R., "Aphasia and Other Language Deficiencies in Children: Research and Teaching at Central Institute for the Deaf," *Speech and Language Therapy with the Brain-damaged Child.* Edited by W. T. Daley. Washington, D.C.: Catholic University of America Press, 1962.
84. Meade, Edward J., Jr., "The Changing Society and Its Schools," *Life Skills in School and Society.* 1969 ASCD Yearbook. Washington, D.C.: Association for Supervision and Curriculum Development, 1969.
85. Fromme, Allan, in the introduction to *How Children Fail,* by John Holt. New York: Pitman Publishing Corporation, 1964.
86. Holt, John, *How Children Fail.* New York: Pitman Publishing Corporation, 1964, p. 17.
87. Holt, John, *How Children Learn.* New York: Pitman Publishing Corporation, 1967.
88. Henle, Mary, "Cognitive Skills," *Learning About Learning: A Conference Report.* Edited by Jerome Bruner. Washington, D.C.: U.S. Office of Education, 1966.
89. Fantini, Mario D., and Gerald Weinstein, *Toward a Contact Curriculum.* New York: Anti-Defamation League of B'nai B'rith, 1967.
90. Hammerskjöld, Dag, *Address to the New York Herald Tribune Forum.* October 18, 1953.
91. Beckel, Graham, in collaboration with Felice Lee, *Workshops for the World.* New York: Abelard-Schuman, 1962.
92. Leiper, Henry Smith (a leader in Congregational Churches and in the American Bible Society) as described by Jack Mabley in *The Philadelphia Inquirer,* May 24, 1960.
93. The American Association for the United Nations (AAUN), *Read for World Understanding.* New York: The Scarecrow Press, 1963.
94. Association for Supervision and Curriculum Development, *Action for Curriculum Improvement.* Washington, D.C.: National Education Association, 1951.
95. Gardner, John W., *No Easy Victories.* New York: Harper & Row, 1968, pp. 30, 39.

SECTION II
Sociology
AS A CURRICULUM FORCE

CHAPTER 4

Teachers Examine Interacting Social Phenomena

The Social Setting

Current Concerns

Sociological generalizations and concepts have been probably the most memorized-for-tests and the least understood-in-practice content of educational foundations courses. And yet teachers are faced with mounting and relentless social expectations of a newly demanding society. Significant new discoveries about people and learning create the need for new curricular emphases, new teaching methods, and new roles for teachers. But a great deal of foundations material prescribed for prospective teachers still brings to mind the gibes about sociological jargon that have plagued education courses for decades.

What is desperately needed to generate new understandings is *social awareness* and practical understanding of the *implications* of sociological generalizations in curriculum development and in field practice.

Must teachers understand children as sociological beings in order to plan curriculum experiences for them? Is it important for teachers to understand themselves as socially conditioned individuals? Does it really matter in curriculum planning whether young people and adults have preconditioned life styles related to their particular series of social learning environments or what their patterns of interpersonal relations and gaining status are? Do teachers need to know and understand about cultural differences related to child-rearing practices, socioeconomic status, or socially sanctioned occupations and life goals? If schools are social forces themselves, should they attempt to be change agents?

Of course we answer these questions in the affirmative, because schools cannot afford to be blind to the emerging needs of a great, complex society.

Schools can no more divorce themselves from individuals as social beings than they can from them as emotional and intellectual beings. What modern educators need to accomplish is a marriage between sociological generalizations and educational applications that have been too long estranged from one another in the departmentalization of college curricula. Ideally, each generalization should be studied in relation to what it means to human beings in social settings, and particularly in relation to what it means to children in the elementary school setting.

The most striking thing about the current social scene in America, and worldwide, is *social change and upheaval.* Swift, stunning changes are accelerating daily and these present schools with constant and significant new challenges that paralyze them when they are unprepared or unwilling to cope with them. Great breakthroughs in technology have not been paralleled by social awareness either in communities or in their schools which mirror the character of their surrounding social complexes. The chasms between *available knowledge and technology* and the *social implications* of these are causing intense social upheavals universally, and schools that cling to past traditions and stale curricula in the midst of these changes serve only to widen and deepen the chasms. Boys and girls learning at firsthand about the tragic divorces between the outsides and the insides of schools drop out of school psychologically long before they actually discontinue their "formal education" or join student protests in upper schools in an attempt to bring living and learning into consonance with one another.

It is risky to attempt to isolate the *most significant* social forces currently operating to change national and international social scenes. Nevertheless, the ones which follow will serve to remind the reader that schools must be concerned about the role of education as a social extender and as a social change agent:

- High school and college student protests.
- Civil rights movements and legislation.
- Larger numbers of youth and aged people.
- School and societal dropouts.
- Adult re-education and welfare problems.
- Population increases and problems of control.
- Attendant health, education, and welfare needs.
- Urban ghetto conditions and urban redevelopment.
- Vocational guidance in an age of specialization.
- Increased sexual freedom and changing morals.
- Changing influence of religion and religious institutions.
- The use of leisure time made available by mechanization.
- Drug and alcohol use and abuse.
- Social and cultural mobility.
- Greater visibility of the poor and indigent.

- Changing family patterns and family disorientation.
- The influence of mass communication media.
- Discovery of new sources of power such as atomic energy.
- Intergroup and intercultural animosities and mutual needs.
- Worldwide challenges of emerging nations and regimes.

When we consider the enormity of these conditions and forces, there is little doubt that schools must deal with social perplexities through the development and use of graduated programs of life skills for understanding and dealing with them. By concentrating on life skills preparation and social action curriculum in elementary schools, a great deal of human waste and unnecessary "unlearning" can be avoided in upper schools and in out-of-school life. Furthermore, today's students will see the relevance between *living* and *learning*—each contributing to, and enriching, the other.

Conscious of the steady march of future generations through their classrooms today, teachers must understand that these children will live under societal conditions not of their own making and now only dimly imagined by most adults. To continue to serve our boys and girls a smorgasbord of outmoded and irrelevant curricula is worse than serving them nothing at all. Education must not only help children cope with and understand what is happening in the world around them today, but must also help them grow as effective and affective social organisms now and in the future.

Curriculum that provides practical sociological implications for educating children in school settings will include learning to understand more about the following generalizations: human groupings, the intricate systems of relationships in human groupings, and the behavioral patterns that occur in the midst of social systems. This very general, but educationally practical, definition of sociology may be found wanting by professional sociologists who are engaged in academic exchanges concerning the nature of sociology—its goals, its procedures, and its appropriate place in intellectual inquiry. But it does place emphasis on social growth of individuals in a series of environments of which the school is perhaps the most important one (1).

The current concerns which plague society and education today have been noted and documented by sociologists and by writers who have foreseen them for generations, it seems. Take, as an example, poverty, with its attending degradation and hopelessness. Even in the early 1960's, Michael Harrington (2) spoke of the invisibility of poverty, and of the reasons why the enormous culture of want and desperation in the midst of plenty had been overlooked by educated and well-meaning Americans. He talked about the unskilled workers, the aged, the minority groups, the alcoholics and derelicts, the migrant farm workers, and others who lived then, and live now, in our social and economic underworlds. It is only very recently that writers speak about the visibility of poverty because sheer numbers of people who have migrated to urban centers have made it visible—have forced Americans to recognize their presence and their problems as well as to seek possible solutions to the conditions that caused the poverty in the first place. In the world of the 1960's and 1970's, America's poor are finding powerful voices and they affect the minds, hearts, consciousness, and pocketbooks of the middle and upper classes in many ways every day. In so doing, they should also affect what is taught—or not taught—in schools.

It is true that the majority of Americans still find themselves with economic sufficiency and more time for recreation, education, and travel. But America has two faces and this is the bright and shining one. The other one is listless and lackluster and reflects the helplessness of those who have bare levels of existence. The others—the poor—have been twisted and deformed in spirit by a society that requires higher skills, more education, and social mobility. They are pessimistic and defeated; new technology and social upheavals have left them behind. From the sharecropper shacks of the South, from the valleys in Appalachia, and from isolation and invisibility, America's undereducated, unskilled, underfed, ill, and indigent have migrated to cities where their families have continued to multiply and where their lives become even worse because they are urban misfits. Not only are they now visible, but they are also voluble. They are an army without guns, but not without strength, according to Martin Luther King (3), who also described it as an ever-growing army into which no one has to be drafted, composed of blacks and whites of all ages, with adherents of every faith, members of every class, every profession, every political party, and united by single ideals. Of course, Martin Luther King was also talking about civil rights as well as the *effects* of poverty and social degradation on every other living person, whether affluent or not.

The disparity of economic and social conditions between majority-group and minority-group Americans is probably a chief contributing factor to the difficulties educators are having in designing curriculum that has relevance to all children. But this same disparity can help educators create the most exciting and challenging curriculum experiences ever envisioned by schools. They can study at firsthand the factors that affect the economic status of communities and that determine community cultural levels, attitudes, and personal and group expectancies. Young children can understand a great deal about the fluctuation of economy—not, of course, in grandiose terms but in terms of its effect on people and institutions.

Middle-aged adults of today will remember the depression of the 1930's but they are hard put to remember that it was even discussed in their schools at the time. While society was witnessing the impact of fortunes lost, banks closed, rampant unemployment, Wall Street tragedies, and unmitigated poverty, schools continued the "regular curriculum" of *Little Red Hen*, the multiplication tables, and "place" geography. In the same way, the child still living in Appalachia today can see the rows of rotting company houses, the muddy roads, and the black, dirty soot left over from the now idle coal mines; and he knows that those who have migrated to the city have left closed churches, empty district schools, and abandoned lodge halls, farms, and mills. But when he migrates to a larger and more affluent community on a school bus each day, he learns little that helps him relate the world of the school and the world to which he returns each evening.

The child living near Disneyland in Anaheim, California, or Cape Kennedy spaceport in Brevard County, Florida, sees daily and can be helped to understand the enormous population growth and the accompanying impact on changes in all community institutions including students, teachers, and schools. They should also understand that were Disneyland or Cape Kennedy to be moved or eliminated, the process would reverse itself as whole communities of workers and supporting institutions and services travel elsewhere to leave ghost towns like those in Appalachia.

Children read about community efforts to attract business and industry to their communities or regions, but they are not helped to realize that new industries and businesses do not necessarily mean that the people who are already there will have better jobs, or even any job at all. If the people now living there are unskilled and uneducated, labor and supporting services will have to be imported until people can be retrained, if possible. Nor do new businesses and industries always mean better educational facilities and programs, because the net result is often that schools are overcrowded, parents upset and demanding, students unchallenged and apathetic, and teachers discouraged and resentful. Bigness is often mistaken for quality, but when growth of a sound economy accompanies bigness in expanding communities, there will be higher expectations and greater support for good educational programs in the area's schools. It seems reasonable to assume that when there are more well-educated people, they will demand better and better education for their children. It also seems important to stress the fact that communities who are well situated economically now will not remain so for long if they ignore the educational needs of the community.

It is true that the men of business and industry often see the needs for good education and the social implications of improving education in a more realistic light than educators do. They have helped boys and girls, with their teachers, understand that people who are educated and have marketable skills are powerful attractions for new business and industry, and they have participated in forward-looking elementary school curriculum plans. When community leaders know that educators have the same concerns they do, they will support quality education and be instrumental in securing better school budgets and helping to create and support more modern curriculum emphases.

Boys and girls, as well as their teachers, are well aware too that the community and the school often disagree on definitions of "good education" and on recommended budgets to achieve it. There are vast sociological implications for educators in the arguments, pro and con, regarding the merits of "mass education," and yet all of the children of all of the people who cannot afford to send their children to private schools are in the nation's public school classrooms. Boys and girls do know that they are grouped, as we have previously stated, and they often have either remarkably correct or fallacious ideas about why they are grouped as they are. Sometimes they find themselves in situations where the school's social purpose seems to demonstrate that its best educational resources are for the education of an ability elite. Many groups and some individuals, such as Admiral Rickover, espouse the education of such an "ability elite" and feel that we are trying to educate too many students who do not have the ability to learn. The child who lives in the social climate created by their educational schema knows whether he has been segregated from the less able or labeled one of the less able. He knows, in either case, who is given preferred treatment.

In a school social climate like this, it is unclear what the critics recommend for the masses, but it is clear to children that someone thinks they either have little to contribute or that they should be written off as soon as possible. Students and their teachers must have a better understanding of the principles of sociology which lend support to the *real purposes and values of groups* in supplying goals and expectancies, especially in school settings which are often the only ones in a position to accomplish diverse groupings and personal growth through flexible individual and group programs.

More than ever before, teachers and their students need ways to assess their own and other societies as they fluctuate and change. Together they can learn how to observe, analyze, and appraise conditions so that meaningful opinions and actions result from progress to higher levels of understanding about people and as a people. America has placed its confidence in teachers and charges them with the responsibility of understanding society and helping children formulate ideas and attitudes that will lead to behavior patterns and social action to improve society for everyone.

It is our intention and purpose to discuss in this section the *ways* that educators and communities can work together to help children understand and shape their attitudes and values in the light of new knowledge and modern times. The teacher's background in sociology should enable him to help himself and his students become more emergent-oriented so that he and they can function effectively, not only in the communities where they now live but in others they have not yet known.

As Patricia Sexton (4) has said so well, the doors of opportunity have been opened, but they have still not been opened very wide. Those who "pass through first are simply newer generations of the same groups . . . mostly they are members of the old elites of wealth and status, disguised now as an elite of ability." We agree with her that a few others do also "pass through" before the doors close, but that their numbers are frighteningly small when we consider the "size of the crowd that is left waiting," and that everyone in a stratified society incurs a disadvantage because the weight of the handicap decreases with the approach to the summit.

If we are indeed an affluent society, we have a great social responsibility. We cannot rest on imagined, or even real, laurels. That way lies the glory that *was* Rome!

Cultures and Teacher Attitudes

If schools are to fulfill new social purposes, it is essential for teachers to have basic understandings of the cultures that are inherited and influential in each of the communities where they study and teach. We use the word *culture* to express a number of related concepts among which are the following:

1. Family and community environments that constitute individuals' modes of living.
2. Moral, spiritual, and ethical standards of conduct are determined by, and also determine, the fabric of social living of individuals and groups.
3. Expressions and aesthetic appreciations, sometimes referred to as the "people's taste," include sculpture, painting, music, dance, literature, and the use of color and design.

When we use the term *community* we will be referring to the various geographic communities, or areas, a given school serves. If it is a small school, it may serve only one or two very similar communities; but if it is a larger "school park" type of school, it is designed to bring children from several very diverse communities together. Thus, it serves a variety of communities that are more widely separated geographically and culturally.

When we discuss *teacher attitudes* we will be considering their *influence* on the social setting or settings—on the possible ways these attitudes operate to understand and use constructively the cultural and community resources.

What do teachers *need to know* and what will they *want to know* about cultural and community representation in their schools? How are they to demonstrate concern for children's social growth as it relates to the community–school setting? How should they work with other institutions in the community, including the family, so that there are compatible and mutually agreed-upon contributions to a child's social growth?

First, they adapt principles of sociology regarding man's common humanity, the nature of culture, specialization and interdependence, concepts of social progress, and concepts related to the responsibilities of a democracy in national and international affairs to the community–school setting in which they find themselves and to curriculum planning that has relevance for the boys and girls with whom they will live and work.

Second, they consider the institutions in the immediate community that contribute to every child's internal environment, environment created by family units, environment created by the community microcosm, environment created by the school complex, and the larger environment created by forces and elements in national and international cultures and concerns.

Third, they demonstrate concern for children's social growth as it relates to the community–school setting by

- Visiting children's homes and neighborhoods.
- Considering the community as an extended center of learning.
- Learning as much as possible about children's cultural mores.
- Valuing children as they find them.
- Helping children grow in their own direction when ready.
- Helping families understand education's real goals.
- Planning diversified activities to help counteract socioeconomic environments whether overprivileged or underprivileged.
- Differentiating and personalizing curriculum experiences on the basis of what they learn about cultural environments and social understandings of students.
- Planning interpersonal and intergroup learning activities that will have enough duration to accentuate the positive.
- Counteracting prejudices and stereotypes with facts and experiences that are significant and meaningful enough to bolster facts in utilitarian ways.
- Keeping anecdotal notes and records of individual learning and life styles observed in behavior patterns while the student is in school and outside of school, as well.
- Noting language as social expression and encouraging children's culturally approved expressions while demonstrating that these and other forms of language exist for different purposes.
- Gearing communication growth—speaking, writing, reading, listening, seeing, and understanding—to present interests and needs as well as future needs and potential.

Fourth, the truly professional and competent teacher will be able to conceptualize these principles and actions with his knowledge and understanding of child growth and development, observed learning characteristics in the school setting, individual differences in behavior, and patterns of influence in the school grouping situation.

Sociological principles mean little unless we study them in actual educational settings. As you read the following accounts, try to decide how the teachers involved operated to change social concepts of individual children, of groups, and of social growth. Also study the ways that individual teachers established contact with parents and involved them in planning and progress.

A Migrant Child

When Richard came to the classroom door, many memories of other schools, teachers, and classmates swept through his consciousness. Some memories were pleasant, but there were more memories that were bitter than there were memories that were sweet; for Richard was the child of migrant workers who moved with the seasons and traveled often to the next crop-picking site. In spite of their migratory life, or perhaps because of it, Richard's parents urged him to attend school at each new site even though they would be there for only a few weeks.

Richard usually walked or took a school bus if one was available from his group of migrant workers' shacks to the nearest school. He did not really know the meaning of the word *home* in the traditional sense of the word, but home for him was wherever the family was camping at the moment. His community was the extended family of migrant workers who happened to be occupying the other so-called dwellings on the crop-harvesting site at the moment. They changed almost as often as his family moved, and they afforded little reinforcement for his family's educational aspirations for him. Many of their children went to the fields to work with their parents and thus increase the family income rather than attending school.

Richard had learned to "read" new teachers rather quickly. He was apt at deciding from their facial expressions, tones of voice, bodily gestures, and general behavior toward him whether he was accepted or rejected. In his new classroom he quickly decided that his new teacher accepted and valued him, and in the days that followed he reinforced his original attitudes. He had "read" his teacher correctly—she liked him and he liked her. She accepted him with his "foreign" accent, his clean but ragged clothes, his academic frailties, and his inability to provide for many of his daily necessities such as paper, pencils, and lunch.

Richard remembered teachers who had shunned physical contact with him, who had tolerated him in the classroom but not in their hearts, who never took the time to visit his parents who worked from sunup to sundown and could not visit his schools. This teacher accepted and loved him—he knew it! She was like that with the others, too, because she knew that each one needed approval from her as well as from one another. Another thing was that she visited his family almost right away, and his family seemed to forget all about their shabby and degrading surroundings the night she came. They all sat together for a long time on the shabby "stoop" and agreed about the importance of an education for Richard. Richard saw a new ray of hope in his parents' eyes as she left them with the heartfelt wish that the family would soon be able to find more permanent employment so Richard could attend school more regularly.

His teacher had other ways of making new students feel at home in the new classroom, particularly new students who would probably not have the time or the opportunity to make lasting friendships and to become fully accepted members of the group in the ordinary course of events. Each new student was assigned a "buddy" who was actually the student who was the next newest to the classroom. Each new student then became the buddy of the next one to join the class. A buddy's responsibilities included introducing the latest arrival to other students, explaining school policies and routines, and helping him locate and use the school's resources. Jack was assigned to be Richard's buddy, and he was an alert one—pointing out the unfamiliar ways of the school because he had a fresh memory of how recently they had been strange and puzzling to him. They toured the school and the school grounds together, and the buddy system helped both the buddy and his partner to become an integral part of the school more quickly.

The teacher respected children's right to belong, even temporarily, and she involved Richard in activities that had meaning and importance to him from the first day. She found many opportunities for him to contribute his knowledge of travel, climate, and geography; she encouraged him to keep a diary about the good things that happened to him at school each day; she saw that lunch was provided for him and that he had a group to sit with at lunchtime; and she kept in touch with his parents through written messages about Richard's positive progress and contributions at school and through more prearranged home visits. While she could not accept some of Richard's behaviors and sometimes too colorful language, she did accept Richard. Richard may not have known the meaning of the term "the right social climate," but he was fortunate enough to be in the middle of one.

One day, Richard taped a short reading selection and played it back as he and his teacher and classmates listened. Another day he learned how to operate the film projector and was allowed to show a class film. Each day his teacher found time to talk with him individually and to help him feel good about himself and his accomplishments. At the same time she was helping him to understand and value himself, she helped him understand the other children and them to understand him.

Richard and his family moved on at the end of the hop-picking season. A home and a school of his own were not to be his for some time yet, but his teacher had seen his growth in accepting and understanding and trusting himself, his peers, and his teachers. She had also seen intellectual growth that developed and kept pace with his social growth. And she knew in her heart that Richard took with him to his next school inner resources and convictions that would help him whether the new experience was a pleasant or a bitter one. Knowing that every teacher makes decisions that set the tone of social well-being with, for, and among children in classrooms, she also knew that teachers' attitudes about and toward children set the quality of the school social setting; and she prayed that Richard's next teacher would be wise enough to know these things, too, so that Richard would have the chance so earnestly sought by his family and by Richard himself.

Dealing with Prejudice

Problems related to prejudice and to thinking in culturally approved stereotypes begin in the home and community long before children come to school. One of the main tasks of education is to find ways to change these social attitudes and the stifling values they represent for the future social development of individuals.

It has been widely assumed that the mere acquisition of education as it has been traditionally practiced in our schools will reduce the level of prejudice found in children, youth, and adults. If teachers doubt that children, even very young ones, harbor severe prejudices about themselves and others by the time they come to school, they should be familiar with facts revealed by research and be willing to put these implications to work in school curriculum from the very first day of school.

One study shows that 400 young children, ages five to seven, of different races, creeds, and nationalities:

1. Used specific group labeling repeatedly in their conflict situations.
2. Held fixed notions about other groups and thought in stereotypes.
3. Were aware of group differences.
4. Nine per cent expressed open rejection of Catholics, twenty-seven per cent of Jews, and sixty-eight per cent rejected Negroes even though many of them were themselves Negro (5).

Another study concludes that "there is little evidence that school consistently causes stereotypes to be rejected, or that the educated are less prejudiced or discrimination-minded in their personal lives. On many issues, the educated show as much prejudice as the less educated, and on some issues they show more" (6).

Classroom teachers have daily opportunities to counteract statements and attitudes that represent in-group prejudices, but they often miss the most teachable moments to do so because they do not want to be involved in controversy. If they could only realize that they are reinforcing prejudices by ignoring them or failing to deal with them, they would at the very least have the courage to present the *facts* in the hope of modifying them. In our opinion, not to do so is to shirk an educational responsibility. Good teachers know that each child's association with one teacher is relatively short but that concepts reinforced may last a lifetime.

Mr. Samuels was such a teacher. He had the courage to correct misinformation with facts on the spot and he designed curriculum experiences that included firsthand opportunities to counteract prejudices he discovered.

His clues to children's prejudices were picked up in comments and observations they made in different situations. He was often astonished to learn that ten-year-olds harbored such antipathies and misunderstandings. Examples of comments he noted and the situations in which they occurred include the following:

1. *After a visit to a newspaper plant:* Did you hear the funny way that Jew-editor talked?
2. *During a bus ride through a slum area:* All niggers are dirty and they like to live like this. Besides, they got different brains and blood—more like animals!
3. *At an Italian restaurant where the class had gone to have lunch together:* My Dad says all Italians are swarthy and gangsters besides! He says you can spot 'em and smell 'em a mile away. (*This child pronounced Italians as Eye-talians.*)

Mr. Samuels realized that even though he was always quick to counteract such statements and tried to counteract them with facts, his "lessons" were not effective. He must deal with prejudice in his classroom in deeper and wiser ways as long as his students were not responding to facts with behavioral changes. Here are some of the experiences devised to emphasize firsthand knowledge of intergroup curriculum and intercultural understanding.

1. The question of different language patterns and speech accents was deliberately brought up often by the teacher. He asked his students whether it was unusual in this country for people to have been born in other countries or to be the children of parents born in other countries for whom English is a second language. Records made by entertainers who have become famous because of their different accents were played and class visits were made to the United Nations to watch people from many nations at work together and to listen to speeches made in their own languages and translated into English by translators who often had "accents." Other questions and investigations that elicited good thinking and helped to change attitudes included these: Would we do as well as some people from other countries do in our country if we were in their country and had to use their language? Should we be laughed at and ridiculed for trying to use someone else's language to communicate with them?

2. Since it was to focus on creative writing that Mr. Samuels had

planned to visit the newspaper plant with his students, a writing assignment was made with the stipulation that each imagine he had participated in a little-known facet of a worldwide leader's life. After the celebrity had been chosen, his country of origin was listed, and the children shared with one another their imaginary adventures in connection with a little-known part of the selected celebrity's life. With their teacher's guidance, generalizations began to emerge concerning people who have reached prominence and made outstanding contributions on the national and international scene. These people came from all walks of life, many races, different cultures and ethnic groups, a variety of creeds and personal philosophies, as well as many nationalities. Furthermore, said the children, their different attitudes, values, and backgrounds explained in many cases how and why they became famous for their special contributions and insights.

3. Using the school "Human Resource" file, which Mr. Samuels and other teachers had helped to develop, different volunteers were invited to visit the classroom and share their special interests and hobbies. This school community, like so many others, was privileged to have residents with varied cultural backgrounds and with vocations and avocations that covered a wide range of school curriculum enrichment possibilities. Children and teacher prepared carefully for each visit. Questions they wanted to ask were noted and information they wanted to share was discussed ahead of time. Although teacher and children knew many of the people who came because some were parents and others were known through civic or religious groups, others were completely new to them. Whether known or unknown, the classroom and community experiences mutually shared were productive and positive contacts were made with people who might have been casually labeled "different."

4. Eventually, students were able to verbalize their innermost thoughts easily and comfortably. Some thought that "foreigners talked so funny" they couldn't help laughing in the beginning. Others observed that even people who have lived in this country for a long time speak differently because they come from different parts of the country. Some children who had labeled any accent that was different as a Jewish accent were surprised when they learned that one person so labeled was Scandinavian. Understanding grew perceptibly after the teacher had read Anne Frank's *Diary of a Young Girl*, a chapter a day, to the class. As he read, he asked questions related to the prejudiced feelings exposed by characters in the story, and students were asked to react in terms of personal feelings if they were to have been a Jew in Nazi Germany. When the story was finished, the class was asked to consider how the Nazis had treated German Jews, and their list read:

Jews were treated as an inferior group.
They were not allowed to hold office.

They were physically assaulted and killed.
They were forcibly removed from homes and businesses.
They were forced to try to escape, hide, or lie.
They could not use entertainment or recreation facilities.
Their synagogues were destroyed.
Their possessions were taken.
They were treated like beasts in concentration camps.
They were burned in incinerators by the thousands.

Sadly, the class came to the conclusion that "we will never know how many of them might have been like Einstein or Sam Levinson" or what contributions "a bright young girl like Anne Frank might have made." Other books that provided a great deal of insight and social introspection were books such as these: *To Kill a Mockingbird, Black Boy, The Story of Albert Schweitzer, All About Us, People Are Important, One God, Call Me Charlie, And Now Miguel,* and *Red Man, White Man, African Chief* (7). Their lists of treatment of particular ethnic groups evolved from individual reading, small group sharing, and large and small group discussions. One list that was eventually displayed prominently on a classroom chart summarized their insights about the bases of prejudice. Prejudice, it said, is based on:

Ignorance, not knowledge and understanding.
Hate, not love and compassion.
Emotion, not reason.
Hearsay, not objective evidence.
Denial of man's dignity, not recognition of it.
Disregard for the individual, not respect for the individual.
Authoritarian attitudes, not democratic ideals.
Fear, not trust.

In this classroom social understanding grew and prejudiced statements and attitudes were diminished. But this teacher knows that he and the teachers who follow him must find every opportunity—incidental and planned—to reinforce these concepts, to help parents and community understand and practice them, and to bring the teaching of positive social values into children's in-school and out-of-school curriculum. Teachers like this one know that attitudes and values are more often "caught than taught." Because this teacher sees himself as a social change agent with a responsibility that goes beyond the mere doling out of facts and reading assignments, he makes certain that attitudes and values of social significance are both *caught and taught.*

Teachers influence the social setting in their schools and communities in formal and informal ways. Informally, they meet parents and children on the street, at church, in the supermarket, at recreation centers, at street fairs, at concerts or art exhibits, or at youth centers and clubs. The way they greet parents, the kinds of interests and enthusiasms they demonstrate, and their general ability to feel comfortable and at ease with people from many walks of life set the tone for the effect they will have. In addition, teachers gain knowledge about communities through these everyday contacts because the myriad values and cultures of the people are reflected in their informal conversations, in their interests, and in the activities in which they participate.

Each teacher also needs to learn as much as possible about

- Other educational institutions in the community.
- Facilities for health and safety of children and families.
- Mental health facilities.
- The extent to which the community supports various movements.
- What welfare and emergency provisions there are.
- General socioeconomic patterns.
- Existing pressure groups, and their influence or threat.
- Who initiates or influences various activities.
- What cultural institutions are available to the school.
- What governmental structures operate within the community.
- What political and power groups are operating there.
- Various religious sects and social groups.
- Service organizations and clubs.
- Businesses and industries operating in the area.

Generalizations from Sociology

Because sociology is the study of the social relations men develop in their interaction with one another, and since educational sociology is concerned with the way these interactions and relations affect young people growing up in different school environments and community settings, it is important for boys and girls to understand that the work of society is done through organized groups in schools and in communities. The following generalizations with some illustrations of their possible application are useful whether the topic at hand is the immediate community, a series of communities, or national or international communities with which students have only vicarious experiences. They are useful to teachers and to students because they apply to the situation in which both presently find themselves and they will apply in other settings in the future. They are also useful because they help teachers develop curriculum cooperatively with their students. Having applied them in situations which are known and more familiar to students, they can then be transferred to thinking about people who live in distant parts of the world, people who have lived at various times and places in the past, and people who will live at future times and places. The important thing about them, also, is that they help children understand the *implications* of social groups for themselves and others.

As you read these generalizations (8), think of other possible applications to curriculum development.

Groups, Society, and Communication

Organized groups are the vehicles for the work of society, and group membership requires people to undertake varied roles in society. In other words, children learn early in their lives—in the family group, for example, before they enter school—that individuals must assume varied responsibilities, rights, and privileges. The responsibilities, rights, and privileges that have been theirs before school entry have been part of the culture that is transmitted first by the home and the immediate community of which the child is a part. As a child enters school for the first time, he sees the culture of his society and often the culture of other societies extending into the school. As he arrives at school, teachers must realize that the physical and spiritual environment into which he has been born and reared determines many of the traditions he already accepts and treasures. It also determines what responsibilities, rights, and privileges he has had or of which he has been deprived.

If a young child comes to school for the first time without having had to assume the responsibility for dressing himself or controlling his temper tantrums, he has already learned that he received the rights and privileges of his family unit whether he assumed these responsibilities or not. In some cases, he learned that he benefited more *because of* his temper tantrum or his continued dependence upon someone else to tie his shoes, put on his rubbers, or button his shirt. He enters school with its new expectations concerning responsibilities, rights, and privileges with his acquired goals and expectations; and in the new social setting his old methods of gaining status and recognition do not work. His peers, who have learned to dress themselves or who have learned that tantrums get them nowhere while other forms of behavior do, seem to be gaining the status he seeks. He learns in another group, or social, situation that approval is dependent upon a different role for him, and thus the new group begins to supply different self-expectations and new responsibilities, rights, and privileges toward which he must work.

When a young child enters school for the first time, he also begins to learn another of the lessons from the generalizations about sociology— that groups differ because of their different purposes, institutions, heritages, and locations. School groups, he learns, have different purposes and goals than his family group or any of the community groups with which he has had any experience, such as his church, the playground, or the swimming pool groups. It is easy to see that there are many possible extensions of this generalization for every age level. At six years of age children may be very interested in studying human and animal families in their own areas and elsewhere in the country and the world to compare similarities of organization, structure, and properties, as well as cultural differences. As they grow older, they are increasingly able to apply the concept of differences of purpose, institution, heritage, and location with the basic similarities of organization, structure, and properties of many kinds of groups.

Because most people belong to several groups, group membership overlaps. This concept has many possible applications from the simplest to the most complex. For example, a young child may see that some of his school-mates are also part of his church and his neighborhood group. As children grow older they belong to groups that take various kinds of music, danc-ing, swimming, or other kinds of lessons. They belong to different special interest groups during and after school. As they begin to participate in departmentalized school programs, they may be with different groups in different classes and will see some of the same peers in different groups. Because an individual participates in several groups at the same time, groups may produce conflicting demands and involve an individual in several roles at the same time. Each role has attendant responsibilities and opportunities. As boys and girls mature, they must develop the ability to analyze their relationships to the various groups to which they belong or think they would like to belong to see what the conflicting demands are or may be.

Children should grow in their understanding of self-identification so that they identify themselves both as people and as members of various social groups. They also need to grow in their understanding that any group can change both its membership and its objectives from those for which it was originally established. This is an important learning which can be injected into curriculum planning often because children tend to permit the pressures and approvals of the group to override their own personal convictions at times, and they can be helped to see this societal illustration appropriate to their level of understanding at each age. Per-haps a group of "best friends" starts out as just that but shortly graduates to petty thievery in the variety store. Or possibly an older group organizes for a special purpose but deviates from that purpose. The question of leadership and followership also enters into a consideration of groups, since these also change—sometimes almost imperceptibly, and members of the group are involved whether they originally intended to be or not.

Another significant concept about groups is that in a democratic, or open-class society, individuals can move up or down in the social system and thus experience significant personal and social change through group membership. If schools are sincere about developing this concept, they will deliberately plan to expose children as early as possible after school entry to different group experiences and memberships. If a child learns in everyday living at school that he is always a member of a certain group or class and that opportunities for him to participate in other groups are denied him through an administrative labeling and organizing system, he cannot be expected to have much respect for democratic concepts. If, on the other hand, his school experience is a rich and diverse one, he has the opportunity to know people from different cultural and social systems and to learn from them that there are other worlds than his own. We agree with Fischer (9) on the essential importance of bringing children of all races into schools together. His recommendations include a mandate for educators: "Action to accomplish this must be taken deliberately, systematically, and rapidly wherever it can be taken without clear damage to the educational opportunities of the children involved."

Another reason for planning to have children experience membership in diverse groups, so that they can know at firsthand and participate in significant personal and social change through group membership, is to help reverse the processes of alienation and disassociation from school that even very young children are seeing daily, reading about daily, and affected by daily. One of the greatest deterrents to cross-grouping of diverse cultures is the attitude held by so many adults about their children's associations with groups other than their own. Particularly, many more affluent parents, black and white, have been acculturated to feel that they have "gotten away from all of that" and that there is no reason for them or their children to return to it. But lower-class life is also seen by its membership as a contemptible and humiliating set of experiences. It is most often fear on the part of groups at both ends of the scale that prompts strong protests, and the fear is not limited to the extreme ends of the social scale. It is sometimes strongest at the middle where groups who are just beginning to pull themselves "up" are the most easily threatened.

Educators must place increased emphasis on the importance of the nature of the social groups from which children come and on the significance of children's social experiences out of school as they affect the nature of learning. Friedenburg (10) feels that the school would have to accept the lower-class child's language, dress, and values as a "point of departure for disciplined exploration, to be understood not as a trick for luring" children into middle-class groups, but as a "way of helping them to explore the meaning of their own lives." This, he says, is the way to encourage and nurture potentialities from any social class.

There are differences in significance and importance of membership in different groups, but many stereotypes ignore the most important characteristics of groups. Therefore, children must also be helped through graduated curriculum emphases that give them the experiences and the tools with which to recognize stereotypes and look for the real values and purposes of groups.

At every learning level, boys and girls should have many kinds of experiences, firsthand and vicarious ones, with the concept that organized groups do the real work of society, and that individuals have wide choice

Language is only one of the ways that individuals and groups communicate. Even very young children can be involved in thinking about different ways of communicating in various times and places.

(Photo courtesy of 3M.)

concerning the groups in which they will participate and the varied roles they will assume.

Communication is basic to culture and to groups. Later in this section, we will develop the idea of communication more fully. Here, it is important to emphasize that language is only one of the many ways that individuals and groups communicate. Some culture groups gesture more than others and within their own groups the gestures are understood to mean certain things, although when the same gesture is used in another group it is misunderstood or misinterpreted.

Even very young children can be involved in thinking about the different ways of communicating in different times and places. Drum signals, smoke signals, code flags, Morse code, hand signs—these and others in the world of human affairs in different times and places stress the essential idea that, basically, communication takes place between individuals and that the tools of communication are essential for every individual. Also, membership in some groups requires knowledge of oral and other communication skills that are not needed in others. All types of communication involve symbolisms that vary to greater and lesser extents from one group to another.

Many revealing and exciting illustrations can also be found in the world of wildlife—birds and animals, for example—where naturalists have studied and documented group communication patterns related to migrating, courting, mating, feeding, warning, scolding, punishing, raising families, teaching the young, and the like.

Probably the most serious distorting elements in the communication process and in the social processes of individuals and of groups are *stereotyping* and *ethnocentrism*. These words are often used together or synonymously, but they actually have different meanings. *Stereotyping* means that one has a tendency to see members of certain culture groups as unvarying in form or pattern from all others in the same group. They are not seen as the individuals they are with characteristics that are both similar to and different from all others; rather, they have fixed expressions, notions, characters, mental patterns, physical characteristics, and so on, in the eyes of the stereotyper. *Ethnocentrism* is the attitude by which we look with uncritical favor upon the ways of our own group, and judge others by the values of our own. The familiar ways of one's own group are not only thought to be superior to the less familiar ways of other groups, but are also thought to be right and natural. In the extreme, it is believing that the ways of one's own group are the best and that the ways of other groups are unnatural and inferior (11).

In the illustrations given early in this chapter, Mr. Samuels developed several techniques for counteracting the stereotyping and ethnocentrism he found in his class. Both are corollaries of *prejudice* and when they are unchecked and unheeded they destroy not only communication but progress and democracy as well. Working familiarity with the tools of assessing pupil needs and attitudes are particularly needed, and some of these tools include: sociometric procedures, participation schedules, social distance scales and other measurements of prejudice, role playing (sociodrama and psychodrama), projective techniques, pupil diaries and attitude inventories, teacher logs of class procedures, and anecdotal recordings of students' informal discussions and reactions in different situations and circumstances.

Teaching techniques for counteracting tendencies to stereotype and tendencies to be ethnocentric require extra sensitivity and skill, but the curriculum experiences that need to be developed are essential for students and rewarding for both students and teachers. They encourage children to reveal hidden thoughts and feelings and they help to remove the teacher from the traditional role of telling or moralizing. Some specific techniques also include these, which are adaptable to many age levels:

- *Using drawings or photographs* that deliberately force children to project feelings and reveal personal reactions in response to interracial situations or to specific culture group activities. The teacher's role is simply to ask questions that will keep discussion open, to accept whatever is said for the moment, and to make mental notes about possible follow-up another time. The kinds of questions that get discussion started and keep communication open can be similar to the following: What do you think is happening in this picture? What is your personal reaction to what you see? How does it make you feel? How do you think they feel? Can you tell us some more about that? What makes you think that might be so? How do we know?
- *Role playing or sociodrama* through which children identify themselves with the feelings of others in given situations and act out these feelings. Situations can also be set up in which children have the opportunity to practice social skills or to resolve conflict situations.
- *Buzz sessions* can be effective techniques, especially for older elementary schoolchildren. Small, informal groups are organized to discuss specific topics. Each group has a recorder and a reporter whose responsibilities include relaying the key issues and discussion in each session to the entire group later. This is a very good technique for maximum involvement of the entire group since it encourages speaking out in smaller, more intimate groups. The large group can choose the topics cooperatively and then break up into smaller groups to discuss them, or the teacher can assign the topics to be discussed.
- *Story completion* is another good device for encouraging individual expression. The *NEA Journal* and *Read* magazine has published incomplete episodes of in-school and out-of-school social-perception-type episodes. These present a problem or a conflict situation and then ask, "What would you do in this situation?" Teachers can develop some of these themselves, and older students like to develop

them and then exchange with a colleague for the completion or resolution part of the exercise. A great deal can be learned about how
students think and what their feelings and values are. There is also
a great deal of value in comparing possibilities and solutions when
several children or an entire group complete the same situation.

· *Newspaper headlines and clippings* can be used in a variety of ways
that help elicit feelings and perceptions. *Films, dramas, books, music,
art, games, dance, pageants,* and *festivals* can serve as social sensi-
tizers and feeling elicitors.

Personality and the Socialization Process

1. The way man expresses his biological drives is influenced and modified by his social environment and the groups to which he belongs.
2. Self-realization is influenced and modified by contacts with others.
3. Socialization results from the methods and experiences of child rear-
   ing, and from educational opportunities in the community and in the
   school.
4. Social controls and pressures tend to force a child's acceptance of the
   mores and folkways of his family and community culture groups;
   having accepted these at an early age, he finds it difficult to accept
   conflicting attitudes and values of other groups and of the traditional
   school.
5. The various roles are determined for individuals by the expectations
   of others. Nonconformity, for example, is perceived in one culture or
   social group as leadership behavior, but in others nonconformity is
   seen as damaging and threatening to society. Thus, the same person
   has different social roles in different groups because of the expectations other group members have for him.
6. Status is also achieved in different ways and is influenced by the
   expectations of others. Status means the prestige that a certain culture attaches to such differences as caste, vocation, class, age, sex,
   physical characteristics, and individual personality traits.
7. Individual organization or disorganization and group organization or
   disorganization reflect the presence or absence of coordinated and
   integrated behavior.

Teachers should be intimately familiar with this group of generalizations and concepts which relate to development of personality and the
socialization process so that they can include appropriate concepts as
goals and objectives in their lesson planning. The value of contacts with
varieties of social environments and knowledge about different national
and international social and cultural situations becomes apparent when
one realizes the progressive conditioning that results from contacts with
only one group or culture.

Social Relations and Culture

Similarly, the imaginative teacher curriculum-planner will see the rich possibilities that these concepts related to social relations and culture make available.

1. A social group, society, or association, once established, develops patterns of learned behavior accepted by, and common to, its members. These patterns, together with their accumulated institutions and artifacts, make up what we call the "cultural way of life" of a society and its various people.

2. Social relations are generally shaped by a set of culturally defined rights, duties, and responsibilities shared by the members of a group. Cultures vary from society to society, and any given culture changes over a period of time.

3. Changes and variations within a culture may generate from factors within the culture itself such as contact with other cultures and societies, or the invention and use of machines to replace men's work. However, some behaviors and institutions within a culture are universal while others vary widely, even when time and change are held fairly constant.

4. Within any large and complex society, there are subsocieties with varying cultures. These subsocieties are usually people who have migrated and are regarded as minority groups in the larger society. Minority groups usually inherit the least desirable geographic areas and poorest living and working conditions and opportunities until they begin to be accepted by majority groups.

5. People with a common culture tend to think of themselves as a certain social class with certain statuses (positions in society) and roles (functions in society). Societies that become so rigidly stratified that interaction between strata are not allowed are described by sociologists as "social caste systems."

6. Culture tends to standardize human behavior and to stabilize societies by developing large numbers of interrelated and elaborate institutions. When societies fail to continuously re-evaluate their institutions, redesigning and modifying them intelligently, cultural lag develops. Cultural lag is the term used to describe maladjustments between different parts of the same culture. When this happens, social disorganization is the inevitable result.

7. Cultures that cannot make adjustments between their parts in order to avoid cultural lag tend to be absorbed or exploited by more aggressive societies. Older cultures that have become too stratified are overtaken by more rapidly developing cultures whose institutions are newer and have not atrophied. Sometimes societies are completely annihilated because of cultural lag.

8. Internal cultural crisis tends to provoke social revolutions with which groups purport to bring about sweeping changes in the old social order as cultural lag develops.

In the present age of social ferment, the pleas for more meaningful school experiences come from many sources and even very young children cannot help but know about them. They know that their older brothers and sisters question the extent to which what is being taught them in school is relevant to their needs and to the needs of a changing society. Subcultures within America's diverse cultures are urging the modification of curriculum to meet specific as well as diverse cultural needs. Astute observers admit that there is often more education going on in the streets and in public halls and gathering places than there is within schools.

Curriculum in elementary schools, and in upper schools as well, needs to deal directly with the important contributions of all ethnic groups because distortions have operated for too long to create and support negative self-images among some culture groups.

Boys and girls and their teachers can plan curriculum cooperatively, that is, centered on human problems simply by selecting from among the varieties of problems that surround them daily. These exist in schools and in their communities and form subject content that has relevance to children and youth today. Approaching the 1970's and entering them, teachers must assume vigorous new leadership to meet the expectations of a demanding society that feels the necessity of bringing about sweeping changes in the old social order if America is not to be absorbed or exploited and if today's youngsters are going to be able to participate in the future they must face.

Demography and Human Ecology

1. Many individual and group social problems are influenced by changes in population or population relocation. Problems which influence groups include considerations of old age, youth, migration, war, housing, famine, employment, government, transportation, recreational activities, education, vocational opportunities, sanitation, social controls, living habits, and medical facilities.
2. National migration and greater population mobility develop cultural diversity within a group and cultural diffusion among groups. These are often deeply resented by the members of the same culture groups who do not migrate and who continue to adhere to the expectations and perceptions of the original group.
3. Environment influences man's way of living, and conversely man modifies and changes his environment. As man becomes more efficient technically, he is not only less influenced by and dependent upon his environment, but he is also able to modify and change his environment.

4. Human ecology is the study of the spatial and temporal distribution of populations and their institutions, and it includes the processes that bring about their patterning. Human ecology is concerned with the study of reciprocal relationships between the community and its physical and social environment. It involves, for example, methods of importing, exporting, and acquiring food, water, clothing, shelter, power, and other necessary resources to satisfy human needs and wants. It also involves climate, social environments and institutions, and folkways and mores.

5. Individuals generally function as members of communities, and although the community has a fixed geographic location, its essence and power lie in the interaction of the persons that are part of it. The people are grouped together in a locality for purposes of cooperation and competing with one another for sustenance, survival, cultural values, and social purposes. Modern inventions for communication and transportation have extended and increased the communities of man, making geographic location and immediate environment less significant than they once were.

If educators face facts realistically, they know that schools are still suffering from the effects of curriculum that was really devised for colonial America and never really has "fitted" immigrants who arrived on the American scene speaking other languages, practicing different religions, and coming from diverse cultures. Schools began to assume cultural burdens they had not borne before as these groups arrived, but they were never really prepared to cope with their new responsibilities. Unfortunately, we in the schools of the past and in the schools of today rationalize our failures to meet the simplest educational needs of many segments of our diverse school populations; but the problem is not new and it has existed too long. The study of human ecology and its cultural implications can help us to identify and meet emerging needs of all communities and all cultures as we move away from the concept of indoctrination-centered schools to the concept of inquiry-centered schools.

From the main generalization and from the subconcepts about demography and human ecology, educators have within their grasp the possibility of making relevant the requests of long-neglected ethnic groups in America's potpourri of cultures, traditions, attitudes, and values among people living in rural, suburban, and growing urban complexes. All groups in a democracy deserve opportunities to help shape their future social worlds and prepare themselves for changing social sensitivities and purposes.

For example, let us look at a group of twelve-year-olds whose interest in the problems faced by older people stemmed from the fact that three members of the class had one or both grandparents living with them and two members of the class lived in the homes of their grandparents. One day a film about Eskimo life was shown, and the class was shocked to learn that among Eskimo nomads when older people become too infirm or ill to travel with the tribe they must be left behind to die. This custom was characterized as an inhumane and horrible custom that, said the children, no "civilized" people would participate in.

Within a ten-mile radius of the school there were three nursing homes that had been built within the past five years, one after another. When the director of one was invited to come to the classroom to discuss some of the reasons why elderly people needed a facility such as a nursing home, he suggested that students and their teacher visit him instead. That way the class would be able to see the kinds of facilities, see how the elderly who lived there were accommodated, learn at firsthand about some of the medical and personal needs that were met by the facility, and then discuss the growing need for homes for the aged.

On the day of the visit, the director was well prepared with statistics about the smaller homes and the greater mobility of the average family today, longer life spans due to improved medical and health knowledge and techniques, and other factors that have to do with the specialty of modern geriatrics—a science that has developed from a modern social need. The students saw the special ramps that make walking or manipulating a walker or a wheelchair possible for older people. They saw the recreation rooms and witnessed volunteers writing letters, cutting men's hair, dressing women's hair, and giving manicures. They saw the special therapy rooms and equipment, visited the doctor and nurses in the health suite, and noted the special rails that lined the hallways. At lunchtime the children ate the lunches they had brought with them in the pleasant inner courtyard, which many of the occupant's rooms faced, but not before they had had a peek at the dining room where they saw the kinship and pleasant comradeship that had developed between and among older persons with interests and concerns in common. They also saw the pleasant reception rooms and observed visiting friends or relatives who lived near enough to call.

In follow-up curriculum experiences, the class divided into subcommittees to learn as much as possible about several aspects of geriatrics. Among the topics pursued were the following:

- Aged people in colonial times in America.
- Aged people in modern times in America.
- Aged people in American Indian cultures.
- Aged people in selected modern world cultures.

The variety of attitudes and practices in regard to older people discovered in class research ranged all the way from abandonment to great veneration, from the concept of their uselessness to a concept of great usefulness, and from a sense of personal responsibility to one of social responsibility.

Informally, the teacher often heard discussions among the children about their own grandparents and the conflicts and changes that occurred in their families' lives after grandparents became a permanent part of the family. Especially interesting were reports of parental confusions and tensions in making the decision to live with Grandpa or Grandma or to have them live in their own homes.

The methods used to develop knowledge about this modern concern were later applied to the study of larger youth groups, the problems of housing, and to other service, facility, and necessity needs influenced by population growth and population relocation. Imaginative teachers will find many ways to develop the concepts implicit in this group, for this is just one example of one teacher's attempt to help his students understand the social realities of today. And it is only one example of a teacher's effort to use social realities to make curriculum more relevant and to influence, shape, and control it.

Social Processes

Societies develop according to recurring sequences of interaction called social processes. Communication and social interaction are the general processes which are umbrella concepts for the following more specialized processes.

1. *Association, dissociation, and stratification.* Human beings in interaction with one another continuously organize and join groups and societies (association). In time, groups dissolve and lose their members to new groups (dissociation).

Individuals, families, and groups tend to become ranked by society into a hierarchy of social classes according to heredity, wealth, education, occupation, group memberships, and other status factors (stratification).

2. *Cooperation and accommodation.* Family members and members of other intimately related social groups tend to work together to carry out necessary functions of community living and to attain mutually agreed-upon goals (cooperation).

Those people who cannot completely accept all members of their intimate social groups, other social groups, or the way of life of these groups, often are able to make compromises or adjustments in order to stay in the groups and to enjoy the status of the group or benefit by the values of the group. We refer to this as *accommodation.*

3. *Competition and conflict.* Individuals and groups who become rivals of other individuals, groups, and group members may also compete as well as cooperate (competition).

Competition can be a healthy force for social change and progress, but rivalry tends to be followed by open clashes and struggles when either group of either opposing side feels that it must defend its social institutions and values or superimpose them on the other group (conflict).

4. *Assimilation.* Assimilation is the process through which individuals

and groups lose their acquired modes of behavior when they migrate to a new environment. As they are assimilated, they gradually take on the behaviors, attitudes, values, and mores of the new society.

Social Control

Societies require systems of social control in order to survive. Social control is secured by uncodified rules of behavior (mores and values) in most primitive societies and partially at least in all societies.

Some of the methods and techniques that individuals and groups use to ensure social control and to secure conformity are shunning, ostracizing, gossiping, jeering, praising, approving, and accepting. Infraction of uncodified rules of behavior considered understood by the social group to which an individual belongs or in which he finds himself will bring on these and other similar kinds of pressures in the group's efforts to make him conform. These informal kinds of social control are the strongest factor in forcing conformity to group standards.

Social control, particularly in large and complex societies, is also partially secured by formal, codified rules of behavior (laws), and infractions of these laws bring formal penalties. Formal legal controls and penalties are imposed on those areas of social life and society which are considered by the particular society to be too important to be left to the chance custody of informal, uncoded controls.

Examples of Curriculum Applications

Examples of curriculum experiences that reinforce the generalizations related to social processes and social control are legion as we have worked with teachers to use them in curriculum construction.

The idea of association can be easily understood by very young children in the family unit, the extended family unit, and in comparing these units with similar units in other societies. Very young children can also undertake simple investigations of community units with which they and their families interact. A classroom unit is an association and a total school is an association. Older children can understand more sophisticated ideas about association.

Dissociation can be understood by children, also. The simplest dissociations take place when someone marries and thus leaves his own family unit to become a member of another unit and start his own family. Older children can understand more complicated dissociations such as changing political parties, starting new religious sects, or forming a group to protest certain practices.

The concept of stratification is the most sophisticated of this group and is probably best applied to older elementary schoolchildren's curriculum because of the danger of oversimplifying and because of the danger of misinformation about stratification. We know one group of ten-year-olds who studied stratification through studying the housing patterns from the core of their city outward and comparing these with per capita income and the various culture groups who inherited certain neighborhoods.

Their study revealed that the poorest people lived in the heart of the city with the most multiple housing, the lowest income, the largest number of children, the fewest skilled parents, and the largest number of newcomers to the city—largely Negro and Puerto Rican. The outward rings had progressively better housing and greater numbers of single-family dwellings, income scaled from low average to high, fewer children, skills that ascended from the skilled tradesman through shopkeepers and professional people, and people who were second and third generation dwellers to those who were long-time well-established dwellers in the suburban collar of the city.

The concepts of cooperation and accommodation can also be studied in the community complex. The students in the class that studied about stratification also observed that certain parts of the city were Italian, certain parts Jewish, certain parts Polish, certain parts Irish, and certain parts Negro and Puerto Rican. Clubs and churches in these sections included similar memberships, as did groups working for community improvements such as parks and other recreation facilities in each part of the city. Political representation on the city council also reflected the ethnic and cultural nature of each area.

Accommodation was the catalyst for lively discussions about how far one should compromise himself to win the approval of a group in one class of eleven-year-olds. One student believed that it was necessary to make accommodation all of the time if you wanted a group of friends and said that "sometimes you have to do things you don't believe in in order to get in a group." This started a whole new discussion about whether or not it was worth being in any group that required you to do things you didn't believe in. At this point, the teacher was able to redirect the discussion back to the generalizations about the purposes of groups and the main reasons why groups form.

During the time that the class focused on these issues, current concerns in the city included a microcosmic mix of many problems now becoming familiar to cities—strikes of policemen and garbage collectors over wages and hours, flurries of civil disorder, a threatened teacher strike, a school boycott, and a city council divided over how to handle recurring problems. The daily newspapers were full of charges and countercharges of members of various groups in turmoil. One new coalition of teachers took place when a courageous group who disapproved of the recommended procedures of two main contending groups started their own new group with the support of a group of parents. Within this group, a fourth group formed to call themselves the Black Teachers League. Various groups of students were forming and re-forming at upper school levels and some of the students had older siblings in these various groups.

The "content" of curriculum relevant to students, to the times, and to the generalizations and concepts related to social control and social processes was always near at hand and teachers and students did not need to look far for the raw material or firsthand experiences. Significantly, though, this has probably always been so to some degree, but often classes have continued to be assigned bland mixtures of next chapters in textbooks whether they have any relevance or validity or not in the midst of it all.

A false assumption that also sometimes deters teachers from using significant current events even though their students and they themselves are in the midst of them is that elementary schoolchildren are "not ready" to consider these issues. Nothing could be further from the truth. They could never be more ready than when they are in the midst of the event and it is swirling all about them, affecting them, and having effects on others around them.

On the other hand, we have known teachers who were unable to abstract the simpler concepts appropriate to a particular age level or a particular group as a starting place. It is the ability to do so that gives the teacher control and appropriate pacing of curriculum, because more sophisticated ideas can be understood as teachers observe internalization of the simpler ideas. When the foundation has not been laid with the less advanced concepts, interest and understanding can be killed when teachers make the mistake of expecting students to understand and analyze situations that are too advanced.

Two other factors enter into teachers' failures to understand and use generalizations and concepts. One is traditional dependence upon students' ability to memorize so that schools have a basis for a report card and grading system; it is more difficult to assess the quality of thinking than it is to assess the ability to memorize. Among changes needed if teachers are to use generalizations and concepts as the basis for improved curriculum is the elimination of the traditional report card and the substitution of new evaluation measures of a child's growing ability to think. The other factor is the hangup of embeddedness to which we have referred often—fear of controversial issues and new encounters.

Suggested Follow-up

1. For each of the six generalizations (or one of their subconcepts) create a possible curriculum experience appropriate for six- or seven-year-olds. Include notes about the school and community setting, the general characteristics and cultures of the students, possible classroom topics and experiences, and the use of the community itself as a laboratory for learning.
2. For each of the six generalizations (or one of their subconcepts) devise a similar curriculum experience for ten-, eleven-, or twelve-year-olds. Include notes about the school and community setting, the general characteristics

and backgrounds of the students, possible classroom topics and experiences, differentiated homework assignments, and the use of the community agencies and representatives in developing knowledge and understanding pertinent to the general topic.

3. Devise an imaginary curriculum experience in which the teacher uses a concept that is either too sophisticated or too simple to be successfully developed.

4. Role-play with a group of your own colleagues an imaginary conversation among a group of twelve-year-olds about a current social issue in which you think they have great interest and divided opinion. Have one of your group serve as an observer to note general tone of discussion and emotions. Have another serve as recorder to record key agreements and disagreements.

5. Choose a book such as Michael Harrington's *The Other America,* Claude Brown's *Manchild in the Promised Land,* Kenneth Clark's *Dark Ghetto,* Robert Coles' *Children of Crisis,* or David Lavine's *The Mayor and the Changing City.* Analyze it for its sociological implications for today's living and future portends.

References

1. Inkeles, Alex, *What Is Sociology?* (Foundations of Sociology Series). Englewood Cliffs, N.J.: Prentice-Hall, Inc., 1964.

2. Harrington, Michael, *The Other America.* New York: The Macmillan Company, 1962.

3. King, Martin Luther, *I Have a Dream.* New York: Grosset & Dunlap, Inc., 1968.

4. Sexton, Patricia, *Education and Income.* New York: The Viking Press, Inc. Distributed in Canada by The Macmillan Company of Canada Ltd., 1961.

5. Trager, Helen, and Marian Radke, "Early Childhood Airs Its Views," (Report of the Philadelphia Early Childhood Project), *Educational Leadership.* Washington, D.C.: Association for Supervision and Curriculum Development, Vol. V, No. 1, October, 1947.

6. Stember, Charles H., *Education and Attitude Change.* New York: Institute of Human Relations Press, 1961.

7. Wright, Betty Atwell, *Educating for Diversity* (for chapters on activities, films, and books to counteract prejudice and implement socially sensitive intergroup education). New York: The John Day Company, Inc., 1964.

8. California State Central Curriculum Commission, *Generalizations from the Social Sciences.* California State Department of Education, 1961. (The statements are adapted from the original document.)

9. Fischer, John H., "The Inclusive School," *Teachers College Record,* Columbia University, October, 1964.

10. Friedenburg, Edgar Z., "An Ideology of School Withdrawal," *The School Dropout.* Edited by Daniel Schreiber. Washington, D.C.: National Education Association, 1964.

11. Wright, Betty Atwell, *Educating for Diversity* (Chapter III, "Prejudice, Stereotyping, and Ethnocentrism," pp. 64–81). New York: The John Day Company, Inc., 1964.

CHAPTER 5

Teachers Study Social Growth

The School as a Social Institution

There is no other social institution that should be more concerned than the school with the structure of groups, group interaction phenomena, and the role of individuals in various kinds of groups that the school sponsors. These sociological generalizations apply as teachers attempt to understand their communities, group children for various kinds of learning adventures, and develop curricula that will eliminate cultural lag in school-centered laboratory experiences.

Among children of upper elementary school age, teachers will find that loyalty expressed between child and child is stronger than that existing between teacher and child, for example. Knowing the inevitability of peer group formation even within groups, the wise teacher does not seek to destroy them but rather to work with them and use them to improve the total social climate. Children vie for status among their classmates and most children want and need the security of belonging to a special group within the group.

In studying the structure of the large group and the structure of smaller groups within the large group, teachers find that all peer groups have both formal and informal goals and codes of behavior just as groups in society generally do. There are also formal groups with specified goals and informal groups who simply share a feeling of needing one another. Teachers learn how to work subtly with groups, formal and informal, to channel their loyalties and talents toward the mutual benefit of the teaching–learning relationship, individuals, and formal and informal groups.

Occasionally there are children who seem to belong to no group. The teacher attempts to understand the reasons and find ways for each child to become an accepting and accepted member of a group. Mr. Roth had this problem in a class of ten-year-olds. Noting that Elizabeth was a class reject, he began to solicit a group change of attitude toward Elizabeth and to lead Elizabeth toward attitudes that would cause her to be accepted by the group.

As an only child, Elizabeth had been indulged and spoiled by her parents. She had been given piano lessons since she was five years old and had undergone five years of constant reminders from her mother to practice her piano lessons by the time she reached Mr. Roth's classroom. Mr. Roth noted that her performance at the piano was highly technical and had little depth or feeling. He also noted that she had an excessive amount of clothes and toys, and that she was a self-centered child with a strong desire to have her own way.

Scarcely a day went by that Elizabeth did not have an argument with someone in the class. She was never chosen for any of the games, but instead Mr. Roth always had to assign her to someone's team amid much grumbling and fussing. Sometimes she refused to play at all.

Finally she voiced her complaints by petulantly telling Mr. Roth that "they don't like me and I don't like them!" Mr. Roth welcomed this opportunity to ask Elizabeth, "Why don't you like them? And why do you think they don't like you?" When Elizabeth did not answer, Mr. Roth suggested that she think about it and see if she could think of any answers to these questions. "I believe you can find some of the answers if you really think about it," he said.

Within the next few days, an opportunity arose for the peer group to help her or hurt her. There was to be a school-wide talent show for a PTA meeting, and each class was asked to send a representative. Mr. Roth asked the class to select the person they wanted to represent them from among several who wanted to participate in the talent show. The class decided to have a room talent show and vote on the best talent to represent the group. Elizabeth naturally assumed that she would be selected, but the class chose someone else.

Realizing that there would be strong reaction from Elizabeth and her mother, the teacher asked each child to write a brief reason why he had voted for a particular contestant. When Elizabeth and her mother demanded to know why she was not representing the class at the talent show, Mr. Roth shared the children's honest evaluations. Victor's statement seemed to sum up the class attitude: "I voted for Elizabeth because I thought she played the hardest piece. But now I am glad Mark won, because he is nicer, and I guess it is better for nice people to win sometimes."

Ever so slowly, Elizabeth, with Mr. Roth's support and help, began to conceptualize the reasons for her defeat. With each new insight, her attitude began to change from animosity to friendliness. As this happened, classmates began to meet her halfway because they knew that their vote for a talent show representative had been based more on popularity than on talent. Privately Mr. Roth made special opportunities to discuss with Elizabeth the difference that friendlier relationships with others would make in the way she felt, not only about others but also about herself.

He also discussed with the class behavior which, like Elizabeth's and like their own, was based on emotion and not on objective evidence. As Elizabeth was gradually included in more group activities, and as she began to respond in less demanding and self-centered ways, rewards deserved and graciously accepted began to be hers. When the group hosted a musical program in the spring, Elizabeth was elected room hostess, one of the many demonstrations of change of social approval by the group and social growth for Elizabeth.

Peer-to-Peer Relationships

Another source of influence which the teacher often overlooks in analyzing the social elements of the classroom setting is the positive influence of a close buddy or dearest friend. Many times when a true allegiance is reached between two individuals, an individual is able to weather the sarcasm and derisions of the large group, reject feelings of inferiority and insecurity, or withstand rejection by his family. The secret lies not in the numbers of close associations, but in the quality of support and approval of one person. Knowing the value of having a confidant, teachers sometimes attempt to encourage one close association for a child who is a loner.

It is the newcomer to a group who is most often a loner. He comes to a group where other children have had longer associations and time to develop special friendships at school and in their neighborhoods. Teachers need to be especially aware of the lonely, empty feelings of being a newcomer to an established group. Children can be sensitized to the problems of a migrant worker's child, or to the problems faced by a child whose parents are transferred from job to job and community to community, or to children who are culturally different from the established group.

Richard was such a boy, and his teacher knew that his migratory life had not allowed him to make deep or lasting friendships with any other boy his age. Jimmy became his special buddy and friend, and each was good for the other. Jimmy's father owned a clothing store and Jimmy had always lived in the community and attended the school to which Richard came briefly as the child of a migrant worker. But the special friendship that was aided and abetted by the teacher may have been the first real friendship Richard had ever known. His visits to Jimmy's home may have been the first opportunity to see how a more "settled" family lived. Richard's father sponsored both boys on Boy Scout Father's Night and Jimmy's family shared his clothing with Richard. Richard's pride in his new friend, his new clothes, his new school, and his new teacher were obvious. But most of all, his new ideas about himself showed in many ways. And they were not accidental.

The boys' teacher deliberately and consistently sponsored the kind of classroom environment that helped children understand and come to grips with some of the major dislocations and disturbances of our times. Unless this is done, the sheltered and artificial environment that the school often projects will crumble at the first touch of reality and practicality. Teachers find themselves on the horns of a dilemma in courageously trying to mediate between a child and his culture. And yet, teachers like Miss Viti welcome the opportunity presented by the building of a migrant workers' housing complex within the environs of a school community that had been relatively stable and was inclined to be stratified and static. She could have moaned, as some teachers do, about the disastrous consequences of "having our *nice* children be in the same classroom with those!" Instead she used the new associations to help her children understand that there is an America other than the one they have always known. Her classroom has become a center of discovery about human interrelationships and concerns and a center of intervention when necessary to change social attitudes. These will stand her students in good stead as they grow toward futures so uncertain and so unpredictable.

Some of this teacher's sensitizing curriculum includes

1. A visit to the fruit farms where migrant workers will be arriving when the fruit is ready. She deliberately goes with her class during off-season, before migrant workers are on hand. She explains the need for temporary help when the fruit is ready, and discusses with the class where and how the families who come will live.
2. Asking children to read and report on books like these during the early part of the school year:
   a. Jerrold Beim's book, *The Smallest Boy in the Class,* a book that cleverly illustrates the importance of peer relationships and individual worth.
   b. Marguerite Di Angeli's *Bright April,* a story about home and school experiences that help "little brown April" experience kindness, love, and understanding.
   c. Florence Hastings' *Skid,* a story about a boy whose family moves from a small town in Georgia to a town in Connecticut. As the only Negro family in an exclusive white community, Skid and his family deal with the feeling and actions of other children about teams, scholastic honors, parties, and other afterschool activities.
   d. May Justis' *New Boy in School,* another story about the first Negro boy in an all-white school in Tennessee.
   e. Mina Lewiton's *Candita's Choice,* a frank portrayal of a little Puerto Rican girl's adjustments and difficulties faced by new arrivals in New York City.

    f. Virginia Sorensen's *Plain Girl*, a story of an Amish child who is torn between family ties and culture and the outside world.

    g. Sidney Taylor's *All-of-a-Kind Family*, the story of the joys and sorrows of a Jewish family arriving in this country at the turn of the century.

    h. Yoshida Uchida's *New Friends for Susan*, a sensitive account of life in a Nisei family and the experiences of a Japanese-American child when she goes to a new school.

    i. Florence Means' *A Great Day in the Morning*, in which a Negro girl experiences the bitterness of racial prejudice and severe deprivation but has the courage to continue and become a nurse so she can help others.

    j. Natalie Carlson's *Tomahawk Valley*, in which two present-day Indian children cope with a stubborn grandmother who insists that the old tribal ways are best.

    k. Don and Betty Emblem's *The Palomino Boy*, a story that develops a Mexican orphan's realization that the discrimination he experiences because of his brown skin does not make him inferior any more than black, brown, or white color makes one of his horses better than another.

    l. William Pène DuBois' *Bear Party*, in which koala bears live and play happily until the fact that they look exactly alike causes grievances and quarreling and they decide to wear masks so that they will look different from one another.

    m. Eva Evans' *All About Us* and *People Are Important*, effective scientific presentations of facts about people in group relationships that help combat intolerance and prejudice.

3. Having children develop an imaginary friend who is completely different from them in some respect. The friend may be of a different color, nationality, religion, sex, or social group. For a period of two weeks or so, the children keep a diary of imaginary conversations they may have or things they do together. Small groups and larger groups share and compare imaginary friends.

4. Using films such as these available from the National Council of Christians and Jews: *The Greenie, Our People, Your Neighbor Celebrates,* or *Boundary Lines;* or these available from the Anti-Defamation League: *Heritage, One People, Skipper Learns a Lesson,* and *The Rabbit Brothers;* or *American Counterpoint* from Philadelphia Fellowship Commission; or *The Toymaker,* available from Contemporary Films.

Sociometry

The companion-deprived child is a socially deprived child. The loner is easily overlooked, for he is quite often quiet and conforming. The teacher who is not sensitive to the special needs of the loner may breathe a sigh of relief and mentally thank the powers that be that there is at least one child who "doesn't cause any trouble." But the socially deprived child may be saying more loudly than words or demands for attention that he is already in deep trouble. The socially conscious teacher makes special efforts to single out these individuals and to provide opportunities for them to participate in classroom interrelationships.

There are some techniques to help teachers. None of these should be overused, and, as in all other forms of measurement and information-gathering about and from children, teachers should not accept all information at face value.

Some techniques that can be used include:

1. Asking questions such as these: Who would you choose to go on a field trip with you? Who would you choose to sit nearest you in the classroom? Which person would you prefer not to work with? Name the three people you would like to have work on your project. Choose two people whose teams you would prefer to be on.
2. Carefully asking questions in informal situations to get information about how children feel about one another. Information gained can be noted informally on cards or the data can be compiled in a sociogram.
3. Making a sociogram or graph. The social climate changes quickly among children. A sociogram which is a week old may be completely outdated. However, teachers can use the results to advantage to structure situations for isolates, to mix members of different peer groups, and to broaden significant contacts among children of different academic and social abilities. The sociogram illustrated here was compiled from data obtained by Miss Viti in Richard's class, and Miss Viti knew that it would change as Richard changed.

Richard's Sociogram

This sociogram shows student number 6 (Richard) as he related to others in his class. Note the positive and negative choices. Number 6 indicated two positive and one negative choices; he was accepted by two others and rejected by one class member.

—————————positive choice
· · · · · · · · · · · negative choice

Self-image and ego development were discussed in Chapter 2 of Section I. The attitude a person holds about himself appears to affect the classroom social climate, both for the individual and for the group. The classroom that is characterized by individual isolation, hostility, aggressiveness, rivalry, intolerance for differing ideas, and attitudes of prejudice and ethnocentrism indicates that the teacher is either unable or unwilling to set the tone for productive social climate. Before any learning

This sociogram shows student number 6 (Richard) as he related to others in his class. Note positive and negative choices. Richard indicated two positive and one negative choices; he was accepted by two and rejected by one class members.

——————————— Positive Choice
— — — — — — Negative Choice

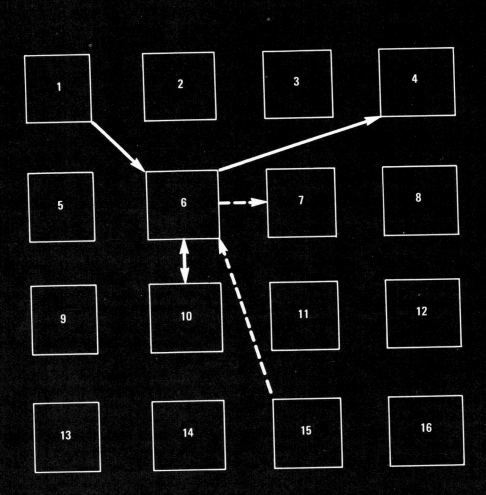

of any kind can take place, a great deal needs to be done even to secure simple cooperation.

Just as there are many facets to individual personalities, there are also limitless dimensions to the personality of a group. It is apparent in many classrooms that the world of the teacher and of the children varies substantially. Differences in economics, recreation, education, religion, government, family, sex, and age play important roles in the peer–peer and teacher–pupil relationships basic to good curriculum planning. As teachers develop more understanding of themselves as social organisms, and of their students as social organisms, they will respect and use differences to fortify and enrich individuals in groups in classroom situations.

No longer is the home the center of children's interests and activities as it was in early America. Home is often a place where one or both parents are absent. One third of American homes exist under poverty levels. In another large percentage of homes, divorce has taken its toll. So too have military service and greater mobility of 70 per cent of American families. Home is a stopping-off place amid the rush of day-to-day living. The social climate for today's children is generally in a state of flux regardless of socioeconomic circumstances.

Teacher Status and Acculturation

In discussions with teachers, there is a tendency to identify the upperclass parent as one who can provide ample money and material needs for the family, but one who is too busy with professional and social obligations to really know and spend time with his family. They picture middleclass parents as providing love and material comforts to the best of their ability. They also describe middle-class parents as having higher standards and morals for their children. The lower-class parent is often seen as one without financial means to supply family needs, lacking reading and speaking ability, often lacking ambition, and frequently of a "foreign" culture.

These broad generalizations that teachers are prone to make are dangerous and may stem from teachers' own early training. Ethnic and economic backgrounds do affect the way teachers teach and the way children learn. This is true, not because people from different cultures are different in innate abilities, but because they have been nurtured in different environments. Certain groups have certain social expectations for themselves and others, and majority group cultures have certain attitudes toward minority group cultures. The opposite is also true—minority group cultures have certain culture-conditioned attitudes about majority group cultures.

Spindler (12) speaks of the social classes from which most teachers come. His conclusions are mirrored by other social scientists who have investigated the backgrounds and behaviors of teachers:

I hypothesize that the child training of most of the people who become teachers has been more traditional than emergent value-oriented. They are drawn largely from the middle to lower-middle social class groups in American society, and this segment of the class structure is the stronghold of the work-success ethic and moral respectability values in our country (even in a culture that is shifting away from these values). Furthermore, it seems probable that a selective process is operating to draw a relatively puritanistic element into the public school teaching as an occupation. Self-denial, altruism, a moralistic self-concept, seem to be functional prerequisites for the historically derived role of the school teacher in American Society (I might have said "school-marm").

If teachers do in fact acquire their personal cultures in more tradition-oriented environments, then they experience what social scientists call a *culture conflict* when they come into contact with parents and children of different kinds of cultures. When people encounter a new culture, discontinuity in the old enculturation of an individual occurs. Many people experience great "culture shock," as for example, when a middle-class white teacher first goes to work on an American Indian reservation, or goes to teach in an all-black ghetto school, or takes a foreign-exchange teaching post.

We discussed the characteristics of open and closed individuals and described what happens to each when they have a new encounter as we looked at the changing roles of teachers in Chapter 1. If culture conflicts remain stable or exist for too long between teachers and children, the teacher becomes nonfunctional as a teacher and the students become nonfunctional as students.

Ours is a culturally fluctuating, polyglot society. The open individual we discussed earlier, and the emergent-oriented person Spindler describes are very similar. Spindler says that the emergent-oriented teacher is one who has "social adaptability, relativistic outlooks, sensitivity to the needs and opinions of others and of the group." He warns, too, that the emergentist can also become a group conformist—just "an average person proud of his well-rounded averageness"—unless his emergence from acculturation is goal oriented.

The teacher who is really sincere about learning as much as possible about children's out-of-school experiences and cultures will deliberately court new kinds of community experiences with the goal of understanding children and their individual learning styles as a basis for planning curricular experiences that are relevant.

With more experience in home visiting and community participation, teachers learn to depend less on their own cultural orientation for interpreting what they experience and more on generalizations that have broad social implications. For example, Miss Blake, as a beginning teacher, was assigned a cross section of socioeconomic cultures in her classroom and noted these kinds of generalizations during her first series of home visits:

1. Some homes of the very poor are untidy but clean; some are dirty and really unsanitary; some are immaculate, even though there are few material things.
2. Some homes of the very poor do have a set of encyclopedias that the family is purchasing on "time" and that are proudly displayed; others have no books, magazines, or newspapers. In either case, there is a role that the school can play in building upon this information in the school setting.
3. Even though some of the middle- and upper-class homes do have books, magazines, and newspapers, their children seem to spend as much time watching television as most of the poorer families.
4. Conversation with children is often lacking in middle- and upper-class families because of overdependence on television or because of the busy social schedules of adults. Conversations are lacking in poorer homes because of lack of education, and because speech is used more often to give orders or directions, rather than for the purpose of dialogue.
5. Often there is little evidence of family reading or conversation in *any* of the homes visited.
6. In middle- and upper-class homes, there are more manipulative materials such as crayons, pencils, games, puzzles, mechanical and other kinds of toys, picture books, children's scissors, and so forth.
7. Regardless of social affluence, in homes where people have recently immigrated from another country that uses a language other than English, children hear the native tongue used generally at home and English is the *second* language.
8. Parents who live in poverty or slum conditions are often embarrassed when teachers or others they consider to be from another class visit them. It is important to join the family for coffee or a soft drink, if offered. If there is no extra chair and the edge of a cot is available, join those sitting there. Stand as the others do if there is no place to sit at all or if everyone else remains standing. A good conversation opener is generally "Where did you live before you moved here?" It breaks the ice and gives people a chance to explain that they didn't always live like this, even if they did.

This teacher's other initial notations following home visits indicate her willingness to look for actual similarities and differences rather than her preconditioned responses to some situations. In contrast, one new teacher visiting with the school nurse remarked, "Honestly, I'd rather die than do that again. I thought I'd vomit before I got out of there. There was a pile of dirty diapers that stunk up the whole place—it smelled just like their son, Joe, usually does."

Another tendency is to assume that people who are poor have no talents to offer. This just isn't so. Teachers who assume that every individual has something to offer and that every individual will be a more supportive and productive person if he has the opportunity are having wonderful experiences with paraprofessionals and teacher aides in their classrooms.

Dan Davies (13), associate commissioner for educational personnel development in the U.S. Office of Education, has said, "My feeling about our experience of the last couple of years is that people with very limited education, very limited opportunity, with poor records of academic achievement can, in fact, be effective as teacher aides. They can help teachers and children significantly. I have seen it happen. This has also been a source of some surprise to experts who have said that introducing people, who have not been successful academically, into the instructional program, just simply wouldn't work. It can work if we want to make it work."

In fact, if teachers are really concerned about *changing* moral and ethical values, they will involve parents whenever possible in the school's program. Both parents and teachers will gain new respect and admiration for one another's attitudes and values, and children will benefit immeasurably. "Parents play a most important role in better communication between home and school. As members of the community they are in contact with other parents and students in neighborhoods and larger community activities. They have opportunities to know at firsthand, as few teachers do, about students' families, circumstances, activities, interests, needs, problems, hopes, and aspirations" (14). Parents can also serve as culture buffers when teachers do not understand certain attitudes and values held by people in different neighborhoods; they serve as intergroup emissaries as culture conflicts are being resolved.

New Grouping Approaches—Teachers, Children, Parents

Human Resources for Living Curriculum

Teachers have differing talents, characteristics, and cultures. And children and their families have differing talents, characteristics, and cultures. Why not build new school organizational plans that deliberately group parents, teachers, and children in ways that ensure cross-fertilizing one another? If we agree that one of the goals of education is to teach all people to live better with one another, to be more human, and to relate to peer groups in the real world now and in the future, then *planned intergroup education* makes sense.

Teachers feel an inevitable uneasiness when someone they think is less qualified than they seems to encroach on their sovereignty in the classroom. This holds true whether the "encroacher" is a student teacher, a younger team teacher, a peer-age team teacher, or a parent. Why? Because education in traditional schools has been a closed door, ivory tower affair! And because teachers, often with a great deal of justification, have been threatened by so many forces—community pressure groups, administrative policies and personalities, and academic freedom.

Life skills education demands open schoolroom doors and open hearts. It demands effective, relevant, and universal education. Ashby (15) contends that "to the astonishment of most of our people and the discomfiture of some, we are discovering that this country does in fact depend on its educational system. In lessons that are hard to ignore, we are learning that where schools decline, the community is diminished; that where schools are not promoted, the country remains underdeveloped. Maintaining schools can no longer be viewed as an optional exercise in charity. Effective, relevant, universal education has become a condition of national survival and an indispensable means of social, political, and economic progress. Even those who are reluctant to face the implications in policy and finance now recognize that without a sound educational system neither the community, the state, nor the nation can prosper."

And James (16) adds another dimension when he says, "The evils of our time, particularly as reflected in interracial conflict, . . . appear to be growing at a pace so rapid as to defy control by government, an omen almost certain to portend social revolution if present trends continue. Consequently, when we look to the future costs of higher education, I hope also we can come to weigh its benefits measured in terms of increasing understanding of man in relation to his environment and in terms of our continuing search for the meaning of human existence and viable rules for governing ourselves."

Interracial and intergroup education have neither been goals nor results obtained by the schools of the past. The evidence showing that the well educated are as prejudiced as the undereducated and in some cases show even more prejudice than the undereducated is persuasive. Someone has said that as an institution-builder man has a notable gift for making the same mistake over and over. Let's take a brief look at the ways nature and men have grouped people for learning during this country's history. People have been variously grouped in formal and informal educative situations by geography, religion, socioeconomic levels, color, culture, nationality, languages spoken, sex, reading ability, age, grade level, general achievement, intelligence quotients, and by physical and mental handicaps. Undoubtedly the reader can think of many other ways that chilren are still grouped.

Admittedly, some people have profited and progressed under these various grouping systems. But not enough, if one looks at the symptoms of social disease that can easily threaten national survival, and in so doing threaten all of mankind. The skills that these groupings purported to develop may have served some well in limited and limiting ways, but they never included the skills that would help all people come out of their embeddedness to face the world in other times and places.

Seeley (17) talks about some "skills of being" and says that

Just as "education" has been a magic word, a talisman, in the general theory of the American people, so "the development of skills" has been a magic slogan for those charged with the tasks of education. Education is to redeem America; skills are to redeem the education that is to redeem the nation.

Yet America has not been redeemed by education, and education has not been redeemed by the development of skills. Never has education been so blessed with means so firmly directed to ends so false, so trivial, or so wanting altogether. . . . And, happily, more and more of the young respond with alienation and revolt against the educational diet of stones for bread, training for education, and skills for substance. How can it be that the school has produced the maleducation, miseducation, and non-education that we see?

Seeley also notes that, paradoxically, the revolt of the young is one of the few things for which educators may be able to take credit, and from which they certainly should take heart. He says that even if educators did not set the revolt up, or help set it off, they did not at least kill it even though they may have resisted it.

Teachers are more vital and necessary to keeping the social system open and going than are the people in any other profession. We have said before that their attitudes and actions affect more lives—children's, parents', and other teachers'—than do doctors, lawyers, ministers, government officials, merchants, or chiefs. We have stressed their roles in the school community and in the world of social affairs. And we have known individual teachers who are the finest intergroup emissaries anywhere. What we propose are new intergroup, professional and paraprofessional alliances. We propose that the best way for teachers and parents to bring education up to date for children and to help them gain the skills of living is to have them actively involved in dialogue and mutually supportive programs to improve education for children.

Parents and Teachers Team Up

Bringing parents and teachers together in imaginative and different ways calls for creativity and imagination. Parents are tired of being "invited" to supply a cake for a cake sale or straighten the books on the library shelves. Parents are often more aware of the problems and implications of changing times than are teachers. "Often they have led much more mobile and realistic lives than many traditional educators. They are more inclined to try to understand the modern world through the eyes of their children and their children's peers. To be a good parent and to be a good teacher require many of the same qualities. In parenthood, as in teaching, one experiences and practices knowledge of child growth and development, mutual respect and concern, love, patience, empathy, and deep personal interest in guiding children wisely. Many teachers would like to make changes in curriculum and in school patterns of living and working, but need the help and support of parents in order to do so. While some parents and some teachers do cling to past standards of living and education, they will become less traditional when they are convinced that new ideas, new ways, and new patterns of living and learning are better than the old" (18).

It takes only one teacher and one parent to make a good beginning. Remember Miss Blake, the teacher described a little while ago as the

Industrialist?

Psychologist?

Psychiatrist?

Doctor or Nurse?

Tutor?

Social Service?

Union Members?

City Planning?

Musician?

Sculptress?

Storyteller?

Scientist?

Dancer?

Artist?

Businessman?

Journalist?

Politician?

beginning teacher who applied generalizations, rather than stereotypes, to observations during her first home visits? Miss Blake didn't stop with those first visits, because she made them to establish contact for further and more meaningful involvement of parents in their children's education. She wanted them to be a vital part of their children's in-school as well as out-of-school education. During her visits, she was thinking about ways to bring about new interrelationships. She had already noted that there were no "Human Resource" files in her school, and that the main involvement of parents was in standard PTA activities. During her home visits, she had reminded parents about PTA and had been told by several that they had attended sometimes but the meetings were dull, uninteresting, and "cut-and-dried," "controlled by a few busybodies." Although Miss Blake made a mental resolution to work with colleagues and parents to make the official parent–teacher association more vital as time went on, she wanted to begin with her own class parents. And so she began by finding one interested mother who was willing to work as chairman of a group to find and organize talent for use in the school program.

The parent Miss Blake persuaded to take on the job had never been chairman of a group before, but she was willing to try because of Miss Blake's interest in her child and the fine classroom experiences she felt her child was having. Although the mother chosen was not highly educated, she had a natural ability to contact and catalyze people, and her results amazed both teachers and other parents. She and her committee organized house-to-house visits, devised questionnaires, and even interested a local business establishment in sponsoring a spot radio announcement. Many of the people who volunteered did not have children in school, and many were fathers who could arrange some time off from their businesses and professions. The chairman personally interviewed each volunteer and explained the purposes of the Community Resources Talent Program. She compiled a file of information with pertinent data about special talents, exhibits, and contributions people were willing to make, when they could be available to do so, where and how to reach them, and materials and equipment they would need when they came to visit the school. This information was also mimeographed and given to the other teachers in the school. Because of the vision of one teacher about involvement of parents and parental influence, four hundred students from ages five through twelve became acquainted with housewives, businessmen, sculptors, chefs, philatelists, ornithologists, doctors, social workers, juvenile court workers, lawyers, and many others who represented not only a variety of talents and interests but also a variety of cultures.

How fallacious to assume that the only one who teaches is a teacher. This just isn't so. Young people have been learning from one another and from their families and neighbors for centuries. But learning from families, neighbors, and a school environment that are identical in culture does not help children have the person-to-person contacts they need in order to *practice* good *intergroup relations* with people of different cultures and different talents and professions.

Traditional schools have managed to avoid at all costs real-life problems and controversial issues that parents and teachers should be deeply concerned about. Among the topics not often handled are race relations, alcoholism and drug use, materialism in society, religion, politics, consumer competency, illegitimacy, birth control and the population explosion, and the implications of family life and sex education. When one eliminates all of these, school is a pretty sterile and unlifelike place. Many parents and teachers will agree that these emphases, which are of prime concern to young people, should be included in school programs for life skills development. Many parents are willing to help schools carry on cooperative programs of education. The plain fact is that neither homes, schools, nor communities as single institutions have available to them all of the resources needed to sponsor accurate and wide-ranging education in any one of these areas of mutual concern. Parents are deeply concerned about new sexual freedoms, growing dependence upon drugs and alcohol, and moral and spiritual values in an age of flux, and so must educators be. The problems may *manifest* themselves in upper schools, but the influences and attitudes which precipitate the problems must be dealt with in our lower schools as well.

New City Parents and Teachers Team Up

New City is a medium-sized, fairly old city that remained relatively static and predictable until about a decade ago. Today it is undergoing all of the rapid change and traumatizing experiences of its larger sister cities. In its center are the slums and ghettos left by earlier waves of English, Irish, Jewish, and Italian immigrants and inherited now by the newest groups of Puerto Rican, Cuban, and African Americans who have come to the city. Around the central core and extending outward beyond the main business districts are mixtures of these various cultures who are a little better off socially and economically. They are employed in trades and small businesses, although many of the factories in which some of them once worked have moved out of New City. The "collar" of the city and the suburbs immediately surrounding the city proper are composed of well-established families who have moved "up and out" and who come into central city only to operate their prosperous businesses, practice their professions, shop, or attend concerts, lectures, or exhibits at the university or city auditorium.

Nearly 40 per cent of the young people attend private or parochial schools, and these are from the two outer rings of New City. The other 60 per cent attend public lower, middle, and upper schools. Of this number attending public school, about 15 per cent are from the outer ring, 20 per cent from the middle ring, and 65 per cent from the core city.

The teachers, like the city, remained fairly static too until about ten years ago. Generally they grew up in New City, went to Teachers' College nearby, did their practice teaching in New City, and returned to teach in New City. Few had ever lived, traveled, or taught elsewhere. Promotions were from within the system and were often based more on *who* people knew than on *what* they knew. But about ten years ago, the first "outside" superintendent of schools was finally hired, and he began to scour the country and bring to New City other "outside" talent—teaching and administrative. New City now has about 40 per cent "outside" teachers, and 60 per cent "inside" teachers. The 40 per cent who have been brought in from outside are of widely divergent cultures, talents, and places of origin. The 60 per cent who once represented the cultural composition of the city are no longer representative of the city population, and average twenty-five years of teaching experience in New City.

The "native" and the "outside" parents and teachers of New City are all worried, and they have good reason to be. Student revolts against teachers, peers, and curriculum occur frequently in the middle and upper schools. Juvenile delinquency, drug use, teen-age marriages and divorces, illegitimacy rates, and incidents of venereal disease have more than doubled in the past five years. Teen-agers who have to attend clinics for medical care of infectious syphilis and other veneral diseases have been found to have no knowledge about their diseases, and young, unmarried, pregnant girls have been found to have little or no biological knowledge in relation to what has happened and is about to happen to them. Many students are leaving school as soon as they legally can, and are multiplying the unemployment and crime figures. Unemployment and illegitimacy costs are straining the city budget and further demoralizing residents who must accept public welfare payments. Summertime riots have caused small businesses to leave the core city and housing there to deteriorate further, but redevelopment is slow and expensive.

The teachers who are newer to New City complain that the curriculum in the schools is far behind the times, but many of the older teachers defend the traditional fare which, they point out, has helped to produce a lot of outstanding local citizens. Some elementary school teachers know they should be as concerned as upper school teachers about the problems that are developing, but others say that these are not problems that lower schools have to be concerned about. Even though evidence shows that the problems are citywide and not centered in just one or two socioeconomic groups, the tradition-oriented teachers tend to scapegoat and blame all of the recent ills of New City's society on "those people down there in the rents." Emergent-oriented teachers countered this oversimplified, stereotyped view and insisted that not only are the problems equally existent in outer city and suburbs, but that responsibility for doing something about the problem is citywide.

And so the recriminations and counterarguments went while the problems developed and got worse. It was not until advisory groups, composed of many segments of the city's culture and of both newer and older teachers, got together to study various aspects of the problems that constructive actions began to take place. As time went on, these groups were joined by teachers and administrators from lower, middle, and upper schools and by people with special knowledge and talents in city agencies, the university, churches and synagogues, and clubs and organizations. New guidelines and programs have evolved in New City's schools and in their neighborhood and community institutions. These projects have special relevance to the lives of the city's young people and are designed to strike directly at the heart of current concerns. They can, and will, change when times and concerns change but the patterns of cooperative concern and action will, it is hoped, remain. Among the outcomes of the interacting lay-professional groups are these programs that are helping to change young people's lives and life skills:

1. *Teacher aide programs* to involve other professionals and paraprofessionals with educators at various school and community sites. Aides for teachers are both paid and volunteer.
2. A *youth-and-the-law project* involving lawyers, social workers, juvenile court workers and officials, and teachers.
3. A program of *family life and sex education* for children from kindergarten through high school and for parents and other interested adults. Cooperating were teachers, church leaders, social agencies, the city health department, private doctors and nurses, psychologists and psychiatrists, and university professors with various specialties.
4. A *talent-search project* involving teachers and people with special vocations and avocations in the arts and humanities.
5. A *Head Start program* for preschool children.
6. A series of *intergroup education seminars* for adults, teachers, parents, and other interested persons. This was accompanied by cooperative curricular experiences for students.
7. A *volunteer tutoring program* involving high school and college students, as well as interested citizens, wtih younger students.
8. *Neighborhood youth centers* and *summer-camp and recreation programs* involving teachers, parents, and others.
9. A *sister-school program* in which teachers and students planned cooperatively with parents a variety of intraschool projects and activities.
10. K–12 *social studies and American history curriculum* to include more emphases on current events and problems and more up-to-date information about the role and contributions of Afro-American and other culture groups in American society.

Among the outcomes of interacting between lay and professional groups are school-community programs that are helping to change young people's lives and life skills.

Photo courtesy of American Friends Service Committee.

We will tell you more about some of these shortly, but for now we want to emphasize the far-reaching significance of New City's approach to school–community curriculum that is germane to the lives of its boys and girls. New City has not licked all of its problems, of course. In fact it has only begun to set goals toward which to work and to work out mutually supportive school–community techniques for accomplishing them. But teachers in New City are not facing the problems alone, nor need they defend their procedures and outcomes; the responsibility for success or failure is being shared by the community. There is a new sense of purpose and direction as more *lay professionals* (the term educators use for people in professions other than teaching), *paraprofessionals* (a term for people with no special training but who can also help in various ways), teachers, and parents team up. And the youth of New City are the beneficiaries, as will be other New Cities of tomorrow.

Teachers Team Up

Team teaching is not really new; James Hosie (19) and his colleagues developed forms of team teaching that were called *cooperative group plans* in the 1930's, and by the mid 1950's Anderson and Keppel were sponsoring *team teaching* in Massachusetts schools. Describing the Lexington, Concord, and Newton experiments in Massachusetts, Morse (20) says that they were designed to "narrow the gap between research and practice by linking the university with public schools systems to make teaching more attractive and effective and to extend the influence of gifted teachers." He quotes Keppel as saying, also, that "the time has come to recognize the difference between those who make a lifetime career in education and those who stay only a few years, or who teach part time."

Team teaching plans we have observed in operation vary from teams of two teachers to teams involving several teachers. Grouping of children with teams of teachers, student teachers, and teacher aides also varies widely. In general, the organization and objectives of team teaching are described thus (21):

> Basically, team teaching is an arrangement that provides for having two or more teachers, with abilities and skills that complement each other, assume joint responsibility for directing the learning activities of a group of students. Together, the members of the team take charge of planning lessons, developing appropriate methods and materials, and teaching and evaluating a program of studies for their student group.

In all of the descriptions of team teaching we have found, three important dimensions of team influence are not mentioned. First, the potential for pairing or teaming teachers so that members of the team represent different cultural groups is important. Not only will an intercultural team of teachers cross-fertilize one another, but the children for whom they are responsible will have before them a model of intercultural cooperation at all times. Ensuring that there are intercultural teams of teachers in every school is a prime responsibility of those recruiting teachers and staffing schools. This does not mean that a white teacher is added to a team of black teachers simply because he is white. His preparation and background must also be appropriate for the job description. But it does mean that recruiters deliberately use broader yardsticks for measuring potential benefits of the team teaching situation. Having intercultural teams also means having people who have lived in other parts of the country or world, who speak other languages, or who come from different socioeconomic groups as well as being of different colors, creeds, or sexes.

Concomitantly, it also seems important for teams of teachers and prospective teachers to be composed of both males and females so that each group of children has contact with both sexes in teaching–learning situations, and so that the team can help one another be more aware of the different ways that sexual acculturation affects teacher attitudes about children.

Second, the deliberate inclusion of student teachers and teacher aides offers a great deal of potential that has not been emphasized strongly enough. Student teachers and aides are often relegated to those duties that have been traditionally considered appropriate for "noncertified personnel." These are generally in areas defined as "relieving teachers of nonteaching chores." This, we think, is unfortunate. Student teachers may be closer to students, in age and in empathy, than are many certified teachers. Aides from children's own neighborhoods and cultures may be able to get through to them when others cannot.

Third, the team of teachers responsible for the *total* program for children must make sure that they consider their various responsibilities in connection with community affairs and home visits just as important as planning appropriate lessons, methods, and materials. Team teaching has often bogged down in more departmentalization and tighter grouping with emphases on subject matter and pigeonholing children rather than on broadening community and cultural life skills. Often, the team leader becomes so involved with administration that he has little contact with children, although he may originally have been designated the leader because of his superior relationships with young people. And unless out-of-school responsibilities to children are taken seriously, no one on the team really knows or works directly with children and their parents. Ideally, team teaching is designed not so much for better subject matter teaching as it is for ending the isolation of the individual classroom teacher, for counteracting the sometimes detrimental influence of one teacher, and for creating "learner-centered organization where our activities are not hampered as in an egg crate organization" (22).

Our purpose here is not to point out the advantages or the disadvantages of team teaching—there are numbers of both—but rather to emphasize the importance of bringing together teachers, children, and other adults who will deliberately foster through the very act of their being together *intergroup* and *intercultural* education.

Children Team Up

We come now to the necessity for breaking the rigid grouping patterns that have caused children in the tradition-oriented school to be labeled at early ages as unsuccessful, fairly successful, quite successful, or very successful, or to put it another way, unworthy, fairly worthy, quite worthy, or very worthy. These groups quite often correlate closely with family income and minority-majority culture groups. The teams of teachers, parents, student teachers, aides, and children we are recommending have the potential to make every child feel more successful and more worthy from the first day they ever attend school whether we are talking about preschool, elementary school, middle school, or upper schools.

"You can't learn to tango with someone who knows only the foxtrot! Every bit of evidence we have tells us that whether we are talking about so-called social learning or specific subject-oriented learning, the quality of learning that occurs is influenced by the individuals with whom we associate. How does one learn to play a better game of bridge or golf? Certainly not by playing with those who know as little as, or less than, we do about these games. Nor can one learn to sing from a nonsinger or to read from a nonreader" (23).

The way children are grouped in school may be the only chance many children ever have to be associated with people of other culture groups or of different socioeconomic groups; and the way they are grouped may very well determine whether their school experiences will be rich and profitable ones or harmful and demoralizing ones. We know that society generally sees certain segregated, homogeneous groups as either inferior or superior. We know, too, that children's self-egos have already been conditioned by some of this before they come to school.

We already know that grouping should be used as a social force for personal development, and we know that sheer numbers of students in our schools make it necessary to group children. We also know that "the uneven growth patterns of individual children make grouping hazardous" (19).

Cross-grouping among different culture groups has received a great deal of attention in this decade, and has most often been proposed as a force for counteracting the attitudes and interests of low socioeconomic groups. But Meil and Kiester (24) point out that, "although other races, other nationalities, other generations have a great deal to teach them, there is little in their education to familiarize them with the rich diversities of American life. In this sense, despite the many enviable features of their environment, the children of *suburbia* are being *shortchanged.*"

Class and caste grouping based on immediate school neighborhoods, and academic achievement scores is deplorable grouping practice. It often results in inferior teaching because teachers think they are teaching to an assumed level; and studies show that when teachers think they are teaching to "an assumed level" of achievement or intelligence, they are apt to do more lecturing, more teaching by *telling*, more rigid rote teaching–learning activities, more teaching for test scores, and to have more rigid and formal classrooms. Children in these situations are literally *forced* to conform, cheat, or give up entirely.

No emergent-oriented teacher can agree that children should be put into groups for the purpose of having the same experience in the same way at the same time with others who are supposedly "like" them and "need" these experiences. Any emergent-oriented school will look for new and imaginative ways to group children. A very good beginning will have been made when school staffs make sure that diversified groups of teachers, student teachers, parents, aides, and volunteers will be working together with children. The stage is then automatically set to group children for learning for some of the same purpose we use in combining teams of adults who will be helping them.

Let us begin to think about new ways to group children by saying that all children will probably make more academic and social progress when they are provided with opportunities to have sufficiently long contacts with wider ranges of talents, interests, abilities, attitudes, and cultures. They will be better prepared to live in the diverse social climates of the future, and they will be better able not only to adapt to change, but also to effect constructive changes.

Since school and neighborhood out-of-school grouping is probably as detrimental to children's learning opportunities as any other one factor, let us make sure that school environments bring together children and adults grouped for *multiformity* rather than *conformity*. Heterogeneous, diverse groups will have different parts, elements, and qualities; and regrouping can occur in order to combine different ages, interests, special aptitudes, and cultures for individuals and for individuals in groups.

Think about these possibilities, find out more about them, and make your own observations about why these statements are or are not feasible:

1. If underachievers grouped together "tend to give one another negative support," as Bowman (25) has found that they do, why not group children of different achievement levels together? The school could ensure learning from one another, and benefit by helping one another learn.
2. If "not only later educational opportunities but also subsequent job opportunities become increasingly fixed by early school performance," as Bruner (26) claims, and the way children are grouped causes them to "become victims of an often senseless irreversibility of decision," then doesn't the school have a definite responsibility to sponsor flexible, often changed grouping arrangements?
3. If "the myth of homogeneity can be a dangerous one, leading teachers to impose a stereotype upon a group, and by teaching to an as-

sumed *type,* make less provision for the unique individuals than they would in classes they know to be heterogeneous," as Wilhelms (27) and others state, on what grounds can so-called homogeneous grouping be defended by educators? What grouping conditions would best ensure that teachers make better provisions for the unique individuals in groups?

4. If "a child tends to produce in his behavior anything that the culture demands, if it is in his repertoire of possible responses" and if "groups thus supply goals toward which children aspire and grow," as Olson's (28) research implies, how can grouping be arranged so that there are goals toward which to aspire and grow, especially when his neighborhood groups do not provide higher aspiration goals?

5. If the reason some schools put children into "ability" groups for reading, arithmetic, and other subjects is "because schools historically have been dominated by the data of curriculum construction and teaching methods rather than the evidence on growth," as Strauss (29) says, how can children be grouped so that emphasis will be on various evidences of growth? Can you justify grouping on the basis of subject matter and teaching methods rather than on principles of child growth and development?

6. If "the effects of racial composition of schools are cumulative; [and] the longer Negro students remain in racially isolated schools [and classes], the further they fall behind" (U.S. Civil Rights Commission, *Racial Isolation in the Public Schools,* 1966) is a verity, how can school systems justify some schools that are almost entirely or entirely composed of Negro students even though it is more convenient for children to go to the school nearest them? What are the advantages and disadvantages of pairing certain classes or certain schools? How will you handle parents of different cultures who fear the effects of another group on their own children if schools are intermingled? And what effects do you think these parental fears will have on children and the success of pairing plans if parents are not involved in making the experiment a success?

7. If stratification of society has resulted from education of the past, and if democracy means elimination of stratification among social classes and true equality for all men, how can schools create models through grouping procedures that will help to eliminate the attitudes and behaviors that perpetuate stratification?

Albert Cohen (30), a sociologist, has this to say about how children left to their own devices group themselves if there is nothing in their lives to make them feel that they are of some importance:

If by the rules of the game, you are no account, one thing you can do is get together with other losers and change the rules. Good becomes bad and bad, good. Toughness, indifference toward school becomes the new norm. You may even acquire stature in the group by defiance of authority and by being punished. Middle-class families equip a child before he gets to school with much of the behavior and skills that the school is called upon to inculcate. Teachers, faced with the problems of keeping order in the classroom, like children who show ambition, achievement, are willing to stick to a job, speak correct English, and are neat and able to control their emotions. This is not because the teachers are undemocratic, but their democracy takes the form of judging all by the same standards, and these are the standards of the middle-class home.

Compare this statement with Sarah Lou Hammond's (31):

There are those who say that homogeneous grouping offers more chance for success and happiness, eliminates snobbishness and conceit of bright pupils, and that slow children do not experience the discouragement of daily failures. These ideas are based on the assumption that homogeneous grouping provides for better attitudes in pupils.

We do not propose answers to the questions we have raised. We hope, instead, that new teachers just beginning their teaching careers will *use* their knowledge of what has been discussed here to question rigid grouping practices and to experiment with new grouping arrangements they can defend with action research. It is our contention that children need to live, work, and play with people of all ages, representing diverse groups, and that the school is the only logical place in the real-life world of today that can provide centers of discovery and laboratories for intergroup cooperation, action, and education for democratic living and for democracy itself. We say that our hope lies in new teachers who will *use* what they have learned, because past generations of educators, who have also had some of this information available to them, have not tried to put it into practice. Tradition-oriented themselves, they quickly fitted into the patterns they found in the schools to which they went and were soon vowing that these were "best."

Furthermore, assumptions about grouping are inescapably linked to assumptions about human potentialities. Just as children who have the misfortune to be grouped on the basis of frailties or problems not of their own making tend to give one another negative support, so children who have the good fortune to be grouped on the basis of their strengths and diversities will tend to give one another positive support. As teachers learn from one another and from children, so will children learn from one another and from teachers. The very act of learning from and with someone else will improve one's own performance if the interaction and exchanges are planned to produce positive results and create new directions.

Problems in Intergroup Relations

Intergroup relations are among the most controversial, explosive, and divisive of all human relationships. Even though lower schools and colleges give considerable attention to the less controversial aspects of human relations, teachers need better preparation for the problems they will face that come about because of circumstances of race, religion, social class, nationality, and varying intellectual and social immaturities.

As in all aspects of human behavior, knowledge alone does not ensure adequate preparation for teachers to deal with children as persons, to work with parents of all races and cultures, and to understand and use community conditions to affect children's development as fully functioning individuals. What really counts is not so much what people *know*, but what they *believe* and how they *behave*. There are often no experiences, either before or during college, that give teachers and others the *direct learning experiences* they need in order to understand and practice the rich possibilities for improved human behavior that are inherent in human diversities.

That there are problems, strong feelings related to individual and group prejudices and ethnocentricities, and strong controversies that develop even when teachers *think* they are practicing good human relations is irrefutable. Unless the human equation is taken into account, classroom communication breaks down, community communications break down, and human relationships are mutilated by fears, feelings of inferiority or superiority, and by indifference and hostility. Any realistic preparatory programs for teachers must face these problems honestly, knowing that simply having high ideals for the human race is not enough, and knowing that teaching better human relations really means changing attitudes, biases, prejudices, and ethnocentrism.

Race and Race Relations

The decades of this century have been witness to racial horrors without precedent in history—gas ovens for millions of Jews in Nazi Germany, starvation for Biafrans in Nigeria, open conflict and death on the streets of our cities. As race pits itself against race, those who fall on the wrong side of the color line or the wrong side of the religious culture line suffer most. When only one-seventh of the world's people are Jews or Christians, when one-third of our own nation is economically deprived, and when three-fourths of the world's population is nonwhite, we cannot postpone direct teaching of good, positive human relations and cooperation.

For the uninitiated who insist that "we don't have any race problems here—the children are all white (or all black, orange, or purple)," let us investigate a few disquieting incidents.

1. In New York City, racial overtones become apparent when fighting broke out around the issue of who should have the right to hire, assign, fire, or transfer teachers in the Ocean Hill-Brownsville experimental school district in Brooklyn. The conflict erupted into overt antiblack, anti-white, and anti-Semitic incidents, and when the smoke began to clear, much more than union-management antagonism was revealed:

Less than a week after the teachers struck in September, 1968, Jacques Torczyner, president of the Zionist Organization of America, warned that "thousands of Jewish school teachers" faced expulsion because black extremists played a major role in the decentralized school boards in New York. "We have a new brand of anti-Semitism," said he. Several black proponents of decentralization later attacked the Jewish leadership of the teachers' union. A teacher at Ocean Hill, who claimed he only wanted to demonstrate the depth of feeling on the subject, read a pupil's anti-Semitic poem on the radio. A consultant to the Metropolitan Museum misedited an introduction to the catalog of its Harlem exhibition. Several paragraphs originally intended to explain the roots of black anti-Semitism were distorted into sounding anti-Semitic themselves. The Anti-Defamation League rushed out a poorly researched study on the rise of black anti-Semitism. Newspapers helped to raise the temperature of the Jewish community. White anti-Semites sat back and enjoyed the conflict of their enemies, Jews and blacks (32).

2. New York is not alone in its racial tensions and overt racism. In one smaller New England city, Italian heads of families armed themselves with guns and vowed "they would shoot any nigger who dared walk up our street" when ghetto residents rioted. On one Saturday night alone, thirty-two cars in that neighborhood were found to contain firearms, although few firearms were confiscated in the ghetto. The problem in this city seemed to be that Irish domination of the city was waning and two groups of people were demanding new management and control powers. The Italian-Americans felt that they were "due" to inherit power next, and the Negro Americans felt that they were long "overdue." In this same city, striking teachers called all other teachers who crossed the picket line "dirty nigger lovers" regardless of their race or nationality.

3. One prominent Afro-American community official tells of his own child's rejection of him because he was darker skinned than the boy's mother. Parents' day at school was approaching and their son reminded them almost nightly, always adding casually, "You'll be there won't you, Mom? And you'll be too busy to come, won't you, Dad?" Both parents assured their son that they intended to be present, and that neither was ever too busy to attend something that important. When the big day finally arrived, both parents attended open house, saw the usual displays of children's work, talked with the teachers and other children, and toured the school. They noticed that their son seemed withdrawn and unhappy during their visit, and later that evening they questioned him about why

A professional teacher seizes every opportunity, planned and unplanned, to help children develop insights basic to understanding peers and adults and to help them grow in interfaith and intercultural understanding. What really counts is not so much what people know, but what they believe and how they behave. Good teachers seek direct experiences that will help them and others understand and practice the rich possibilities for improved human behavior that are inherent in human diversity.

(Photo by Reginald Jackson.)

he had seemed so unhappy. He turned angrily to his father and demanded, "Dad, why are you so *black?*" It had never before occurred to either parent that their child's predominantly white school culture was white-oriented and white-dominated. The mother might have "passed" had she visited school alone, but the darker-skinned father was not a desirable sire in this situation. Furthermore, the father reported to school officials, there was nothing in the classroom or in the school—no books, pictures, or other indications—to indicate to white or to black children that families were other than white, blonde, and blue-eyed.

4. Another Afro-American father, who is an elementary school principal, tells the story of his son's observations soon after beginning kindergarten. The family was well educated, with a long history of backgrounds in the ministry and in education. They had never used epithets of any kind in their home, and even though their son knew that he was a Negro he had never heard derogatory words for Negroes or any other group. "Hey, Dad, there's some niggers in our class at school," he announced at the dinner table one evening. His parents were forced to explain to him that this is the word some people who don't know any better use to describe people like them. "But the other kids say that only some people are niggers," was his reply.

Awareness in Young Children

What is actually known about how early and at what age children become aware of racial differences? Remember that in a study described earlier [The Philadelphia Early Childhood Project (10)], the findings revealed that among kindergarten and first-grade children, (1) there is repeated labeling of specific groups, especially in conflict situations; (2) young children already hold fixed notions of other groups and think in stereotypes, and (3) young children are very much aware of racial group differences. Furthermore, it was found that 9 per cent of these children already expressed open rejection of Catholics, 27 per cent rejected Jews, and 68 per cent rejected Negroes.

Clark (33) found that young children are not only aware of racial differences, but also begin to associate darker skin color with being "dirty." When they studied the attitudes of 253 nonwhite children between the ages of three and seven, half of them attending a segregated southern school and half attending an integrated northern school, they found strong attitudes of self-rejection. When these children were asked to choose the doll that "looks bad" (between a brown doll and a white doll), 59 per cent chose the nonwhite doll. When asked to choose the doll that "looks nice," 42 per cent of these children chose the white doll. In similar types of studies, white children have shown even greater degrees of rejection of darker skin colors and of prejudice when asked to choose between dolls of light skin and dark skin.

By age twelve, behavior rejection replaces verbal rejection, and at about age nine or ten, children cease to choose individuals of other races or ethnic groups as playmates or as friends they would like to sit near in class. The problem of racial rejection, in terms of both attitude and behavior, begins before a child comes to school and develops in predictable degrees and kind as a child grows older. We have discussed Stember's conclusions in relation to the effects of traditional education on reducing prejudice and stating that merely raising the educational level will not necessarily reduce prejudice against minority groups by community majority groups.

This does not say that education cannot be a powerful force against the development of prejudice, or that different types of education cannot counteract existing prejudices. But it certainly does imply that traditional education has not been able to counteract race biases. Each of us is a product of acculturation germane to our race and to other races, and surely we can assume that no child is born prejudiced. We can assume that prejudice and ethnocentrism develop in home and neighborhood cultures, that they are acquired somewhere in the process of child-rearing and home influence.

Minority-Majority Group Racism

A common misunderstanding is that prejudice and racism are problems of majority groups but not of minority groups. Many studies of racial attitudes show that minority groups also have antipathies and stereotypes about other groups as well as about their own groups. Several studies have shown that there is a greater average ethnic prejudice among people with darker skins than among people with lighter skins. Recent conflicts have illustrated vast discrepancies between militant and moderate blacks. One study compared the attitudes of black and white college students, high school students, and adults regarding their willingness to have varying degrees of association with twenty-four different racial, religious, and nationality groups. The study revealed that in each comparison, whites were agreeable to closer association with each of the other groups named than were Afro-Americans (34).

Other studies confirm the existence of prejudice among Jewish groups, even revealing anti-Semitism among Jews. Descendants of Irish immigrants describe the intra-attitudes of early Irish settlers and include in their explanations the disdain of the "lace curtain" (or more highly educated and affluent Irish) for the "shanty Irish" (or "lower" class Irish). In the New England cities to which some Irishmen first came, the "lace curtain Irish" stoned the "shanty Irish" and chased them back to their homes on the other side of towns or rivers if they found them out-of-bounds after dark.

The most serious aspect of prejudice is its effect upon the members of those groups toward whom it is directed. It is often expressed in discrimination against the out-groups, in acts of segregation, and, in extreme forms, in physical attacks against the persons and properties of the out-group. Less extreme expressions of prejudice include jokes and name-calling. Thoughtlessly worded epithets are as inflammatory as billy clubs when used by police, for example, and the word "nigger" is supposed to have set off the Watts riots in Los Angeles. The Washington, D.C., police force has available to them a list of "insulting words," and this "prohibited list" has included all of the well-known and frequently used slurs on ethnic groups, among which are: *spic, wop, kike, chink, burrhead, dago, nigger, polack, bohunk, limey, frog, kraut, Shylock, chocolate drop, boy,* and *darkie.* All of these lists, however, overlooked the fact that the fore-most minority group in Washington in 1968 was white (there were 292,000 whites compared to 506,000 blacks). So the city's Human Relations Coun-cil issued some "separate but equal" word of advice to the black recruits on the police force during their orientation training. The Council warned that blacks dealing with nonblacks (minority group people) must take special care not to use two additional inflammatory words—*whitey* and *honkey.*

Sociologists caution us that not all behavior of minority-group persons is the result of prejudice or discrimination against them—that a great deal of it is a consequence of their social class status. However, aside from social class influences, they indicate that prejudice develops precisely those qualities of behavior that the dominant group dislikes.

Expressions of Racism and Prejudice

According to Simpson and Yinger (35), expressions of racism and preju-dice related to racism have the following kinds of consequence on those who are the recipients, or the objects, of the prejudice.

1. Feelings of insecurity, often expressed in hypersensitiveness.
2. Feelings of inferiority often to the extent of self-hate.
3. Feelings of superiority, which take the form of increased prejudice, not only toward the dominant group, but also against other minorities and even against members of one's own group.

They also say that distinct kinds of behavior seem to result from atti-tudes formed because of prejudice.

1. Resignation and passivity, including the lowering of aspirations and mo-tivation, as protection against further frustration.
2. Symbolic status-striving that takes such forms as flashy displays of jewels, clothes, and automobiles; clowning and other forms of exhibitionism.
3. Clannishness.
4. Aggression toward the dominant group, other minorities, and one's own group. Among lower socioeconomic groups this often takes the form of physical aggression.
5. Neuroticism and, in its extreme form, mental illness.

We have said that there is intergroup competition for the economic and political rewards of income, prestige, and power—and this competition is often the impetus for making use of racist tactics. In the competition between Oriental and native white Americans in labor crews on the West Coast of the United States, prejudice against the Oriental "newcomers" served the purpose of this kind of conflict. We see the same kind of strategy in the struggle between rival politicians in the Deep South, where antiblack and prosegregation pronouncements often appear to be prerequisites to campaigning and to winning elections.

Traditions of culture seem to be equally powerful sources of racial prejudice. It is true that maladjusted, neurotic personalities may predispose individuals to racial prejudice, but well-adjusted people can be "expected to exhibit about the same amount of prejudice" as their parents and their subcultures, according to Saenger (36). It is, then, the influence of culture that determines the accepted expressions of racism and prejudice and the singling out of groups against whom it is directed. Horowitz (37) wrote that "attitudes toward Negroes are now chiefly determined not by contacts with Negroes, but by contact with the prevalent attitude toward Negroes." This kind of cultural attitude is conveyed by the mere observance of, and participation in, the in-group patterns of discrimination, segregation, and racism.

The power of cultural influence can be illustrated by the fact that even people with substantial degrees of racism have been found willing to participate voluntarily in unsegregated situations when their fellow participants seem to indicate that such participation is appropriate and will be accepted and welcomed (37). A great deal of racism is a sort of "clinging to the vine," a blind conformity to prevailing folkways. It does not serve any functional purpose and is detrimental to the potential development of individuals.

Racism in School Curriculum

Racial and class biases are implicit as well as explicit. Since they are prevalent in society generally, they exist in classrooms in the composition of groups of children who attend school together, in the attitudes of the adults who work with children in schools, and in the learning materials that have existed in traditional schools.

Textbooks and children's library books, films and filmstrips, and pictures and charts have been, until very recently, reflective of white-oriented America. "As a taxpayer, I object to federal money being spent for books which perpetuate outmoded racist doctrines," Dorothy Sterling (38) told the House Committees on Education and Labor hearings on the *Treatment of Minority Groups in Textbooks and Library Books.*

Another prominent American, Lerone Bennett (39), says that "The American school system has made the fourth R—racism—its traditional three R fare . . . it permeates the entire curriculum . . . it is reflected not only by *what the schools are* (location and staff-student make-up) but also by *what they teach,* or to be more precise, by *what they do not teach."*

James Baldin (40) thinks that "if one managed to change the curriculum in all schools so that Negroes learned more about themselves and their real contributions to this culture, you would be liberating not only Negroes, you'd be liberating white people who know nothing of their own history." And Wright (41) told the teachers at New York State's Summer Institutes on Integration that "Quarantined as he is in a school segregated by de facto racism, and having only companions like himself and books oriented only to his own world and history, the white child, too, is robbed of knowing about the real world he soon must join."

"The venality of publishers is appalling. They have a moral responsibility to stop pandering to the racial mentalities of the North and the South," insists Herbert Hill (42), author, teacher, and National Labor Secretary of the National Association for the Advancement of Colored People.

Several years ago a panel of historians from the University of California were asked to review the history texts used in California's schools. After studying a dozen or so books, they reported that the texts reflected "views on racial and sectional themes that have been rejected or drastically modified by the best of current historical scholarship." They found that in many books the Negro American simply did not exist, unless he was shown picking cotton. In others, slavery was sugar-coated, the Reconstruction period after the Civil War was greatly misrepresented, and the role of the African Americans in the Civil War was either grossly distorted or omitted entirely. They were concerned that much of the material in the books was not only bad history, but that it was the kind of bad history that reinforces "notions among whites of their superiority and among Negroes of their inferiority."

Dorothy Sterling describes a group of New York City high school students who had been designated as the best history students at their schools and who were chosen to interview her on a radio program a few years ago. In the course of the discussion, they informed her that American Negroes were the only people in history who had not fought for their own freedom. When she asked them where they had picked up this bit of misinformation, one of them told her that he "read it in a book" and another said "my teacher told us." She remembers one of the first adult biographies that she read as a young girl—a Literary Guild selection, *Meet General Grant,* by William E. Woodward, and quotes a few sentences from that book which said, "The American Negroes are the only people in the history of the world, so far as I know, that ever became free without any effort of their own. . . . They had not started the War nor ended it. They twanged banjoes around the railroad stations, sang melodious spirituals and believed that some Yankee would soon come along and give each of them 40 acres of land and a mule."

This, she says, is one of the many lies and legends that we were all brought up on and that are still being passed on to our children today. The truth, which can be verified from official government records, is that more than 200,000 Negro Americans fought in the Union army and navy during the Civil War, and that although there were great waves of German and Irish immigration in the decade just before the war, Germans supplied 176,000 fighting men and the Irish supplied 144,000. Negro American soldiers were much more numerous than any other minority group; 37,300 of them lost their lives, 17 soldiers and sailors were awarded Congressional Medals of Honor, and Abraham Lincoln said that, "without the military help of black freedmen, the war against the South could not have been won." When teachers, too, have been taught myths and have never learned the true facts, and when books are based on fiction instead of fact, young people do not get reliable information, as was shown during the radio interviews with the "best" history students.

When black and white schoolchildren do not see black as well as white people in their schools and in their learning materials, both races can only conclude that there must be something wrong with being black. Similar instances can be found in which other groups have been misinterpreted or libeled—Italian Americans as gangsters, Jewish Americans as caricatures, Oriental Americans as washermen, and American Indians as dirty savages. Every race has its share of humanitarians and scholars who are prominent in history and in contemporary life. The civil rights revolution has forced changes in some textbooks, library books, magazine and newspaper advertising, television programs, and films and filmstrips. But many textbook publishers still publish three editions of the same book —one with all white children, a second with a few suntanned children, and a third similar to the first except that the teachers wear nun's garb. One edition for the South, one for the urban schools in the North, and one for Catholic parochial schools! These educational materials are just as bigoted as the ones we had before.

Antidotes for Racism
1. *More reliable, representative, and relevant teaching materials* are becoming available. Selecting unbiased and historically accurate materials, creating one's own accurate materials if necessary, and making sure that every classroom has bulletin boards and other learning centers well filled with multiethnic illustrations is the responsibility of a professional teacher. All schools, whether presently racially isolated and segregated or not, should mirror the composition of the larger society, and all classroom and learning resource center materials should measure up to new criteria so that each child will have an up-to-date concept of society and of history. Materials that do not measure up to new criteria for accuracy and diversity should be destroyed. Under no circumstances should they be passed on to "less fortunate" schools as sometimes happens. The condi-

tions that newly purchased materials should meet and the materials from periodicals and other sources used in schools include these:

a. They must be historically accurate.
b. They must be racially and ethnically representative.
c. They must not label or stereotype any group.
d. They should represent new research and scholarship.
e. They should support intercultural and intergroup education.
f. They should provide wide personal choice and relevance for students.
g. They should represent rural, suburban, and urban concepts.
h. They should include contemporary literature as well as classics.

But in spite of national hearings, the urging of civil rights groups, and wide national and local publicity, the adoption of new and better books and other teaching materials is slow and spotty. For one thing, textbooks that will "sell everywhere" omit most of what is real and accurate in American life. Dolmatch (43) says that "With new eyes, publishers and educators have looked at their older books, only to see blonde children, suburban homes, white-collar fathers, and grandparents on farms. They have now begun to produce and use what one Negro educator has called color-me-brown books as naive in their own way as their predecessors." He goes on to say that in some cases hardly more than a tan or a sunburn has been applied, and in others we have books about Negro heroes and courses on Afro-American history and culture instead of books about heroes and history—black and white. In a way, these are replacing previous exclusions and distortions with a new kind of separatism and a new type of segregation.

For another thing, selection and adoption procedures are slow and unwieldy, budgets for new materials are woefully inadequate, and worst of all, local power structures are slow to change. Publishers' accomplishments are still modest because power structures refuse to buy "radical" books, and so suitable books that are available have not made the impact they should in educational marketplaces. Local power structures usually represent the provincialism of an area, so their viewpoints and perceptions are the ones they want to have reflected in the materials they approve for selection.

Books and other learning materials keep adults and children *provincial* almost as surely as segregation itself does. They could help unshackle teachers, school administrators, parents, and students. Provincialism causes materials selections committees to pander to the mentalities and perceptions of the local politicos, for the real provincialism of people is not a matter of geography but rather of lack of education for cosmopolitan issues. The importance of saturating all schools with books, illustrations, exhibits, and audio-visual learning materials representative of cosmopolitan life is a relatively new concept for teachers and most other adults. They delude only themselves when they say that they "have no racial problems," for national and international problems in today's world are everybody's problems.

Nancy Larrick (44) states the case forcibly when she says that "the impact of all-white books upon 38,600,000 white children [in 1965] is probably even worse [than for Negro children]. Although his light skin makes him one of the world's minorities, the white child learns from his books that he is the kingfish. There seems little chance of developing the humility so urgently needed for world cooperation as long as our children are brought up on gentle doses of racism through their books."

2. *Prolonged,* rather than casual, *intergroup contacts* are another effective antidote for racism. The Cornell University studies of intergroup relations involved fourteen different research surveys and about six thousand persons and confirms the fact that contact between individuals of different groups, whether youths or adults, reduces prejudice in individuals of both minority and majority groups. Two key studies related to the effect of intergroup contact also indicate that such contact reduces prejudice whether the contact is voluntary or required by law, court, or administrative decision. Therefore, it seems logical to create opportunities for intergroup contacts before group tensions and racist overtones have a chance to develop, because forced integration often takes place under strained, tense circumstances.

Of the two key studies mentioned, the first was conducted by the Research Branch of the Army Information and Education Division. It compared the attitudes of white officers and noncommissioned officers in Europe before and two months after black and white companies of soldiers were first integrated in the same armed forces units. After two months of living, working, eating, and socializing together, 77 per cent of these officers were more disposed toward having black soldiers in their companies and none were less favorably disposed toward having them. In a similar survey of white enlisted men, the army found that in those divisions with black soldiers, only 7 per cent of the white enlisted men were opposed to the proposal that black platoons be brought into their companies. Of the men in divisions with no blacks, 62 per cent were opposed to blacks being brought into their companies (45). Obviously, those men who had had the opportunity to know *personally* people of a different race were predisposed to live and fight on their team; but those who had not had that opportunity still harbored their racial antipathies.

Rose (45) also describes a second key study dealing with the effect of integration of races on attitudes of tenants of public housing projects. In this study, Deutsch and Collins studied the changes of white tenants' attitudes toward black tenants in two racially integrated public housing projects. They found that the integrated living pattern created "more frequent and more extensive favorable attitudinal change toward Negro people in the project and also toward Negroes in general." Ending separate black and white units and facilities made intergroup contact possible, and proved that when people are involved in a common undertaking or project for a sufficiently long period of time, racism and prejudices related to race are reduced. We can assume, then, that when these circumstances exist, racial discrimination will at least be lessened.

Since our main concern is to be able to understand and use the techniques that will lessen racism and racial biases, it is also important to know about those situations where interracial and intergroup associations have increased hostilities.

There is a great deal of evidence available to show that complete isolation and insulation heighten racial prejudices and tensions, and increase the potential for interracial conflicts.

There are also some research studies that show that casual contacts or once-in-awhile associations are more likely to increase than to decrease prejudice. This happens when persons meeting under brief, casual circumstances have no real interest in moving toward mutual goals and satisfactions. They are not likely to have enough contact to counteract the ethnocentrism and racial biases they bring to the situation or contact. In a brief encounter, individuals tend to perceive only those traits which confirm their preconceived notions; this is why difficulties develop when children are brought together in schools and then separated again on the basis of a few narrow traits. Frequently the groups that have been educationally disadvantaged over a longer period of time are grouped with one another if one of the grouping criteria is either academic achievement test scores or culture-conditioned I.Q. measures. Often the lowest groups under these circumstances are again frozen into isolated groups that have one color—black. This is just the same as maintaining segregated schools, the only difference is that, within the same schools, some doors are marked "for white only" and some are marked "for black only."

Increased hostilities between and among different races are also more apt to result when integration has taken place among protests, intense community objections based on lack of proper communication and preparation, and civil strife. The observer can see these hostilities when studying the attitudes of parents (both black and white) whose children have been arbitrarily assigned to another school farther from their neighborhood school. They can be seen in the attitudes and behaviors of teachers who have been used to teaching children of only one race or one achievement level and students of other races or different achievement levels are placed in their classes. And they can be seen in the attitudes of students who are acculturated with their own family's racial myths at the dinner table every night—racial myths that reinforce either race inferiority or race superiority.

Recognizing that prolonged intergroup contacts can be a strong antidote for racism, and that the contacts need to be planned so that once the group has been brought together there will be mutually agreed upon goals and expectations, educators should not wait for court mandates. Knowing that the earlier and the longer the contact, the better the intended results will probably be, educators will make sustained efforts to bring children of many races together as early as possible in their school experiences. Realizing that intergroup association, like all other educational dilemmas, has its limitations because of housing patterns and differences in previous school experiences, educators will be sure that the quality of the experiences during the associations they plan will be positive ones for parents and for children, and they will involve parents in the planning before the actual educational experience for children begins.

Under these circumstances, intergroup and interracial associations will begin to affect larger numbers of people before their prejudices have had a chance to jell and to close them off forever from others who can add immeasurably to their happiness, productivity, and general well-being.

Ethnic Origins and Religion

The only people who are really ethnicaly indigenous to our land are American Indians who live either on isolated and insulated reservations or have married across ethnic lines. Immigrants from other nations to America lose their immigrant identifications of other languages and customs by the second or third generation in this country, but there are families newly arrived in the country who are more easily identified by their language, accents, and culture patterns as belonging to a particular ethnic group. In a secondary school and college survey, anecdotes of tension situations that arise in classrooms noted that "in the North Central States are pupils newly come from Italy, Lithuania, Germany, Poland, Scandinavia, Mexico, Latin America, Latvia, Hungary, Belgium, Ireland, and Afghanistan" (46). Other distinct ethnic groups who have come to live in American cities are Puerto Rican, Cuban, and Mexican, and many of these children speak Spanish or use English with difficulty. Although the latter groups speak a common language, the Spanish that is spoken is different, depending on ethnic origin, and Spanish-speaking people do not necessarily understand one another. In addition, their culture patterns differ and many of them find themselves again culturally deprived, the term most often used for lower-class status, in American cities. Prejudice against these groups is widespread and they suffer economic and social discriminations that carry over into school life to cause numerous tension-ridden situations. As we already know, teachers themselves are often prejudiced against certain groups who are different from their own.

Interreligious prejudice is still widespread, although a great deal has been done to ameliorate conflicts and antagonisms created by religious differences. Many families encourage their children to give up associations across religious lines, fearing intermarriage and loss of religious identity. Bitter controversies have been waged during recent decades around the issue of separation of church and state and the elimination of religious observances in schools. Conflicts between Christians and non-Christians arise over Christmas celebrations in schools and on mutually owned community property. Atheists, civil libertarians, and Supreme Court decisions influence sectarian practices in schools as, for example, when the Court handed down a decision excluding sectarian prayers and Bible reading in public schools, causing bitter recriminations by some and applause by others. During the 1960's, waves of anti-Semitic desecrations of synagogues and burial grounds swept across the States, especially in cities. During the 1960 presidential election campaign for John F. Kennedy, anti-Catholic activities reached a new high, and anti-Catholic and intra-Catholic tensions are causing tremendous divisions and antipathies today.

Questions that teachers in service and teachers in preparation have asked about tensions and problems created by ethnic origin and religious differences in classrooms include the following:

- If I find it hard to reconcile my own values and those of some of the families of children in my classroom, what can I do to at least *cope with* and *tolerate* others?
- Are there techniques I can use to help children accept minority group children and to make minority group children feel and behave in less resentful and antagonistic ways?
- Do I have to refrain from mentioning Christmas and Easter entirely if I am teaching in a predominantly non-Christian neighborhood?
- What do you do if a child's religion forbids him to salute the flag or to have any medical or dental attention?
- Is it wrong to instill our own values in the minds of students?
- Why include controversial topics in school curricula at all if they are going to offend some ethnic or religious group?

You will remember that one of the qualities of teachers who are "open individuals" is the ability to bring controversial topics into classroom curricula without attempts at rancor or indoctrination, and that open, emergent-oriented people recognize their own in-group acculturations and try to modify them even though they experience culture shock at new encounters. They are able to understand and accept ethnic and cultural differences, and these become the bases on which rest teachers' abilities to develop new social awareness for themselves and for the children they teach.

While the controversies about prayer versus no prayers in schools have been stirring emotions and tempers, some teachers have used the inter-religious controversies to create vital curriculum experiences for and with their students. When one school district became embroiled in the bitter arguments that centered around whether or not there would be a traditional Christmas crèche on the village green, teachers capitalized on local headlines to have some meaningful lessons about religion. Their objectives included agreement that they would not espouse any one religion, that personal opinions would be accepted if they were not attempts at indoctrination, and that emphasis would be on the role of religion in history, art, music, literature, science, international relations, and various forms of government. Each teacher was to work with groups of concepts that seemed appropriate for the age of the children he taught.

Now picture a group of seven-year-olds discussing people who help them to live with one another well in their communities. Along with the policeman, the fireman, the postman, the doctor, one child wanted to list the minister and God. "Let's put priest instead of minister and God," said another child, "because we don't call ours a minister." "We call ours a rabbi at our synagogue," said another. "Well, we've got a minister!" insisted a third.

Come with us next to a classroom of eight- and nine-year-olds. Most of the children celebrated Christmas, but Johnny's family celebrated Hanukkah. His teacher, who knew little about Hanukkah, borrowed library books to study more about it herself and talked with Johnny's mother to see how the class could learn more about the Festival of Lights. Johnny brought to class records, children's books, a dreidel, and his Menorah. As he lit the candles, explaining that one is customarily lighted each night for eight nights, he told the meanings of each—charity, love, courage, faith, freedom, honesty, knowledge, and peace. He also explained the origin of the celebration and the significance of "eight days of light" for Jewish people. What a wonderful way for children to learn to appreciate one another and to see that values they think are different are also values all men have in common. Johnny's teacher will tell you that for her, too, this was a spiritual experience. She spent the fifth night of Hanukkah at Johnny's house and participated in the family's ritual. Best of all was Johnny's remark to his mother, "She hasn't told me, but I think my teacher must be Jewish."

In another classroom of ten- and eleven-year-olds, representatives of Jewish, Catholic, and Protestant institutions were invited to visit the classroom and explain the major tenets of each religion. The children were fascinated with the differences in the history of the development of the various religions, and in the vocabulary that was used to express the same basic ideas. The origins of Christmas, Yom Kippur, Hanukkah, Epiphany, Lent, Whitsun Eve, Easter, and catechism led into the study of some functions of present-day religious institutions and how they have changed as society has changed from rural to urban and from agrarian to technological patterns of living. They learned about the values of co-operation between religious institutions when they received an invitation to participate in a nondenominational welfare drive sponsored by all of the churches to collect clothing and money to be used in disaster areas throughout the world.

This class got a "good feeling from the inside out" when they gave up their usual holiday room party and brought gifts that they themselves would like to receive to send to a farm school for children in foster homes. Their illustrated bulletin board shared with the rest of the school their understanding of the Biblical admonition "It is more blessed to give than to receive."

We see professional teachers creating the atmosphere, the opportunities, and even the incidents in which children can participate in experiences that will help them to resolve interfaith conflicts and learn the real meanings and roles that religion has played in the lives of men. And we see the modern school planning a total program which is varied and flexible enough to allow participation and encourage contributions by children with widely differing talents, interests, capabilities, and backgrounds. A professional teacher seizes every opportunity, planned and unplanned, for helping children develop insights basic to intercultural understanding.

We asked a kindergarten teacher whether there are opportunities to teach about religion, and she replied, "Goodness, yes! Nature, for instance. Just the other day a rainbow appeared after a shower and we all went to the window to see it. One child said, 'How I wish I could touch those colors'; another one asked, 'What makes all those beautiful colors?'; and a third answered the second with, 'Don'cha know it's the sun shining through the rain? God makes it do that!' Nature walks are a wonderful way to help children appreciate the wonder of the world regardless of what church they go to. But they have to be taken with a grown-up who has a genuine feeling for beauty in creation and for the universality of nature . . . I mean someone who sees the rose, instead of the thorn that snagged her nylons."

Other opportunities present themselves when teachers are conscious of tension situations that develop in classrooms. Teachers are often confused in regard to how to teach about religion, the role of religions in history, and the significance of religion and ethnic origins in American life. Some teachers, consciously or unconsciously, make remarks that reveal anti-Semitism or anti-Catholicism and are deeply resented by parents and students. For example, one teacher assigned his students to select one aspect of religion in American life and write a short paper about it. When he read the papers, he commented to the class that they had dealt with religious matters "illogically," whereupon the children accused him of being prejudiced. He himself believed that the pupils "were not able to think" and said that "they only quoted parrot style things that they did not understand." This teacher not only let his own biases show, but he also missed some excellent opportunities to help children understand the basic differences between and among religions. Further information gathering and group discussions could have helped to open new avenues of thinking, but the teacher's remarks and defensiveness heightened antagonisms and misunderstanding and closed off further inquiry.

Some teachers, fearing charges of partiality, say that they are more severe in criticizing children of their own religious or culture group. Others report hesitancy and discomfort when discussing current affairs that involve religious or cultural minorities when there are members of the group under consideration in the immediate class, as, for example, Arab-Israeli relations. They do not know how to reply when asked for their own opinions, and their silence often says more than a direct, honest reply would. A number of teachers report classroom situations created by members of Jehovah's Witnesses or Adventist groups who, because of religious customs, refuse to salute the flag, to participate in dancing or other social activities, or to attend any functions on Friday or Saturday nights. If teachers cannot find ways to help other classmates understand these kinds of differences, they will not know how to ease the resulting tensions. In some cases notes excusing students from certain activities are required by the school, and a simple explanation quietly given by the teacher helps to eliminate gibes and name calling that occur when such exclusions go unexplained and misunderstood. In a country founded on religious liberty and the freedom to worship in any way one sees fit, meaningless conflicts and tensions arise when the school does not see its role in relation to reinforcing this concept.

Schools need to share with home and community the responsibility for developing in children awareness of the importance of religious and cultural difference in the world of human affairs. Behaviors and actions of inferiority, superiority, exclusion, and rejection are reported in schools where the basic population groups are predominantly of one or another religious or culture group. Often the minority group accuses teachers and others of discriminating against them, and too often teachers merely report these incidents instead of trying to change the negative attitudes that cause the accusations. Reports come from science teachers that there are conflicts that arise between religious teaching and science teaching, for example, difficulties over the teaching of evolution, or difficulties over diet and balanced meal study when some groups have religious taboos against food such as bacon or milk.

Music teachers have problems with some students of particular faiths over the singing of religious music other than their own or over the issue of cultural bias in some folk songs. They report difficulties encountered when Jewish students are unwilling to sing Christmas carols or to participate in a Christmas play, and when Catholic children refuse to go on class trips to churches other than their own. Usually, however, these difficulties can be avoided when teachers take the time to plan ahead of time with parents and community, as well as their students, so that the goals of the activities involved are understood as part of an over-all study of appreciation of history and culture rather than criticism or indoctrination of different ideas and ideals of which parents may disapprove. With sensitivity to the rights and feelings of all concerned, teachers can help children learn to respect and understand one another. Other examples will be given concerning the "how" in the last chapter of this section.

Social Classes and Social Immaturity

Although the newest term for the poor is *culturally deprived,* we all know that the ideas basic to class and caste still exist in society and are therefore matters of deep concern for schools as social institutions. Schools are the most strategic and logical institutions for affecting change in both social status and in ego structures that determine social maturity. Both are directly related to minority culture groups in American society because the largest number of poor people living in the most depressed areas are from minority groups here, and these are the people with the least education and the fewest skills to help them move upward socially and economically. Because of their inadequate skills, lack of education, and minority group membership, they are discriminated against and are often unemployed or are employed in low-paying, menial jobs. Poverty and the conditions imposed upon children and their families by a society of which they cannot be a part deprive young people of the cultural experiences that prepare the middle- and upper-class child for traditional school experiences.

When teachers are unprepared to deal with social and cultural deprivation, the children of the poor are predoomed to failure. By seven or eight years of age they are apathetic, hostile, withdrawn, alienated, convinced that they cannot learn, and have often dropped out of school and society psychologically if not in actuality. At least, they are certainly potential dropouts whom many schools do not hesitate to push along and push out.

Teachers have described classroom situations caused by differences in social levels. Among the problems they mention that cause them concern in classrooms are these: ridicule of pupils who are richer or poorer; derisive treatment of those who are badly dressed or unclean; incidents of name calling and excessive teasing; sensitivity about race, economics, slums, and welfare; formation of cliques based on socioeconomic levels; animosity toward out-group children who try to join the in group; gossip and character assassination; feelings of rejection, superiority, or inferiority which affect ego development and self-esteem; excessive absence and truancy; conflicts over "right" and "wrong"; food served in the school cafeteria (as, for example, recent demands of black students for "soul food"); and feelings of inadequacy because of lack of clothing or money to spend for school supplies. Some teachers say that they themselves lack understanding because they have had no previous experience with lower-class children, other teachers reject the behaviors of students from high economic levels, and still others prefer to work with middle- and upper-class children because they say that "they are generally easier to work with."

All of the social responses that children give are evoked by the social group into which a child is born, and the larger community of which the school is a part. We can assume, certainly, that social behavior is modifiable, and that it is either maintained at the same level or altered by a person's response to animate objects in his environment, that the young social being is not fixed but, rather, flexible. Every member of any group, from the family unit to the larger community, is a potential caretaker of the social development of others if we do not limit the term *caretaker* to its narrowest definitions. An individual displays social behavior toward others and they toward him; they are the social organisms to whose behaviors he will respond. Whether his social group produces favorable results or produces additional anxieties and learning problems is the crux of the dilemma that faces educators.

Knowing that race, religion, ethnic origins, socioeconomic status, and social maturity, or lack of it, are the factors that affect people, and that these are the same factors that affect national, international, and community relations, and being able to modify and redirect them so that they can be channeled in positive and productive directions is the job of social institutions such as the school. It becomes increasingly clear that attitudes and achievements of individuals are affected by their group associations, and that the way teachers perceive children and their possible contributions affects what they expect of them and what and how they teach them. Teachers must, first of all, know more about the effects of social-economic disadvantage on children who are its victims.

The Disadvantaged Rural Child

The disadvantaged rural child is born into a family that is among the 46 per cent of the country's low-income families; his family, by this criterion, earns less than $3,000 per year. He is the country cousin of the urban ghetto child at whom we shall shortly take a closer look, but he is much more isolated than his city cousin. He is isolated by distances, by fast-disappearing agrarian economies and ways of living, by poor education and health programs, by lack of social and cultural opportunities, and by lack of opportunity to associate with others of differing cultures, races, religions, and social status.

Because he does not have available to him proper medical and dental services and may live a long distance from doctors, dentists, or clinics, his health needs often go unmet. His family's extreme poverty may cause him to have been nutritionally starved even before birth, and some researchers are beginning to accumulate evidence to show that this prenatal deprivation adversely affects his potential intellectual development. Even if he has not been nutritionally deprived and his intellectual capacities are normal or above, he gets lower IQ test scores because of his social and cultural isolation. He does not have high occupational aspirations or career hopes for himself because he comes in contact with so few people who live or work differently than his own family does.

He is often absent from school in order to help with farm work or to travel with his family in search of migrant work if he is from a subsistence farming family, a sharecropper's family, a migrant worker's family, or a tenant farmer's family. He is, therefore, not successful in school when he does attend and he becomes an early dropout statistic as soon as legally possible.

Statistics show that he is a low participator in youth clubs and activities, and that he will eventually seek a low-status farm or nonfarm job. The work he will seek is already being automated and will not require his unskilled abilities, so he faces a continually receding horizon of job opportunities whether he remains in the country or migrates to the city.

Since nonwhite families still number about three million on farms, he is apt to be nonwhite although he may be from another race or cultural background. If he is nonwhite, his family is apt to be about a third larger than the average white farm family and his family will have only about half of the income of the average white family. In 1960 he was one of approximately three million nonwhite youths in rural areas of the United States, and thus he suffers both from being poor and from being black.

The probabilities are that he comes from a family whose parents have eight years of schooling or less, and the out-migration of families from his rural area has already caused the accessible churches, schools, and lodge halls that once helped bring his family and neighbors together to be closed. The sparsely populated regions and the geographic isolation of the area where he lives make him hard to find, hard to know about, and harder to reach and help.

He spends less time with peer groups than his city cousin does, and he spends more time with his own family than children in more populated areas do. Because of his isolation, he seems to be freer of rules and regulations that urban and suburban children are, but the seeming freedom and lack of knowledge about rules by which more organized societies live makes him less prepared and less able to cope with life in the more populated areas to which he will probably eventually also migrate. He will be less sympathetic to regulations which he will see as restricting his personal freedom.

Poor health causes earlier death of his parents, whose life span is ten to fifteen years less than that of the average American. Death and premature births have already taken some of his brothers and sisters in larger proportion than in the average American family, and he is less apt to have the numbers of aged relatives that the average American family has. Thus, he may already have lost one or both parents, both grandparents, and a number of brothers and sisters through death even though his family is still larger than the average American family.

Much of what can be done to help the rural impoverished child must now be undertaken by schools. As small district schools have been closed and as the rural child travels farther and farther to attend school, he is beginning to come in contact with more well-qualified teachers, more guidance consultants, more summer school and recreation programs, better equipped and staffed libraries and learning resource centers, and better school programs and course choices. The school is now the main social institution with resources to give him encouragement and help, whether he elects to stay in the country or migrates to the city; his chief hope of upward mobility, of escaping poverty and disadvantagement, rests with education.

The Disadvantaged Urban Child

Like his country cousins, he is also one child among the 46 per cent of the country's low-income families who earn less than $3,000 per year. He differs from his equally poor country cousin in that he probably lives in a city slum or ghetto area and is surrounded, not by space, but by junkyards, equally dilapidated homes of his friends and neighbors, ancient and crowded schools, and bankrupt or abandoned shops and factories. At the school, from which he and his friends play hooky as often as possible, he is an occasional drop-in until he is pushed out or drops out for good to become another statistic in an unskilled urban population no longer needed by a highly skilled technological society.

He is apt to be a member of a gang, both for protection and for companionship. When he and his peer groups do attend school, they are distrustful and resentful of adults, and they sometimes go to sleep there because their living quarters are occupied by too many relatives and friends for them to be able to sleep at home. Home is a place of noise and crowds; there are too many people in too little space with too much leisure time and too little to do with it—a place, also, to avoid as much as possible. This place he calls "home" also knows hunger, disease, and often hopelessness beyond description. There is sometimes a landlord trying to collect rent money the family does not have to pay for the rats, lack of sanitary facilities, cold, and filth they do have. The arrival of the landlord, the welfare worker, or the truant officer is a dreaded event and is about the only time there is absolute quiet until these unwelcome visitors go away.

His family has almost forgotten his father, who came with them to the city in search of work, for he gave up in self-loathing some time ago and disappeared, or spends his time at the cheap gin mill down the street. If the family is fatherless, there are a series of "uncles" who also leave when the "welfare lady" arrives or when another new baby is born.

Most often the urban disadvantaged child has ghetto neighbors who are black, brown, or tanner than white, like his own family. They, too, are the most recent in-migrants to inherit the neighborhoods and schools abandoned by the last out-migrants, but they are more insulated than past waves of newcomers to the city because of their color. They are all victims of urban decay and its handmaidens, in addition to being victims of poor education, broken families, discrimination, malnutrition, and poverty. This child is a prototype of millions of urban poor children whose surroundings and isolation from more affluent areas trap them and dim hope that they will perform differently from the way their families and neighbors perform unless there is immediate and intense intervention by coordinated social agencies and institutions.

Recommendations

"Our nation is moving toward two societies, one black, one white—separate and unequal" is the warning sounded in the *1968 Report of the National Advisory Commission on Civil Disorders* (47). This comes more than a decade after the 1954 Supreme Court Decision (48) ruling that segregated school systems were unconstitutional under the Fourteenth Amendment. The National Advisory Commission Report further states that "what white Americans have never fully understood—but what the Negro can never forget—is that the white society is deeply implicated in the ghetto. White institutions created it, white institutions maintain it, and white society condones it."

Teachers should be familiar with the decisions and recommendations for eliminating isolation of the poverty-stricken and racially insulated groups in this country, as well as with the federal funds being made available for special programs of this nature. The guidelines for fund disbursement change as programs are evaluated and eliminated or extended, so we shall not attempt here to give specific guidelines for this or any other year. Rather, these are general criteria which undergird most of the new recommendations and funds to implement them.

Realizing that integrated schools will not become a practical reality for some time to come, except on a limited basis, because of housing patterns and the objections of white and nonwhite parents to long-distance bussing of their children, the National Advisory Commission of 1968 nevertheless gives the highest long-run priority to integration, saying that "Racial isolation in schools is detrimental to white and Negro. Opportunities for interaction between races must be expanded." If these opportunities cannot be immediately expanded, the recommendation is for "drastically improved quality of ghetto education" with the goal of equality of results for nonwhite schools and all white schools.

Other highlights of the Commission's report include these:

1. Sharply increased efforts to eliminated de facto segregation through urban-suburban and rural-suburban joint educational efforts.
2. Vigorous enforcement of the Civil Rights Act of 1964 and the Supreme Court decision of 1954 to eliminate racial discrimination in northern and southern schools.
3. Expansion of the teacher corps to attract to the teaching profession well-

qualified and highly motivated people who can work effectively with disadvantaged students.
4. Extension of early childhood education to every disadvantaged child in
the country, building on programs such as Project Head Start and preschool education programs, and continuing into and beyond the early
primary school years with programs of educational intervention similar to
present programs known by such names as Higher Horizones, Project Follow Through, and Project Keep Moving.
5. Dramatic improvements in disadvantaged area schools which include
twelve-month compensatory and enrichment programs, and expanded
research and experimentation.
6. Greater federal support for adut basic education to help eliminated adult
and child illiteracy.
7. Enlarged opportunities for parent and community participation in public
school programs and program determination.
8. Expanded opportunities for higher education through federal assistance
for poor people, and revitalized vocational programs emphasizing work
experience, work training, and partnerships with business and industry.

Presently, financial assistance is being given by the federal government
for lay involvement in school programs, breaking up segregated school
groups, implementing the above recommendations, and for additional
special help for two of the groups most often previously ignored or forgotten entirely, the rural disadvantaged and the urban disadvantaged.
For example, Title III of the Elementary and Secondary Education Act
(ESEA) charges the U.S. Commissioner of Education with "the alloca-
tion of 25 percent of the funds to be used for projects of national
significance, with special consideration of *problems of big cities and problems of remote, sparsely settled rural areas.*"
The *Rural Education Studies Teaching Guide* (49) reminds us that
teachers in cities inherit children with problems that are created in rural
areas:

> To focus only upon the problems that rural migrants create *after* they have
> moved to the city is much the same as treating a disease without concern for
> its causes . . . many disadvantaged will continue to stream into our cities,
> but many more will remain in the country and seek subsistence where they
> are less visible.

And the *Urban Education Studies Teaching Guide* (50) reminds us
of the challenges brought about by social revolution and conflict:

> The challenge to schools, to communities, and to universal education itself
> is whether we can rise to the challenges presented by social revolution and
> conflict; whether we can advance human dignity and equal opportunity in a
> precarious, uncertain, and changing world. . . . If we believe that the aca-
> demic and social development of each student go hand in hand and that the

kinds of materials and procedures we use in schools can make real differences, we need to develop and experiment with ideas that help meet modern diversities.

Pressure and Special Interest Groups

Freedom is a precious commodity and it is relatively young in the world of human affairs. Freedom is also a fragile thing, and, for those who put their trust in freedom, the right to choose, to have alternatives, to act for oneself, are important prerequisites. Freedom also includes having responsibility for oneself and the ability to see the needs of others and of the state and nation and world.

Public opinion is often formed by pressure groups within communities as, for example, when a community bands together to stone or deface property of one family they do not wish to have in their community or to threaten and intimidate the members of the family so that they will move. When the dignity of one man or one family is diminished, everyone loses a little of their freedom and their right to choose because they leave themselves and others fewer alternatives. Children need to understand the background of prejudice and discrimination that have led to fair housing practice laws and they can be helped to understand how, and why, pressure and special interest groups develop, how to evaluate their real objectives, and how to maintain individual responsibility in the midst of pressures to conform because "everyone else is doing it."

One group of eleven-year-olds studied the history of bigoted groups in America (e.g., Ku Klux Klan, Know-Nothing Party, American Protective Association, John Birch Society). Next they reviewed the possible influence of gossipers, lobbyists, advertising, political organizations, professional groups, and mass demonstrations. One group studied the history of religious intolerance and conflict including anti-Catholicism, anti-Semitism, and oppression of Protestants and other religious sects. Another group examined voting-rights history including the poll tax, "white primary," "grandfather clauses," woman suffrage, voter-registration drives, and property-education-character requirements for voting. Among their observations at the conclusion of their study were the following:

1. Just because facts can be found to substantiate the position of an individual or pressure group does not mean that what they are doing is right. Each person should find out all he can before he joins a group for a certain cause.
2. Just because everyone seems to be following certain trends does not mean that the trends are morally or ethnically right.
3. Varying views on a single issue are bound to exist among the citizens of any one community, and people have a right to their opinions unless their actions are harmful to others.
4. It is difficult for any pressure group to be completely objective in its

presentation of facts, and people should learn to listen carefully for mis-representation of facts.

5. Goals of pressure groups are not always in the best interest of the entire community, but may be for the benefit of a single group or cause.

All children can be helped to understand the extent of power or leadership, as well as the positive and negative effects of pressure groups in community structure. They can also study the direction in which different groups and community agencies are moving in regard to areas of living such as health services, recreation, housing, taxation, community improvements and renewal, political and governmental functioning, and equal opportunities to use public facilities.

Within the school culture, too, are many opportunities for students to study and analyze the effects of special interest and pressure groups. Extracurricular activities would be one example of an area of school life where teachers might learn a great deal about peer group pressures exerted upon individual students. Taba (51) found that students learn "verbal allegiance to democratic values while practicing habits of authoritarian control, social indifference, and dishonesty of group purposes." School programs, she found, "tended to reflect the pressures, biases, emphases, and prejudices of the surrounding environment, instead of consciously supplementing gaps in them or correcting their flaws." And to accept the premise that the school can only reflect the culture leads to serious difficulties as the educational dilemmas of today will illustrate clearly.

References

12. Spindler, George D., "Education in Transforming American Culture," *Harvard Educational Review*, Vol. 25, No. 3, summer, 1955, pp. 145–156.
13. Davies, Dan, a statement reported in *The School Administrator*. Washington, D.C.: The AASA Newsletter, February, 1969.
14. Wright, Betty Atwell, *Teacher Aides to the Rescue* (Program Guidelines for Better Home-School-Community Partnerships). New York: The John Day Company, Inc., 1969, pp. 4–5.
15. Ashby, Lloyd W., *Man in the Middle? The Superintendent of Schools.* Danville, Ill.: Interstate Publishers, 1968.
16. James, Thomas, dean of School of Education, Stanford University. Reported in the AASA Newsletter, February, 1969.
17. Seeley, John R., "Some Skills of Being for Those in Service in Education," *Life Skills in School and Society*. Washington, D.C.: Association of Supervision and Curriculum Development, 1969, Yearbook.
18. Wright, Betty Atwell, *Teacher Aides to the Rescue.* Op. cit.
19. Hosie, J. F., and others, *The Cooperative Group Plan for the Organization of Elementary Schools*. New York: Teachers College, Columbia University, 1931.

20. Morse, Arthur D., *Schools of Tomorrow Today.* Garden City, N.Y.: Doubleday & Company, Inc., 1960, pp. 21–22.
21. National Elementary School Principal's Association, *Elementary School Organization: Purposes, Patterns, Perspective.* Washington, D.C.: National Education Associations, 1961, p. 115.
22. Orr, Hattie, "UTTO: Ungraded Team Teaming Organization," *Oklahoma Teacher,* December, 1963.
23. Shane, Harold G., "Grouping in the Elementary School," *Phi Delta Kappan,* Vol. XII, No. 7, April, 1960.
24. Meil, Alice, and Edwin Kiester, Jr., *The Shortchanged Children of Suburbia.* New York: Institute of Human Relations Press, American Jewish Committee, 1967.
25. Bowman, Paul H., "Personality and Scholastic Underachievement," *Freeing Capacity to Learn.* Washington, D.C.: Association for Supervision and Curriculum Development, 1960.
26. Bruner, Jerome S., *The Process of Education.* Cambridge, Mass.: Harvard University Press, 1962, p. 77.
27. Wilhelms, F. T., and D. Westby-Gibson, "Grouping Research Offers Leads," *Educational Leadership,* Washington, D.C.: Association for Supervision and Curriculum Development, Vol. 18, No. 7, April, 1961.
28. Olson, Willard C., *Child Development.* Boston: D. C. Heath and Company, 1959.
29. Strauss, Samuel, "Looking Backward on Future Scientists," *The Science Teacher,* December, 1957.
30. Cohen, Albert, Professor of Sociology at Indiana University, in a speech given at Michigan State University. Reported in Patricia Sexton's *Education and Income.*
31. Hammond, Sarah Lou, "Homogeneous Grouping and Educational Results," *Curriculum Newsletter #10.* Middletown, Conn.: Wesleyan University, 1967.
32. Astor, Gerald, "New York, Dream or Nightmare," *Look,* April 1, 1969.
33. Clark, Kenneth B., *Prejudice and Your Child.* New York: Beacon Press, 1955.
34. Gray, J. S., and A. H. Thompson, "The Ethnic Prejudices of Negro and White College Students," *The Journal of Abnormal and Social Psychology,* Vol. 48, 1953, pp. 311–313.
35. Simpson, George E., and J. Milton Yinger, *Racial and Cultural Minorities: An Analysis of Prejudice and Discrimination.* New York: Harper & Row, 1953.
36. Saenger, Gerhard, *The Social Psychology of Prejudice.* New York: Harper & Row, 1953.
37. Dean, John P., and Alex A. Rosen, *A Manual of Intergroup Relations.* Chicago: University of Chicago Press, 1955, pp. 58–60.
38. Sterling, Dorothy, "Negroes and the Truth Gap," statement made at hearings on *Treatment of Minority Groups in Textbooks and Library Books,* Washington, D.C., summer of 1966.
39. Bennett, Lerone, Jr., "Reading, 'Riting, and Racism," *Ebony,* March, 1967.
40. Baldwin, James, "A Talk to Teachers," *Saturday Review,* December 21, 1963.

41. Wright, Betty Atwell, "Projects and Plans to Help Educate for Diversity," paper presented at Summer Institute on Integration sponsored by New York State Education Department in New Rochelle, N.Y., summer of 1966.
42. Hill, Herbert, "Integrating the Texts," *Newsweek*, March 7, 1966.
43. Dolmatch, Theodore B., "Color Me Brown—I'm Integrated," *Saturday Review*, September 11, 1965.
44. Larrick, Nancy, "The All-White World of Children's Books," *Saturday Review*, September 11, 1965.
45. Rose, Arnold M., *Race, Prejudice, and Discrimination: Readings in Intergroup Relations in the United States.* New York: Alfred A. Knopf, Inc., 1951.
46. North Central Association of Colleges and Secondary Schools, *Human Relations in the Classroom: A Challenge to Teacher Education.* No. D-14, Chicago, Ill., 1963.
47. U.S. Riot Commission Report, *Report of the National Advisory Commission on Civil Disorders.* Washington, D.C.: Government Printing Office, 1968.
48. U.S. Supreme Court decision of May 17, 1954, in the case of *Brown v. Board of Education of Topeka.* This reversed an earlier decision (*Plessey v. Ferguson*, 1896) which declared that "separate but equal" facilities were constitutional.
49. Wright, Betty Atwell, *Urban Education Studies.* New York: The John Day Company, Inc., 1965.
50. Wright, Betty Atwell, *Rural Education Studies.* New York: The John Day Company, Inc., 1967.
51. Taba, Hilda, *School Culture, Studies of Participation and Leadership.* Washington, D.C.: American Council on Education, 1955.

CHAPTER 6
Teachers Investigate Social Action Curriculum

In Retrospect

Education's Social Values

Childs (52) said that "schools always exhibit in their purposes and their programs of study that which the adults of a society have come to prize in their experience and most deeply desire to nurture in their own children." The values reflected by educational programs in schools in different societies differ because the values of societies differ.

The idea that children and teachers should demonstrate changed social behaviors as a result of what is included in school curriculum is not new, nor is the idea that education should become a tool for social actions. Dr. Harold Benjamin (53) dealt satirically with the social problems of education in an era of change in his story of Paleolithic education. Prior to the Ice Age, New-Fist, a social thinker and doer for his times, devised a new curriculum for children of his tribe; his curriculum included fish-grabbing-with-the-bare-hands, wooly-horse-clubbing, and saber-tooth-tiger-scaring-with-fire. Conservative members of the group resisted the new education that New-Fist devised and taught, and they accused him both of defying the "Great Mystery" and of being a "damned fool for trying to change human nature" by teaching the young people how to get adequate meat, skins, and security before they "needed" this knowledge.

But generations passed and the "new" curriculum was not only accepted, it became a traditional way of life. It worked quite well, too, until a new Ice Age brought muddy water so that people couldn't see fish to catch with their bare hands, marshy lands which caused the small wooly horses to seek higher grounds, and damp air that gave the saber-tooth tigers pneumonia which killed almost all of them. However, there still existed men of the old New-Fist breed who had the "ability to do and the daring to think," and they saw the necessity for new skills to get meat, skins, and security for members of the tribe. Their innovations in curriculum included:

1. Fishnet-making-and-using so that fish could be retrieved from the new muddy waters.
2. Antelope-snare-construction-and-operation to catch antelopes who were much more fleet than the small wooly horses that had formerly been their source of meat.
3. Bear-catching-and-killing to combat the new threat to security posed when bear came to swampy areas in place of the saber-tooth tiger.

Even though these innovations were much more appropriate to the needs of the tribe during new Ice Age times, there now existed also a new group of conservatives who thought that the old curriculum was better and that adding anything to it that deviated from the "standard cultural subjects" would make the curriculum too crowded. New-Fist, they said, would turn over in his burial cairn at the very thought of changing the standard curriculum. They declared that the real trouble was that the young people were not getting a thorough grounding in the old subjects, that even the teachers did not know how to fish-grab properly. And, worse still, teachers and students were swinging their wooly horse clubs awkwardly and had no flare at all for tiger-scaring. After all, the elders had learned these subjects so well that they never forgot them!

But even as the conservative members of the tribe bemoaned student–teacher disinterest in curriculum that was no longer needed, there were others like the first New-Fist who "ate a little less heartily, slept a little less stupidly, and arose earlier than his comrades to sit by the fire and think" of ways to improve life for the tribe by preparing its young people to live more effectively in changing times. These new radicals believed that what was taught must be more relevant to the present and future lives of their children and that education should become a tool for social action to benefit the tribe. And each group of New-Fists to succeed them has had to face the same dilemmas they faced—the conflicts with those who would maintain the status quo curriculum in spite of its obsolescence.

Social action curriculum that demonstrates concern for social understanding and functioning and results in changed social behaviors undergirds this country's efforts to acculturate its conglomerate citizens. The foreign-born constituted between 60 and 75 per cent of the children in large city schools by the end of the first decade of the twentieth century, and Cremin (54) suggested that the immigrant character of American society explains, in part, why American schools were more receptive to reform than were European schools. He also stated that schools that wanted to educate these children could "not get by with surface changes" such as teaching them the English language, but also had to deal with problems of

manners, cleanliness, dress, the simple business of getting along together in the schoolroom—these things had to be taught more insistently and self-consciously than ever. And long before Spencerian talk about "health," "citizenship," and "ethical character" began to replace "mental discipline" in the ponderous reports of NEA committees, teachers found themselves pursuing these ends in the day-to-day business of teaching (55).

Edgar (56) explains that the "present cultures out of which central, southern, and eastern European immigrants came placed a low value upon education" and that this was also true of Mexican groups arriving in this country. Thus schools offered

immigrant children the opportunity to learn English and to acquire skills and social attitudes that would enable them to rise from the low social and economic position in which practically all ethnic groups began life in America. . . . The value placed upon education in the culture native to the immigrant was an important factor in determining the ease of assimilation.

A great deal has been written about the dominant social values that have controlled American education. According to Kluckhohn (57), the dominant values of American culture are those of an evil-but-perfectible definition of human nature, mastery over nature, future, doing, and individualism. Myrdal (58) says that there are conflicts between moral values on various levels of consciousness in this country, between valuations on the "general plane" which he calls "The American Creed," where

the American thinks, talks, and acts under the influence of high national and Christian precepts, and, on the other hand, the valuations on specific planes of individual and group living, where personal and local interests, economic, social and sexual jealousies, considerations of community prestige and conformity, group prejudice against particular persons or types of people, and all sorts of miscellaneous wants, impulses, and habits dominate his outlook.

Centers of Social Conflict

It is inevitable that schools are centers of conflict of social values, for, although they have been called "common schools," they have never been "common" in fact. Because of segregation of nonwhite minorities (Japanese, Chinese, Filipino, Mexican American, Indian, and Negro) in housing, politics, employment, and social relations, schools have been segregated by white and nonwhite. In the South, the Negro minority in 1870 was 13.5 per cent of the population of the entire United States and there were severe problems that had their roots in slavery, the economic, social, political, and emotional effects of the Civil War and Reconstruction, the laws that prohibited intermarriage, and other laws that legalized segregation. As more recent laws have been passed to reverse these decisions, some statistics have appeared on "compliance, tokenism, and defiance" (59) but these do not indicate the deep social convulsions and the dreadful personal ordeals that families, especially children, have undergone as society has attempted to reconstruct itself through its schools.

Success of educational efforts toward social reconstruction depends upon fundamental changes in the values educators and laymen hold for their children's education and upon changes in the institutions of society as a whole. Teachers have not been notable in past decades for their social consciences; their voting and registration habits are not equal to those of other college graduates or those with comparable professional standing, according to Grobman and Hines (60), although participation in civic and social groups requires "educational qualifications, adequate income, control over blocks of time, and social prestige or status." Of these qualifications, the teacher possesses only the college degree.

Theodore Brameld (61) is one who continues the social reconstructionist theories of Counts and Rugg, but he also recognizes that there are "powerful resistances to consciously directed change that are typical of cultures." And although Hutchins (62) declares that "education should be everywhere the same," he also has stated that "whatever is wrong with education" has a great deal to do with "what is wrong with the country" because the educational system will always cultivate "whatever is honored in a country."

Hidden Experience Curriculum

One reason curriculum in "common schools" becomes obsolete so quickly is that the hidden curriculum of experience, whether one is referring to food, clothing, and protection for a group or concern for social understanding and functioning of more advanced nature, provides young people with a great many experiences, some of them are quite rich; but they do not provide them with the abstract concepts, symbols, and manipulations that confront youngsters in the traditional school curricula.

If, as many fine educators have recommended, the curriculum finally demonstrates concern for changed social actions and behaviors, there must be courses of study aimed at innovative social reconstruction because the reconstruction theory is more relevant than ever in the last decades of the twentieth century.

Fantini and Weinstein (63) propose this idea pertinent to the reconstruction theory. They say that it represents the "only definition of the social function of education which, today, offers any hope that education may play a significant role in the resolution by consensus of social conflicts and problems." What they are really saying is that the social action process which is basic to the democratic way of life is mandatory for keeping society healthy, vital, and strong. When people are uninvolved, they cannot be really committed. To be isolated from the process is to be ignorant of it and, therefore, not dedicated to it in any real sense of the true meaning of dedication to an ideal, the solution of a problem, or a needed innovation.

"It is inconsistent to ask more and more teachers of the disadvantaged to read, study and try to understand the pupils as much as possible, to attempt to perceive the child's frame of reference, interests and effects of his hidden curriculum, at the same time to limit the teacher's freedom to put such knowledge to use by boxing him in with curricular mandates. . . . What we finish with is a curriculum geared to uniformity rather than to diversity," insist Fantini and Weinstein.

In order to free teachers to use the information that they gather from records, families, and children themselves, they must not be bound by "detailed content recipes," but, rather, knowing the most crucial concepts of each discipline or subject area, they can be more flexible in designing curriculum experiences relevant to each child and to each group of children. It is then possible to diagnose carefully the individuals in a group, or even in a school population, to determine which content and what methods will help them understand particular concepts and to decide upon sequence and time allotments.

Essential, also, is the ability to use cross concepts as well as horizontal concepts, inasmuch as a well-designed curriculum helps students relate one subject area to others. For example, mathematics and science should enhance one another and there is no reason why they should not also enhance the language arts. Or take the whole thing in reverse; there is no reason why language arts should not enhance mathematics and science. The social studies are a fertile field for the development of language and the study of communication systems with, or without, the use of formal language. It is in being able to relate and synthesize what is learned that the individual is able to process and apply knowledge in decision making and in actions. The idea of the spiral curriculum is based upon using children's "hidden curricula of experiences" as springboards for the next things to be learned. As we know, a concept is not formed in a certain way at a certain time; nor is there one specific way to "teach" a concept, or even to be absolutely certain what concepts children are actually forming. They are constantly adding to what they have already understood or experienced and each background is different. What teachers can be certain of, however, is the accuracy of the information and concepts which they try to convey while a group of children is under their tutorage. The hidden experience curriculum provides many children with experi-

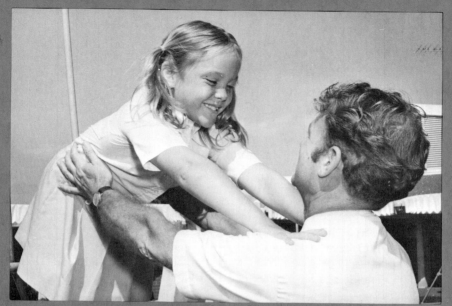

Play in the life of a child is a factor that recognizes the significance of autonomous, self-directed learning ... active exploration and manipulation ... opportunities and facilities that permit full functioning of their organisms if they are to meet the many demands, restrictions, pressures and tensions they must encounter as they grow and develop. It is a way to translate into the education of children ... a belief in the worth of the individual personality ... for the dignity and integrity of the child.

(Lawrence K. Frank, "The Role of Play in Child Development," Childhood Education, *October, 1964.) (Photos courtesy of Florida Atlantic University.)*

ences that are quite rich, even though the children are quite poor, but often it does not provide them with the abstract symbols and manipulations that confront them in the traditional school curriculum. Furthermore, the traditional curriculum may be as obsolete as the saber-tooth variety.

This kind of a statement usually brings up the question "but what about the skills? Don't they *have* to be taught?" This immediately suggests that there are groups of *absolute skills* and *facts* that must be taught regardless of what else is taught. Concerning the speed with which facts go out of date, Hutchins (64) says that "almost every fact" he was taught "from first grade through law school . . . is no longer a *fact*. Almost every tendency that was proclaimed has failed to materialize. The facts and tendencies of today are those that nobody foresaw fifty years ago." He also says that he is especially embarrassed by the facts and tendencies that he himself proclaimed during his years of teaching; "I can only hope that the students in the Yale Law School have forgotten what I taught them. The courts have overruled and legislatures replaced most of what I know."

Understanding Significant Events

Seeley (65) talks about "people knowledge," personal knowledge, and the skills that "flow out of such knowledge." He says that these are the "skills we must seek."

By "people knowledge," Seeley explains that he means the trinity of "me knowledge," "them knowledge," and "us knowledge." The skills, he believes, will emerge as we seek these kinds of knowledge and they will become the "skills of being" which are basic to all real learning, relating, and functioning.

> The least and littlest child is wise enough to recognize that morality and compassion are much preached but little practiced in the classroom. Perceiving the teacher's own lack of the essential "skills" of knowledge, insight, and human art, which partially accounts for the discrepancy between what is taught and what is practiced, the child learns to protect himself, as he must, with quite other skills; putting up barriers, resisting indoctrination, negating authority. These are the "skills" which children are forced to develop in today's schools.

Seeley refers to teachers and to others who help children learn as "educative persons" or "helpers," and he uses a shorthand expression, "the external world of children" to describe three quite different concepts related to what it means to be a child: understanding what it is to be a child, especially a child in Western culture in a modern age; what it is to be a child in a particular peer-group and child-culture in any particular year of his life stage; and what it means to be *this special* and *particular* child. In connection with these "external worlds of children," he says that without the teacher's, or "educative person's" reconstruction of his own "skills of being" he cannot properly apprehend or understand any of these concepts related to children.

Rubin (66) speaks of what should comprise a blueprint for the future schooling of children and a basis for curriculum experiences the school sponsors. He says that we can fashion

> alternative approaches to teaching and learning by varying the basic ingredients in the educational formula. We must experiment, for example, with methods of transmitting knowledge through the child's different sensory apparatus. We must find new ways to blend, in accordance with the individual's nature, behavioristic and cognitive learning procedures. Perhaps of greatest importance, we must revise our pervasive beliefs that many children do not respond to learning stimuli and are only capable of limited attainment. We must reinforce initial learning through imaginative uses of repetition and through attempts to make the classroom more relevant to the learner's intellectual appetite.

Regarding *how* to fashion alternative approaches to teaching and to create the kind of environment in which children will thrive, Rawson (67) again looks toward new roles for teachers when he suggests that teachers function

> in a new attitude and a new faith. To watch, to help, to aid growth, but not to impose standards and views that will stand between the child and the direct experiences from which alone he can truly learn. Such an attitude requires a teacher with poise and self-control that must be built up from within and . . . the creative source within the teacher himself, his love and understanding that alone will call into operation the creative powers of his pupils, and perhaps our greatest need today is to find ways of enabling him to make contact with this inner source of strength.

As the more thoughtful, articulate, and constructive of today's alienated youth find fault with their parents' generation, they criticize obsession with material things and possessions, passive attitudes and lack of involvement in vital and constructive social action, mass conformity and apathy, blind adherence to middle-class morality and thoughtless dedication to tradition, repression and distortion of human individuality and creativity, and, most serious of all, unquestioning and passive acceptance of man's present state of being.

What they are really saying, as they get old enough to say it, is that there is a lot of unfinished business if we are ever to have a true democracy and that society must keep in step with the times if it intends to remain alive and vital. Our earliest, most continuous, and most extensive curriculum tasks, then, will help to make students aware of the unfinished business of democracy, of unemployment and poverty, and of human rights for all Americans. Programs of skills will respect both the mind and the emotions, for they will evolve from the content that helps children experience and know, think, feel, value, and act.

Community Microcosms

Curriculum can no longer be isolated from the dynamic flow of daily events. Even the youngest child learns more by working on a social or political cause of his choosing than from reading or being told about the process. One class of upper elementary school students, for example, became involved in a project to "get out the vote." Not of legal voting age themselves, they were, nevertheless, concerned about the small percentages of people who had a record of voting. Previous to the local primaries, they studied the voting records of the city according to statistics from the last primaries and elections. These were located at the newspaper publishing plant in back issues of daily and weekly summaries. Armed with this information, they designed a questionnaire which they took from house to house in their own and other neighborhoods, tallying information when each block survey was completed.

Classroom sessions were lively as the investigations continued. Some entire blocks were found to contain apartment dwellers who moved often and thus thought they had to lose their votes. Others did not think they would be allowed to vote; and still others were ill and housebound, or apathetic, feeling that their vote would not "make any difference, anyway." The results of student investigation in neighborhoods, which was approved by their parents who sometimes drove some of them to more distant neighborhoods and parked to await their return from each dwelling, confirmed the newspaper statistics from former elections; the areas or wards with the lowest voter participation were the same ones where students were finding the greatest apathy, the largest number of problems, and the least knowledge about current issues and citizen responsibilities.

They studied the data they had collected, decided what information and incentives would be needed to get people more interested in the issues to be decided, prepared tapes and posters with accurate information about both the issues and voting rights, and returned to each home they had originally surveyed. They were well prepared and enthusiastic about their missions, and their parents, too, became concerned and involved by volunteering to serve as distributors of their literature and posters and by having their homes become information, message, and transportation centers.

When the voter registration and participation statistics were studied following the project, everyone involved felt a real sense of accomplishment as the areas that had been saturated with personal attention and pertinent information showed considerable increases in voting records.

By then, many parents had become personally involved not only by visiting other neighborhoods with their children, but also by offering to drive those with no transportation of their own to the registration and polling centers.

The voting participation issue was only the beginning of social action curriculum for these boys and girls, for they learned many other things in the process of becoming personally involved in some of the unfinished business of democracy in their own community. For one thing, they had met people in their homes whom they had only seen previously in positions of servitude or as menial day laborers, and they found that they had common bonds that could be established in spite of differing backgrounds. They began to gain some inklings about what it means to be poor or more affluent, well established in a community or unknown to it, black or white, young or old, from a large family or a smaller family, from a two-parent home or a one-parent home, and skilled or unskilled.

They had had satisfying experiences with more advanced social behaviors such as assuming responsibilities beyond their own needs, contributing to social welfare, inspiring confidence in others, promoting civic progress, sharing community responsibility, and advancing general welfare.

In their class project to help "get out the vote," they had helped to establish the goals and objectives, decide upon the jobs to be done, and assign and participate in different tasks.

They had learned that when everyone understands the goals, they will all work to accomplish them. And their personal involvement and commitment to the first project gave them a much-needed feeling of "helping to remake society in the light of mankind's needs."

Among the other kinds of problem situations that have to do with everyday living that they had discovered were issues that formed the basis for continuing study of their own community microcosm:

1. How can government be brought closer to people so that it will know their real needs and so that they will become involved and participate?
2. If the annual incomes from either wages or welfare payments are lowest in the areas with the greatest number of minority group people, would they change if people were scattered throughout the city rather than being confined to certain sections of it?
3. What is the city or the government doing about scattered housing? Decent low-income housing? Homes for large families? Getting children out of ghetto schools?
4. What agencies are available to help the aged? To help the ill and infirm? To help unemployed adults learn new occupational skills?
5. How do statistics of juvenile delinquency, illegitimacy, teen-age pregnancies and marriage, social diseases, and drug addiction in

poverty areas compare with those in more affluent areas? What agencies are there to help poor people when they have these problems?
6. What are the student dropout rates in the most poverty-stricken areas? How do these compare to more affluent areas?
7. How can people be helped in the most positive, productive ways? Whose responsibility is it to help them?
8. What are human rights and what does it really mean to be an American?

As they studied these various issues, their quest for information and firsthand experiences took them to health clinics, social work agencies, the public health department, the juvenile court, employment agencies, a job training center, and to the city administration offices.

One of their continuing classroom projects was a bulletin board labeled "What is an American?" The teacher had started the idea by placing a few pictures there one day and asking:

1. As you look at these pictures that show some characteristics of American citizens, what are your impressions? Do you think this is a true picture of American citizens?
2. If you say it is not representative of all of our citizens, why isn't it? What have we failed to include?
3. If you were a citizen of another country, what impressions of Americans would you get from looking at only these pictures?
4. If we were to add other pictures, what should they be?
5. If you were to write on the subject "What is an American?", what would you write?

As students planned, collected, and displayed more composite pictures of Americans and included representatives of minority groups, multiracial and multiethnic people in many kinds of activities, and current problems being discussed in newspapers and periodicals, the teacher continued to ask questions that stimulated new inclusions and considerations. At times, the headline center of the bulletin board was changed to a new theme such as

Liberty
Equal Opportunity
Democracy
Affluence and Poverty
Civil Rights
Housing
Occupations
Education
Recreation
Social Welfare

Sometimes the teacher mineographed a copy of a current newspaper clipping that featured a community debate or local, national, or international social concern. At other times, he used the article to be discussed on an overhead projector, and the class read and discussed it together. Was the headline misleading? Did it really represent what the article said? How did it compare with another newspaper's interpretation of the same issue or event? Where was it placed in each newspaper? Why? What had the feature writer done to encourage people to read beyond the first paragraph?

Another activity which had more meaning in the light of class investigations and interest was the study of the country's great documents such as the

Gettysburg Address
Preamble to the Constitution
Bill of Rights
Bill of Human Rights
F. D. Roosevelt's Second Inaugural Address
J. F. Kennedy's Inaugural Address
Martin Luther King's Lincoln Memorial Address
Presidential Oath of Office
F. D. Roosevelt's Four Freedoms Address
Washington's Farewell Address
Lincoln's Second Inaugural Address
The message at the base of the Statue of Liberty

Words such as these took on new meanings: created; equal; unalienable; rights; civil; pursuit of happiness; government of, by, and for the people; instituted; just powers; consent of the governed; conceived in liberty; dedicated to the proposition; union; domestic tranquillity; liberty; posterity; respecting religion; religious freedom; human rights; convert; retreat; wretched; teeming; homeless and "tempest tossed."

Another activity that had high appeal and interesting revelations was asking students to develop one of the following topics either pro or con and to substantiate their opinions:

- Americans are status conscious.
- Americans love their children.
- Americans are competitive.
- Americans are progressive.
- Americans are materialistic.
- Americans love all children.
- Americans are prejudiced.
- Americans are nonprejudiced.
- Americans use leisure time well.

Biographies, fiction, and drama were read and were found to be valuable ways of sensitizing students to the feelings, attitudes, and problems of representatives of different cultural groups and for developing more respect for individual and group differences and similarities. Discussions in connection with differentiated reading centered around patterns of family life, community contrasts, economic and social differences, adjustment to new places and situations, belonging to groups, and experiences of acceptance or rejection. Through concentrating on the people in biographies, fiction, and drama, students began to learn some of the distinguishing characteristics of facts, fiction, opinions, rumors, and generalizations that are used by different authors in thinking and writing about people.

When they wrote descriptions of a trait which they thought peculiar to members of a racial, religious, national, or specific socioeconomic group followed by research to substantiate what they had written, their own evaluations of the original article's accuracy revealed that they were beginning to understand the nature of prejudiced remarks, the effect of epithets and labeling on their own attitudes and the attitudes of others, and some of the ways one might effectively respond to them.

One of the most revealing learnings centered around the concept that as family life in America has changed so have the agencies and institutions. The kinds of changes are indicated by the degree to which other institutions now supply missing needs and services that were formerly considered family functions. Elementary school teachers should establish concepts related to institutions as they exist to serve the needs of today's families, and even very young children can have exciting and purposeful activities in connection with this concept. And in building these concepts, the teacher needs to guide children through elementary education toward school–community involvement. To help children see the interrelatedness of individuals to society, there are practical approaches for introducing concepts about housing, food, air, water, health and welfare services, and communications. Some of these practical concepts and conceptual approaches follow.

Population

Primarily because of the technological and medical advances of the past century, there has been a tremendous increase in population growth in this and other countries. Organizations like the Planned Parenthood Association, and books like William Vogt's *Road to Survival* and *People* have sounded warnings about the implications and the dangers of too many people on this planet; there will not be enough food to go around, for example, and the planet cannot support life for burgeoning populations in other ways. Even today, it is estimated that one third of the earth's people go to bed hungry, and for the first time mankind faces an era in which it is possible to reproduce himself into extinction. We may be living with the last generation which has free choice in deciding the number of children a family will have, for future parents may be required to think of the quality of the children they will produce rather than the quantity as they plan their families and raise their children on a shrinking and overcrowded earth.

Besides the food supply issue, excessive human growth is creating other problems threatening our right to quality living environments—lack of privacy, inadequate housing, wasteful land use, inadequate sanitation, the necessity for protecting life and property, overcrowded schools, unemployment, pollution of natural resources; and the psychological effects of overcrowding, strangling traffic, excessive noise, and eventually a lower standard of living for all. Since the planet cannot continue to support uncontrolled growth, the solution to overpopulation must come from the medical profession, religious leaders, and a determination by world citizens through education to conquer this problem. Teachers especially, must help meet the task by developing curriculum content and concepts about problems dealing with increasing population.

Housing

Expectations of the public regarding family housing have grown from the small, simple, adequate concept to a more sophisticated and complex idea that the "home" should be a status symbol. Needed attention is currently being focused on ghetto and slum areas, and federal assistance is available for urban renewal and slum clearance projects. Urban renewal includes attracting new businesses and industry to blighted areas as well as building "scattered" housing that includes low, middle, and upper income housing intermingled in neighborhoods. In the Eighty-ninth Congress, the passage of the Demonstration Cities Bill was designed to provide massive aid for rehabilitating substandard living conditions, and three federal agencies now exist to help with home construction and financing—the Federal Housing Administration, Veterans Administration, and the Federal National Mortgage Association. In addition, vast model cities projects are in process and there is a Department of Urban Affairs with a special subunit on housing.

The federal government proposes further restriction against racial discrimination in the sale and rental of housing, and some individuals and businesses question how much and how far government regulations should be allowed to reduce or eliminate discrimination when they think it encroaches on individual free enterprise to sell or rent homes. Attempts are being made by public and private agencies to provide low cost or subsidized housing for low-income families, and many of these attempts have resulted in dismal failure, with the new housing accommodation turning rapidly into new slums and ghettos. The realization that people cannot just be moved into new and better housing without accompanying education to help them maintain and care for their accommodations with the zeal that middle- and upper-class families exhibit comes slowly. New steps are being taken to remedy this situation; they include involving families to be moved in the planning of the housing project; adult education for more rewarding employment; family counseling and help; and a program to educate people in the proper use and maintenance of new facilities and property.

The moral and constitutional aspects of federal housing are topics which older elementary schoolchildren enjoy discussing and investigating. Another class developed questions with their teacher that were related to housing:

1. What is meant by "substandard living conditions"?
2. Who finances federal housing?
3. What effects does substandard housing have on people?
4. What responsibilities should occupants assume?
5. What are some experiences commonly shared by the child who lives in a federal housing project and one who lives in an expensive high-rise apartment?
6. Why do people leave their rural homes to come to cities?
7. When and why do people move from the city to the suburbs?
8. Would it be better to plan new cities rather than to attempt to rehabilitate old ones? If so, how could they be planned to avoid the problems that have developed in old cities?

Closely associated with the problems of housing is the question of land use. As the more desirable properties are used up, the land that is left must be put to the best possible use. Rental apartments, cooperative and condominium apartments, and housing developments are growing in number because so many more people can live on a given piece of ground with shared services and facilities. A great deal of land is now simply too expensive for single-family dwellings; in addition, in many areas of the country today, new housing is divided into special sections for older and retired people, special sections for families with young children, and special accommodations for handicapped persons. These trends will undoubtedly intensify as population grows.

Zoning ordinances affect housing possibilities in most communities now, so teachers can encourage children to study the effect of zoning regulations to decide whether they are beneficial for better housing arrangements or whether they hamper improved housing for families. Zoning can be a very beneficial and protective device for home and apartment owners, as can building inspection. If buildings are constructed and maintained according to prescribed codes that help guard against inferior workmanship and irresponsibility of landlords in facilities and maintenance, there is a better chance that there will be less substandard housing. Children can investigate the building codes and zoning regulations of their own communities, invite city or community officials to discuss them, and visit different kinds of areas to see how regulations affect new building plans.

As we have said before, seldom does a teacher return from a home visit without more understanding of his students and increased awareness of home problems that affect school life. The child from a bleak home and decaying neighborhood is most often the same one who has the fewest background experiences for learning, who is handicapped from the beginning in the traditional school program, and who becomes a school dropout with the most disadvantages in life and in work available to him. This chain of misfortune needs to be corrected and the school must accept a great deal of responsibility to educate for its correction.

Air

One of the attractions in the early days and settlement of this country was the "wide open spaces," and early colonists associated space with clean air, fresh water, new land, and other physical resources, including soil and minerals. Until fairly recent times, natural resources seemed so abundant that there seemed little need to be overly concerned about conservation or purification. Even though conservationists were warning of the misuse of natural resources shortly after the turn of the century, the general attitude of people was reflected in statements such as "Why? We have no problems here!"

As industry and technology grew, increasing use of fuel to operate machinery became a necessary part of our progressing civilization. Even when the fumes from private and public sources became initially noticeable and objectionable, there was no thought about curbing air polluting activities. It has taken years of population and industry growth, millions of automobiles, the disappearance of our forests, and the pollution of our streams of fresh water to awaken citizens to the detrimental effects of the loss of natural resources, and particularly to the effects of polluted air on health and property. Disturbing atmospheric conditions such as smog and "smaze" result from a combination of such air pollutants as smoke, soot, fly ash, and chemicals. Factory smokestacks, home incinerators, automobile exhaust fumes, and heating fuels are the major causes of filth in the air; and pollution is a national problem. As one approaches the New York metropolitan area by air, sea, or road the heavy concentration of smog that actually obliterates the area and cuts out the sun is the first thing one sees. The same is true of many other major cities of the world.

Some local communities and a number of major cities have taken action to reduce air pollution by regulating industry and by limiting incoming and outgoing traffic. Some have placed certain restrictions on private incinerators. New cars are being produced with mechanisms to eliminate exhaust fumes. Other restrictions are being placed on heating facilities, and other fuel usage that contaminates air. The government will soon require all new automobiles to come equipped with devices which will reduce, but not eliminate, air pollution; and federal agencies are generating momentum to educate the public to the necessity for clean air.

Teachers know that one way to help inform the public is through their children, and that a really informed public will take action if they perceive the problems to be serious enough. Joan Adams was such a teacher, and one day when one of her students brought up the topic of temperature inversion, she decided to correct his misconceptions by developing accurate knowledge and concepts about air. She discovered that John seemed to know that warm air blanketed the cold air below it, thus making the air stagnant, but that he did not understand why this disturbed people with lung diseases or why it made eyes burn and fill with water. She explained that the atmosphere tended to clean itself through wind currents, settling, and rejuvenation through chemical changes. In estimating the depth of the earth's atmosphere, most of the class felt it extended for miles above the surface of the earth. The teacher pressed a sheet of paper onto the classroom globe model of the earth, and explained that in proportion to the earth's size the sheet of paper represented the depth of the atmosphere. The children were amazed and began to have some idea of the need to conserve and appreciate the air we have available to us to breathe.

The class also considered these questions:

1. Why is it dangerous to play in an empty refrigerator?
2. What makes a person drown?
3. Why do people die in fires when they are not burned?
4. How do miners breathe when they are in mines?
5. What is the biggest danger of fire in a mine?

Some of the concepts which became apparent as information was gathered and experiments were conducted included these:

1. A chief cause of suffocation is lack of oxygen, and oxygen is necessary in our air supply. When an individual is trapped or confined in a small area with no ventilation he will use all of the oxygen in the air. (One demonstration of this is to place lighted candles of the same size under different-sized jars, timing the length of time it takes each candle to go out. The smaller the jar, the sooner the flame is extinguished.)
2. Drowning and smoke inhalation also cause death through a different kind of suffocation. In either case, there is a deficiency of good air and individuals can endure for only minutes.
3. All people need uncontaminated air. It is necessary to force clean air mechanically to areas where ventilation is inadequate, in places such as mines, tunnels, subways, and airplanes.

Water

As the class talked about air pollution, some children branched out in another direction. They wanted to know if water also became polluted and how it was possible to know if water they drank was polluted. The teacher indicated that contaminated water was another problem which was nationwide, and it was decided to ask the director of the city water department to explain what steps were being taken to ensure pure water in their area. When he was contacted, he invited the class to the water treatment plant to see some of the actual operations there.

During the tour, it was explained that for water to be potable in the area, several obstacles had to be overcome. The water director stated that the water in the area contained a great deal of calcium, and because it was "hard" water the color was light tan, and it had an odor resulting from hydrogen sulfide. He made the following observations about overcoming the objectionable properties of water:

1. Water is softened by taking out the calcium. Less soap or detergent is needed in soft water and therefore there will be less pollution from the homes where it is used. All traces of iron are removed to eliminate stain to fixtures and clothing.
2. Filtering the water removes the other impurities and clears all color from the water.
3. Disinfecting the water with chlorine destroys all bacteria and prevents illnesses such as diphtheria that used to be carried by water.

He explained that the county board of health requires reports indicating periodic checks on analysis of the water supply, and that his local system runs checks on water purity every two hours to ensure a continuous supply of pure, clean water.

In their field trip follow-up, the class summarized their major learning experiences as

1. Understanding the steps involved in pumping, cleaning, purifying, and distributing water to its ultimate destinations.
2. Appreciating safety controls on water supply.
3. Recognizing the need for conserving water because of its limited supply.

Other topics recommended to teachers for helping children develop concepts about water as a vital resource are

1. The need to control raw waste and sewage in fresh water.
2. The pollution of large bodies of water by irresponsible dumping of waste and by-products from factories.
3. The loss of fish and wildlife through pollution of salt and fresh water.

4. The closing of recreation areas because of infectious and contaminated water.

Noise Level

Earlier we spoke of the psychological and physical effects of constant noise on city dwellers. One of the newest problems affecting people's rights to a physically safe and psychologically tolerable environment in congested areas is an excessively high noise level. Noise is measurable in decibels, and studies show that continued exposure to 80 decibels or more of noise will produce loss of hearing. Jet pilots are victims of this steady overexposure as are some workers in heavy machinery in factories. But the problem is more widespread in residential communities as science invents more transportation devices, and labor-saving machines and appliances. For example, a food blender makes 93 decibels of noise, a power lawn mower 107, and a jet plane 117 (to persons on the ground) as it comes in to land. In tests with animals, these levels of noise cause them to become neurotic; thus the danger is both physical—loss of hearing—and mental—the possibility of neuroses.

Pressure is mounting for jet airports to be located far from inhabited areas, but as population increases this becomes more and more difficult. Industry is being pressured to produce quieter motors for all kinds of machines. Schoolchildren are aware of the effect on their ability to concentrate when the noise of jets landing nearby interferes with their concentration or conversation. They can analyze the advantages and disadvantages of their particular school and community setting as it relates to the problem of noise. They can have experiences in the classroom with the principles of sound and vibration, and they can measure sound in decibels and discriminate between loudness and softness, highness and lowness, and pleasure or displeasure of sounds.

In classrooms where concepts are developed from community problems such as air, noise, water, or the use of natural resources, the teacher does more than relate content to practical use. He helps children perceive the needs of the total community and of people everywhere, and to relate them to social action by citizens.

Conservation of Natural Resources

The conservation of natural resources can be an exciting real life theme that runs throughout the school year and intermeshes with many areas of the elementary school curriculum. There are many resource people available to schools from state game and fish departments, state forestries, soil conservation services, fish and wildlife services, garden clubs, ornithologists, chambers of commerce, and leaders in agriculture and boys' and girls' clubs such as 4-H Clubs. They can be solicited to help develop accurate information and concepts about conservation that young children can understand.

Other classroom experiences suggested to help children understand modern man's relatedness to his environment include field trips to zoos, hatcheries, state forests, bird sanctuaries, nature centers, parks, or public recreation areas. Oceanography is a new and fascinating area for study and if students are anywhere near a center where oceanographic studies are conducted, they can learn at firsthand about research efforts to study the potentials of living afforded by the sea, including growing food on the ocean bottom and man's potential for one day living under the sea.

Among the many possibilities for providing direct experiences for children in connection with the use and preservation of natural resources, teachers can select those that offer the most opportunity for investigation in their own communities. From these, it is possible to move to more abstract and vicarious experiences and concepts; the important thing is to develop general concepts about man in relation to his environment which are applicable to both concrete and abstract situations comprehensible to children.

Health and Welfare Services

We have said that curriculum needs to be part of the dynamic flow of daily events and that curriculum that uses current concerns as springboards for learning will be more relevant to boys and girls. Surely every child today is being made aware through mass communication media of the problems of people who need public medical and welfare assistance even if they are not part of a family that needs such help. Because nearly half of our population exists at or below the poverty level, millions of children desperately need to be educated to the help available; and all other children need to know that whether the problems are theirs or someone else's makes no difference in every citizen's responsibilities.

Children need to know that many local institutions provide medical and dental care and that there are other welfare services that work in interlocking and cooperating roles. These various agencies and institutions vary from community to community, but teachers should know which ones exist in their areas and how they function not only so that children and their families can have the help they need when they need it, but also so that all of the children in their classrooms can be sensitized to health and welfare needs and services. Minimal services for most communities include family services where counseling, psychological, and psychiatric help are available; medical and dental clinics; and agencies that sponsor projects of educational and preventive natures, such as immunization programs and venereal disease clinics.

The main concerns of health and welfare departments are food, shelter, and health care for the indigent, aged, and individuals in need at the moment. Every taxpayer contributes to the support of public services and to old-age assistance funds even though the funds come from the federal government and are administered by individual states and localities. Visiting nurses and social case workers are now available to even the most rural areas, and assistance is provided after a social case worker has investigated and made recommendations regarding kind and degree of aid. Each state has different requirements for aid, but generally they include: employment, financial need, and length of residence. The Eighty-ninth Congress funded the Medicare Bill which provides financial assistance in matters of health to senior citizens who enroll in the program. In addition to tax-supported assistance, various civic and private organizations help needy children with hospitalization, eyeglasses, hearing aids, clothing, and school lunches.

Language and Communication

Closely allied to advancing social behaviors is advancement in communication behaviors. The more advanced of the communication behaviors discussed earlier include participating in group discussions, following and discussing current events, and speaking up for causes and for justice. Communication is basic to culture and to groups, and in today's world news is common knowledge almost as it is happening via television, radio, and newspapers. Communication satellites circle the earth and beam intercontinental news, thus making other countries' and nations' news as near as our own.

Man is distinguished from other animals by his ability to use language to communicate, although children are fascinated to learn about communication systems in the world of birds, domestic and wild animals, and water life. Opportunities to teach skills and develop concepts about language are not limited to periods designated as reading, writing, or language arts, but are, instead, implicit in every academic discipline and social occasion. Since language is a system of vocal symbols by which people communicate, it can be spoken, heard, read, and written; and language represents experience.

The spread of the English language throughout the world has been called a "linguistic accomplishment of the twentieth century," for more than 400 million people speak English as a native tongue and over a billion people speak it as a second language. It is fast becoming the international language of commerce, aviation, diplomacy, science, sports, and scholarship. There have been countless complaints that American schoolchildren are not mastering their own language, that they cannot spell correctly, write effective messages or letters, read coherently, or express themselves orally with any degree of proficiency. It has become increasingly obvious to educators and to others that what was good enough in language instruction in the past is simply not adequate for today.

As educators and linguists directed their attention to the failures and asked themselves why the traditional curriculum was falling short of its intended goals, scholarly study by linguists interested in language from a scientific viewpoint has emerged. A number of these are descriptive linguists who are primarily concerned with analyses of the ways we communicate, and as a result of being able to analyze and describe our language, we now have available ways to help us understand better how language functions.

The work of linguists is not new. Leonard Bloomfield published *Language* in 1933 and this was perhaps the first important synthesis of linguistics as a force in the study of the English language. There were earlier grammarians such as Henry Sweet, Alonzo Reed, Brainerd Kellogg, H. Poutsma, Otto Jespersen, and George O. Curme who helped lay the foundations for the linguistic movement and who also produced books that introduced the scientific spirit of inquiry into the description of the English language. Members of the American armed forces were able to take advantage of the principles of linguistics in learning other languages quickly and well, and their experiences soon affected the teaching and learning of foreign languages generally. The teaching of English in schools, however, was not much affected by the results of linguistic studies until the works of Z. S. Harris, George L. Trager, H. L. Smith, and Charles C. Fries were published in the 1940's and 1950's. Research in the field of linguistics continues at a rapid pace, and the knowledge that has already been acquired provides complete descriptions of English language as a system, but few linguists consider themselves qualified to determine what children should learn. This is left to the experimentation of educators who have available to them the results of linguists' studies. It is important here to note that the work of descriptive linguists, as well as of historical and geographical linguists, brings important insights to teachers.

Understanding How Language Works

With new ways of looking at our language, we have better bases for studying about language and how it operates. Today we expose children to language in such ways that their understanding of its use will be far greater than was that of the child involved in traditional English curriculum. Today we help children expand their experiences and their knowledge in order to help them apply the greater insights they develop to speaking and writing their own language more effectively. Teachers today no longer rely on rules, but instead help children see how language works and they use spoken language as a base for written language since written language is really a transcription of what one person says to another person; thus writing becomes a code.

Most children are fascinated with codes. One teacher, for example, in order to lead students to make some interesting discoveries about language used examples of language intuitively familiar to most of his students, and helped them to see the structure and the purpose underlying communication. These students lived in an area where a large number of fathers and other male relatives were truck drivers. The teacher visited a local roadside diner and was fascinated to hear two men discussing a third whom they described as a "sheepherder" or "cowboy" who had been "deadheading a dog" or "a sick horse." This person, they said, was now outside "spotting the body." Would you have been able to participate in this conversation with truck drivers if you had overheard it and been invited to participate?

Translated, this conversation describes a reckless truck driver with questionable ability who has been driving an empty truck with very little power and who is now outside parking his trailer. Almost every profession today has some conversational brevities understood by colleagues in the profession but extremely unintelligible to those outside of their professions or industries.

Using the social experiences of language that a large group of children in the class would understand and associate with, and that all children would find of interest, the teacher and the children categorized some of the jargon used by truck drivers but not found in Funk and Wagnalls. Here is their list:

1. Drivers are categorized according to what they transport. A "bean hauler" transports fruits and vegetables, a "bull hauler" or a "goat'n shoat man" hauls livestock.

2. A truck driver may be described as a "boll weevil" (a novice truck driver); a "floater" (a driver without a steady job); or as a "woodchuck" (a driver with low job seniority).

3. There are many colorful ways drivers have of describing the way other drivers operate their vehicles. A driver may be a "gear bonger" if he grinds his gears when he shifts; and he is "dusting" when he is driving with wheels on the shoulder of the road.

4. There is another interesting group of words that are used to describe the kind of trucks drivers use. They may work with an "agitator body," "bareback," "bob tail," "bumble bee," "cherry picker," "pajama wagon," "peg leg," "possum belly," or "reefer." These expressions refer to the fact that they may drive a truck with a body designed and equipped to mix concrete in transit, a tractor without its trailer, a tandem tractor with only one power axle, a livestock trailer with a drop frame to haul small animals such as chickens or rabbits underneath the heavier cattle, or a refrigerated truck or trailer designed to haul perishables.

5. One thing the trucker dislikes intensely is a "tattle tale" or "squealer," the name they give to the tachograph which is a device used in a truck cab to automatically record the number of miles driven, number of stops made, speed, and other factors during a hauling trip.

This teacher and his students had a fine experience with the *conventions of language*, with the choice of forms appropriate to a particular context and a particular situation. From these, they were able to move to certain generalizations that apply to jargon, dialect, and other kinds of language used by specific groups. Through using language samples that were relevant to the lives and interests of his students, the teacher was able to lead them toward choices in terms of sensitivity to the appropriateness of language for given situations. The groundwork was laid for helping them to become increasingly aware of usage as convention that is subject to change from time to time and from place to place.

The important thing, also, is that teachers such as this one recognize and value children's cultural backgrounds, start where they are in the truest sense, and help them use what they already know.

Listen to those around you and you will note that people have one way of talking when they are speaking informally to you, and another when they are giving a report or lecture. When making speeches or attempting to put our thoughts in writing, we are apt to use more formal language; in other words, each one of us uses different language and uses language differently, depending upon the occasion. Linguists sometimes refer to these differences as "levels of language usage." Newer generations use some words, both known and unknown, in ways that their elders do not understand, for example, *man* and *cool* or *square* and *fuzz*.

It is all a matter of viewpoint and, whether correct or not, it is highly improbable that the youngster of today is going to stop using our language as he now uses it. The school can refine his use and help him to understand his language; and, of course, he must be led to an awareness of the suitability of language in certain social situations. However, the uses the youngsters of today make will inevitably result in some changes in our language (68).

Oral Language Development

A child's speech patterns and usage are closely allied and interwoven with family speech patterns and usage, and they have their roots in early childhood. It is when a child enters school that he begins to have problems with his own concepts of personal language competency, because until that time everyone in his family has become accustomed to his speech and his own personal ways of expressing his needs, wants, and ideas. His natural and spontaneous language has been effective in communicating with his family and his neighbors. But even though the child's natural language may be colorful, forceful, and descriptive, it is frequently not the language that the school expects or accepts. When he feels that his language is rejected and knows that he is not familiar with the patterns of language the teacher seems to want, his means of communicating are blocked.

Recent studies of disadvantaged children suggest that it may not be feasible to habituate every child to the oral use of standard English during the *elementary school years;* in fact, trying to do so may do more harm than good for the child's oral language growth (69). Speaking of the importance of a child's ability to think and to express himself clearly and with honesty, precision, and imagination in the language of his family and neighborhood, Mackintosh (70) says that "Later, when he can realize the social and economic penalties of a limited command of standard English, he can be motivated to accomplish crucial changes in these matters. Since language is a living and dynamic instrument, being continually modified by people and events, he and his social group, if representative of a large population, are likely—over a period of time—to induce changes in standard English."

We know that relationships with other human beings are often directly related to being able to communicate orally, and that social growth is intricately involved with advanced communicating behaviors. How a child meets others, how he performs with colleagues in work situations and in other social situations, and whether he is increasingly able to master the tasks of formal learning are increasingly dependent upon his use of oral language, his ability to listen and interpret, and his ability to express and respond.

At the very least, most children come to school with some kind of language even though the school may reject it and they have also generally had the freedom and the opportunity to use it before coming to school. The school has the responsibility of helping children extend their language usage and understanding, but "quiet" classrooms do little to encourage real oral communication among students and teachers. Oral language must be used in order to be mastered, and oral language is probably the principal skill a child needs to help him think, to write, and, eventually, to read. In order to grow in his command over language, a child has to have genuine needs to describe, distinguish, classify, generalize, and qualify. Making associations and opportunities like these will benefit him more than all of the drill and grill that he gets in innumerable "exercises" and contrived rote memorizations.

Again, referring to the work of Loban (69), who has done intensive research into the oral language of elementary schoolchildren, children with the greatest proficiency in language use the same basic sentence patterns as those who lack proficiency. The differences lie in the precision and the complexity of thinking, in the ability to make distinctions, modify ideas, handle emphasis through subordination, control unity through transitions and arrangement, provide for expression of cause and effect or concede exceptions. Very few of these characteristics which represent power over spoken language can be learned through mechanical means, because language and thought live and grow in situations where one must think and where one must be involved and concerned.

Most authorities agree that listening and speaking serve as bases for reading and writing, and that when these are rooted in experience, listening and speaking furnish the much-needed background of meaning for written and printed symbols, for using and deciphering the graphemes that represent the phonemes of English, or the combinations of phonemes that make up the morphemes in English to form a base, a prefix, or a suffix.

Furthermore, it is easier for most people to master oral language than it is to master the coding of it in writing. The reason for this is that when people speak they use *pitch, stress,* and *juncture* to help them communicate the *meaning* of what they wish to say. By *pitch,* we mean low, normal, high, or very high voice intonations; by *stress* we refer to degree of loudness; and *juncture* is the joining or pauses between sounds, words, and word groups that help us separate speech into units and patterns of meaning.

In modern programs, for example, the student uses his joinings or pauses to help him punctuate written material; patterns of intonation can help him to identify the physical characteristics of a sentence, especially if one proofreads orally. In the act of writing, we are unable to lower or raise the pitch of our voice or to change the tempo, so we hope to carry the reader along with us by the use of punctuation and by doing such things as underlining to show what we want to emphasize. The modern teacher is not so concerned with definitions as traditional teachers were but, instead, concentrates on the learner's ability to speak and write effectively and creatively. In the process of helping children *use* language orally, it is possible to examine certain structures, to study what they consist of, and then to learn about generalizations in relation to poor construction, run-together sentences, and nonsentences or "partials."

During the elementary school years, it is more productive to help children learn about these generalizations by giving them many opportunities for creative oral and written expression, for hearing good literature well read, for hearing themselves on tapes or recordings, and for encouraging them to participate in group discussions and to follow and discuss current events.

Mass Communications Revolution

There is no doubt that the printed media, books, newspapers, magazines, and the like, will continue to exert powerful influences on curriculum in our schools and in society. But equally certain is the fact that, to use a phrase of David Riesman's, print no longer "monopolizes man's symbolic environment."

Think of the effects that new kinds of mass communication began to have beginning in 1839, when Daguerre developed the first practical method of photography; in 1844, when Morse perfected the telegraph; in 1876, when Bell transmitted the first telephone message; 1877, when Edison invented the phonograph; 1894, by which time movies had been introduced; 1895, when Marconi sent and received the first wireless message; 1906, when Fessenden transmitted the human voice by radio; 1920, when regularly scheduled radio broadcasts began; 1923, when a picture was televised between New York and Philadelphia and when

Henry Luce and Briton Hadden created a totally new idea in magazines with *Time;* 1927 when the first "talkie" appeared; 1928, when Disney's first animated cartoon was made; 1935, when E. H. Armstrong developed FM radio; 1936, when *Life* magazine was inaugurated; and 1941, when full commercial television was authorized.

These, of course, are just some of the mass communication inventions that began to revolutionize people's lives. To these we could add the tape recorder, LP records, comic strips, comic books, tabloid newspapers, electronic computers, paperback books, and communication satellites. New mediums of communication have engaged "learning by books alone" in serious competition, although people will continue to learn by way of the printed word, naturally. But we must accept the fact that children in classrooms today have become used to all of the audio-visual methods of communication and may prefer them over the printed word because they, and many of their parents, have become accustomed to these as their "more natural mediums." Educators have not yet really assessed what the burgeoning of mass media means and will mean to teaching, to learning, and to society in general. Neil Postman (71) thinks that perhaps we can only seek the answers to questions such as the following:

1. If the telegraph made nothing so old as yesterday's newspaper, have radio and television similarly made some of the functions of *today's* newspaper obsolescent?
2. If photography changed the character of painting, has film challenged the novel to invent new means of expression?
3. Now that the flow of information in our culture is so continuous and its sources so various, do we run the risk of being overwhelmed by facts? (One thinks of the little girl whose one-line book report read: "This book told me more about penguins than I wanted to know.")

Actually, we need to find ways to make students "literate" in a number of media because they coexist as forms of communication in today's world. Postman reminds us that whatever the future may hold, teachers can face it with equanimity if they avoid the temptation to pit television or any other medium against print, helping students to become knowledgeable and literate in the various media. "Any other policy," he says, "would be unbecoming to a great profession."

We have used the terms *mass media* and *mass communication* here because speech, writing, print, and all the newer media we have mentioned are capable of transmitting messages to large numbers of people simultaneously and over periods of time. Actually, boys and girls can study the distinctions between the various instruments or media of communication and the uses to which they are now, or have been, put. Because communication of all kinds is really a process of exchanging various symbolic meanings, the media that serve these purposes are many and varied:

Sound as in spoken language.
Sound as in music.
Graphics and paper for the written word.
Photographic images, still or projected in rapid succession.
Stone for carved messages and images.
Various art media of painting for conveying feelings.

All of these can be "mass" media, but obviously some can also have limited usage and would not be considered mass media—for example, the home movie, the personal or business letter, or closed-circuit TV used for a limited purpose. However, certain media become mass media because the cost of producing a good documentary film or broadcasting through the air is prohibitive for individuals. Thus television, radio, movies, newspapers, and magazines are mass communication media and they are used in different ways than are great music, art, architecture, or languages, each of which communicates meaning and symbolisms to large masses of people in quite different ways. The mechanized media transmit messages that are generally received simultaneously by large audiences—they do not necessarily convey the same *meaning* to all audiences or elicit identical responses because people "take in" and "process" information differently depending upon individual backgrounds and interest. Additionally, the members of mass audiences have no way, or at least only limited ways, of communicating with one another or with the medium; they are anonymous and passive "receivers" rather than participants.

Older elementary schoolchildren can begin to consider some of the economic, institutional, and legal forces in connection with the use of television, as one example. Here are some of the possibilities:

Invention: With each new invention there must be a reshuffling of existing facts, materials, and effects. Most "inventions," such as television, are built upon the contributions of various other inventors. Since television is a process that involves the transmission of electromagnetic energy, it uses some of the principles usually associated with earlier inventors like Faraday, Morse, Marconi, De Forest, and others. What are the implications inherent in the idea of "invention"?

Legislation: 1. The first legislation in the United States to deal with radio is noted in 1910, when radio transmission was still in its infancy and consisted of what we now call "wireless telegraphy"—the dot-and-dash Morse Code signals. A Congressional amendment in that year brought wireless and wire communication (telegraph and telephone) under federal jurisdiction, and the Wireless Ship Act dictated certain requirements for the installation of radio equipment on passenger vessels. No further legislation seemed necessary until other technical advances or "inventions" made it possible to transmit speech and music. With growing interest in radio, people with relatively little training could send messages and began to build their own radio receivers and even their own transmitters. The air soon became full of conflicting signals from ships, commercial communication companies, government agencies, high school and college physics classes, and hobbyists; and new social problems dictated new legislative needs.

2. The first Radio Act was passed in 1912 partly as a result of the *Titanic* disaster. Radio communication with the mainland was partially obstructed by the conflicting and interfering signals uncontrolled by assigned frequencies or license. What effect do you think was achieved while the government's discretionary powers were still restricted to the assignment of a limited number of frequencies? As more and more applicants asked to be licensed, what do you think happened to the channels assigned to broadcasting?

3. Why did the Federal Communication Commission have to lay down more limitations regarding the use of "space" and "standards" between 1922 and 1925? And why was further legislation needed in the Radio Act of 1927 and in its extension into the Communications Act of 1934? (*Note:* These are suggested only to demonstrate the type of thinking and investigation that will help students think about the *why—* the *social implications,* and the responsibilities of our technical abilities to broadcast information. Make notes about other social implications.)

Politics: Students can begin to think about the *political* implications by using a section of the *Amended Communications Act of 1934* which follows:

Sec. 315 (a) If any licensee shall permit any person who is a legally qualified candidate for any public office to use a broadcasting station, he shall afford equal opportunities to all other such candidates for that office in the use of such broadcasting station: Provided, That such licensee shall have no power of censorship over the material broadcast under the provisions of this section. No obligation is hereby imposed upon any licensee to allow the use of its station by any such candidate. Appearance by a legally qualified candidate on any—

(1) bona fide newscast,

(2) bona fide news interview,

(3) bona fide news documentary (if the appearance of the candidate is incidental to the presentation of the subject or subjects covered by the news documentary), or

(4) on-the-spot coverage of bona fide news events (including but not limited to political conventions and activities incidental thereto), shall not be deemed to be use of a broadcasting station within the meaning of this subsection. Nothing in the foregoing sentence shall be construed as relieving broadcasters, in connection with the presentation of newscasts, news interviews, news documentaries, and on-the-spot coverage of news events, from the obligation imposed upon them under this Act to operate in the public interest and to afford reasonable opportunity for the discussion of conflicting views on issues of public importance.

Sec. 326. Nothing in this Act shall be understood or construed to give the Commission the power of censorship over the radio communications or signals transmitted by any radio station, and no regulation or condition shall be promulgated or fixed by the Commission which shall interfere with the right of free speech by means of radio communication.

The teacher might use the following kinds of questions and considerations to help children think about the social implications here:

1. Does this describe specifically the public responsibilities of broadcasters? If not, why not? (Vague legal language.)
2. What does it mean to "broadcast in the public interest"?
3. What social implications do these parts of the Communications Act have?
   - Prohibition of profane and obscene language.
   - Provision of equal time and facilities for political candidates.
   - Treatment of controversial issues that will ensure fairness to differing points of view.
   - Prohibition of the Commission from passing judgment on a program before it is broadcast and from interfering with the right of free speech.

Teachers and students can also investigate, often at firsthand, the responsibilities and problems of the sponsor, the networks, local stations, educational television, and other checks and balances imposed by the FCC, the advertiser, and the public.

Teachers begin to help students and their parents be more critical in their viewing and listening habits in some of the following ways. Add others that occur to you.

1. Tell children and their parents about an especially good program that is going to be broadcast—a travelogue, a play, a movie, a concert, or visits to national shrines or exhibits. Some teachers have prepared a short, weekly or monthly news sheet to send home with children; others have had students copy lists to take home; others have a special bulletin board to remind children and their families about something important that is on the way via radio or TV.

2. Rotating student television and radio committees are even more effective than the teacher's announcements after a period of time because this technique gives students the responsibility of keeping students abreast of current offerings; as we have stressed previously, successful teaching cannot really begin until students begin to assume responsibilities that involve them actively in the learning process. Students can keep the bulletin board, write announcements on the chalkboard, make class announcements, and report to one another on programs seen or heard. The bulletin board and the individual reporting provide students with the opportunity to express and share a wide range of talents and interests. For example, a jazz program may lead students to make a bulletin board display on the origins of jazz, including written reports, photographs of jazz musi-

cians, and book jackets of important books about jazz. Other ideas for students include "team watching," in which a group of students assembles at the home of one to watch a specific program together; this is an especially good technique where some children may not have TV or where the program may interfere with other family plans. Occasionally, teachers should give students a list of particular things to watch for, such as the plot, theme, and characterizations of a play, so that students themselves begin to compare, analyze, and be more critical and thoughtful in their viewing habits. Occasionally, a short reading on or about the same subject can be assigned previous to the viewing or listening experience, or two conflicting versions of the same incident can be read by more advanced upper elementary school students for the purpose of comparing and analyzing.

Other ideas and implications can be found in the following bibliography. It is suggested that the reader select several of these for background reading and for further study and thought:

Asheim, Lester (ed.), *The Future of the Book.* Chicago: University of Chicago Press, 1955.

Bachman, John, *The Church in the World of Radio-Television.* New York: Association Press, 1960.

Barnouw, Eric, *Mass Communication.* New York: Holt, Rinehart and Winston, Inc., 1956.

Blum, Daniel, *A Pictorial History of Television.* Philadelphia: Chilton Company, Book Division, 1959.

Educational Policies Commission, *Mass Communication and Education.* Washington, D.C.: National Education Association, 1958.

Head, Sydney, *Broadcasting in America.* Boston: Houghton Mifflin Company, 1956.

Henry, Nelson (ed.), *Mass Media and Education.* Chicago: The National Society for the Study of Education, 1954.

Himmelweit, Hilde, A. N. Oppenheim, and Pamela Vance, *Television and the Child.* New York: Oxford University Press, 1958.

Hogben, Lancelot, *From Cave Painting to Comic Strip.* London: Max Parrish, 1949.

Innis, Harold, *The Bias of Communication.* Toronto: University of Toronto Press, 1951.

Journal of the American Academy of Arts and Sciences, *Mass Culture and Mass Media.* Middletown, Conn.: Wesleyan University Press, 1960.

Klapper, Joseph, *The Effects of Mass Media.* New York: Bureau of Applied Research, Columbia University, 1949.

Klapper, Joseph, *Children and Television: A Review of Socially Prevalent Concerns.* New York: Bureau of Applied Social Research, Columbia University, 1954.

Klapper, Joseph, "What Does Research Show?" *Child Study,* Vol. XXXVII, 1960.

Klapper, Joseph, *The Effects of Mass Communication.* New York: The Free Press, 1960.

Larrabee, Eric, "Our Face to the World," *Horizon*, Vol. II, May, 1960, pp. 4–9, 122–123.

Schramm, Wilbur (ed.), *The Process and Effects of Mass Communication.* Urbana: University of Illinois Press, 1954.

Seldes, Gilbert, "Radio, TV, and the Common Man," *Saturday Review*, Vol. 36, August, 1953.

Siepmann, Charles, *Radio, Television, and Society.* New York: Oxford University Press, 1950.

Winick, Charles, *Taste and the Censor in Television.* New York: Fund for the Republic, 1959.

Wright, Charles, *Mass Communication: A Sociological Perspective.* New York: Random House, Inc., 1959.

Creative Writing

Teachers know that simply bringing children and books together is not enough to help children be good writers. Most assuredly, it does help budding young authors to hear, read, and enjoy the best of literature, and being able to read well does help to give children a constant flow of new ideas, words, and patterns of language with which to express their own ideas.

Most important of all, however, good teachers encourage and accept children's thoughts and feelings because they are unique to each individual. Teachers can capitalize on the ideas, concepts, and language each youngster brings to school with him, for even the most educationally handicapped have listened to, seen, and participated in experiences undreamed of even a few short years ago. The school helps the child enlarge and interpret his knowledge of himself and of the world around him—the world that he knows intimately and the more vicarious world. It follows that teachers must know, understand, and accept the language each child already knows and uses as well as to help him pursue new ideas and language that are basic to thought development.

Regardless of social dialect, paucity of traditional language or experiences, or native languages spoken in homes, each child brings ideas, words, and mannerisms of his own to school with him. These can be used as springboards for examining feelings and ideas and for generating new feelings and ideas as children become increasingly aware of who and what they are and of their interrelationships with one another.

The history of mankind is known to us through various kinds of record keeping that can be loosely described as writing—the signs and symbols man designed to tell those who came after him about his existence. Initially he drew pictures of himself, his family, his environment, and his adventures; later he designed symbols to record his spoken language, and thus began the process of teaching others to interpret these signs and symbols. The same process is repeated by each child as he develops language and thought; his *self* is first revealed through his attempts to speak, later through his drawings, and eventually by symbols representing his words.

At each stage of a child's development listening and speaking develop simultaneously and eventually so too do reading and writing. To teach any one of these skills as an isolated and separate one to the exclusion of the rest is to fracture the learning experiences so necessary to the development of good skills of communication.

Prerequisite to success in reading and writing are the elements that must be incorporated in all phases of language, thought, and communications instruction at every age level after a child enters school (72):

- Having many informal opportunities to talk in conversations, creative dramatics, puppets, "play corners," and the like.
- Exchanging ideas and participating in new experiences with others.
- Recording ideas and experiences using pictures, symbols, and notations.
- Having varieties of sensory and motor experiences.
- Learning about logical sequence and relating new information and ideas to those already known or understood.
- Being read to and talked with, taking trips together, seeing films and other visuals to be discussed, and participating in planning.
- Drawing or illustrating in some other manner or media one's impressions or understandings.
- Dictating individual and group accounts, ideas, dramas, or conversations.
- Selecting books for picture-story and eventually for special interest reading.
- Doing some meaningful writing every day using chalkboard, paper, or typewriter, with emphasis on thoughts and ideas.
- Understanding that when, and if, a piece of writing is to be taken home, put in the school newspaper, mailed, or displayed it can be proofread and grammar, handwriting, and spelling can be corrected *later.*
- Having regular individual and small group conferences to receive needed guidance and instruction with small groups changing as needs change.
- Keeping personal dictionaries of new words learned and used, and eventually learning to locate needed new words and information independently.
- Being able to develop individual creativity and ideation.

Sharpening the Senses

In newly emerging concepts of intelligence, a great deal of significance is being given to the full development of the senses to raise intelligence quotients and to sharpen mental acumen. The ways that information is acquired, organized, stored, used, and communicated are underscored and described as "the techniques that a child acquires for processing information furnished by his senses. Information pours into the brain through sound, sight, touch, smell, and taste. The brain appears to reduce this vast jumble of inputs to coded symbols which can be logically organized to solve problems, achieve goals, and carry on a meaningful existence" (72).

Following are some of the kinds of experiences that help children to develop and use their senses more fully:

Sound: Use materials and equipment such as records, tapes, sandpaper, chalk, coconut shell halves, different kinds of bells and whistles, motor and engine sounds, wind and rain, leaves rustling, bird songs, animal sounds, cellophane being crumpled, tapping different objects such as wood or metal, or different voices and tones of inflection. Have children close their eyes and guess what made the sounds or give one word that best describes the sounds. Open a window and listen to the sounds outside, or describe the sounds one hears at an airport or other terminal. List interesting, unusual, and different words that are given. Another good listening activity is provided when teachers read stories and poems that play on colorful and unique words to evoke memories and mental images.

Sight: Take field trips, look at slides, use film and filmstrips, study photographs and paintings, examine artifacts or rocks or shells, look at different kinds of tree bark, notice the changes in the sky, study colors in different light and at different times of the day, observe the changes that take place in shrubbery at different seasons of the year, observe the habits of a bird or an animal, talk about the different expressions on people's faces. Children like to keep records of what they see, such as:

"A bird floating like a piece of paper."
"A haystack sitting like a fat old king."
"A bare, cold tree just waiting for spring."
"One lonely cloud in a sea of blue."
"Soft, white sand that was once big, rough rocks."
"Leaves going to leafland for the winter."
"One lone star waiting for the others to come out and play."

One imaginative third grader *really looked at* the snow and discovered that he saw colors even though most people say that snow is white. Here is what he wrote:

Is snow white?
     No, it's blue at night.
And when there's sun
     I can see yellow:
When it's cloudy snow turns green
     and sometimes I can see a
Whole rainbow of colors.

Touch: Children like the "Touch and Guess" game in which they or the teacher bring objects such as an orange, a ball, an egg, sand, sugar, sandpaper, a furry animal or bird, other vegetables or fruits, a doll's hands or feet, tree bark, ice cubes, or cotton. Again, the experience of having eyes closed so that the sense of sight is eliminated elicits some very interesting descriptions and observations. Some teachers have used a book such as *Find Out by Touching* by Paul Showers and children have tried some of the experiments in touching suggested. One seven-year-old girl wrote this after touching a bird that had flown in the classroom window, resting there until it was strong enough to fly again:

> I touched him before he flew up high;
> Now we both know just how he feels—
> The little yellow bird and I!

Here are other comments children have made after "touch experiences":
A kindergartner said that a pumpkin "feels like a big, cold ball with lines in it."
A six-year-old described sand as "like sugar only not sticky."
A seven-year-old described his new baby brother as "soft and he won't get hard until he has been away from God for awhile."
Sand caused an eight-year-old to observe that "it feels like the bottom of the bathtub in the summertime."
Nine- and ten-year-olds described wood as "a piece of tree that is glad it didn't get burned up"; an apple as "like what I feel when I'm in my tree house at my Grandmother's"; and a kitten as "a little ball of fur that doesn't want to grow up."
These kinds of reactions represent language and "poetry in communication" that do not "just happen"; they are the result of deliberately planned curriculum experiences to help each child develop his senses more fully.

Smell: We are told that our sense of smell and our emotions are closely related. Note the relationship of the two in this poem by a nine-year-old boy:

> When I come home from school
>   And open the door of my
> Father's bakery, it
>   Smells just great.
> It smells like all the things
>   I'll have for supper
> And breakfast and even lunch.
>   It smells so good that I
> Don't want to wait.

This poem was an outgrowth of a classroom "smelling experience" and the catalyst was a piece of fresh bread. With eyes closed, students can smell and describe such things as soap, apples, other fruits or vegetables, bread, perfume or sachet, flowers, spices, leather, cheeses, cosmetics, or tobacco. These can be placed in small plastic cups so that the sense of touch will not be involved. Teachers list the different words and phrases children use to describe the same item.

Or teachers can use poetry such as *Smells* by Kathryn Worth to encourage experiences and discussions about how minds receive and send various messages. We like this poem written by a twelve-year-old after a series of sensory experiences in the classroom:

> I'm here—I can taste and smell and feel.
> I *am*—I can breathe and dance and see and hear.
> I'm *free*—I CAN!

Taste: It is interesting to experiment with one's sense of taste in at least two different ways. The first, with eyes closed, eliminates the sense of sight and helps children understand how much their ability to see conditions how they think things will taste. The second way is to hold one's nose while tasting to learn how much one's sense of smell affects the sense of taste. Children will think of other things to taste and so will their teachers, but here are a few suggestions: salt, sugar, bread, various fruits or vegetables, cheese, various greens, crackers, various juices, water, milk, tea, coffee, spices, and pickles. When asked what various tastes *remind* them of, children are apt to say things such as: a picnic, a walk in the woods, a cookout, a bakery, a supermarket, a restaurant, a department store, a bureau drawer, a closet, a TV snack, or a walk in a park.

The idea in each case of trying to isolate and develop one particular sense is that seldom do we take the time to really experience some of the common, everyday kinds of things and rarely do we appreciate the full importance of each one of our senses. These are the kinds of experiences schools should be providing and they are the kinds of experiences that transcend economic and social privileges or disadvantagement. Just a few suggestions have been given, but the reader should note others that have occurred to him as he read this section. And at the first opportunity, use some of these ideas with a group of children to test for yourself the new avenues of learning that will be opened to you and to the children.

These and other suggestions can be found in *Books for Children by Children,* which also discusses creative language and thought development (73):

> Each child has his own growing edge. This is especially true in language skill development. His expression of ideas and special ways of acquiring them are as unique as his looks and personality . . . there is none other in the world just like him. Each moment of his life should be an opportunity to satisfy his need to know, to achieve, to laugh, to feel deeply and express feelings, to understand others who are both alike and different, to create, to

appreciate beauty, to succeed or fail and try again, to empathize, to belong, to feel secure and needed, to love and be loved. . . . He must discover for himself the seemingly undiscoverable, to touch the untouchable, and accept the marvelous and possible as his own.

Family Life and Sex Education

The students and teachers of New City's schools instituted a program of family life and sex education as the direct result of involvement of many community agencies, parents, and teachers in studying the needs and recommending programs. They are also learning that social conflict can result even when a great deal of careful groundwork has been done and there seems to be general agreement about a new program or curriculum emphasis.

The program had been going rather smoothly for two or three years and had been based on recommendations such as this resolution passed in 1964 by the Joint Committee on Health Problems in Education of the National Education Association (NEA) and the American Medical Association (AMA) (74):

> Whereas, the altered structure of our society has resulted in greater permissiveness, and changing moral values, and
> Whereas, the years when sexual drives are recognized to be approaching a peak present the need for important and even urgent decisions on the part of youth, and
> Whereas, the exploitation by all forms of mass media of the sensual aspects of sex has placed undue emphasis on erotic behavior, as opposed to mature, responsible love relationships, and
> Whereas, the disparity between expressed beliefs and observed actions of many adults has not passed unnoticed by the youth of our country, and
> Whereas, the persistent occurrence of out-of-wedlock pregnancies and of venereal disease has been paralleled by a lessening of the restrictive effect on sexual behavior by either of these conditions, therefore be it
> Resolved that the schools accept appropriate responsibility for reinforcing the efforts of parents to transmit knowledge about the values inherent in our family system, and about the psychic, moral, and physical consequences of sexual behavior, and be it further
> Resolved that this be done by including in the general and health education curriculum the physiology and biology of human reproduction beginning at the elementary level and continuing throughout the school years at increasing levels of comprehension, and that the study of venereal diseases continue to be a part of communicable disease education during early adolescence, and be it further
> Resolved that the concept of the family as a unit of society based on mature, responsible love be a continuing and pervasive educational goal.

They had been assisted in launching their program by these groups, by a large and well-known university in their city, and by other national groups such as the Sex Information and Education Council of the United States (SIECUS) which was organized in the mid-1960's, and which stimulated concern of communities and offered aid for sex education in its broadest aspects with a statement of purpose (75):

> To establish man's sexuality as a health entity: to identify the special characteristics that distinguish it from, yet relate it to, human reproduction; to dignify it by openness of approach, study, and scientific research designed to lead toward its understanding and its freedom from exploitation; to give leadership to professionals and to society, to the end that human beings may be aided toward responsible use of the sexual faculty and toward assimilation of sex into their individual life patterns as a creative and re-creative force.

Funds for the new program had been made available through churches, civic organizations, the university medical school, and the board of education as well as federal funds available through the U.S. Office of Education and the state department of education. New City had the approval and support of both its state and federal offices of education, and had available funding through the following kinds of programs:

1. Aid to schools in low-income areas.
2. Supplementary education centers and services for elementary and secondary schools.
3. Community service and continuing-education programs, such as University Leadership for Urban Progress.
4. Vocational and technical education, under which home economics activities and the training of home economics teachers and health professions personnel are supported.
5. Guidance and counseling institutes, and institutes for advanced study, in which family life and sex education may be included as appropriate for the subject matter of the Institute.
6. Adult basic education programs, in which course materials for teaching reading, writing, arithmetic, and speech are related to such "adult experiences" as homemaking and family relations.

Teachers and laymen in New City had welcomed a policy statement made in August of 1966 by the man who was then U.S. Commissioner of Education, Harold Howe, II, and which explained the extent and control of the government's support:

> The United States Office of Education takes the position that each community and educational institution must determine the role it should play in the area of family life education and sex education; that only the community and its agencies and institutions can know what is desirable, what is possible, and what is wise for them in this realm. To assist communities and educational institutions which desire to initiate or improve programs in this area,

the Office of Education will support training for teachers and health and guidance personnel at all levels of instruction; it will aid programs designed to help parents carry out their roles in family life education and sex education. The Office will work closely with other agencies, both Federal and State, to ensure the most effective use of our resources in the implementation of this policy.

The school system had developed concept outlines for teacher–parent guidance and had teacher–laymen teams investigating and evaluating the various curriculum publications which are now being published to give aid and support to school teachers and administrators (see Sex Education Reference List at the end of this section). Included among these are: curriculum guides from other school systems and from commercial publishing companies, guidelines, courses of study, textbook supplements, discussion guides, pamphlets, resource units, and suggested programs of audio-visual aids.

The *Conceptual Approach of the School Health Education Study* (76) became their general model:

> The conceptual approach consists of a hierarchy of concepts developed into a framework for the health education curriculum. Health, defined as "a quality of life involving dynamic interaction and interdependence among the individual's physical well-being, his mental and emotional reactions, and the social complex of his existence," is the comprehensive, generalized concept appearing at the highest level of the hierarchy. This concept embodies physical, mental, and social dimensions which are the characteristic of all levels of the hierarchy.
>
> The next level of the conceptual model focuses on three key concepts which characterize the processes underlying health and serve as unifying threads of the curriculum. These are:
>
> *Growing and Developing*—a dynamic life process by which the individual is in some ways like all other individuals, in some ways like some other individuals, and in some ways like no other individual.
>
> *Interacting*—an ongoing process in which the individual is affected by and in turn affects certain biological, social, psychological, economic, cultural, and physical forces in the environment.
>
> *Decision Making*—a process unique to man of consciously deciding whether or not to take an action or of choosing one alternative rather than another.

Parents, teachers, and others involved in devising the initial pilot projects felt that the program was twofold and the pilot projects soon spread throughout the city as other schools and groups became involved and as more teachers were trained and capable. First, they agreed that it is easier and wiser to get across the basic facts of reproduction *before* students are old enough to be emotionally involved in the subject. And, second, that rather than merely describe human reproduction, sex education should try to help children understand the meaning of sexuality, to give a comprehensive view of how sex affects personality, the family, and society.

But trouble was in store for New City just as it was for many other cities when in 1968–69 new pressure groups started new vendettas against the schools and against family life and sex education, particularly. Even though the illegitimate birth rate was rising, incidents of venereal disease were increasing, drug addiction was becoming a serious problem, and most parents felt that they needed the cooperation of the school to help them combat societal problems to which their children were being exposed, there were groups, such as the John Birch Society and others, who stated publicly that the program was "little more than slick smut" and that the entire thing was "a communist plot."

One father, a conservative Catholic, asserted that a statement such as the one in a SIECUS study guide for teachers and parents that "attempting to indoctrinate young people with a set of rigid rules and ready-made formulas is doomed to failure in a period of transition and conflict" was particularly galling to him. "In my church," he said, "children go to catechism classes just to learn a set of moral rules—to learn their faith including Church teachings on sex. I don't want them taught in school that this is just all a matter of opinion or that they can decide for themselves." Antagonists in the New City sex-education debate regularly accused one another of being warped by sexual hangups or obsessions. Proponents called the right-wing attackers "very, very sick people." Each side accused the other as the controversy grew, and accusations included statements about "calculated deceptions" and "base conspiracies."

A newspaper article during the controversies quoted the Birch Society's Mr. Welch as saying, "Deep-laid plans have been carefully initiated to spread this subversive monstrosity [sex education] over the whole American Education system" (77). This same account also says that the result of the crusades to eliminate sex education from schools is that "after about five years of surprisingly smooth sailing, sex education is as bitter and emotional as any controversy that ever rocked the nation's schools." Stunned educators, they say, who "thought they had won support for sex education through intensive efforts to tell parents about the courses, are asking, 'Why now?' Nobody really knows."

The educators and proponents of sex education in New City, as in other cities that have been attacked for their innovative and imaginative programs, consider that it is an important facet of their total health education program. They see that there is some danger in rushing to institute programs, and have felt that they moved slowly and logically. They agreed with Dr. Calderone (78) when she said that "The rush to climb on the sex education bandwagon is ill advised if it results in poor efforts, half-baked programs, and mistakes so glaring as to arouse community opposition to a pitch that will slam doors that may not be reopened for another generation." But they feel that theirs has been a good, solid effort and that the program is not only necessary but also approved by the majority of parents.

The arguments are pointless, and we hope that the teachers and parents of children in New City will persist in their efforts to continue good health education including family life and sex education. The sexual revolution is only one part, although a very important part, of the changing world of the twentieth century. Schools need to help children and youth understand more about themselves, and sexuality is part of understanding oneself. After all, each person has a self and a sexuality even before he is born, and long before children come to school, families and communities have been giving informal, and not always positive, instruction in self-concept, home and family living, and sex education. There is no magic age when children are more "ready" for such instruction, but *things* change faster than people and institutions do.

Family life and sex education of broad scope need to be included in the elementary school curriculum; many of the concepts from model frameworks will be legitimate for a long, long time to come and only the facts may change from kindergarten through college.

> The modern definition of sex education is no longer merely a recital of the facts of life but is concerned also with the importance of moral values in interpersonal relationships and with the family's role as a social unit. It also includes the teaching of male and female roles to children, and thus permits an integrated approach to the whole problem of role fulfillment in a changing society. Though there was always a need for sex education, there are many reasons why the need is greater today (79).

Among some of the reasons detailed by Wright are these:

- Statistics show startling increases in numbers of teen-age marriages.
- Divorce rates for teen-age marriages continue higher than any other age group.
- Teen-age parents tend to produce a higher percentage of premature babies, with a consequent rise in mortality and morbidity rates due to lack of prenatal care.
- Infectious syphilis has increased over 200 per cent among teen-agers in the past several years.
- Studies in cities reveal that very few teen-agers attending venereal disease clinics have any knowledge of their disease.
- Modern developments in urbanization, homes broken by death or divorce, accelerated social and scientific changes, the population explosion, delinquency, the increasing productive span of life, the changed attitudes toward previously accepted moral values—all of these increase the need for education to strengthen community and family living.

What does all of this actually mean to elementary school teachers? What are the responsibilities of elementary schools? Do they have *any* responsibilities? They certainly do.

Life management and social action curriculum must start early to teach children about good mental and physical health, and sexuality is a very important part of this. In conjunction with families, church, and other community agencies, including clinics and universities, a young child should have continuing education in the following areas:

Physical Facts

Physical facts include accurate knowledge of not only the "facts of life" —reproductive physiology, correct terms for bodily functions, developmental changes, venereal disease, and so on—but also the relationship of these to good mental health. Naturally, these are presented and discussed in a gradually ascending conceptual framework in proportion to children's ages, abilities, and readiness.

Emotional and Psychological Development

Feelings and attitudes are immensely important, and should include respect and reverence for life, sex, marriage, the family, parenthood, for one's own and the opposite sex, and for general societal responsibilities. A child should grow in his understanding of the psychology of men and women, the nature of love, the place of dating and courtship, the need for self-control whether married or unmarried. Attention should also be given to the problems accompanying emotional and physiological development (e.g., those of approaching puberty and adolescence) and the understanding and knowledge necessary to help a child deal with these.

Moral Values

Sex, marriage, family life, and participation in community affairs are deeply and essentially tied to moral values in American life. Since education is not merely a matter of imparting information but also of attitudes, values, and habits, the school emphasizes that knowledge, by itself, does not give license nor does it produce virtue; rather it should buttress the moral teachings of home and church.

Socioeconomic Context of Life

Sex education should be an integral part of general education, integrated into a total view and into a unified pattern of life. There are tremendous pressures and changes in modern living; these have been mentioned and discussed throughout this book as we have tried to relate them to implications for modern elementary school curriculum. Each is now, and will continue to be, related to each person's concept of his role in society as an individual and as a member of a family unit.

Launching Programs

Even though cities and communities across the country where programs have been launched or are being launched are having difficulties with right-wing pressure groups, it is important to study the guidelines used by communities that have proceeded in thoughtful and well-organized ways. Two programs serve as models here, one in Washington, D.C., and one in New Haven, Connecticut:

1. When educators and laymen have agreed about the necessity for the inclusion of family life and sex education in school curriculum, even though there are some dissenters, *curriculum guidelines and supporting* staff policies should be developed.
2. Budget is provided for in-service education and purchase and development of curriculum materials. This can be mutually provided by community agencies, the federal government, and the local board of education.
3. There should be continuing close cooperation with community groups who serve in an advisory and supportive capacity as the program is launched and as it continues to grow. These advisory groups can change as needs change but should always include representative community and civic action groups as well as educators.

WHAT IS INCLUDED? *In kindergarten and primary school,* children care for and observe small growing things such as hamsters, tropical fish, baby chicks, seeds, and plants. The different ways that life begins among animals, plants, and humans becomes a naturally observable and discussable phenomenon. Everyday events at home and at school are catalysts for wonder, observation, discussion, information gathering, and questioning; young children are interested in families of all kinds, human and animal, and extend their knowledge and understanding through curriculum experiences that can be made a normal part of a number of subject areas such as science, health, language arts, mathematics, and the arts.

During the upper elementary school and middle school years, boys and girls extend their understanding of the beginnings of human, plant, and animal life. They deepen their appreciation of human ways of living. Instruction continues through actual observation of animal life, and through films, reading materials, models, and photographs. Again all subject areas are really involved—science, social studies, literature and English, health and physical education, mathematics, and the arts. Preadolescents are helped to understand themselves and the various changes that are taking place socially, emotionally, physically, and intellectually.

In the middle and upper school years, young people learn more about puberty, masturbation, the sex drive, homosexuality, venereal disease, dating, courtship, marriage and its responsibilities, parenthood, various methods of birth control, drug and alcohol abuse, and the social implications of the family unit.

Throughout the curriculum for family life and sex education, the observations and questions of youngsters guide the pacing and emphasis of information given, and discussions are natural and flexible. Often boys and girls are in the same classes and sometimes they are separated if it seems that there will be more free and frank discussion when they are separated temporarily. At all levels, young people's need for private counseling and instruction are recognized, respected, and provided for. Because *the most important part of curriculum is the teacher,* they must be very carefully chosen and properly trained and supported if they are to deal with such sensitive and potentially controversial areas of instruction. In addition to technical background provided with the help of doctors, psychiatrists, social workers, and psychologists, *personal equilibrium and confidence* are necessary personal attributes. The teacher must have not only sufficient knowledge, but also must have sound values, a healthy emotional outlook, and integrated and accurate views of sex and sexuality.

Discussion Questions

1. Would classroom teachers, members of the school's faculty qualified by temperament and training, or "experts" from community agencies experienced in leading groups be the most desirable persons to work with children and youth in a family life and sex education program? Give your reasons for deciding which.
2. Does the existence and availability of the oral contraceptive pill affect the need for sex education? If so, at what levels of instruction?
3. Do the world's population explosion and health and welfare problems affect the responsibility of the school? If so, how?
4. The board of education is reluctant to include a program of family life and sex education in the curriculum. The PTA suggests that it be allowed to sponsor a series of discussions led by a doctor or a staff member from a community service agency skilled in family life and sex education. The discussions are to be held after school hours, in school buildings, open to all parents who wish to take part, and a nominal charge is to be made to cover expenses. The demonstration project, if successful, would be assumed by the board of education and lay-educator groups would begin to integrate family life and sex education concepts into the regular course of studies in the schools. What advantages and disadvantages do you see in this proposal?
5. What do you think curriculum content should include in the elementary, middle, and upper schools?
6. Do you agree or disagree with the following definition of family life and sex education? Give your reasons and your suggested changes:

Definition
Family life and sex education in its broadest meaning may be defined as any approach which helps the individual to live a more satisfying life, creatively enriched and productive, as a member of his family, his community, and his wider society—national and international. It may best be described as edu-

cation for personality maturation and increased self-understanding. It includes instruction designed to develop understanding of the mental, emotional, social, economic, and psychological, as well as the physical phases of human relations as these affect and are affected by male and female relationships. Contributing to such education are numerous fields of specific knowledge—each with emphases necessary to well-rounded personality development. These include: health and medical sciences, psychology, sociology, physical education, physiology, nutrition, housing, clothing and home management, family economics, religion, philosophy, literature, and the arts.

7. Do you agree or disagree that the school must acknowledge and share with the family and religious leaders a responsibility for family life and sex education?
8. Do you think the school's *avoidance* of this crucial area conveys certain values and attitudes to parents and children?
9. What pretraining and ongoing training do you think teachers should have?
10. What do you think evaluative procedures for teachers and for programs should be? Can you list desired behaviors of children?

Additional Suggested Reading

American Social Health Association, *About Family Life Education*. New York: The Association, 1968. Lists particularly good curriculum guides and resources.

Anschen, Ruth Nanda (ed.), *The Family: Its Functions and Destiny*. Rev. Ed. New York: Harper & Row, 1959.

Benedict, Ruth, *Patterns of Culture*. Boston: Houghton Mifflin Company, 1961.

Bossard, James, and E. S. Boll, *The Sociology of Child Development*. New York: Harper & Row, 1960.

Burgess, Ernest W., "The Family in a Changing Society," *American Journal of Sociology*, Vol. 53, 1948.

Delli Quadri, Fred (ed.), *Helping the Family in Urban Society*. New York: Columbia University Press, 1963.

Goode, William J., *World Revolution and Family Patterns*. New York: The Free Press, 1963. Traces reasons for family disruption and diminishing family influence.

Hess, Robert D., and Gerald Handel, *Family Worlds: A Psychosocial Approach to Family Life*. Chicago: University of Chicago Press, 1959.

Kroeber, Alfred L., *Anthropology: Culture Patterns and Processes*. New York: Harcourt, Brace & World, Inc., 1963.

Selected Books on Sex Morality, YWCA, 600 Lexington Ave., New York. This book offers a bibliography of religiously oriented books on sex and values.

Selected References on Sex Education, American Academy of Pediatrics, 1801 Hinman Street, Evanston, Ill. Includes some references for teen-agers that are not usually on reading lists.

Stycos, J. Mayone, *Family and Fertility in Puerto Rico*. New York: Columbia University Press, 1955.

Following are organizations and publishers from which materials on family life and sex education can be obtained. It is not intended to be complete, and the listing is not exhaustive. Some of the organizations have many titles, others only a few. Most have materials for sale, and some have free materials. Some have films that can be used free, others have a rental fee. For these reasons, it is wise to write asking for the catalog or list of publications concerning family life, sex education, or child guidance before ordering.

American Academy of Pediatrics, 1801 Hinman Street, Evanston, Ill. 60204.
American Association for Health, Physical Education and Recreation, National Education Association, 1201 Sixteenth St., Washington, D.C. 20036.
American Home Economics Association, 1600 Twentieth St., N.W., Washington, D.C.
American Medical Association, Department of Community Health and Health Education, 535 North Dearborn St., Chicago, Ill. 60610.
American Social Health Association, 1740 Broadway, New York, N.Y. 10019
Child Study Association of America, 9 East 89 St., New York, N.Y. 10028.
Family Service Association of America, 44 East 23 St., New York, N.Y. 10010.
Florence Crittenden Association of America, Inc., 608 South Dearborn St., Chicago, Ill. 60605.
National Congress of Parents & Teachers, 700 North Rush St., Chicago, Ill. 60611.
National Council on Family Relations, 1219 University Avenue S.W., Minneapolis, Minn. 55414.
Public Affairs Committee, 381 Park Avenue South, New York, N.Y. 10016.
Sex Information & Education Council of the United States (SIECUS), 1855 Broadway, New York, N.Y. 10023.
U.S. Department of Health, Education, & Welfare, Children's Bureau *or* Public Health Service, Washington, D.C. 20201.

Human Resource Volunteers and Aides

There are various programs and help available to teachers. These have not been utilized effectively in schools of the past, but modern schools are beginning to realize the potential value of teacher aides, volunteers, and human resource paraprofessionals.

New City parents and teachers are finding that through the use of parents and other paid and volunteer human resources who share their special insights, talents, hobbies, experiences and interests with teachers and with boys and girls, their schools and their communities are vastly more relevant and exciting places for learning and doing.

Resource places and resource people may be suggested to you by the following list to help you use the human community more effectively in schools:

Airports	Labor organizations
Animal shelters	Libraries
Armories	Lumber—woodworking
Art exhibits	Markets
Associations	Museums
Bakeries	Music groups
Banks	Nurseries
Broadcasting stations	Nursing homes
Businesses	Orphanages
Churches	Other kinds of schools
Civic groups	Packing plants
Colleges	Park departments
Construction	Planetariums
Courts	Political headquarters
Crime prevention	Processing plants
Dairies and produce	Professional societies
Drama groups	Publishers
Dredging and harbors	Race relations groups
Economic councils	Railroad depots, airports, etc.
Employment agencies	Redevelopment agencies
Exchange teachers	Religious agencies and groups
Exchange students	Senior citizens' groups
Family counseling	Service clubs
Farms and farming	Slum clearance projects
Feed and grist mills	Social service groups
Filtration plants	Sports clubs and events
Fraternal clubs	State schools and homes
Government agencies	Theaters
Hatcheries	Telephone companies
Health agencies	Traffic centers
Historical sites	Travel and transportation agencies
Hobby clubs	Trust companies
Hospitals and clinics	Union headquarters
Housing agencies	Waterfront facilities
Human relations groups	Welfare agencies
Industry	Youth counseling groups
International groups	Youth organizations
Juvenile courts	Zoos and nature centers

Two of New City's programs that evolved as the direct result of educator–citizen planning that we described earlier in this section were the *Art Goes to School* program and the *Youth and the Law Project*.

Art Goes to School

Teachers and parents agreed that there were neither enough special art teachers nor adequate art facilities in New City's schools. New City, with a large university in its midst and more than its share of professional and semiprofessional artists, was in an ideal position to provide encouragement and support for school arts programs, but until teachers and community got together on the needs and the possible resources, nothing was done about improving the art education program. It was decided that volunteer groups might start by contributing to art appreciation and later expand to co-sponsor actual school-community centers for instruction in the various media. A visual arts committee was formed, and agreed that early exposure to art appreciation would serve three purposes:

> To heighten children's perception of art in traditional forms and in the world around them.
> To supplement children's knowledge and interest in history by making it more visual and therefore more vital.
> To make children aware of art as both vocation and avocation.

The first pilot projects consisted of three forty-minute lecture discussions to be presented by volunteers from the visual arts committee and followed up by teachers and their students in nine-, ten-, and eleven-year-old groups. Each group had three sessions with the volunteers dealing with the development and changes in American art forms from 1600 to the present, the colonial period, the Revolutionary period, and the last two centuries. Volunteer lecture-discussants were chosen carefully, the slide talks were carefully researched and written, the art gallery and the university assisted and advised, and from the beginning there were enthusiastic reports from children, teachers, parents, and volunteer teachers.

In advance of the lecture discussions, teachers received suggested activity lists, word lists, and bibliographies. Following each visit, prints of the paintings discussed were left and teachers were asked for evaluations that included suggestions for improvement in the presentations by volunteers. From a small beginning and a few pilot project classes, the project soon spread to other grades, more schools, and other lecture discussions such as pop art and history through architecture.

Prints-in-progress was added during the third year of the school-volunteer project, and involved volunteer printmakers who demonstrated the making of an original print and helped children create original prints. Portable presses were taken from school to school or were set up at a center convenient to several schools, thus bringing children from different schools together. With the presses and volunteer printmakers, it was possible to demonstrate and to involve children in creating silk screens, wood blocks, monotypes, and rubbing processes. Previous to and following classroom or art center demonstrations, students and teachers are encouraged to visit museums, art galleries, exhibits, historical and modern buildings, or art fairs; and students' work is exhibited in schools, stores, community centers, and at the annual arts festival.

In addition, Project Talent Search is now evolving in New City. It will bring together students with special talents in drama, dance, art, music, writing, and other areas with volunteers who can work directly with the students in either school settings or other settings such as private studios, university facilities, or civic centers. It is difficult to tell who benefits most by the creative activities in the graphic and performing arts in New City —volunteers, students, or teachers. But it is safe to say that the cooperative enterprises are making significant changes and real differences in the program of the schools, and in the lives of teachers and children.

Youth and the Law Project

Another New City project that uses volunteers and that evolved from the combined interest and concern of educators and parents is the Youth and the Law Project. As in many cities, New City's juvenile delinquency was increasing and many young people were found to lack knowledge of the reasons for having laws and the consequences of breaking them. Educators worked with women's clubs and the Bar Association to evolve a series of three lecture discussions to be conducted by lawyers and classroom teachers in each fifth and sixth grade classroom in the city. Lawyers were sought because of the derogatory ideas students, especially inner city students, had about police and juvenile authorities. The younger lawyers were especially effective, and they donated their Monday afternoons because this was the time they were most free from appearances at court sessions. The topics discussed ranged over wide varieties of questions and interests, but were generally grouped around these topics:

- Laws that affect young people.
- How laws come into being.
- How laws can be changed when times and need change.
- Juveniles and the court system.
- Noncriminal and criminal acts.
- Guilt by association.
- The liabilities of a criminal record.
- Civic responsibilities and the law.

Evaluation of the ongoing project includes reactions supplied by attorneys, students, teachers, school principals, and parents in regard to the following questions:

1. Was the program beneficial? If so, how? If not, why not?
2. Were attorneys (or students or teachers) cooperative?
3. Were lawyers on time and well prepared? Please comment. (Were students and teachers prepared? Please comment.)
4. Where do you recommend that the program is most appropriate if it were to be changed to another grade level?
5. How can the program be improved?

6. What curricular suggestions and activities can you share with other teachers, students, and attorneys? Please be specific.

7. Please give examples of student questions and concerns that impress you as illustrative and representative.

The convictions of parents and teachers that "one child in trouble is one too many" thus led to volunteer lay participation that has already benefited thousands of children in New City, and the possibilities for extending and improving it are infinite because it has been so enthusiastically supported by students, parents, teachers, attorneys, and other civic and fraternal groups.

Teacher aides, both paid and volunteer, are making a real difference in schools across the country as this is being written. They are helping school people revise outmoded ideas about nonprofessional educators and education, and we hope that the day is not far away when the teaching profession, realizing that it is impossible to be all things to all people, will *demand* the services of other professionals in the sciences, the humanities, and vocational and technical education. Educators and "laymen" need but to use their imaginations and their powers of persuasion to attract talent scarcely dreamed of to teaching partnerships in schools of the future, because the school of the future may well include many centers other than the traditional school building.

References

52. Childs, John L., *Education and Morals*. New York: Appleton-Century-Crofts, 1950, p. 7.

53. Benjamin, Harold, *The Sabre-Tooth-Curriculum* (by J. Abner Peddiwell, who really is Dr. Benjamin). New York: McGraw-Hill Book Company, 1939.

54. Cremin, Lawrence A., *The American Common School*. New York: Teachers College, Columbia University, 1951.

55. Cremin, Lawrence A., *The Transformation of the School*. New York: Alfred A. Knopf, Inc., 1961, p. 72.

56. Edgar, Earl E., *Social Foundations of Education*. New York: The Center for Applied Research in Education, 1965, p. 21.

57. Kluckhohn, Florence R., and Fred L. Strodtbeck, *Variations in Value Orientations*. New York: Harper & Row, 1961, pp. 10–19.

58. Myrdal, Gunnar, *An American Dilemma*. New York: Harper & Row, 1944.

59. Leeson, Jim, "The First Ten Years," *Phi Delta Kappan*, Vol. XLV, May 1964, pp. 362–370. (The title refers to the ten years following the 1954 *Brown v. Board of Education* decision saying that "in the field of public education, the doctrine of 'separate but equal' has no place" and that "separate educational facilities are inherently unequal.")

60. Grobman, H. G., and V. A. Hines, "The Private Life of the Teacher," *The Teacher's Role in American Society*. Edited by Lindley J. Stiles. New York: Harper & Row, 1957. 14th Yearbook of the John Dewey Society.

61. Brameld, Theodore, "The Meeting of Educational and Anthropological Theory," *Education and Anthropology*. Edited by George D. Spindler. Stanford, Calif.: Stanford University Press, 1955.

62. Hutchins, Robert M., *The Higher Learning in America*. New Haven: Yale University Press, 1936. Also see Hutchins' *Education for Freedom*. Baton Rouge, La.: Louisiana State University Press, 1947.

63. Fantini, M. D., and Gerald Weinstein, *Toward a Contact Curriculum*. New York: Anti-Defamation League of B'nai B'rith, 1967.

64. Hutchins, Robert M., *The Higher Learning in America*. New Haven: Yale University Press, 1936. Also see Hutchins' *Education for Freedom*. Baton Rouge, La.: Louisiana State University Press, 1947.

65. Seeley, John R., "Some Skills of Being for Those in Service in Education," *Life Skills in Schools and Society*. Washington, D.C.: Association for Supervision and Curriculum Development, 1969 Yearbook.

66. Rubin, Louis J., "The Object of Schooling: An Evolutionary View," *Life Skills in Schools and Society*. Washington, D.C.: Association for Supervision and Curriculum Development, 1969.

67. Rawson, Wyatt, and William Boyd, *The Story of the New Education*. London: William Heinemann, Ltd., 1965, pp. ix–x.

68. The American Book Company, *What's Happening to Our Language Today?* New York: The American Book Company, 1967.

69. Loban, Walter D., *The Language of Elementary School Children*. Research Report No. 1, Champaign, Ill.: National Council of Teachers of English, 1963, p. 93.

70. Macintosh, Helen K., *Children and Oral Language*. Washington, D.C.: U.S. Office of Education, 1964.

71. Postman, Neil, *Television and the Teaching of English*. New York: Appleton-Century-Crofts, 1961.

72. Lageman, John Kord, "Can We Make Human Beings More Intelligent?" *Reader's Digest*, May, 1965. (From an interview with Dr. Joseph McVicker Hunt, who is the author of *Intelligence and Experience*.)

73. Wright, Betty Atwell, *Books for Children by Children*. (From *Teaching Tips*, the teaching guide which accompanies the books which children develop themselves.) New York: The John Day Company, Inc., 1966.

74. "NEA-AMA Joint Committee Resolutions," *Journal of Health, Physical Education, and Recreation*, Vol. 35, No. 7, September, 1964, p. 14.

75. "Why the Need for a Sex Information and Education Council of the United States as a New, Separate Organization?" *SIECUS Newsletter* 1, February, 1965.

76. School Health Education Study, *Health Education: The Conceptual Approach to Curriculum Design*. St. Paul, Minn.: 3M Education Press, 1967.

77. Reported in *The Wall Street Journal*, Friday, April 11, 1969, in a feature article written by Neil Ulman called, "A Delicate Subject: Sex Education Courses Are Suddenly Assailed by Many Parent Groups."

78. Calderone, Mary S., and Sally Fox, "SIECUS as a Voluntary Health Organization." Special Issue: "Human Sexuality and Education," *California School Health*, Vol. 3, No. 1, January, 1967, p. 8.

79. & 80. Wright, Betty Atwell, *Teacher Aides to the Rescue*. New York: The John Day Company, Inc., 1969, pp. 148–159.

SECTION III
Philosophy
AS A CURRICULUM FORCE

CHAPTER 7

Teachers Review Philosophy

Philosophical Contributions

Introduction

Just as philosophers refer to logical and consistent formulations, *theories, ideals,* and *ideas* about man's place in the world and as scholars and writers develop outlooks that help them view man and explain his existence, so teachers derive from their knowledge of past and present-day emerging philosophies personal philosophies for thinking about educational issues and values. Since the major issues of education are really philosophical, the professional teacher is concerned about philosophy not only as a student of human behavior but also as a student of human behavior within the context of the conditions and consequences of institutionalized school life.

From his own personal experiences in the world, from the study and contemplation of these in relation to the experiences of others, and from the structure of formal philosophy, the teacher evolves his own philosophical concepts. Basically, the teacher's previous study of philosophy, the structure and nature of formal philosophies, has been for the purpose of making available to him the tools of logic, scientific method, and ethical analysis. Additionally, it should have contributed to his social philosophies, political philosophies, and philosophy of history. These are the philosophies that equip individuals to cope critically with questions, problems, concepts, theories, and value judgments that arise in discussions of race, private property, the family, the state, human nature, obligations to others, socialism, free enterprise, civic responsibilities, civil disobedience, classes and class conflicts, self-government, the rights of man, and the relation of religion to morality.

Teachers need to have logical ways to question the concepts, generalizations, and doctrines to which they are subjected as they face controversial issues in changing times with objective examinations of ideas and arguments. Furthermore, they must be able to help students advance in making rational and well-considered judgments, and, together with their students, they will be engaged in various stages of critical analysis basic to reasoned judgments and should be able to circumvent ready-made, "pat" answers, superficial evidence, bigotry, and ethnocentrism. They should not have to be stopped short by avoidance of controversial issues, but rather should be free to handle them without rancor or indoctrination, as we have previously stated in this book.

Special interests, pressures, and even emotionally charged words are also the concern of applied philosophy, for the "entry of interests and of emotionally charged words into discussions of human affairs has itself to be noted and examined. The teacher needs to make clear the how and why of requirements laid down for testing assertions on the basis of evidence and right reasoning and to point out the pitfalls which trap discussions that neglect these requirements" (1).

Teachers and their students will then have grounds for acceptance or rejection of concepts, generalizations, and doctrines which can be brought under review while applications and implications are investigated and explored. To be able to do so is to participate in "the examined life" which Socrates declared to be the life most worthy to be lived by man.

Philosophy and Education

Before the emergence of some of the newer social sciences, philosophy and history were the main tools available to students of human behavior. Examples of this premise include Plato's theory of the ideal and the propositions that eventually derived from it, as well as Milton's description of cosmic forces in *Paradise Lost* and *Paradise Regained* in elaborate constructions of humanistic theory. These will remind the reader that a great deal of past and present-day educational theory is of the humanistic type and therefore highly germane to the study of education.

In order to improve instructional programs and to share innovative practices in, between, and among schools, each teacher contributes by adopting the attitude, *"I make a difference."* The history of education highlights many individuals who have "made a difference." Among them are men such as Francis Bacon, John Amos Comenius, Jean Jacques Rousseau, Johann Heinrich Pestalozzi, Friedrich Froebel, and John Dewey.

Bacon (1561–1626), an English philosopher, influenced education by his scientific method of aiding learning through observation, utilization of the senses, and classification. The Czechoslovakian educator Comenius (1592–1670) developed the first illustrated textbook, the *Orbis Pictus*, with the idea of appealing to children. The French writer Rousseau

(1712–1778) opposed intellectualism as an exclusive right of the elite, campaigned for the rights and dignities of the common man, and is characterized by his belief in educating the child through experimentation in his natural environment. The philosophy of Pestalozzi, a Swiss educator (1746–1827), centered around the natural unfolding of children's abilities and interests; he was among the first to advocate the need for establishing teacher education institutions. Froebel (1782–1852), a German educator, espoused the need for young children to acquire self-realization through creative play, and it was he who founded the kindergarten system. And an American educator, John Dewey (1859–1952), believed that learning originates in life experiences and that learning situations should deal with problems selected from the child's environment.

With emphasis on the teacher as the person who can make a real difference in curriculum and as the primary designer of instructional programs, teachers study philosophy for the wealth of ideas necessary for creative approaches to current educational concerns and problems.

> A knowledge of philosophy is fundamental not only to an understanding of education as a whole, but also to a clear grasp of the actual techniques of teaching and their effective use (2).

You will remember that no philosophy is completely isolated from the others, that there is a great deal of interrelationship among philosophies, and that the work of later philosophers builds upon that of earlier ones. So too no educational philosophy is isolated from all others, because philosophers think in terms of philosophical positions and meanings rather than dogmatic statements and total beliefs. Just as psychology and sociology serve as important teaching forces, the various educational philosophies will serve you, as an eclectic, by helping you to formulate your own philosophy. As you adopt parts of differing philosophies that are acceptable and workable for you, you may adopt or adapt ideas from philosophy that will help you have both general and systematic ways to think about the "whole of reality." Teachers, like philosophers, find the need to think about the whole of reality rather than just a part of it as the scientist is able to do.

Psychology and sociology have assisted you to formulate concepts and understandings about how children learn and how they are affected by their social settings. The information in this section on philosophy is intended to help you:

1. Acquire broad perspectives in personal and professional knowledge and experiences.
2. Discover how philosophy applies in defining goals and purposes of education.
3. Develop concepts for relating content and purposeful classroom experiences consistent with philosophical beliefs.

Even though there is considerable overlapping, labels play an important role when we discuss the various schools of philosophical thought; the labels generally associated with these are: idealism, realism, neo-Thomism, experimentalism, and existentialism. These philosophies have been extended into the educational setting to form the following educational philosophies:

CLASSICAL PHILOSOPHY	EDUCATIONAL APPLICATION
Idealism	
Realism	
Neo-Thomism	Traditionalism
Experimentalism	Pragmatism
Existentialism	Existentialism

Of these, idealism and realism date back to Plato (427–347 B.C.) and Aristotle (384–322 B.C.), when philosophers were asking the questions that have become basic to formal philosophy and philosophers:

1. What is real? (Ontology)
2. What is true? (Epistemology)
3. What is good? (Axiology)

Philosophy and Educational Thought

These brief résumés are for the purpose of reminding the reader about the various philosophies, but the bibliography which is included with each chapter is included so that more thorough study of the meanings, inferences, interpretations, purposes, and values of the major philosophies can be made. The more the teacher attempts to increase his knowledge and to develop consistent patterns of behavior in terms of ontology, epistemology, and axiology, the more seriously he takes his job as he examines critically the assumptions upon which education is based.

Idealism

The ontology (what is real) of idealism is made more obvious when one omits the *l* from the word *ideal* to form the word *idea;* the world of *ideas* in recorded philosophy dates back to Socrates and Plato. Socrates (469–399 B.C.) utilized the process of "drawing out ideas" from man by carefully questioning the individual to help him find truth for himself; the technique of drawing out knowledge from the individual is known as the *Socratic method of teaching.* Inherent in this educational practice is emphasis on man's ideas, on his thinking abilities, on his mental faculties.

Idealism considers man as a spiritual being whose interpretations of reality in the universe are based only on spiritual and mental reality rather than on the physical world and matter. In Plato's allegory of the cave, the world is not really real, but is only a shadow or imitation of the eternal world of ideas. In order to discover answers to what is real and what is true, the theory of idealism advocates the use of one's knowledge and ability to reason.

During the sixteenth and seventeenth centuries, scientific investigations of Galileo and Sir Isaac Newton challenged the position of the idealists, and conflicts arose between churchmen and scientists. The churchmen, following the philosophy of Aquinas, who was a disciple of Aristotle, defended their viewpoints through principles of idealism and realism. To them the spirit of God controlled the universe and through believing in "mind over matter" they perceived the physical world as created by God.

When we examine the epistemology (what is true) of idealism, we see that man is seen as a microcosm, a small world unto himself, with truth originating in his mind and as a product of his ability to reason. Both senses and subject matter are considered important in this view, but most significant is the development of the individual to his fullest potential through mental activity. Subject matter is not an *end*, but is a *means* by which the student experiences free will and expresses his individual nature.

And the axiology (what is good) of idealism is made obvious by looking at the word "ideal." Man's achievements in moral behaviors and aesthetic appreciation is based on values, or ideals, that are absolute and unchanging in this view of man. Attaining the ideal is the objective of the idealist and is accomplished through the organization and structure of man's ideas. In making choices of ethical conduct, according to interpretations given by Immanuel Kant, man must live so that his actions can become "the basis of a universal principle for all mankind."

In a classroom setting, ideas from various subject fields, but mainly from the humanities, are defined to serve as guidelines for intuitive thinking. In selecting the kinds of questions to ask students, the idealist does not emphasize the importance of the subject matter per se, but he concentrates on initiating thinking, attitudes, and insights based on what the student already knows or understands. One example of subject content serving as a vehicle, or means, rather than an end is illustrated by the following attempt to stimulate a group of eleven-year-olds to weigh reasonably moral values of society. These are the questions asked by their teacher during a discussion of Alfred Noyes's poem "The Highwayman."

1. What risks were the highwayman and the landlord's daughter taking by seeing one another? Why were these risks?
2. What do you consider to be the distinguishing characteristics of the landlord's daughter? of the highwayman? Why?
3. Are your sympathies with the Redcoats? the landlord's daughter? the highwayman? the landlord? Why?

4. How do your feelings coincide with our system of law and order? How do you think you came to feel this way?
5. Do you think it is morally right ever to kill oneself? another human being? How can you justify your opinions?
6. What moral values do you hold for yourself? How do you think you came to hold these?
7. What man or woman do you consider great because of their strong moral character or great talent? Is there one person in our local community that you respect for their ideas and contributions?
8. Do you think the social attitudes in the days of the highwayman are the same as they are now? Why or why not?

In this illustration, the student has the opportunity to discover his own *meanings* and to relate these to his own personal experiences; this is a basic principle of idealism. The idealist promotes a variety of methods in seeking self-direction for the student, but basic to success, of course, is the teacher who serves as a model by helping students achieve mental and spiritual growth through ascending powers of reasoning.

With emphasis on the dignity of man, the curriculum of the idealist's classroom provides opportunities for the student to use his own mind to reason and to discover personal realities. The curriculum is built on symbols, ideas, and subject matter in the areas of religion, history, philosophy, and the humanities and is significant only as it activates the child to develop concepts about established truths and verities. A prime objective of idealism is the discovery of the meaning of information and, through its application, development of the individual personality which will be in harmony with family, school, church, and nation. The idealist expresses himself in personality development through *self-discovery* and *free will* rather than through scientific investigation.

In the school of idealism, students are evaluated subjectively rather than objectively. Essay-type and open-ended oral questions are essential to enable the student to express the ways he sees himself in relation to society, and the teacher is more concerned with an individual's rapport with the world than with his mastery of facts. The idealist teacher deals with the concepts of truth and knowledge in helping students reach the goal of self-realization. Absolute idealists, such as Hegel, say that knowledge is valid only to the extent that it forms a system, and both Plato and Hegel believe that the good life is possible only within a highly organized society. But Kant advances less totalitarian ethics when he urges men to treat one another as ends rather than means as in the highly organized society of Plato's *The Republic* where every individual has his own function and purpose.

Record your ideas about idealism as it relates to the following material:

1. How do you see subject content as it relates to the idealists' philosophies?
2. How do you see method as it relates to the idealists' philosophies?

3. How do you think idealism relates to evaluation?
4. What part do you think idealism should play in teachers' personal and professional philosophies?

Realism

Realism stems from Aristotle who was for twenty years a student of Plato. Aristotle is an example of a creative thinker who, in disagreeing with Plato, felt strongly the need to question the principles of idealism and to create a new, more systematic philosophy which would deal objectively with the nature of reality.

In considering the ontological question about what is real, Aristotle answers "matter" or "the physical world." Realists believe that there is an absolute plan for the universe which is permanent and enduring, and that even though change occurs, it is governed by natural laws under which all physical phenomena perform. Objects and items of matter existing in the universe are to be identified by man as they really are and not as he thinks they are; things have an existence independent of man and therefore do not depend upon man's perception of their existence.

Concerning what is true, the realist is objective in studying the universe and formalizing principles and laws as they exist. Man bases his beliefs in the reality of matter through his sense experience with each object, and according to Aristotle nothing can be in the intellect unless it is experienced originally through the sense of seeing, hearing, touching, tasting, or smelling. Consequently, sensory experiences are planned and perception is tested for accuracy.

The realist refers to the physical world and to natural law when he looks at the axiological problem of what has value; he believes that the moral behavior of man is acquired by adjusting to his environment through his knowledge of natural laws governing the universe and structuring human behavior on absolute moral standards. The first principles of the natural law are supposed to be known to every "normal" human being through reason alone. The natural law is not supposed to change, but man's knowledge of it changes. Through training the mind with formal drills, the way is supposed to be prepared for the realist to develop knowledge, skills, and moral standards he will need in order to adjust to the physical world.

In placing emphasis on reality, the realist does not overlook the child in his relationship to objects and to matter, for the child is a part of the physical world and reality is the physical world. The realist's main concern is to have the child observe reality accurately; what is taught should be enduring, contain well-defined values, and provide items of knowledge that aid all living human beings with exact principles and laws. Life adjustment to one's environment is facilitated by this knowledge and the perception of objects and matter in the universe that are orderly and rational.

Mastery of facts is accomplished through the systematic organization of a hard core of subject matter. Studies in science and mathematics are paramount because they lend themselves to an objective analysis of man's world. Accomplishments can be measured objectively, and thus evaluation becomes more scientific and exact. The composition of the subjects of mathematics and science is made up of objects, things, and numbers which can be perceived through the senses and explained by natural and logical laws. Information can be prescribed and dictated because knowledge is considered to be absolute and basic values will remain constant.

Because subject matter is chosen by traditional authority and follows a logical, predictable order, it is supposed to be uncontaminated by the teacher's biases and prejudices. The teacher serves mainly to schedule time for various fields of study and to provide the educational setting that employs sense of perception. While ordering factual mastery of content, the realist presents the subject in logical fashion, beginning with the simple and progressing to the complex. To assist the student in sense perception about the universe as it really is, the realist augments the lecture with concrete demonstrations, experiments, visual aids, and field trips. To illustrate the teaching concepts and practices of one realist teacher, let us examine the work of a class of ten-year-olds:

> The teacher and the children constructed a miniature Acropolis in order to perceive more realistically the relationship between Greeks and the physical world from 300 B.C. to the present. They used maps to gather information about cities, land regions, coastlines, surface features, and natural resources. They conducted a class symposium on Greek gods in which they discussed the events of the day. They also dressed in togas and tunics to play the roles of philosophers such as Plato, Aristotle, and Demosthenes lecturing on various philosophies.
>
> Evaluation of the project included formal tests to determine what had been learned in each of the areas studied. Evaluation was mainly concerned with dates, places, events, geography, people, the gods, and the ideas of the philosophers who had been studied.

Consider the following questions:

1. What do you consider to be the main differences between idealism and realism?
2. What aspects of realism do you think will make learning more effectual?
3. Which are the most important qualities of idealism and realism for personal philosophies and for classroom practice? Why?
4. What are the major differences between *rational realism* and *natural* or *scientific* realism?
5. How do *classical realism* and *religious realism* relate to public education?
6. How do the opinions of the leading neorealists of our day differ from

those of the classical realists? Investigate Bertrand Russell, Alfred North Whitehead, and Ralph Barton Perry, among others.

Thomism

Saint Thomas Aquinas originated the philosophy of Thomism by applying the beliefs of Aristotle to religion. It is important for teachers only to know that religious realism is the basis for not only the Roman Catholic Church but also other orthodox religions, including Anglicans (Episcopalians) Jews, and Baptists. The role of the church and religious beliefs as they affect individuals—adults and children—has been previously discussed, but it is germane to mention here that, from the ontological point of view, the Thomist states that both matter and spirit have been created by God, and that through His supreme wisdom there has been constructed an orderly and rational universe. Thomists agree that man can discern the moral laws through his reasoning ability but that in order to practice them he needs divine guidance. Beliefs are substantiated through revelations from the Bible, from sacred documents, and in the teachings of Christ.

In regard to what is true, the Thomist states that truth is in God and can best be learned through God's scripture and the church. Generally, the belief prevails that revealed truth through God is superior to reasoned truth. When man experiences conflict between revealed truth and reasoned truth, reasoned truth must bow because of some defect in man's reasoning.

1. What conflicts do you see for the teacher from a deeply religious home in public education? For the child from a deeply religious family?
2. How would you resolve the conflict between *revealed truth* and *reasoned truth* in the classroom situation if the topic for discussion were, for example, the theory of evolution?
3. Compare the philosophies of world-famous spokesmen for modern Thomism such as Etienne Gilson and Jacques Maritain; leading American Thomists including William McGucken, Robert J. Henle, Edward A. Fitzpatrick, and William F. Cunningham.
4. Find out what the best-known American exponents of the implications of classical realism for education think. Investigate Mortimer Adler, Robert M. Hutchins, and Scott Buchanan and the meaning of *perennialism.*
5. What is your own opinion about evidence gathered by the senses and subjected to rational or scientific realism? Suggest possible ways that this can be tested in classroom situations.

Traditionalism—Including Perennialism and Essentialism

As the table of *classical philosophies* with *educational applications* cited earlier in this chapter showed, traditionalism reflects principles from idealism, realism, and Thomism. The essentialist and the perennialist are similar in that they select content with complete autonomy and they look upon education as a process of storing up knowledge. The essentialist believes that certain basic ideas and skills or disciplines essential to our culture are formulable and should be taught to all alike by certain time-tested methods.

Basically, essentialism is a combination of idealism, which upholds the belief that the mind is supreme, and realism, which supports the view that universals exist outside of the mind. The essentialist builds his curriculum around the experiences of the race, and the perennialist turns to Aristotle, Plato, Aquinas, and their modern successors dealing with problems of ultimate reality (as the nature of being). The perennialist advocates disciplining the mental faculties of memory, will, and reason, and thereby creates an educational program more for the intellectually elite than do the essentialists.

When Hutchins spoke of that which is distinctly human in man remaining the same everywhere, he also said that "education should be the same for everyone" (3).

He is using one of the six basic principles of perennialism, which are the following:

1. Because human nature is constant, the nature of education also remains constant.
2. Education should concentrate on developing man's rational faculties since his most distinguishing characteristic is his ability to reason.
3. Since truth is universal and unchanging, education need only adjust to the truth and education should lead only to adjustment to truth.
4. Education is preparation for life rather than a replica of it.
5. Curriculum should consist of certain basic subjects which will make young people knowledgeable about the world's permanencies—both spiritual and physical.
6. Permanencies are best studied through what the perennialist calls the "great books."

The basic principles of essentialism are four and include the following:

1. Hard work and application are necessarily involved in learning.
2. Initiative in education should be for the teacher, not the pupil.
3. Prescribed subject matter and its absorption are the heart of the educational process.
4. Traditional methods of mental discipline should not be abandoned by the school.

Both the essentialist and the perennialist view the role of the school as that of an agency charged with teaching the student the traditional mores and customs of the society which he is to uphold. The principles of democracy are to be interpreted as fixed and absolute, and the school as an educational institution is to follow rather than lead society.

From the traditionalist's point of view, knowledge is education, and the acquisition of knowledge is pursued by students through hard work in lectures, recitation periods, and examinations. Method and content remain constant, because the students' objectives are predetermined and well established by the teacher and the course of study. Techniques for individualizing the curriculum are omitted because the same values and techniques hold true for all; consequently, the hard core of subject matter presented by the teacher is the sole prerequisite for the "good life."

In the traditionalist's views, the teacher is dedicated to the task of imparting information to the child and to authoritarian control. The traditionalist teacher is more apt to be rigid in outlook and organization and less apt to be flexibly and intimately involved with process because operations are more perfunctory. Presentations may include demonstrations, instructional television, teaching machines, and human resources, but the repetitive dependency upon textbooks and lectures allows little leeway for spontaneous discussion, discovery, and self-initiated activity. Students in the traditionalist's classroom are conditioned through indoctrination with the idea that definite, prescribed values and experiences are essential to everyone. Conformity of thought and action characterize such classrooms, because the child is expected to regurgitate facts and fears reprisals for nonuniformity and nonconformity.

In the following illustration of an art lesson, the traditionalist's emphasis on intellectual development, logical order of content, and orderly repetition is observable. This is the teacher's lesson plan for a group of upper elementary school-age children:

Teacher objective: To have the children paint a still life and submit a finished product for exhibition and for grading.

Activities:
1. Outline and discuss characteristics of a good painting:
   a. mood
   b. line
   c. color
   d. light and shade
   e. mechanical perspective
2. Show and discuss the painting, "Still Life: Apples, Pear and White Mug," by Jean Baptiste Simeon Chardin, 1699–1779 (French).
3. Set up and discuss still life arrangement of mug, knife, one pear and four apples.
4. Children to draw still life. Call attention to line and mechanical perspective.
5. Children to color in their still life. Have them call attention to natural colors, light, and shade.

6. Analyze each painting in terms of proper conformity to nature and to principles of mood, line, color, light and shade, and mechanical perspective.
7. Collect papers and grade the finished products preparatory to displaying best ones for PTA exhibit.

Discuss the following three quotations in relation to essentialism and to traditionalism. What are the curriculum implications?

The essentialist is no less interested than the progressive in the principle that learning cannot be successful unless it is based on the capacities, interests, and purposes of the learner, but he believes those interests and purposes must be made over by the skill of the teacher who is master of that "logical organization" called subjects and who understands the process of educational development (4).

Essentialism places the teacher at the center of the educational universe. This teacher must have a liberal education, a scholarly knowledge of the field of learning, a deep understanding of the psychology of children and of the learning process, an ability to impart facts and ideals to the younger generation, an appreciation of the historical-philosophical foundations of education, and a serious devotion to his work (5).

Since the environment carries in itself the stamp of the past, and the seeds of the future, the curriculum must inevitably include that knowledge and information which will acquaint the pupil with the social heritage, introduce him to the world about him, and prepare him for the future (6).

Experimentalism Including Progressivism

Ideas contained in experimentalism can be traced to Heraclitus (c. 535 B.C.–c. 475 B.C.), but its evolvement as an American philosophy was initiated and developed by Charles Sanders Pierce, William James, and John Dewey. Heraclitus introduced the *theory of reality of change* and Dewey applied this liberal philosophy to education. As used in this discussion, experimentalism identifies the philosophy; pragmatism is the application of experimentalism to education to form an educational philosophy; and progressivism is the name applied to the school movement and to practices of pragmatism. The three labels of experimentalism, pragmatism, and progressivism are used interchangeably by many authors, but progressivism is essentially the application of pragmatism to education.

One of the first Americans who rebelled against the strict formalism of traditional education (which was conceived as passive learning, drill and grill, and stiff discipline) was Francis Wayland Parker (1837–1902), the first director of the School of Education at the University of Chicago. Basic elements of the Progressive Education Movement can be found in the practices he encouraged—more informal settings, freedom from strict discipline, and more pupil involvement in the learning process. Around the turn of the century, more educators were rebelling against traditionalism, but the movement that later became organized remained largely individualized and localized until after the publication of John Dewey's first major writing, *Schools of Tomorrow*. Although this was published in 1915, the Progressive Education Association was not formally founded for four more years.

Concerning what is real, or what is the essence of reality, progressivism adopts the pragmatist view that change, not permanence, is the only reality. Since education, in this view, is always in the process of developing, educators will modify policies, methods, and content in the light of changes in environment and settings and in light of new knowledge. Dewey (7) talked about a continual reconstruction of experience when he wrote, "We thus reach a technical definition of education: it is that reconstruction or reorganization of experience which adds to the meaning of experience, and which increases the ability to direct the course of subsequent experience."

Progressivism has six basic principles related to growth through the reconstruction of experience:

1. The examined interests of the child should make his education active and related.
2. Learning should be involved with problem-solving projects rather than with the absorption of subject matter because people handle change, perplexity, and novelty of life better when they can break these down into specific problems.
3. Education should be in regard to life itself rather than preparation for life because intelligent reconstruction of experience is synonymous with civilized living.
4. The teacher's role must change from authoritarian dispenser-of-knowledge to guide-adviser as the child learns in accordance with his own needs and interests.
5. Schools should foster cooperation rather than competition because individuals achieve more when they work with and for one another rather than against one another.
6. Education and democracy imply one another and therefore schools should be organized and operated along the principles of democracy.

Probably the greatest misunderstandings and conflicts that arise between traditionalists and progressivists center around the acquisition of knowledge. Basically, the first views learning as the passive reception of knowledge by the student and the second views learning as being actively acquired through experience. Dewey (7) pointed this out when he said that the

most direct blow at the traditional separation of doing and knowing and at the traditional prestige of purely "intellectual" studies, however, has been given by the progress of experimental science. If this progress has demonstrated anything, it is that there is no such thing as genuine knowledge and fruitful understanding except as the offspring of *doing*. The analysis and rearrangement of facts which is indispensable to the growth of knowledge and power of explanation and right classification cannot be attained purely mentally—just inside the head. Men have *to do* something to the things when they wish to find out something; they have to alter conditions. This is the lesson of the laboratory method, and the lesson which all education has to learn.

In this statement, Dewey makes it clear that he does not reject the content of traditional subject matter and, in fact, would retain a great deal of it. He merely says that subject matter changes in light of new knowledge and in the light of men's experiences in physical and social environments. Problem solving is not to be the end result, but only the means used to move from concrete to abstract ideas, from practical to theoretical issues, and from sensory to intellectual development. McMurray (8) says that

> Clearly, the intent of Dewey's theory was to stimulate more and better learning of arts, sciences, and technologies. There was in this program no concern for immediately practical or directly utilitarian bits of information and technique, nor any process of choosing and organizing information around characteristic activities of daily life. On the contrary, in Dewey's version of pragmatism, characteristic activities of daily life were psychologically useful starting points for moving the learner to consideration of meanings increasingly remote, abstract, and related to one another in impersonal systems rather than to practical daily use.

Today we hear a great deal about critical thinking, discovery, and the reconstruction of ideas to fit new times. In the pragmatic view of education, subjects would not be as general as economics, geography, or the social studies, but would center around specific themes or problem areas, sometimes called *units*, such as communication, transportation, import and export, weather, or conservation. These are not fixed in the sense that curriculum was formerly a cut-and-dried affair, but instead, Thomas (9) says that "a curriculum cannot be more than outlined broadly in advance by the teacher and will consist largely of an array of resources which the teacher anticipates may be called upon as the current activities of the class lead on to new interests and new problems. The actual details of the curriculum must be constructed cooperatively in the classroom from week to week."

The pragmatic acceptance of the change in reality does not imply that the individual invents new truths without scientific investigation. The pragmatist considers problem solving and scientific investigation as instruments to test ideas and to fulfill tasks. He evaluates truth in terms of satisfaction of the action performed between the biological organism and the physical world.

Experimentalism is concerned with axiology, since the experimentalist believes the question of what is good or of value is really, "Of what worth is human experience?" He applies the scientific approach to a belief, an act, or a theory in moral and ethical behavior just as he does to the intellect. He is concerned about what is "best" for society and feels that this transcends the good of the individual. Dewey, especially, felt that democracy as "shared experience" was important to the total development of the individual, and that only through practical democracy in school situations can each individual learn how to think critically about his own behavior as he reconstructs experiences that correspond harmoniously with those existing within the society.

Concepts in Pragmatism

From the viewpoint of the pragmatist, the teacher who is fact-oriented does not assist the student in adjusting to society because he isolates knowledge from experience. The pragmatist provides diversity in classroom situations so the individual can experience intellectual curiosity and extend truths to meet personal needs. Pragmatic principles are developed in the classroom by the establishment of a democratic climate in which rules of behavior develop from mutually agreed-upon needs and from experiences within the classroom. They are enforced for class members, and students strive to improve behavior through class analysis of problems. Because of the universality of change in the social world, the teacher constantly involves the class in critical and creative thinking, conclusion drawing, and choice making.

Classroom climate that fosters creativity and flexibility characterizes pragmatic thought and teaching philosophy. A pragmatic approach to teaching is illustrated by the following example of a project to find out how insects of various kinds live:

How It Began: A class of eight-year-olds had learned a great deal about the living habits of dogs, cats, guppies, hamsters, cows, sheep, and rabbits through personal observations, field trips, books, pictures, and films. They became curious about insects such as flies, spiders, ants, and mosquitoes with which they were less familiar and which were not so easily observable. Since ants live under ground, how could they possibly *see* how they live?

What the Teacher Did: He led the children to think of various ways they could reconstruct an underground living situation above ground so that it could be observed and studied. One child said that he had read about a way to make an ant colony in a terrarium, another suggested that they could capture some spiders and put them in a glass cage, and a third suggested collecting lady bugs or lightning bugs. The teacher said these were all good ideas and suggested that possibly one class project, the ant colony, could be a group project and then individuals could devise other experiments with different insects, based on these procedures, observations, and evaluations.

What Happened: Max, the child who remembered reading about how to make an ant colony, was asked to find his reference so that he and his classmates would know how to set up a replica. Teacher and children gathered the necessary equipment to construct a frame for an ant nest, the sand and dirt for the nest, and the ants. As time went on, they studied the social roles of queen ants, workers, and males. They observed stages of the egg, larva, and pupa. They observed the uses of various rooms and tunnels within the colony, and the amount and nature of food given as it affected population and productivity. They read and discussed the differences between their ant colony and various kinds of ant colonies that exist in clay, mud, or hollow trees. They observed the care and feeding of the young and of the workers who were given less care and attention. They observed what happened to the females after laying their eggs, and learned about marriage flights when ants are living in their natural habitats. Their methods of fact gathering, observation, and conclusion drawing were also applied to the problems that ants and other insects cause for people. Ants, they learned, have a high nuisance value, but houseflies and mosquitoes have more serious problems for people because they carry diseases.

Evaluation: The teacher, as a pragmatist, did not think it important for anyone to be able to draw and label the anatomy of the various inserts, although some children became interested in this activity and created some informative charts. Nor did the teacher think it important for every child to know the names of all of the insects studied. One demonstrable outcome that was related to the initial project was the result of a visit by the school doctor who discussed the harmful effects of houseflies and mosquitoes and a visit to the local agricultural experiment station to learn about the damage insects inflict upon crops. The class wrote news reports to submit to the newspaper, and these were published to stimulate interest in the community about the use of indoor-outdoor insecticides, immunizations, and proper drainage. Other observable and testable evaluations accrued when individuals set up experiments with spiders, mealworms, houseflies, and mosquitoes. These children used their methods of observation and information gathering in thinking about new, but related, problems of how insects live and reproduce themselves.

Discussion Questions

1. What roles did the following educational progressivists play in changing educational philosophies? William Heart Kilpatrick, John L. Childs, George Counts, V. T. Thayer, Boyd H. Bode.
2. How are contemporary experimentalists such as Lawrence G. Thomas, H. Gordon Hullfish, George Extelle, Bruce Raup, Frederick C. Neff, Ernest Bayles, and William O. Stanley affecting progressivism?

3. Critics of education blame pragmatism for: (1) the inability of students to master fundamental skills; (2) its failure to establish definite goals; (3) its failure to develop traits such as perseverance and self-sacrifice; and (4) its failure to set up specific criteria for evaluating students. How would you answer these four criticisms?

Reconstructionism

Reconstructionism is the most recent educational *theory* claiming true successorship to progressivism. It is centered around the ontology of the cultural crises of our times (what is real) and contends that the main purpose of education is to "reconstruct" society so that these crises can be met.

Because Western civilization and its values have dictated a great deal of past curricular emphases in schools and a great deal of what has happened in society in America, reconstructionism holds that it is the job of the school to reinterpret the basic values of Western civilization in view of changing times and new scientific knowledge available.

Again, John Dewey suggested this educational theory in the title of his book, *Reconstruction in Philosophy*, in 1920; and in the 1930's there was formed a group called the Frontier Thinkers who felt that schools should be the leaders in creating a more equitable society by encouraging loyalty to a new social order. The leading spokesmen for the Frontier Thinkers were George Counts, who wrote *The American Road to Culture* in 1930 and *Dare the Schools Build a New Social Order?* in 1932, and Harold Rugg, who published *Culture and Education in America* in 1931. Progressives like Kilpatrick and Childs had urged schools to be more cognizant of social responsibilities, but they did not agree with Counts and Rugg that schools should be involved in designating and inculcating *specific* social trends.

Although progressivism declined during the next twenty years, there were some notable attempts to use Dewey's philosophy as a basis for wedding progressivism and essentialism by suggesting that schools should aid and abet social movements to further realization of American cultural values that were prevalent outside of schools rather than to initiate social reforms themselves. Isaac B. Berkson published a major work, *The Ideal and the Community*, in 1958 which advanced these ideas for education.

Probably the most revolutionary of all of the reconstructionists is Theodore Brameld who published *Patterns of Educational Philosophy* in 1950, *Philosophies of Education in Cultural Perspective* in 1955, *Toward a Reconstructed Philosophy of Education* in 1956, *Cultural Foundations of Education—An Interdisciplinary Approach* in 1957, and *The Remaking of a Culture* in 1959.

Brameld has presented some basic principles or main themes of reconstructionism. He includes the following:

1. The real purpose of education is to promote a clearly thought-out program of social reform.
2. The task must be undertaken immediately by educators and schools.
3. Any new social order must be "genuinely democratic."
4. Students should be persuaded democratically of the urgency and validity of the reconstructionist viewpoint and teachers have the responsibility to persuade students in these directions.
5. The means and ends of education need to be refashioned in consonance with new knowledge available in the social sciences.
6. Social and cultural forces shape the child, the school, and education itself.

While reconstructionists agree with progressive definitions of *experience* as "interactions of human organisms with material and social environments," and welcome the *methods of education* that progressivism espouses, they also feel that Deweyism gave education the means but not the end result. Brameld (10) criticizes progressivism and says that it is "the educational effort of an adolescent culture, suffering from the pleasant agonies of growing up, from preoccupation with the excitement of present events, from the cultural period of trying and erring when the protections of infancy have been left behind but the planned autonomies of maturity await future delineation and fulfillment."

Brameld (11) also holds that commitments to the new social order must not be simply tenuous and well-meaning, but must be urgent and direct. He says that reconstructionism

> commits itself, first of all, to the building of a new culture. It is infused with a profound conviction that we are in the midst of a revolutionary period out of which should emerge nothing less than control of the industrial system, of public services, and of cultural and natural resources by and for the common people who, throughout the ages, have struggled for a life of security, decency, and peace for them and for their children.

Brameld (12) uses the term *genuine democracy* in discussing the third main theme of reconstructionism; and when he uses this term he means having major resources controlled by the people themselves, including everything that affects the public interest—pensions, health, industry, transportation, through elected popular representatives. He declares that, "Control by the largest possible majority of the principal institutions and resources of any culture is the supreme test of democracy . . . the working people should control all principal institutions and resources if the world is to become genuinely democratic."

In Brameld's formulations, civilized life is for the most part *group life* and groups are seen as playing important roles in schools for the purpose of having educated adults who will know how to use their talents in the social milieus they will enter. In another of his writings, Brameld (13) advises that we "should recognize groups for what they are. We should neither cynically condemn them nor passively accept their behavior as inevitable, but through sound diagnosis aim to build a social and educational program that will help resolve their longings, reduce their immoralities, and release their human potentialities."

Discussion Questions

1. Can the boast of reconstructionism—based on reliable scientific knowledge about human behavior—be sustained in your opinion?
2. Do you think that America, which is a very pluralistic society affected by hosts of religious, moral, aesthetic, cultural, social, and personal considerations, could ever come to the agreements considered essential by Brameld?
3. Do you see any contradictions of terms in Brameld's theories? For example, would it take a totalitarian movement rather than a "genuine democracy" to create such unity of thought in so diverse a country as the United States?

Existentialism and Analysis—Emerging Philosophies

Two newly emerging philosophies which are growing in importance but have not yet formulated educational programs as specific as those we have already discussed are existentialism and analysis. Both academic philosophers and philosophers of education recognize their importance and their significance in criticizing and counteracting traditional philosophies.

As you consider these philosophies, try to determine which elements of older philosophies are incorporated in their theories and how they complement your own emerging values and philosophy of life and of education.

EXISTENTIALISM. Existentialism is not a single philosophy, but occupies a position embracing a number of commonalities as well as fundamental differences among other philosophies. It can best be described as emphasizing the freedom and uniqueness of choice commitment and personal involvement. Since man's choices are self-legislated, the existentialist alone is held responsible for his actions. Unlike the idealist and the realist, he does not discover what is real in terms of absolutes but, instead, in that which exists for the emerging, experiencing individual.

There are few characteristics shared by all those who have been designated as existentialists, because the theory of existentialism is personalized for each individual. Fixed moral rules are of no real consequence since man is committed to make his own choices at each level of his existence. Through the personal experience of expressing one's inner nature every moment, hour, and day, the existentialist is in a constant quest of discovery or finding his own essence, the *meaning* of his personal existence.

Among the leading existentialist philosophers are Jean-Paul Sartre, Martin Heidegger, Karl Jaspers, and religious philosophers and thinkers such as Paul Tillich, Gabriel Marcel, Nikolai Berdyaev, and Martin Buber. The forerunners of the movement are the Danish Christian philosopher, Søren Kierkegaard (1813–1855), and the German atheist, Friedrich Nietzsche (1844–1900). These men had in common criticisms of traditional philosophy and contemporary Christianity; the first, Kierkegaard, worked to revitalize Christianity from within and the second, Nietzsche, wanted to replace it completely with a morality of a Superman.

In searching for the commonalities of existentialism there seem to be these:

1. Existentialism begins with each individual's passionate awareness of the human predicament and especially of *his own predicament.*
2. Rejecting the traditional view that philosophers should be detached and calm, existentialists welcome perennial encounters with life and are passionately involved with life and the inevitability of death, the agonies and the ecstasies of love, the realities of personal choice, the experiences and the responsibilities of freedom, and the hope or hopelessness of personal friendships.
3. Existentialists view knowledge as indecisive and unnecessary if it does not engage the emotions and the feelings of the knower. Thus they do not believe in knowledge for its own sake.
4. Man possesses absolute freedom because he is not part of any world order or *system of being,* and he must accept total responsibility for his actions.
5. The universe is without meaning or purpose, and the meanings and purposes that man thinks he sees in it are nothing more than man's own projections and desires for order.
6. Because man is free and responsible for his own actions, he must also help expose tendencies in society which undermine man's freedom. Dehumanizing experiences are felt to be the tyranny of the majority in the democratic process, exploitation of the public by mass media, subordination of individuals to an economic system, and the tyranny of groups in social orders and affairs.
7. In regard to education, there is general agreement about true freedom and the uniqueness of the individual, and the existentialist deplores current practices of educating children in groups rather than educating them as individuals. There is a place for groups, however, and existentialists feel that groups should serve to stimulate the development of each group member.
8. Individuals are to use groups for their own personal development and fulfillment.
9. The existentialist also disagrees with the tendency of families to surrender more and more of their responsibilities and their own

educative responsibilities to the school. He also believes that family life is the best possible social arrangement and wants the family to have a greater educative role than it now enjoys.

10. Knowledge has an important place in the existentialist's concepts, but he believes that the school must revise its conceptions of knowledge because knowledge is for the purpose of freeing people, of delivering them from ignorance and prejudice and helping them to see themselves as they really are. Knowledge, then, is seen as "the cultivation of self."

11. Acceptable values are only those which the individual adopts for himself and of his own free will. Values that are superimposed have no value under this conception.

12. The role of the teacher, too, undergoes revision. Whereas realists think the teacher is to impart knowledge, pragmatists believe that the teacher should be a consultant, and idealists think that the teacher should be a model to be emulated, the existentialist wants the teacher to help each personality to achieve self-realization, and to grow toward free, creative adulthood.

Concerning curriculum, existentialists attach a great deal of significance to the humanities, feeling that history, literature, art, and philosophy have more significance for studying man in depth than do other subjects. They also feel that to have only one specialty is a mistake because it limits the individual's perceptions and understandings which should be global. Nietzsche (14) discussed the specialist in science thus: "A specialist in science begins to resemble nothing but a factory workman who spends his whole life in turning one particular screw or handle on a certain instrument or machine."

Kneller (15) speaks of the role of the teacher in the existentialist philosophy, also. "The teacher," he says, "should bring home vividly to the student that, whatever he does, he cannot escape the consequences of his actions; he must accept them as the issue of his own free choice, however thoughtless that choice may sometimes be. He should insist that each man's life is his own to lead and that no one else can lead it for him."

In the classroom setting, existentialism would imply that the feelings and actions of students play an important role in developing instructional programs. Students have the opportunity to agree or to disagree with authority and, through accepting full responsibility for their own actions, they learn the consequences of the right to practice freedom in action and choice. Since each student has the right to do as he chooses, the existentialist would create an environment that presents moral and intellectual questions for each individual to pursue.

As an illustration of the existentialist teacher's behavior in handling a conflict situation between two boys who were threatening to have a fight after school because of a dispute in a baseball game, the teacher asked these questions:

> If one of you succeeds in knocking down your opponent, will it change the score of today's ball game?
> Will the fight decide whether Carlos was *safe* or *out* at the home plate?
> What was one of the main reasons you were playing the ball game?
> In team sports, what attitude do you generally expect from the losing team?
> In team sports, what attitude do you generally expect from the winning team?

Even though team sports are not valued in the existentialist philosophy because of its ideas about groups and competition, the teacher who asked these questions was behaving as an existentialist. He had respect for the values of both boys, showed concern for each, and gave each one an opportunity to question himself. If Jim had stated that he was not accepting the original decision at home plate, the teacher might have stated that he had a right to feel that way if he chose to and that he, as an individual, was responsible for his own actions and feelings. The teacher does not moralize, set up fixed rules, humiliate, or ridicule, but encourages students to reconsider their threats and decide what course of action to take. Using nondirective guidance, he helps each student find self-fulfillment by discussing alternative choices. Think about the following criticisms of existentialism which some educators have voiced:

1. Existentialism is weak because interest in the individual overshadows respect for the group and concern for others. Do you agree or disagree and why?
2. Existentialism is too "open-minded" and indefinite in establishing specific goals and purposes. Do you agree or disagree and why?

Discussion Questions

1. Using ontology (What is real?), epistemology (What is true?), and axiology (What is good?), how would you answer these questions in relation to existentialism?
2. Would an existentialist defend the concept of equality of educational opportunity by educating all children at the same time in the same way? How would he use groups to extend the concept?

PHILOSOPHIC ANALYSIS Finally, we come to philosophic analysis, which believes that the true *function of philosophy is to clarify thought.*

It is a serious challenge to traditional philosophies, and in this respect it has something in common with existentialism. But it differs from existentialism in that it feels that existentialist philosophy is too passionate and personal, theoretically misconceived and, in practice, futile. It states emphatically that philosophy cannot tell us what is or what should be.

There are two main analytic movement schools of thought—*formal* and *informal*. In formal analysis, problems can be either resolved or designated as insoluble when they are translated into the artificial language used in modern logic and following exactly the laws of logic. Informal analysis rejects the necessity for these formal statements and its proponents are often called "ordinary language" philosophers. Both groups believe that the job of philosophy is to clarify questions, not to answer them, to decide whether they are genuine questions or the product of assumptions that are unstated and thinking that is confused.

Wittgenstein (16) says that the object of philosophy "is the logical clarification of thoughts. Philosophy is not a theory but an activity . . . Philosophy should make clear and delimit sharply the thoughts which otherwise are, as it were, opaque and blurred."

Both philosophers and educators feel that until the science of education is much more developed than it is now, formal analysis is largely irrelevant to it. Because education depends upon so many other areas of knowledge and takes many of its concepts from other concepts and disciplines, it still lacks an order of its own. The vocabularies of mathematics, common sense, law, physics, theology, art, sociology, psychology, and education are varied and have systems of logic of their own arising from their uses and ways of being used. Sometimes these become entwined or interchangeable, and this causes confusion about both philosophy and the use of language to express concepts.

Most of formal analysis' present exponents are American, but chronologically Bertrand Russell, the first Ludwig Wittgenstein, the group of logical positivists, and Rudolf Carnap have been its exponents. The informal analysts, or the "ordinary language" exponents, have been by and large British. These include G. E. Moore, the later Wittgenstein, and contemporary philosophers such as Gilbert Ryle, P. F. Strawson, and J. L. Austin.

Basically, *applied analysis*, whether formal or informal, may eventually help education to clear up some of its confusion and ambiguities, but it cannot replace the contributions or the functions of speculative and prescriptive educational philosophy. The student who is seriously interested in knowing more about philosophic analysis is invited to read the following references, in addition to those which represent the annotated portions of this chapter.

Brown, L. M., *General Philosophy in Education*. New York: McGraw-Hill Book Company, 1966.

Hospers, John, *An Introduction to Philosophical Analysis*. Englewood Cliffs, N.J.: Prentice-Hall, Inc., 1953.

Kneller, George F., *Logic and Language in Education*. New York: John Wiley & Sons, Inc., 1966.

O'Connor, D. J., *An Introduction to Philosophy of Education.* London: Routledge and Kegan Paul, Ltd., 1961.

Scheffler, Israel (ed.), *Philosophy and Education.* Boston: Allyn and Bacon, Inc., 1966.

Scheffler, Israel, *The Language of Education.* Springfield, Ill.: Charles C Thomas, 1960.

Smith, B. Othanel, and Robert H. Ennis (eds.), *Language and Concepts in Education.* Chicago: Rand McNally & Company, 1961.

References

1. From Report of the State Central Committee (on the Disciplines) to the California State Curriculum Commission, California State Department of Education, 1961.

2. Kneller, George E., "Philosophy and Education," Chapter II in *Foundations of Education,* 2nd ed. (also edited by George Kneller). New York: John Wiley & Sons, Inc., 1967.

3. Hutchins, Robert M., *The Conflict in Education in a Democratic Society.* New York: Harper & Row, 1953.

4. Quoted by William W. Brinkman in, "Essentialism—Ten Years After," *School and Society,* Vol. XLVII, May 15, 1948.

5. Brinkman, William W., "The Essentialist Spirit in Education," *School and Society,* Vol. LXXXVI, October 11, 1958.

6. Kandel, Isaac, *Conflicting Theories of Education.* New York: The Macmillan Company, 1938.

7. Dewey, John, *Democracy and Education.* New York: The Macmillan Company, 1916.

8. McMurray, Foster, "The Present Status of Pragmatism in Education," *School and Society,* Vol. LXXXVI, January 17, 1959.

9. Thomas, Lawrence G., "The Meaning of 'Progress' in Progressive Education," *Educational Administration and Supervision,* Vol. XXXII, October, 1946.

10. Brameld, Theodore, *Patterns of Educational Philosophy.* New York: Harcourt, Brace & World, Inc., 1950.

11. Brameld, Theodore, "Philosophies of Education in an Age of Crisis," *School and Society,* Vol. LXV, June 21, 1947.

12. Brameld, Theodore, *Toward a Reconstructed Philosophy of Education.* New York: They Dryden Press, 1956.

13. Brameld, Theodore, *Patterns of Educational Philosophy.* New York: Harcourt, Brace & World, Inc., 1950.

14. Nietzsche, Friedrich Wilhelm, *On the Future of Our Educational Institutions.* New York: The Macmillan Company, 1924.

15. Kneller, George F., *Foundations of Education.* 2nd ed. New York: John Wiley & Sons, Inc., 1967.

16. Wittgenstein, Ludwig, *Tractatus Logico-Philosophicus.* New York: Humanities Press, 1955.

Additional Suggested Reading

Barrett, William, *Irrational Man. A Study in Existential Philosophy.* Garden City, N.Y.: Doubleday & Company, Inc., 1958.

Bode, Boyd H., *Progressive Education at the Crossroads.* New York: Newson & Company, 1938.

Brameld, Theodore, *Philosophies of Education in Cultural Perspective.* New York: The Dryden Press, 1955.

Hutchins, Robert M., *The Conflict in Education in a Democratic Society.* New York: Harper & Row, 1953.

Kilpatrick, William H., *Philosophy of Education.* New York: The Macmillan Company, 1951.

Kneller, George F., *Existentialism and Education.* New York: John Wiley & Sons, Inc., 1964.

Kneller, George F., *Introduction to the Philosophy of Education.* New York: John Wiley & Sons, Inc., 1965.

Morris, Van Cleve, *Existentialism in Education.* New York: Harper & Row, 1965.

CHAPTER 8

Philosophy Affects Teachers and Students

Philosophy and Self

The contemporary scene in American education raises many philosophical dilemmas for the professional teacher. Alexander Meikeljohn (17) raises the question of mere professional technicianship versus beliefs, motives, and values when he states that one of the greatest

> failures of our contemporary training of teachers is that they become mere technicians. They learn the tricks and devices of the classroom. But they do not learn the beliefs and motives and values of the human fellowship for the sake of which the classroom exists. The primary question of teaching theory and practice is one of purpose. Why do we teach? What should we teach? For whom do we teach? What is our goal, and what is the source of its authority over us? Those are the questions which must be answered if our teachers are to be themselves members of the fraternity into which they seek to initiate their pupils.

This statement lends support to the philosophical concerns teachers have as they are subjected to the various demands of the educational establishment and of the community, and as they make decisions about whether certain things are worth doing or not. In deciding which principles or philosophies will help one make valid judgments, the professional teacher demonstrates the difference between mere "teacher training" and true "teacher education."

Teachers often have knowledge about individual characteristics of children through personal contacts and cumulative records before school actually begins, and children often acquire information about the personality of a teacher before school begins through the observations and opinions of other students, teachers, and parents. Even if a child is meeting the teacher for the first time on the first day of school, he begins immediately to develop concepts about what the teacher is *really* like; he begins to "read" his teacher. He becomes increasingly astute at "reading" teachers as he goes on through his school career. Teachers demonstrate more than they know they are demonstrating and reveal more of their own personal values than they know they are revealing in such simple everyday things as the way they say "sit down" or "please sit down," "this is *my* room" or "this is *our* room," or "all of the children in this room are too noisy and rowdy" or "all of the children in this room make school a good place for me to be." Gestures, voice, and facial expressions convey a great deal, too, about what the teacher thinks and feels about himself and about children.

The Teaching Idealist

The idealist is a virtuous person and feels that he must be an excellent person in his personal convictions and conduct; he sees himself as a model for emulation. He wants his students to study and evaluate the unchanging moral values which he demonstrates himself in his everyday relationships with them, and he feels that positive societal values are best learned by having students establish patterns of living and behaving similar to his own. Because of the pressure on children in the idealistic philosophy, the idealist teacher views his own behavior most critically and exhibits consistent standards of right conduct. Since the quality of the teacher and of the other adults in a child's life in inculcating *truth* about life and behavior is considered to be of maximum importance for a child, idealist teachers are expected to show great skill in being able to provide opportunities for a student's mind to discover and apply absolute moral truths.

The Teaching Realist

The realist sees himself as a strict disciplinarian who must condition children to subordinate immediate goals and gratifications for long-range goals of education. These long-range goals are seen as reward for effort and achievement, controlled attention provided by environment and lesson organization, and activation to operate intellectually upon content provided.

Because respect for the individual is secondary to the significance of universal truths and natural laws, the teacher is expected to be impersonal in his relationships with students. He is expected to treat every child with fairness and impartiality; furthermore, he expects every child to learn in the same way at the same time. Like the idealist, the teacher who is a realist is expected to know his subject area, or areas, well, and this expert information is to enable him to direct intellectual development and to correct intellectual mistakes and errors.

This teacher is expected to keep the learning environment under constant control so that the attention of children is constantly occupied with the content and objectives of the lesson being taught. The realist does believe that content should be related to the experiences of children, and hopes to use pupil interest and motivation whenever possible while providing both direct and vicarious experiences previous to depending upon abstract symbols of verbalization.

The teacher's function in evaluation of students is also considered important, and since the teacher is expected to require students to recall facts, explain facts, interpret relationships, compare facts, and infer new meanings in daily lessons, the teacher must also be able to test and measure factual knowledge, understanding, and comprehension of the pupil. Evaluation must be objective to eliminate subjective teacher interests or pupil interests, and the kind of testing done must be frequent, accurate, and immediately reinforcing for students.

The Teaching Pragmatist

The pragmatist sees himself as a fellow human being with his students and as a person who demonstrates basic philosophic beliefs in the significance of the individual and in the democratic process. He identifies interests and needs through having his students identify them, and he sees his role as one of providing classroom situations in which all children can make choices and participate in activities that each one finds to be worthwhile for himself.

Teachers and pupils plan jointly, but the objective is to assist each learner to think independently and to develop his own values through a process of continual reconstruction of experiences. Because pragmatists reject the existence of absolutes which measure good and bad, and the tests of value are based upon *human experience,* they believe that

1. *Values are changeable* and will vary with the changes that take place in society.
2. *Values are probable* because there will be different values under different sets of circumstances.
3. *Values arise from social and individual needs* and "good actions" are the result of significant ethical or aesthetic needs.
4. *Values have public consequences* because final tests of morality and aesthetics are their effects upon society—each act or object exists only in the human context or social experience, and an action is therefore good if it is socially worthwhile.
5. *Values are not universal* because societies differ one from another, tastes vary with cultures, and experiences of people in different cultures vary.

Strongly democratic, the teaching pragmatist believes that the democratic form of government and a truly democratic classroom atmosphere enable people to live and grow through the social interactions that take place with others. Each person is then expected to take an active part in the operation of the classroom, and eventually in community, state, national, and international affairs. In addition, each individual must have equal opportunity to choose his life's work, develop his talents freely, be unrestricted by biases, and be free from prejudice and hate. He must also be free to follow his conscience in order to choose his own personal actions, and must not have spiritual enslavements to any one institution— because he is free to worship as he pleases, speak as he thinks, and live in the place and manner of his choice. Everything the teaching pragmatist does is for the purpose of encouraging habits of living and behaving that are consistent with democracy and democratic living. He will help each student "live the good life" through helping each one achieve good health, vocational skills, avocational interests and hobbies for leisure time, preparation for family life and parenthood, and abilities to deal with social problems.

The Teaching Existentialist

An existentialist fosters self-realization among his students by encouraging them to question and criticize views of man. He encourages his students to be critics of their own behavior and accepts trial and error, but emphasis is placed upon an individual being accountable for his own actions and defending his choices of action and behavior.

This teacher is nondirective—that is, his methodology is nondirective. Exact, prescriptive, detailed lesson plans are not possible because these would force upon children adult values and interests, for example. Rather, the existentialist is a guide whose function is to help each student develop his own purposes and learning. When an individual pupil directs a problem to the teacher, the teacher reflects it back in such a way that the student's insight into the nature of the problem is aroused. The existentialist teacher is also a resource person and believes that although he is never to impose his goals upon his students, it is important to plan democratically with them on the basis of their personalized needs and purposes.

Existentialist teachers believe that education exists for helping students learn about the nature of life and that this is best accomplished by helping each student develop individual awareness, have opportunities for ethical choices, grow in self-knowledge, develop self-responsibility, and grow in individual commitments that will involve him in the human condition.

As a person who believes strongly in individual differences and the significance of each individual, he rejects the pragmatist, or experimentalist, view of social concensus, and feels that only indirectly does the school need to be concerned about social improvement generally.

Quite naturally, young students will not identify teachers as idealists, realists, pragmatists, or existentialists. But they do have the ability to see teachers' personalities in perspective, and they do know whether their teachers have real respect for them and for others. They also sense characteristics such as honesty, acceptance, flexibility, cooperation, willing and open guidance and assistance, and personal growth through association with a given teacher. And these reflect both the personal and professional philosophy of a teacher.

Because a teacher is actually teaching, at all times, what is real (ontology), what is true (epistemology), and what is good (axiology) through his own behaviors, it is important for him to understand the dimensions of living and thinking that philosophy can bring to him as a person and as a professional teacher.

Philosophy and Children's Needs

Intellectual Needs

All schools of philosophy are interested in the common objectives of helping children develop their intellectual abilities, but they differ in their theories about *what children should learn* and about *what procedures to use.*

The *idealist,* possessing great culture and believing in absolute truths, serves as a model who is to stimulate children to learn about the great ideas and values which are supposedly timeless. This is best done, he believes, through the "great books," lectures, recitations, reports, drill, and memorization. Lessons are to be logically arranged, orderly, and purposeful, and arranged around eternal, unchanging verities of truth, goodness, and beauty. He believes that there are constant subjects that are essential to the realization of a student's intellectual and moral growth, and that these constant subjects should be required for all students since they constitute the general education of each individual. The purpose of knowledge about psychology is to enable a teacher to personalize assignments within the constant subjects so that each student can develop according to his own intellectual capacities.

Literature, for example, is studied not so much for the factual information it contains, but for the purposes of helping children study the criteria by which men make moral choices; the content is to help a child see what ought to be in the worlds of human activities. Similarly, the child is to study the "best" art, music, and biography. Knowledge and intellectual development are measured by the student's excellence in knowing and understanding the subject material which is logically arranged from concrete, simple concepts to more abstract and vicarious concepts in each subject.

The realist believes in certain "in-puts" and "out-puts"—in the "pouring in" of information and the "drawing out" of factual material. The intellectual diet of children is conceived as a subject-centered curriculum built around science and mathematics, the humanities, and values. Values are not taught normatively, but the value of the scientific and objective approaches are stressed so that students will have the necessary approaches to knowledge. If a conflict arises in which the emotion of the student interferes with the acquisition of the knowledge deemed to be "essential," it is the teacher's responsibility to condition the student to the discipline and intellectual concentration necessary to help a student subordinate immediate impulses to sound, long-range goals.

The pragmatist helps children formulate questions and problems, develop skill in organizing and analyzing data, and relate findings to his experiences in order to help him further his own intellectual development. The child is more involved in the process and learns by doing. There is also more personal relationship between the learner and the teacher. Intellectual development of a child's curriculum content is built around the definition of common social goals (applicable content from history and emerging contemporary problems), democratic planning and actions, and the development of new methods for the release of creativity. Intellectual development is not a matter of the acquisition of knowledge for knowledge's sake but rather to have knowledge serve as an instrument that will help students solve their problems.

The existentialist believes that subjects have no value in and of themselves, and are only of value in helping a child develop self-knowledge and self-responsibility. If the existentialist finds himself in a school situation where the subject-centered curriculum dominates the philosophy of those who plan for the intellectual development of children, he will probably choose to emphasize the importance of the humanities. This is consistent with his belief that intellectual development consists of engaging children in situations where they can search for meanings and develop understandings and insights, and that children will increase their understanding of the world through intellectual and emotional involvement with whatever they study.

As teachers continue to examine philosophical theories and their classroom applications, they need to keep in mind that while the classroom's primary purpose is for intellectual growth, other emotional and social growths are really inseparable from intellectual development. What happens at school can

1. Build or damage a child's self-image.
2. Increase or decrease his self-motivation.
3. Enrich or deprive him of personal and personalized experiences.
4. Build related concepts or isolate and compartmentalize knowledge.

And, furthermore, these negative and positive effects are just as true for the teacher as for the child in the school setting.

Emotional Needs

A teacher's philosophy begins to affect a child's emotional self at the moment he walks into the classroom, and the emotional climate that prevails is a reflection of the teacher's beliefs and behaviors. There are many interpretations of the philosophical meaning of *value*, but values generally represent human needs and emotions. Sigmund Freud is one who asserted that human reason is charged with emotion and that it may possibly serve to defend emotional needs. Beginning teachers often express fear of their inability to maintain an atmosphere conducive to learning and often have not developed their own philosophies of the role of emotions in learning.

Every teacher involves students in developing personal understandings about the sources of authority and the function it serves for individuals through some combination of the "follow me" attitude of the idealist, the "accept what I say" attitude of the realist, or the "let's plan together for problem solution" attitudes and behaviors of the teaching pragmatist.

The idealist teacher is supposed to be able to look beyond what he perceives about each child and enter into the very mind of a child, according to Gentile (18), who says that the teacher "must not stop at the classification of the pupil or at the external observation of his face or behavior. He must enter into the very mind of the child where his life is gathered and centered . . . [He] must not read into the child any spontaneous and independent impulses of his own."

The idealist teacher cannot look at children as simply bodies without spirits, and must try to find the real spirit of each individual child. Herman Harrell Horne (19) talks about individuals as "parts of larger wholes" and thus refers to the social-emotional needs of a person in the idealist philosophy, "The individual is a whole and he is also a part of a larger whole. It is the nature of an individual to be both himself and a *socius*. Individuality is not a narrowly circumscribed sphere, but is a large circle inclusive of one's fellows. The individual really finds his own unity in the service he can render to many selves."

The ideal school, and thus the ideal emotional climate which an idealist teacher would strive to maintain, creates a "brotherhood" according to Boboslovsky (20) who wrote a book called *The Ideal School*. "In the spirit of brotherhood one approaches his fellow men not claiming his rights or declaring their social status, but as a person to person in terms of human understanding, affection, and love."

Horne's (21) definition of education is a famous one, and includes emotional environment among the idealist's objectives for education. It is, "Education is the eternal process of superior adjustment of the physically and mentally developed, free, conscious, human being to God, as manifested in the intellectual, emotional, and volitional environment of man."

According to Horne, to be a good teacher is to be a good friend, and a teacher should be a "maker of democracies"—his classes will practice democracy as well as praise it.

The realist teacher is, in the strictest sense, less personal than the idealist, and maintains a more impersonal classroom climate because of his views about mastering what the teacher feels is important. Since education is seen as a function of the guide, or teacher, it is not a function of the guided (or students). Class discussions which question values meet with strong disapproval because the student is to listen to the teachers and learn what teachers prescribe. Uniformity and conformity are prized, as are diligent study, punctuality, obedience, readiness, neatness, and classroom decorum and order.

The classroom climate, in extreme realist views, would be characterized as undemocratic by most of us; and in some cases strict rules for children's behavior are backed up by penalties for disobedience and an emotionally threatening climate. Yesipov and Goncharov (22) acknowledge the disciplinary climate of the extreme realist's classroom when they say that

> in developing discipline in pupils we may apply at times threats of punishments themselves, if regulations are violated. Also we may assume that the pupil will refrain from such violations because of fear of displeasing adults in positions of authority, fear of disapproval on the part of the collective, fear of the reproaches of his own conscience, and fear of the unpleasant experience of shame.

Democratic classroom climate characterizes the learning environment and the emotional framework of the pragmatic teacher. Values are viewed as changing and are to be agreed upon in open and informal discussions. Joint planning and assessment of growth create confidence and independence in individuals, and children are encouraged to construct learning situations around particular problems, working at rates commensurate with individual abilities and tempos. Where the idealist has clearly defined purposes for studying great ideas and universal truths and the realist determines important factual content and selects the best teaching methods, the pragmatist feels the moral obligation to foster an emotional climate in which children find purpose and relate real life experiences to content. He performs in a more democratic manner with his students and begins to build concepts in the very young child about the individual's role, his responsibility, and his unique contribution to the welfare of others.

In the eclectic's behavior, philosophical values from several philosophies may at times be exhibited. If the teacher's philosophy provides for student responsibility in maintaining an acceptive and understanding classroom emotional atmosphere, the primary outcome will be the joint relationships that guide and support learning in classroom situations.

Teachers need to consider the effects of their philosophies and attitudes upon children's total growth and development. One teacher tells of the effects of his impatient, critical, and negative attitudes toward a child during his first year of teaching. One of the students, Betsy, was a twelve-year-old who lived with her brother and sister-in-law, and had previously been a behavior problem at school. Other teachers warned the new teacher that Betsy needed "a heavy hand" if he expected to have any degree of control over her, or if he expected her to maintain any self-control. Taking his more experienced colleague's advice, he penalized her vigorously each time she misbehaved and she did seem to become more subdued. But her performance dropped from average to below average, and the teacher said that he would always be haunted by what happened on the last day of school of his first year of teaching. As Betsy boarded the school bus, she turned back toward the school and yelled, "I hate this place!"

Because of the difference in teacher personalities and their philosophies of education, and because these differences control to such an extent the ways children behave in classrooms, no teacher should try to adopt "recipes" that have "worked" for others. Rather, it seems to us, throughout each day the teacher's insights into his own and children's emotions and interests should determine the approach he takes with each child. Not only will teaching be more satisfying to the teacher, but school will make an important and self-fulfilling difference to children, to Billy who knows that his teacher will be pleased about the fact that he has learned to swim, to Mary whose stuttering is improving because her teacher listens attentively to what she has to say, and to Sam because his teacher accepts his speech problems or his ragged clothing.

Where good emotional climate and mental health abound in classrooms, you will generally find a teacher who makes it his business to know each child as an individual and as an individual in relation to the groups. You will find a teacher who is aware of the positive values of groups but who does not sublimate the interests, problems, and abilities of individual children to "groupness" and conformity to group norms.

When you think about the various kinds of learning environments in which you have participated or are now participating, can you attribute the theories of any one philosophy to the emotional climate of each? What factors affect you positively? Which ones affect you negatively? Was this the same or different for other members of the class? What philosophies will you draw upon in creating an emotional climate that will effect self-understanding and self-enhancement of each of your students? How do you plan to demonstrate the beliefs, motives, and values of human fellowship for which the classroom exists?

Because of the difference in teacher personalities and their philosophies of education, and because these differences control to such an extent the ways children behave in classrooms, teachers should not try to adopt "recipes" that have "worked" for others. Rather, throughout each day, the teacher's insights into his own and children's emotions and interests should determine the approach he takes with each child.

Where good emotional climate and mental health abound in classrooms, you will generally find a teacher who makes it his business to know each child as an individual and as an individual in relation to groups, who is aware of the positive values of groups but who does not sacrifice the interests, problems, talents, and abilities of individual children to conformity to group "norms."

(Photos courtesy of Florida Atlantic University.)

Social Needs

What does philosophy contribute to the teacher's background in connection with individual and group social needs? Realizing that children belong to both family and school groups, and that both affect children's attitude toward social, civic, political, and professional groups, the teacher realizes that it is practically impossible to believe that all children have the same social needs or that their social needs will be met in the same ways.

The idealist believes that the ethical conduct of man grows out of social tradition, and he sees his role as a transmitter of social graces and attitudes. This is done primarily through emulation and through subject matter dealing particularly with social conventions and ideals.

Plato concluded that everyone in a given society must fulfill his purpose by contributing to the welfare of the social order to the best of his ability, and that society in turn will provide him with his needs. Because each individual varies in his abilities, each will hold or be assigned duties or positions suited to these abilities. Because wealth creates conflicts between those who have and those who have not, Plato would recommend a communistic form of government because social welfare and justice are not possible under any other form of government, in his opinion.

Demiashkevitch (23) wrote about the idealist's idea of social progress as a purpose of education and felt that mobility aspects of modern social life created the danger that each new generation would not be sufficiently in touch with the equilibrium aspects of changing social life. He felt that the school could place emphasis on bringing social mobility aspects and social equilibrium aspects into juxtaposition. He also felt that emphasis should be put on the side of the equilibrium aspect since the mobility aspect gets more expression from agencies outside of the school.

Two other concepts from idealism imply the social role of the school and the social needs of education. They are (24):

1. *The teacher is an apostle of progress* if he fulfills his entire role. It is the important job of helping to give birth to the new generation spiritually and is definitely related to the purposes toward whose [social] realization history moves.
2. *The teacher should also be a maker of democracies.* Depending upon how much such experiences [democratic demonstrations and involvements] capture the devotion of students, they will, in turn, become democratizing influences in other groups.

Some authors in discussing *realism* in education make note of the fact that not all educational practice which corresponds with realism is the conscious expression of a realist philosophy of education. Some educators are conscious of their realism and deliberately practice it but others follow realist practices without thinking about the philosophic applications which they practice in their professional lives.

Believing as they do that it is a necessary and prime duty of any society to educate its children, and that human group life is not inherited but is learned, realists see direction of man's inherited tendencies as the chief task of the school. John Wild (25) says the tendencies inherited by birth are "indeterminate and flexible" and that they therefore lend themselves to the "task of determination and direction."

The realist considers the immediate demands of the individual and society as less significant than the long-term needs of society. Kneller (26) says that for the realist "the purpose of education is not primarily to convert each child into something rare and individual. It is to enable him to become a balanced, tolerant, and well-adjusted person, in harmony mentally and physically with his physical and social environment." He also states, so that there will be no misconceptions about the realist's view of individual creativity, that "adjustment is not hostile to spontaneity and individualism."

Because the pragmatist is supposed to demonstrate and practice true democracy, and to build concepts among his students regarding the individual's role, responsibility, and unique contributions to the welfare of the group, he believes that the student must first accept himself as a person of dignity and integrity and *then* demonstrate democratic values while integrating with peer groups. The teacher who believes in democratic actions and values demonstrates these by encouraging children to participate in social situations that help them to learn social attitudes and social problem-solving techniques. He has faith in students' abilities to govern themselves and to utilize their freedom in assuming individual and group responsibilities.

The pragmatist teacher's philosophy determines how he uses his classroom and the community as learning laboratories for group consciousness and social-mindedness. When he engages young children in classroom situations that permit them to grapple with the principles of self-rule, cooperative planning, individual responsibility, freedom of inquiry, and majority decision with minority protection, classmates will, with guidance and consultation, work with more initiative and effectiveness.

One teacher of ten-year-olds began to develop concepts about the democratic process among a group of children who had come from an extremely authoritarian former classroom situation. After the first few weeks, he moved his own desk from the front of the room to the back of the room. He then suggested that the children might like to rearrange their desks in more informal situations and groups than the rows of seats they had been used to. He observed that by making a physical change in the classroom arrangement, there were also psychological effects. By removing himself as the "central figure" of authority and discipline on which children focused because of his position in the front of the room when seated at his desk, the children began to feel more comfortable in making other flexible classroom seating arrangements.

As time went on, the teacher deliberately brought up the question relating to dual responsibilities of rights in a democracy and in a democratic classroom. As a result of a group problem, for example, this is a chart that emerged from class discussions and decisions about rights and responsibilities:

RIGHTS	RESPONSIBILITIES
1. A student has the right to express himself and to be listened to by others, including the teacher.	1. It is the student's responsibility to try to express himself clearly (facts, opinions) and to grant the same right to everyone else.
2. A student has the right to disagree with someone else, including the teacher.	2. It is his responsibility to find out exactly why he disagrees and to offer something better, or different, in a tactful manner.
3. A student has the right to work at the science table, the reading center, the author's research center, the art center, or any learning activity area.	3. It is his responsibility to use his time wisely wherever he is working, and to leave the area in good order so that someone else can use it.
4. A student has a right to correct another student who may be breaking the rules of the school or destroying another's property.	4. A student must be sure about the rules and he must be sure that he keeps agreed upon rules of conduct.
5. Students have the right to select certain learning goals and learning activities.	5. A student needs to give much thought to what he wants to learn in order to get the best possible results.

These children and their teacher had many opportunities to test the effectiveness of their philosophies as the year progressed, and their teacher feels that they had many good experiences with responsible democratic action. Because of individual differences and because many children have been handled with such authoritarian control at home and at school, it is unreasonable to expect that there will be democratic cooperation and responsibility at all times. But it is reasonable to expect that teachers can give children opportunities to believe in their own abilities to work out problems of living within a democratic framework.

Teachers who value and practice democratic ideals are not threatened by having teacher aides, parents, or other professionals or paraprofessionals in their classrooms. In fact, they deliberately involve people with special talents, interests, and hobbies because it is one of the ways that children can have firsthand experiences in discovering new ideas, new meanings, and new perspectives in viewing human beings and their potential worth to one another and to society.

America's continued development as a strong nation is dependent upon the strength that is embodied in ideas from many cultures and subcultures. For children to learn the potential value of self in relation to others, the teacher and students need to share classroom activities with guests of varied backgrounds and participate in mutually planned activities; by engaging students and diverse adults in social interaction, children are helped to have realistic conceptions of different people and ideas.

Ethical Behavior

In the past it made sense for teachers to use the code of ethics formulated by the professional associations as they grew in influence and in commitments. But we believe that today's teacher should find the basis for his own ethical beliefs and behaviors in his working relationships with his students, fellow teachers, administrators, and parents.

According to Flaum (27), the teacher is one who believes that it is essential for him to have a "core of dedication from which stems his conviction that all the world is possible for man to live in peacefully, honestly, and in happiness if he will learn to live in it." And he also says that the professional teacher tries "to help individuals balance and coordinate the functional and utilitarian with the idealistic and moral attitudes which are essential in giving meaning to our lives" (28).

More than a person in any other profession, the teacher should base his teaching upon reasoned integrity and truth as far as he can find these. Regardless of their philosophy, teachers must be fully aware that students depend upon their examples, their guidance, their creativity, and their judgments; these are the essence of the teacher and the art of the true teacher.

The prospective, as well as the experienced, teacher should know and understand what loyalties he holds, the ideas and ideals he represents, what makes him ineffective or fearful, what stimulates him and gives him courage to enter a new world of experience and make new discoveries about human relationships, what views of true democracy he cherishes and why he does, and what his beliefs about the central purposes of education are.

According to the National Education Association (29) of the United States, the creative teacher feels obliged to provide learning situations that demonstrate democracy at its best and believes that

- Young people are entitled to be respected as individuals, respected for what they are and what they may become.
- Young people, to the extent of their growth and ability, are entitled to deal with the conditions or problems of their times.

- Young people are entitled to such knowledge and experience as are appropriate to the nature of the problems under study.
- Young people should learn that all ideas thoughtfully expressed are entitled to thoughtful consideration.
- Young people are entitled to the opportunity to develop those habits of critical thought which democratic society requires.
- Young people are entitled to build their own beliefs on the basis of facts, theories, forces, and experiences which affect the judgments of citizens on contemporary issues.

And the creative teacher holds beliefs about the end results of his teaching. He believes that these should be

- An individual who possesses skill and discrimination in using language, reading, listening, speaking, and exchanging ideas with others.
- An individual who knows how to govern himself so that he may learn to govern others.
- An individual who possesses skill in improving his personal health habits and the health conditions of his community.
- An individual who respects the personality of every individual, whatever his origin or present status.
- An individual who assumes full responsibility as a sharing member of a family and understands the nature of a family in our society.
- An individual who understands the elements of scientific knowledge necessary for intelligent living and is aware of the relationship of science to human understanding.
- An individual who protects the weak and cares for the needy so that they may maintain their self-respect.
- An individual who maintains the improvability of all men within the limits of their potential.
- An individual who respects the arts, contributes to them, and appreciates their contribution to our continuing culture.
- An individual who relies upon reason rather than force to secure personal or social ends.
- An individual who assumes that all persons have equal rights to education, citizenship, religious worship, and occupation.
- An individual who does not tolerate an enduring social stratification based on birth, race, religion, or wealth, inherited or otherwise acquired.
- An individual who recognizes a desire on the part of people to freely govern themselves and a willingness to assume responsibility for doing so.
- An individual who holds that government derives its powers solely from the consent of the governed.
- An individual who holds that the responsibilities and activities of citizenship are among the highest duties of a man.

- An individual who demands that minorities live in accord with the decision of the majority, but accords them the right to achieve majority status through peaceful change.
- An individual who is willing to sacrifice personal comforts for the recognized general welfare, when necessary.
- An individual who uses legal, peaceful means for promoting and bringing about change.
- An individual who guarantees the right to everyone to enjoy the products and income of one's labor and to use them for their own benefit as long as they do not interfere with the rights of others.
- An individual who holds that the fundamental civil rights to liberty may not be curtailed by anyone or any group.
- An individual who maintains human rights to be the cornerstone of democratic, religious, political, social, and individual living.
- An individual who guarantees freedom from persecution to every citizen without discrimination.
- An individual who believes that democracy provides a form of security, freedom, opportunity, and justice for its members in such degree that they will be willing to voluntarily sacrifice their wealth and their lives in defense of its way of life, if necessary.

Teachers are now engaging in major political activities for the first time in history; teachers' organizations have participated in collective bargaining, teacher strikes, and sanctions. Teachers and the public have had differences of opinion in the past and they are having them now. It is probably a healthy sign if these continue to some degree because dialogue and communication about the problems of education and the tasks of education are kept alive. But the teaching profession is not thought to be worthy of being called a profession by some because it has been unable, or unwilling, to police its own ranks, to weed out the black sheep and the incompetents. It has the responsibility to raise the quality, image, and status of the teaching profession, but some of its new tactics and interests have served to do the opposite; they lower the quality, protect the weak and nonprofessional, and lower the images of teachers.

Progressive, well-trained, and professionally alert teachers are the best insurance for the development of true professional status, for improved teaching, and for improved educational opportunities for children. Until these become the objectives and the model for teaching professionalism, the profession as a whole will continue to suffer because of the indiscretions and weaknesses of a few. The profession has yet to put the quality of person and quality of certification above hours, wages, and protection of incompetent colleagues. But the profession is ethically correct when it demands more and better educational facilities, services, and materials. It is also ethically and morally defensible to demand a better deal concerning the welfare of children.

If William James was right, the philosophical system accepted by a philosopher is the result of his temperament and it follows that the philosophies adopted by teachers are the result of their temperaments.

Discussion Questions

1. One of the contributions of existentialism is the belief that man cannot be entirely objective. Whereas in the past, idealism and realism have established codes to define norms, existentialism accepts the premise that man often rebels against objectivity because his feelings influence his thinking and his thinking influences his emotions. With which philosophy do you identify most closely in regard to man's objectivity?
2. In replying to or quoting another person, it is easy to use "language that threatens," thus closing the door to free interchange of ideas. Give some examples of what you consider to be "threatening language."
3. Do you believe that it is more important to determine *who* is right than to be concerned with *what* is right?
4. Do you agree or disagree that the main reason some people feel threatened by excellence in others is that they have not learned to be enriched by the talents of others?
5. Do you believe that you can disagree with a basic philosophy of education in the school system where you are teaching and still put parts of your own philosophy to work? Give examples of how this might be done.
6. What do you think are some of the reasons, or factors, that lead some to assert that teaching is not yet a profession?
7. What do you believe the role of educators in academic freedom should be?
8. Why should ethical problems be of serious concern to the modern educator?

References

17. Meikeljohn, Alexander, *Education Between Two Worlds*. New York: Harper & Row, 1942.
18. Gentile, Giovanni, as quoted in *The Educational Philosophy of Giovanni Gentile* by Merritt Moore Thompson. Los Angeles, Calif.: University of Southern California Press, 1934.
19. Horne, Herman Harrell, *The Philosophy of Education*. Rev. ed. New York: The Macmillan Company, 1930.
20. Boboslovsky, B. B., *The Ideal School*. New York: The Macmillan Company, 1936.
21. Horne, Herman Harrell, *The Psychological Principles of Education*. New York: The Macmillan Company, 1908.
22. From the Russian text on pedagogy by B. P. Yesipov and N. K. Goncharov, *I Want to Be Like Stalin*. Translated from the Russian language by George Counts and Nucia Lodge. New York: The John Day Company, Inc., 1947.
23. Demiashkevitch, Michael, *An Introduction to Philosophy of Education*. New York: American Book Company, 1935.
24. Horne, Herman Harrell, *This New Education*. Nashville, Tenn.: Abingdon Press, 1931.

25. Wild, John, "Education and Human Society: A Realistic View," *Modern Philosophies and Education*. Edited by Nelson B. Henry. Chicago: University of Chicago Press, 1955.
26. Kneller, George F. (ed.), *Foundations of Education*. New York: John Wiley & Sons, Inc., 1967.
27. Flaum, Laurence S., *A Credo for Teachers*. San Francisco: Fearon Publishers, Inc., 1960.
28. Flaum, Laurence S., *Credo for American Public Education*. Minneapolis: Burgess Publishing Company, 1962.
29. *Forces Affecting Education*. Washington, D.C.: National Education Association of the United States, 1953.

Additional Suggested Reading

Barnett, George, and Jack Otis, *Corporate Society and Education*. Ann Arbor, Mich.: University of Michigan Press, 1961.

Broudy, H. S., and John R. Palmer, *Exemplars of Teaching Method*. Chicago: Rand McNally & Company, 1965.

Butler, Donald J., *Four Philosophies and Their Practice in Education and Religion*. 3rd ed. New York: Harper & Row, 1968.

Carr, Edward H., *The New Society*. London: Macmillan & Company, Ltd., 1951.

Counts, George, *Dare the Schools Build a New Social Order?* New York: The John Day Company, Inc., 1932.

Daley, Leo Charles, *College Level Philosophy of Education*. New York: Monarch Press, Inc., 1966.

Hook, Sidney E., *Education for Modern Man*. New York: Alfred A. Knopf, Inc., 1963.

Hutchins, Robert M., *Freedom, Education, and the Fund*. New York: Meridian Books, 1956.

James, William, *Principles of Psychology*. New York: Holt, Rinehart and Winston, Inc., 1890.

Lerner, Max, *It Is Later Than You Think*. New York: The Viking Press, Inc., 1943.

Nash, Paul, *Authority and Freedom in Education*. New York: John Wiley & Sons, Inc., 1966.

Peters, R. S., *Ethics and Education*. Glenview, Ill.: Scott, Foresman and Company, 1967.

Russell, William F., *Liberty versus Equality*. New York: The Macmillan Company, 1936.

Shaw, George Bernard, *Man and Superman*, "The Revolutionist's Handbook." New York: Dodd, Mead & Company, 1948.

Trueblood, D. E., *The Predicament of Modern Man*. New York: Harper & Row, 1944.

Wooten, Barbara, *Freedom Under Planning*. Chapel Hill, N.C.: University of North Carolina Press, 1945.

CHAPTER 9

Philosophy and Curriculum

What Teachers Believe

Aims and Values

Daley (30) writes about *value theories*, saying that they underlie every single educational activity and that statements of aims of education constitute "a statement of what is of value in life, applied to the education process. The content of education is suggested upon the basis of what is good education. The teacher considers the motivation and discipline within the classroom according to his value outlook." According to Daley, he also evaluates pupil progress against his own personal value objectives.

For general purposes, groups of theories and theorists can be arbitrarily divided into two groups, *intrinsic* and *instrumental:*

1. *Intrinsic values* are more *absolute* values like the values that exist in the nature of things and are considered to be unchanging. They may also be *permanent* such as the values that remain constant in human relationships—friendship and intellectual pleasures—or those that people consider to be religious "truths." Or they may be categorized as *higher* values that human beings discover and arrange in a kind of hierarchy. Virtue, truth, and happiness are among the values that the intrinsic theorists consider to be worthwhile in and of themselves since they do not need extrinsic objects to activate them.

2. *Instrumental values* are *relative* and only value "things" because they may be useful to achieve some other value, depending upon the individual's or society's judgment for their existence. They may also be *subjective*, that is, they may be determined within the human mind as feelings, needs, or thoughts. And instrumental values are

held to be *equal* because values vary within cultures and because value statements cannot be factual since they are determined by verification of their consequences in different cultures and situations. They then become the means by which problems are solved in a given situation and cannot be sorted into any kind of hierarchy.

The experiences that the school sponsors or that are considered to be the responsibility of the school are loosely described as the curriculum. The curriculum is often devised and evaluated in the same ways that values are set and described; and since values are theories held by people, put into practice by people, and evaluated by people, curriculum is really people in various stages of being and becoming.

It is the differences among people and the values and beliefs they hold that make school programs unique. As teachers strive to help young people develop personal values and beliefs about themselves and others, and to develop concepts about how they fit into a democratic society, psychology, sociology, and philosophy help them analyze and apply the various techniques they devise for and with each child. Practicing a particular educational philosophy, the teacher may react in the following ways or in combinations of these:

1. As an *idealist,* he serves as a model to demonstrate democratic behavior and good human relationships.
2. As a *realist,* he may teach beliefs about individual rights as outlined in the Constitution of the United States.
3. As a *pragmatist,* he involves students in real-life situations in the school–community setting.
4. And as an *existentialist,* he focuses on the freedom of individuals to discover themselves.

The system of public education in this country possesses traits and characteristics that are admired, respected, and emulated around the world. Our country was the first to espouse free public education for all its citizens, but critics still persist that we cannot provide education for everyone and at the same time provide a high quality of education.

Conflicts always exist among educators and among lay people as to the effectiveness and validity of certain educational practices. This is healthy because it causes educators to appraise their philosophical beliefs and practices and to restate principles inherent in day-to-day contacts they have with children. It also encourages cooperative lay-professional evaluation and, more often than not, results in clearer goals and understandings. Most American schools include at least four philosophical principles in their aims. Not all teachers accept and practice these in their classrooms, but the authors feel that the position each teacher takes in regard to these influences every aspect of the learning situation he will design.

Respect for Individuals

If a school faculty's philosophy states that it intends to show respect for each individual, then its practices must reflect this philosophy. It is contradictory and dishonest to state this value as an accepted principle and then fail to put it into practice by using excuses such as oversized classes, segmented subjects, limited time, undemocratic supervision, or too many interruptions. Children and parents soon realize that teachers give only lip service to the concept, buffering their failures to follow through with excuses and diversions. Granted, obstructions and frustrations like these do exist, but educators, teachers and administrators, need to appraise the circumstances and institute changes that will enable them to demonstrate their stated philosophies.

When parents see their children's reactions to changed grouping procedures that recognize and support individuality, when they see efforts to draw out children's creativity, when they see teachers working in teams to bring their best talents to bear on children's intellectual development in flexible settings and rearranged scheduling, when they see that individuals can proceed at their own pace in some kinds of programmed instruction, when they see opportunities for independent study and research in areas of special interests, and when they see teachers designing new projects and programs, they will be more supportive of the school's efforts to add personnel, learning materials, and space for their children's education.

As teachers demonstrate respect for each individual in spite of handicaps and problems, they demonstrate their intention and determination to implement their stated aims. Obviously, the day is long past when any well-trained, professional teacher would consider that he is demonstrating respect for the individual needs, problems, and interests that differ because of dissimilar cultures, emotions, health, and innate abilities if he teaches everyone the same thing at the same time in the same way.

Self-defined Objectives

Included in the concept of self-defined objectives are the practice of self-realization, self-direction, and the development of individual creativity. These imply help for children by instructing teachers in ways to detect and interpret specific behavioral signs in students' classroom performance and in how to identify negative-positive conditions that will help teachers and children select and organize experiences for developing productive abilities through self-direction. Lindsey (31) mentions the use of direct approaches to self-direction but also mentions the general climate a teacher fosters:

> Although direct approaches should be employed in helping students with concepts and skills that contribute to their full use of creative potential, much of what a student learns about teaching and teachers, himself, other people,

ideas, security in uncertainty, and the need for continuing to learn, he gets through experience not directly designed for the purpose.

Torrance's (32) discussion of promising new areas of development in relation to self-defined objectives and self-initiated activities includes greater emphasis on

1. Self-initiated learning (supplemented by the development of skills in research and inquiry or learning how to learn).
2. Learning on one's own (encouraging children to do things on their own).
3. Responsive environment (an adult or the environment responding promptly to the child's following of his own curiosity).
4. Revision of readiness concepts (re-examining notions of "holding back" children and helping them instead to cope with frustrations and failure from overly difficult tasks).
5. Developing a child's self-concepts about his own potentialities.
6. Recognizing the uniqueness of the individual and its consequences for the nature of creativity.

Although Torrance is speaking here of teaching methods and classroom conditions that encourage productive thinking and specifically creative thinking, it is interesting to note how self-definition and self-initiated learning are basic to self-realization.

When "self-defined objectives" are part of the school's statement of aims, but neither teachers nor students are seen by parents and the general public to have opportunities for self-definition and self-initiated performance, the aim again becomes a "lie," a pencil-and-paper unreality.

The question becomes one of whether or not teachers can actually modify their methods so that they are able to allow children to set their own objectives and participate in self-directed learning. Gallagher (33) feels that the skills of productive, self-initiated thinking can be taught if teachers have a model such as Guilford's structure-of-intellect model and plan accordingly. "The model," he says, "enables the teacher to have always before him the global picture of intellect, so that he can keep in perspective the area being stimulated at any given time. As much as possible, the exercises should be integrated into the curriculum so that they are a true part of the curriculum and are not viewed merely as pleasant games by the students."

Examining the lesson plans of one teacher of nine-year-olds, you will see his efforts to include elements of self-defined objectives and self-initiated activities into the regular curriculum through plans for a health unit on diet and food. The general topic is "What Creates Your Appetite?" and the major concepts are to center around the ways that both food and conduct affect the health of individuals. More specific concepts are included in the teacher's objectives and hoped-for outcomes of the study, namely, that children will learn that

1. Good food, well served, increases appetite.
2. Smells, color, and attractive arrangement increase appetite.
3. Physical atmosphere and good manners affect appetite.
4. Exercise increases appetite.
5. Balanced meals improve personal well-being and health.

Suggested activities included the following ones, but children are free to suggest and develop others:

1. Research the process of burning up body energy.
2. Research the process of food preparation.
3. Compare the kind and weight of space diets with regular diets.
4. Illustrate (using magazine cut-outs or a method of your choice) various kinds of diet such as well-balanced, high-protein, nonsalt, nonsugar, and nonfat.
5. Illustrate, in some way of your own choice, an attractive food display or table setting.
6. Find out what foods need to be imported to this area and why.

Included in the lesson plan were visits from the school doctor, the school nurse, and the school dietician who would discuss various aspects of the digestive system, proper rest, food, exercise, and eating habits.

During the time spent on the topic, the teacher noted these additional activities that were suggested and carried out by the class:

1. A menu collection from local restaurants.
2. A study and analysis of a month's sample school cafeteria menus.
3. A sample breakfast planned and cooked by the group and served to the class.
4. News reports covering the discussions with the school nurse, doctor, and dietician.
5. A role-playing demonstration of pleasant mealtime conversation.
6. A study of comparative prices at a small grocery store and at a large supermarket.
7. A scrapbook of attractive table settings.
8. A collection of poems about food.
9. Imaginative stories about food's journeys through the human digestive system, the journey of certain foods to market, and the heart's reaction to mild exercise, strenuous exercise, or no exercise.
10. An exhibit of canned and packaged foods from other countries.

This teacher's primary purpose was, obviously, to involve students in projects of their choice within the framework of a unit of study recommended in the school's curriculum. His practices gave children the opportunity to plan independently and to work in groups or individually. Parents, children, teacher, and others could observe that children were having practice in self-direction and self-realization, and that the teacher was able to modify his own concepts and methods so that children could participate in a democratic classroom atmosphere. The teacher also demonstrated respect for individual choices and directions taken by the students and thus reinforced his belief in respect for the individual.

Development of Maximum Potential

In respect to helping each individual develop his own maximum potential, the American school is unique in the twentieth century. Philosophy differs, however, in the methods and techniques that are to be employed. The idealist interprets his responsibility as that of transmitting well-established ideas and truths to generation after generation; the realist sees his responsibility in terms of disciplining students' minds; the pragmatist considers the needs of individuals and builds his problem-solving situations around the individual in an ever-changing society; and the existentialist helps individuals determine their own personal essences through living and being able to choose from among alternatives, believing that the school must not provide any preconceived goals for individuals and that the teacher's main purpose is to be guide and resource.

In studying these four basic viewpoints of philosophy, we see that each is interested in the individual as a contributing member of society. They differ mainly in their ideas about how the individual can best be prepared to be a contributing member of society and accomplish self-realization at the same time. Obviously, a student must meet effectively his own needs and self-fulfillment and he must also be able to participate effectively in society. During the past half century, great progress has been made in attempting to understand the components that will help individuals develop their maximum potentials, and a great deal of time, thought, and effort have gone into advancing understanding of the human condition and human intelligence, learning, and mental development.

If the teacher fails to develop his own professional competence and the qualities necessary to integrate theoretical and practical knowledge to promote his own maximum potential realization, students will not have the opportunities they need for an unknown future.

The history of educational innovation suggests there are several major steps that need to be taken before such innovation appears in any significant degree in the educational system itself. First of all, there must be a thorough comprehension and knowledge of the new ideas that necessitate the change. Second, there has to be a translation of these ideas into practice. Through demonstration of their worthiness in practical situations, others are convinced to modify their own performance. Third, a training program for teachers should then be developed utilizing these ideas (34).

Our work in this book is intended to raise the issues basic to the need for change, but it cannot hope to give each teacher the thorough comprehension and knowledge necessary to comprehend each issue. This will take concentrated present and continuing study. We are attempting to show how some teachers transfer their ideas into practice and to suggest other possibilities. But we know that the prospective teacher and the experienced teacher will be convinced to modify their own performances only after they have had a chance to try some of these ideas and practices for themselves. The third step of making these ideas and practices significant in the thought and preparation of teachers from the beginning of their experiences in preparing to teach is the real purpose of this book.

In Chapter 2 we devoted a great deal of space to the various concepts and philosophies basic to helping children develop their innate and creative abilities and Chapter 1 spoke to teachers in the same vein. Teachers who nurture maximum potential in their students must first be attempting to reach, at all times, their own maximum potential. If researchers are now pointing to educators as *inhibitors* of creative behavior and development of maximum potential, then teachers and administrators must investigate innovative techniques, practices, and philosophies that will *facilitate* the development of these.

Equal Opportunity for All

The real meaning of equal opportunity for all must be widely studied, understood, and implemented with confidence if the promise of American education is to be realized. We have made it abundantly clear, we hope, that this does not mean the same thing for everyone. Our ideas come closer to those of Thomas Jefferson, who was both a statesman and an educator, and who wrote in the Declaration of Independence that "We hold these truths to be self-evident, that all men are created equal, that they are endowed by their creator with certain unalienable rights, that among these are life, liberty, and the pursuit of happiness."

In a democratic society, all human beings are equal in their possession of certain basic rights and responsibilities, but unique and individual differences come into play after that. One cannot be so idealistic as to think that all have the same talents and potential, nor so realistic as to think that there are fixed limits on the development of whatever potential exists in an individual. Care must be exercised in distinguishing between *equality of opportunity* and *equality of achievement*. Teachers can foster the first, but they can never expect the latter.

Experimentalism and existentialism both advocate individual freedom and choice. They place equality of opportunity high on their list of priorities for education. However, all educational philosophies in our country subscribe to equal opportunity. Every student, including the gifted and the disadvantaged, deserves opportunities to make discoveries for himself in a climate and environment that lends dignity and provides the freedom for him to become a responsible lifelong learner. For the teacher and the

Equal opportunity for all means that each child shall

- Be provided direct experiences to help him make sense out of his immediate environment and to help him build concepts about others.
- Be helped in the techniques of communication so that he can better understand himself and communicate with others.
- Be given the opportunity to associate with others of different socioeconomic backgrounds and culture groups.
- Be adequately fed, clothed, housed, valued, and educated as a person who enjoys equal fruits of the democratic way of life.

(Photo courtesy of Florida Atlantic University.)

learner, the tasks that lie ahead are then exciting, significant, and rewarding.

Equal opportunity for all means that each child shall

1. Be provided direct experiences to help him make sense out of his immediate environment and to help him build concepts about others.
2. Be helped in the techniques of communication so that he can better understand himself and communicate with others.
3. Be given the opportunity to associate with others of different socio-economic and culture groups.
4. Be helped to have sensory contacts with reality on perceptual levels.
5. Be involved in a progression of experiences that will help him further his cognitive and creative development.
6. Be helped to move from perceptual experiences to concepts so that he can understand relationships and parallels.
7. Be adequately fed, clothed, housed, and valued as a person who enjoys equal fruits of the democratic way of life.
8. Be afforded equal opportunities for further education and skill training at each continuum in keeping with his abilities, needs, and interests.

Principles in Practice

In answering your own questions related to "For what purpose does the school exist?" it is not so important that your answer support any one philosophical viewpoint. But it is important that it include respect for the individual, maximum development of his potential, provision for self-defined objectives, and equal opportunity for all. Every child deserves a teacher who bases his practices on sound beliefs about these, and whose behavior demonstrates his beliefs in these.

Review this case study of Joe Williams whose two teachers viewed him so differently. When he moved away from one community at the end of the fifth grade, his teacher made these comments in his cumulative record folder which followed him to his new school:

Family Background: Joe comes from a family of nine children known by teachers as "those Williams children!" Joe is always in the same kinds of trouble that has given the other children such a bad reputation—he is always into some mischief, is inattentive in class, is not very intelligent, creates problems for himself and others, and should not be in a regular classroom.

Comments: Joe is eleven and looks very anemic. His grades in my class and in other classes have been average or below average. He is a behavior problem, a troublemaker, and an irresponsible pupil. His grades in citizenship are lower than his other grades. He is a bully on the playground, a show-off in the classroom, and a menace in the cafeteria, washroom, and halls.

What a send-off! Joe had three strikes against him before he ever faced his teacher in the new school he attended that fall. The new teacher, Mr. Lee, read his school record and felt that he already knew more about Joe's former teacher than he did about Joe. His former teacher had, for one thing, experience with some of Joe's brothers and sisters and was preconditioned to look for the same kinds of behavior in Joe. For another, there seemed to be little understanding of the relationship of "citizenship" to academic performance, and no attempt to study the underlying causes of Joe's personal or academic problems. It was also fair to assume that Joe probably did not have a high opinion of teachers or of school and that some reconstitution of experiences would have to be effected before he would change his opinions.

Mr. Lee set the stage for a memorable event in Joe's life the moment he walked into the classroom. Joe arrived at school late, as had been his habit, but instead of ignoring him or expounding the virtue of promptness, Mr. Lee held out his hand and shook Joe's hand warmly, saying, "Good morning, Joe. I'm glad to have you here." Joe, quite discomfited by now at the reaction he felt from a warm reception at school, was introduced to the rest of the class and assigned a seat with a group of four of them. This, too, was a surprise, because he had most often in his school career been told to "sit up front by the teacher's desk" or "go to the back of the class!"

Joe took a second look at Mr. Lee. He was tall, smiled often, and moved around the room a lot. There were a number of things different about him from the other teachers Joe had known. He listened to students, and when they talked to him you could tell that he was interested in what they had to say. Joe intuitively knew that this was not an act, and guessed correctly that Mr. Lee would accord him the same courtesy. That would be quite a switch, he thought to himself; he couldn't remember that teachers had ever wanted to hear what he had to say. After his first contributions to class discussion, he found that he was indeed accorded the same courtesy as the others.

He felt the need to talk with Mr. Lee some more, and he caught Mr. Lee's enthusiasm for learning and his genuine acceptance of students' contributions to his own and their learning. Within the first week of school, Mr. Lee received a telephone call from Joe one evening. "Teacher," he said, "tune in Channel 2 right now. There's one of them Chinese Buddhas we saw in that book on China today!" Mr. Lee knew that the first step, true communication with a student, was under way. During the next two months, he maintained a diary of Joe's progress, since he believed that accurate descriptions of Joe's behaviors would give valuable clues in guiding and directing his accomplishments toward more self-defined and self-directed goals. Here are Mr. Lee's recordings of Joe's behavior in a variety of classroom situations:

LANGUAGE ARTS: SEPTEMBER 2

On the first day of school each pupil was to write a "get-acquainted" story, using the last names of the class members. Only one person was able to work in all thirty names—Joe! Names like White, Oaks, Winters, etc., presented no problems to anyone, but Joe alone was able to include names like Adie and Comacho. Example: "He was a man who had seventy Winters, but actually looked more like 'Adie.' He was a Comacho Indian, a companion tribe of the Comanches," wrote Joe.

ART: SEPTEMBER 15

Cleo asked whether she could draw a flower on a stencil and run off a copy for each child on the mimeograph machine. Cleo needs a little self-image assistance, so I asked the class, "If you each had a copy of Cleo's flower what could you do with it?" Joe's idea, which was immediately forthcoming, was to "let each one of us select a quotation suitable for the flower print. You choose the best ones and post them on the bulletin board." I guess this stems from my abundant use of quotations to help develop attitudes, values, creative writing, and sentence analysis. Anyway, the class accepted Joe's suggestion and each student submitted a quotation. His quotation was posted with a few others that the class agreed were most appropriate, and it was Keats's "A thing of beauty is a joy forever."

MATHEMATICS: SEPTEMBER 28

Members of the class were invited to submit an original design after class discussion of rectangles and triangles. They were to use seven isosceles triangles. The average design was of this nature:

But Joe's design looked like this:

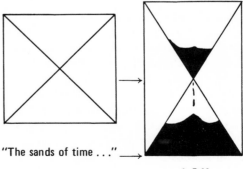

"The sands of time . . ." ⟶

4 P.M.

Theme Writing: September 24

The class was working on alliterative titles, using a list of their current spelling words. The idea was to capture the reader's fancy by using not only alliterative titles but also imaginative and "catchy" ones. One lad said, "How about this one—'A Large Leopard'?" Joe was quick to respond, "Now who would stop to read that story if he could read about 'A Lavender Lion' or 'A Lemon-colored Leopard'?"

Reference Work: October 2

We now call our dictionary-encyclopedia work Research Work. This change of terms came about from a discussion led by Joe, and this has led to the class use of orthography instead of spelling.

Sentence Analysis: October 12

I listed sentences on the board and these were to be classified and analyzed. Among them was this one: "Give me your tired, your poor." Joe had long since accomplished the requirement and was probing into other matters such as: "Why did we use quotation marks with that one sentence? Where did that quotation come from?" While the class was finishing the lesson, Joe was in the library locating the entire text of the inscription on the base of the Statue of Liberty.

Conference with Joe's Mother: October 11

She tells me that Joe has a heart condition that requires corrective surgery in about eight months. Must watch for any feelings of anxiety Joe may have about it. Mrs. Jones is aware of Joe's creative abilities, and she says that, "Joe has something my other children don't have."

Achievement and IQ Scores: November 15

Received results of achievement tests administered in October. Joe has so far achieved above grade level, and the tests indicate an IQ of 125.

As Mr. Lee reviewed these notes, his diary was full of evidences of very divergent and creative thinking. He was aware of a quality that set Joe apart from other children, a unique ability that should be fostered and valued, but that probably caused his other teachers to think that he was a problem. The teacher recommended that Joe be included in an enrichment class that met once a week as part of the school's program for gifted children. And Mr. Lee continued to value and encourage Joe's unique and creative abilities so that he could develop his real potential as he began to establish new goals for himself.

A comparison of the descriptions of Joe's behavior in the original school situation whose cumulative record folder had been forwarded, and the behavior in Mr. Lee's classroom illustrates the effect of two teachers on a child. We do not know what the future holds for Joe, but we do know that for this particular year in his life there was a teacher named Mr. Lee whose philosophy about boys and girls and learning was sound and caused him to accept Joe as an individual who had the right to a fresh start without prejudgment or labeling. In this one year, at least, Joe may have learned that education has special significance for him, and in this one year, at least, he had the privilege of being with a teacher who exemplified

Cremin's pleas for teachers who understand the theories behind the strategies they use (35):

> Education is too significant and dynamic an enterprise to be left to mere technicians; and we might as well begin now the prodigious task of preparing men and women who understand not only the substance of what they are teaching but also the theories behind the particular strategies they employ to convey that substance.

Discussion Questions

1. Philosophy of education offers alternative recommendations about *what ought to be.*
2. Philosophy of education studied historically or comparatively offers explanations for *what is.*
3. Studied historically or comparatively, philosophy of education gives insight into *what could be.*
4. From your own experiences, can you give positive and negative examples of the way teachers have behaved in each of the four philosophical principles of *respect for individuals, self-defined objectives, development of maximum potential,* and *equal opportunity for all?* Try to use different levels of education including primary and lower schools, middle schools, upper schools, and college or university level.

Curriculum and Content

Types of Curriculum

Throughout this book the authors have given emphasis and high priority to the *concept-centered curriculum* because they believe that it facilitates intellectual development over the other two most common curriculum designs which are *subject centered* and *child centered.* So that you can determine what your own philosophy will be, let us take a look at how each curriculum deals with content.

Subject-Centered Curriculum

The subject-centered curriculum allocates time for study of separate subjects generally classified as the language arts (reading, writing, and spelling), mathematics, the social studies (history, geography, economics, sociology, anthropology, philosophy, and so on), science, health, physical education, art, and music. Mastery of content and skills is the chief objective and the teacher uses a text over other educational aids as the primary source of knowledge because the textbook lends itself to preplanning and more precise study and homework assignments. Idealists and realists support the subject-centered curriculum because content is more easily controllable and because textbooks are more easily accessible. The framework lends itself to good, logical organization, precise lesson planning, and organized ways of presenting knowledge, established truths, and natural laws of the universe.

Some critics of the subject-centered curriculum (particularly existentialists) feel that the practice of using identical textbooks in classrooms implies that all children have equal abilities and can learn at the same rate. They also say that textbooks can monopolize the child's time in memorization and drill and rob him of opportunities to engage in more self-directed learning activities. These criticisms lose some of their validity when teachers use multilevel texts, that is, texts with different reading levels, and use them in more personalized and reference-book ways. When this is done, variation of pace is permitted, content can be more selective for individuals, and single mass reading assignments are not the specified objectives.

Child-Centered Curriculum

The child-centered curriculum bases its philosophy on the observed or felt needs of children and provides self-expression through child-selected activities. Froebel, in the 1800's, expressed ideas about helping children develop social and intellectual behaviors through play experiences and self-direction, but the child-centered curriculum did not gain much momentum until John Dewey promoted the concept that school is not preparation for life, but is life itself.

Educators, as a group, have been dissatisfied with the child-centered curriculum because of the many different interpretations given to Dewey's philosophy and because of the lack of guidelines to help correlate child-centeredness with appropriate and accurate content. Criticisms include unclear guidelines for teachers and administrators, the possibility that the child isn't really learning anything at all, that individualism is emphasized too much, that it is too agnostic, and that the individual-social life process is not a sufficient existence base for values. Others have even gone so far as to say that if the individual has too much freedom of choice, he will sink to a "low-level, pleasure-seeking life and ethics."

We previously quoted in this book some statements made by Dewey and others which counteract these impressions and clarify the child-centered curriculum's concepts of content, but the popular opinions of criticism about lack of content are the ones that largely persist.

Concept-Centered Curriculum

The concept-centered curriculum is designed to correct some of the gaps in knowledge and selection of inconsequential knowledge that were attributed to the child-centered curriculum. As teachers become more informed about how children learn and as students of the various disciplines contribute more accurate generalizations to help update the content of curriculum, various conceptual curriculum designs are being developed to include both the individual and his relationship to knowledge and to society.

The course of study that once dictated routine procedures and practices is being replaced by professional guidelines developed cooperatively by teachers and scholars of the various disciplines. These guidelines, as opposed to the fact-oriented curriculum, place emphasis on concepts that are considered to be important. They are opposed to the more restrictive scope and sequence outline and allow the teacher more leeway in selecting materials, activities, units of work, and specific content. These guidelines encourage the use of current events which cannot possibly be kept up to date in textbooks and which quickly render textbooks obsolete in today's world.

In some innovative organizations of teaching and learning, teachers who excel in one particular field are permitted to teach in this field alone and are given time to develop instructional materials to individualize instruction. Occasionally the organizations we have studied smack of the old-time subject-centered curriculum because teachers go back to being more subject-centered than child-centered and because no one person accepts the responsibility for knowing about a child's *total* school program. The most successful specialization efforts are in the use of a team of people each of whom has special talents and each of whom also has knowledge about the child in relation to other aspects of his development such as emotional, social, and intellectual growth in other content areas.

Programmed materials, too, are uniquely suited to combining the best that specialists and generalists have to offer because children can proceed at their own pace in some content areas part of the time and cross-fertilize one another in groups at other times under the guidance of empathetic and informed teachers.

In studying and analyzing your views on curriculum design, you should begin to do reflective thinking as to these problems:

1. Integrating knowledge by crossing subject matter lines.
2. Identifying with knowledge through experience and application.
3. Utilizing maximum teacher potential and capabilities while not losing sight of the child for whom educational programs are designed.
4. Using instructional media and human talents to individualize and personalize instruction.
5. Using groups as a teaching force for some kinds of learning.

Philosophers View Content

Idealists

Because idealists are concerned with education as an intellectual and spiritual pursuit, they seek to de-emphasize facts about the physical world and matter because they feel that facts are not reality; only ideas that matter are real. Idealists encourage reading as an intellectual activity, and prefer reading to audio-visual materials, experiments, or other sensory approaches. This is because of the unreality of physical things, in their opinion, for "Things are not what they seem to be" is the guiding maxim.

Because the idealist believes that there exist common elements concerning the needs and nature of man in every society at every time, the function of education is to preserve the subject matter content which is considered by them to be *essential* for the development of the individual mind. The chief characteristics of the idealist's curriculum include:

1. Constant subjects—those considered to be essential to each student if he is to realize intellectual and moral development.
2. Required subjects—the constant subjects are required of everyone and are for the *general education* of every child.
3. Individual differences—psychological information in modern idealism is for the purpose of helping teachers to individualize assignments within the common subjects that everyone must take.
4. Moral choices—the subject matter is normative, that is, the content should provide students with ideas about *what ought to be* in the world of human affairs.
5. Cultural enrichment is seen as a process of furnishing the child with the "best" examples of art, music, literature, biography, films, and so on, so that he will know and experience the "best" achievements of man.
6. Subject organization is neat, orderly, and logical, arranged in such a way that students proceed from the simple, concrete, and elementary to the more complicated, abstract, and sophisticated.

The idealists have had considerable conflict in the twentieth century because of the growth of scientific and technical knowledge, new psychological and sociological information, and because of the development of materialism that has developed as the result of increased wealth and technical knowledge and has tended to alienate man from spiritual concerns.

Realists

The essential content of education is best organized according to a subject-centered curriculum organized according to the psychological principles of learning by which the subject proceeds from the simple to the more complex depths of the essential body of knowledge (36).

Of least importance in the realist's view of the curriculum is the humanities. The scientific idealist would not ignore them completely, because he feels that individuals must be able to adjust satisfactorily to what is— or the status quo. However, he feels that if they are studied, they should be studied in the light of knowledge about social environments as seen through the eyes and writings of man.

Science and mathematics are of the most significance because they emphasize the accurate accumulated knowledge about man and his physical nature. Math and science are seen to have great value in and of themselves as mental disciplines, because science helps men have scientific approaches to problems and mathematics develops man's ability to reason.

Values must develop through scientific experimentation, and through the reason and objectivity of science and mathematics. To be avoided at all costs are normative value teaching, since the acquisition of values must be disciplined and sublimated to the emotions and to any immediate compulsions or impulses.

The realist feels that there is no need to "tune in" on a supernatural intelligence in order to educate man; rather, he feels that man can deal with his universe through a variety of sensory learnings and arrive at objective understandings that he can substantiate. Those subjects which can be precisely organized, taught, and evaluated are the only ones that are really recognized as legitimate curriculum content, because these kinds of subjects furnish the student with data from which he can make accurate generalizations.

The realist relies heavily on the objective-type test to measure achievement, since the elements of knowledge to be mastered can be identified. The teacher is responsible for deciding what children should learn and employs the conditions and techniques which are thought to facilitate learning of factual knowledge and understandings.

It is apparent that the long-range educational goals of idealists and realists are very similar and center around the development of basic, eternal truths even though they disagree about what these are or how they are acquired.

Experimentalists

The experimentalist feels that the only meaningful content is found in human experiences, and that he must therefore stimulate the student to discover subject matter and curriculum content that will be useful to him. The teacher's breadth of knowledge, background, and creative abilities, together with instructional materials influence the scope of content to which each child is exposed. Subject matter is not introduced in specific bodies of knowledge or blocks of time, but it is made available as data to utilize in seeking solutions to personal needs, problems, and curiosities. As opposed to scholasticism, realism, and idealism, experimentalists do not rely upon exact bodies of content considered appropriate for every child as part of his general education.

Democracy and its study and practice are important, and the primary aim of education, as described by most scholars of experimentalism, is to enable the individual to adjust to an ever-changing society while preparing for intelligent social cooperation, participation, and actions.

Since the democratic tradition is considered to be a self-correcting one, the social heritage of the past is not the focus nor is the transmission of culture. Rather, the curriculum is to focus on experiences that will help children *test* and *verify* democracy through changing and new experiences. The serious social problems of society are to be examined in order to see whether some reconstruction will render them capable of being corrected, and the curriculum must not exist apart from the social context of education.

Thus the curriculum has a social science base in which the pupil who is a product of society is also seen as a force in helping to change that society. The curriculum is viewed as everything that happens within the school environment, and includes student councils and clubs, as well as class and so-called extracurricular activities for which previous philosophies had no recognized place or concern.

The legitimate content of history which applies to the emerging problems of the present demands democratic administrator–teacher, teacher–teacher, teacher–pupil, pupil–teacher, and community–school planning, definitions of common social and educational goals, and the development of new methods to nurture creative skills.

As the variety of ways increase to introduce content, the experimentalist supplements technology, including programmed instruction, multilevel materials, teaching machines, computers, and audio-visual programs, with classroom situations to help children relate content to personal behaviors and understandings. Otherwise, the same lack of understanding and unrelatedness that developed from strict textbook teaching will attach itself to the new technologies now making themselves felt in educational circles.

Because it is the teacher—not the machine or the textbook—who sets the controls in learning environments, experimentalism, say educators, should provide the favorable climate and appropriate experiences that cannot be supplied by technology; in other words, the teacher provides the humaneness. The teacher serves as the guide and facilitator in helping each student to develop self-understanding, self-fulfillment, and to improve attitudes toward self, peers, school, and society. Thus the experimentalist is in a unique position to take advantage of his individual freedom in establishing classroom situations that originate in knowledge based on the psychological and sociological needs of children.

A major issue in American education has been the problem of whether to organize an instructional program by focusing on subject matter content or upon the child. The experimentalist has the best of two worlds for he does not recognize this as a problem since he holds strong beliefs that the curriculum should be child-centered; he views content as important data which excite and motivate further exploration by the individual. Defining problems, exploring major issues, and participating in scientific inquiry in various areas of human experience create learning situations with significant content for the experimentalist teacher and his students.

Whereas content, to the experimentalist, is based on the student's needs and goals, it is paced in terms of his development in skills, concepts, and intellectual abilities. Students are encouraged to evaluate their school experience in terms of self-improvement and to make recommendations for changes in the instructional program pertaining to both content and experience.

Existentialists

The theories of existentialism are similar in some respects to those of experimentalism, but much more emphasis is placed on individuality and free choice, with little regard for society. The existentialist prefers content in the fields of literature, philosophy, history, and art because these subjects lend themselves to involvement of the student spiritually, emotionally, and intellectually. Because the existentialist wants the student to become emotionally involved, content is selected and utilized by student choice. Overspecialization in content is discouraged since the student is expected to be committed to achieve self-realization through a wide variety of content and experiences. Limited and precise content would inhibit self-realization because students would not have the wide exposures from which to select.

The teacher serves as a guide for the student and provides classroom situations in which students develop personal concerns and use these in making their curriculum choices. Individualization of learning experiences is mandatory since learning is an emotional experience for the individual. Because group work is considered to be a method of standardizing thinking, the student is given the freedom to work independently and to assume responsibility for his own actions.

Since subjects have no value in and of themselves and are merely instruments through which individual students develop self-knowledge and self-responsibility, the existentialist, if forced to try to adapt to such a curriculum, would put emphasis on the important functions of the humanities. Because the existentialist teacher is democratic and nondirective, he feels more comfortable with a modified activity curriculum built upon student interests, common activities in which students may work individually or in groups, immediate needs as the vehicles for student involvement in the learning process, and individual differences because of the great differences that exist in the hidden curriculum of experience of each student.

Specific Content Areas

All elementary school teachers working in subject-centered, child-centered, and concept-centered curriculums are responsible for teaching content. The major question a teacher's philosophy seeks to explore and answer is: "What are the objectives to be accomplished through the content of curriculum?"

In America, teachers are free to participate in the planning of school philosophies, aims, values, and ideals, and in developing from these their own educational philosophies about the purpose and kind of content that will further these. As you read the following summaries about content and the teaching–learning aspects of content, direct your attention toward the possible ways to improve practices as you have observed or experienced them in your own education.

Before we investigate specific content areas, it is important to mention that each content area has been drastically changed through the cooperative efforts of teachers and scholars during the past decade. It is also significant to remind the reader that even more changes in recommended content are just beyond the horizon and that even more changes can be expected by the end of the century.

When statements about curriculum content include the relationships between a pupil, his instructional setting, and goal characteristics, the teacher curriculum developer is "in a much better situation not only to plan his content and sequence, but also to assess its merit. For example, a curriculum recommendation in social studies which overlooks such pupil and teacher characteristics as age, race, class background, and other demographic factors leads to an unused, or at best a misused package. Similarly, when naive assumptions about group processes among adolescents are made, so that teachers are instructed to 'put pupils in small groups,' the curriculum design is faulty, and data collected to test it may not prove its worth because of the variety of ways teachers followed the instruction" (37).

Student teachers, as well as experienced teachers, should be able to recognize different types of theories and should also be aware of their appropriate uses, their limitations, and their possible powers. We mentioned previously that most educational philosophy has a humanistic type of theory or theories, and these, although not empirical, can help teachers to broaden their perceptions, their roles in society, and their classroom stances.

Most "new" curricula are based on models of various sorts, and no one expects every teacher and supervisor to attain the specialized skills needed to thoroughly assess these. But teachers and supervisors do need to know how to raise questions about theory and how to read, interpret, and judge the prepared assessments of others. The purpose of knowing about theories, then, is to help educators become more astute as they make professional judgments and as they participate in professional actions.

Any good curriculum recommendation should specify:

1. Student outcomes and behaviors.
2. The process and flow by which content and techniques lead to changes of behavior with certain students.

Failure to specify these "decreases the potency of the recommendation. The research in classroom grouping is a case in point. This administrative device for influencing learning has often been used without specifying why it should be effective, or without indicating what changes in instruction should accompany the administrative change. School organization, as a reflection of manipulation to achieve curricular outcomes, often fails to support its case through research because it lacks theory and precision," state Gordon (37) and his colleagues.

To be able to combine content, students, instructional settings and techniques, and student outcomes and behaviors with educational goals is the confusion, complexity, and phenomenon of instruction. To be able to do these things professionally and effectively is not to seek simple solutions, superficial aims, or purely emotionally satisfying answers to questions.

Language Arts

How a person communicates and what he communicates affect to a large degree the way he functions and the way others perceive him as a person; these actually reflect the kind of person he is. Since young children come to school at an early age with wide ranges of abilities in both verbal and nonverbal language, the teacher faces the problems of helping to direct, select, and individualize content from communication skills that will initiate growth and have long-lasting, ongoing effects.

To define communication as a process which affects how one thinks, how one sees himself, and how one behaves in society, the teacher needs to be able to incorporate good linguistic principles into children's reading, writing, listening, and speaking experiences. The teacher's observation and analyses of children's basic structure patterns when communicating —the sentence patterns, the question patterns, the exclamation patterns— exemplify key language patterns or forms of usage upon which the teacher can structure linguistic content.

Structural linguists have for years been engaged in fundamental appraisals of grammar and their research has resulted in sweeping condemnations of traditional English teaching and particularly of traditional methods of teaching grammar. At least two prominent linguists have concerned themselves with the why and how of grammar teaching. Charles Fries and W. Nelson Frances speak in similar veins about clear and precise thinking as expressed through language. Frances (38) declares that the superseding of vague and sloppy thinking by clear and precise thinking is an exciting experience in and for itself. To acquire insight into the workings of a language, and to recognize the infinitely delicate system of relationship, balance, and interplay that constitutes its grammar, is to become closely acquainted with one of man's more miraculous creations, not unworthy to be set beside the equally beautiful organization of the physical universe.

In the modern school, listening and speaking skills are receiving more attention. The advent of television has greatly increased the amount of listening that children do, and some writers have called the twentieth century "The Listening Age." Witty (39) conducted a series of studies of children's television viewing in the Chicago area beginning in 1949, and his 1962 report stated that elementary school children spent 21 hours a week watching TV. On an average, children in grade two averaged 16 hours per week, in grade four 23 hours, and in grade five 25 hours per week.

The significance of these studies highlights the increased amount of time that is being spent listening, and raises the question of the importance of improving the teaching of listening. Some research shows that people are not very effective listeners. Nichols (40) has shown that the average person remembers only about half of what he hears others say, even if he seems to have been listening intently; two months later, after a particular listening experience, average listeners are able to recall only about 25 per cent of what has actually been said.

Several studies show that listening can be improved through teaching and practice. For example, Canfield (41) found that when the techniques of listening were taught either directly or indirectly, significant gains resulted when compared with groups who had no planned instruction. Trivette (42) found that 77 per cent of the fifth graders in her studies showed improvement when they were given specific training in listening for the main ideas, for details, and for the purpose of making inferences. Listening is not a separate subject, but an integral part of almost everything that goes on in daily life. It can be taught directly or indirectly in almost all content areas in the classroom and as an integral part of everything that is taught.

Similarly, oral language has been undergoing intensive study and research, and researchers have found that children's language patterns are largely set by the time they come to school. Studies conducted by Noell (43), Smith (44), Strickland (45), and Loban (46), as well as those by others, find that most children have already learned to use the sound systems, grammar, and vocabulary characteristic of their homes and neighborhoods by the time they begin school. Smith (44) calls attention to the fact that 98 per cent of all normal children are able to speak and to be understood. Strickland (45) and Loban (46) say that the children included in their studies have vocabularies and speaking habits that are almost completely set by the time they come to school and that they use all of the common sentence patterns that linguists have identified as basic to the English language. In addition, and important to teachers who will remember that we discussed sex differences in learning in Chapter 2, Loban's (46) study shows that boys of elementary school age are typically less proficient in oral language than girls are. Similarly, we have already pointed out that in traditional schools one is apt to find that remedial reading classes in elementary schools generally have more boys than girls in them, and that one's ability to communicate orally is directly related to one's ability to read. These findings suggest that since boys are naturally lower in language proficiency, they should be given many opportunities to use oral language in situations related particularly to their ideas and interest.

A number of researchers who have been working since the 1930's also have accumulated evidence that children of today possess larger vocabularies and use more complex sentence structures than children did a generation ago. It has been proved that listening and speaking are directly related, and that children's reading abilities are directly related to the way they speak. Strickland (45) has provided a great deal of objective evidence about this. Her studies show that there is a higher relationship between speaking and listening than between speaking and all other testable variables; and she concluded, also, that the way children speak influences the way they read:

> Pupils who ranked high in silent reading comprehension employed the most common patterns of structure more frequently than did pupils who ranked low, and they used fewer short utterances. Pupils ranking high in silent reading comprehension had a greater average use of movables and elements of subordination and a greater mean sentence length than did pupils who ranked low in this variable.

In a joint statement issued by the Association for Childhood Education International, the Association for Supervision and Curriculum Development, the International Reading Association, and the National Council of Teachers of English, this statement about the significance and order of the components of good language arts programs is made (47):

> Upon a base of the spoken language are built its written forms; a pupil with inadequate oral language facility is likely to be blocked in most learning, particularly with respect to reading and writing facility which is basic to the total elementary school program. . . . Research in human growth and development and in learning reveals that, for most physically and emotionally normal human beings, learning to communicate beyond the stage of crying or random babbling involves learning to listen, to speak, to read, and to write, in the order listed. Listening and speaking serve as a base for reading and writing and, if rooted in experience, furnish a rich background of meaning for written and printed symbols.

A great deal has also been said and written about improving the language skills of the culturally different and educationally deprived, the study of dialect as it applies to standard English teaching in schools, and the teaching of English as a second language. Some writers have traced traditional attitudes about any English that deviates from the "standard" or "norm" to the rigidity of the traditional American middle class. Calitrini (48) is one of these, and he says that not only do people not want to be Americanized in the same way that "they can be atomized," they do not want to feel that they must develop cultural tastes and abilities to replace what they already have; he also deplores traditional rigidity:

> How rigid we are, we of the educated American middle class! We make Carol Kennicotts of all those who come to our main streets, or else we impose the costume and the makeup of our little stages upon all of the young actors who come to play with us, pushing them into a faceless chorus line. . . . We tell them they must speak as we do, read as we do, follow our customs, and adopt our moral values. We attempt to impose our music and art upon them and insist that they admire our technology as if the very differences that make them what they are, individuals in their own right, make them less than we instead of only different.
>
> . . . The problem, then, is one not only of language and reading, but also of socialization—and beyond that, it is a problem of values and philosophy.

Certainly as a teacher studies a classroom situation for the various ways children express themselves orally, he must value each as he finds him, encourage a two-way flow of conversation, and realize that children from lower socioeconomic income groups generally use oral language on a more limited basis; the linguist would say that they are more apt to speak in "partials." Many of them have already learned that their language is not accepted or valued by the school although it is well understood in their own cultural speech communities. Thus, when it is necessary for them to use language in school, it may be difficult for them to communicate with groups other than their own.

They may use language to express feelings and ideas just as much as the middle class does, but they may use more localisms, colloquialisms, slang, jargon, or obscenities. Linguistically, they can be helped to become more verbal and can be sensitized to the forms of language that are used for purposes other than communication in their own speech communities.

A word needs to be said here about *dialect* because it is often used to describe a variety of speech characteristics that are really quite different. Generally, the term "dialect" means the speech used in cultural or regional communities where people are in constant communication with one another. Within this framework there are:

1. *Localisms,* which are a form of dialect, or a dialect form.
2. *Colloquialisms,* which are forms of speech characteristically used in relaxed, informal conversations.
3. *Slang expressions* that are popular forms of extremely informal language.
4. *Jargon,* which is language that is used in a specialized field or area under discussion.

What new linguistic understandings add up to for the teacher is that, in determining an over-all structure for language arts programs, he must move from the strict approaches of grammarians and "judges" to a *usage approach.*

The traditionalist textbook-workbook approach fails to stimulate a child to express ideas, to discuss things with others, and to *use* his language first in oral expression that leads to competence in the other language arts areas. In Chapter 6, we spoke of the importance of language and communication for understanding the world of significant events. Books are still important, but today's children receive so many messages from so many media that they need to be helped to understand and interpret critically the messages with which they are constantly bombarded. The textbook and programmed instruction can be helpful in teaching children the concrete symbols that represent speech and thought, but they are not a substitute for learning to listen and to speak effectively.

Teacher creativity in planning learning situations that involve children in dialogue, in self-expression, and in imaginative experiences involving puppetry, role playing, and drama should become the rule rather than the exception. Teachers can also make creative use of life experiences, tape recorders, films, photographs, records, and other audio-visual classroom aids. With an imaginative and professional teacher in the central position at the "hub" of the wheel of learning environments, it is possible to select and devise appropriate materials and activities as needed to provide specific linguistic experiences for individuals and for groups. We cannot overstress the importance of helping children learn new ways and new vocabularies to help express their thoughts, feelings, and new understandings.

The knowledge and understanding of a teacher toward ways to utilize content in language arts throughout the school day, as well as during periods specifically earmarked for language arts, will be the mark of his success as a teacher and as a person who really helps children to become self-actualizing individuals. Implicit in the development of any good language arts program is the attitude that there is a place for every child's national or family language, for dialects, for colloquialism, for informal jargon and localisms, and for more formal English. It is not the teacher's role to remind children constantly that his language is "poor" or "incorrect," but it is the teacher's role to encourage children to talk, to keep communication open, to listen, and to determine what kind of help children need at a later time when there will be language drill of some sort. It is the teacher's responsibility to guide children into a variety of situations where language can be *used* and, from these, to help them understand how language operates, what it is for, how it can be manipulated, and why it is such a powerful asset to man.

Social Studies

As the linguists have brought new concepts and content to aid the teacher in language arts, so the scholars of the various social sciences have contributed the generalizations, or large central ideas, around which learning in the social studies is to be organized, patterned, and made meaningful. By working from generalizations, teachers can discern sub-generalizations, concepts, and factual data that will lead young people to understand the generalizations.

These generalizations provide a basis for gathering and organizing facts, for interpreting facts that fit a general category, and for testing the accuracy of ideas and statements. As individuals mature and enlarge their backgrounds of knowledge, concepts evolve into generalizations. For example, a young child may say that any body of water he sees is a "brook," but gradually he comes to understand that there are many different types of water such as rivers, lakes, seas, oceans, streams, creeks, ponds, or puddles. Eventually he learns that there are various name designations for each of these categories, for example, "river"—Mississippi, Amazon, Hudson, Blue Danube, and many others. He also learns that there are many kinds of rivers such as feeders, tributaries, natural, man-made, dirty, muddy, wide, narrow, or fast-running. He also learns that the words which designate some kinds of water formations also have other meanings such as stream of thought, river of dreams, or a lake of daisies; and that rivers have many purposes such as a means of transportation or exploration, a source of food or power, a source of drinking water, a way to irrigate, or the center of a flood control or conservation program. Thus, over considerable periods of time, the learner builds full understanding of concepts involved in his everyday environment, and associates the meanings involved by single terms and ideas.

Social studies content emphasizes the expectations of individuals and of society. It also helps individuals to grasp social generalizations and to make generalizations of their own. Just a few years ago history, geography, and civics were the "content" of the social studies, and these disciplines were taught separately with the expectation that young people would make their integrations and associations for meaningful context from the information they received. These were designed mainly to "bring home the lessons of history," to pass on the culture, to ensure that each child be knowledgeable about place geography, and to improve civic understanding and competence. If the interrelationships and generalizations were ever understood, it was because the student began to make his own associations from dates, names, and places, but no coordinated effort was a specific part of the technique of teaching.

Now newer fields of study and research have been developed and have become recognized as social or behavioral sciences that are making important contributions to the social studies. The biggest problem for educators is the selection of content from among the vast amount of information which is available and which is basic, essential, and contributive to the effective citizenship of young people maturing in a changing society.

Political science, economics, anthropology, psychology, sociology, and philosophy have now been analyzed for the contributions they are able to make to modern social studies curricula, but especially with young children, information from the natural and physical sciences, art, music, literature, health, and safety is needed in order to help them grasp information and meaning about themselves and other people. The important thing to remember is that a good social studies program provides a way for teachers to bring generalizations and contributions of related social disciplines into meaningful activities and concepts for children. In so doing, it serves as a central and very essential aspect of the curriculum.

The teacher must exercise care in planning his social studies program so that there is balance in the total offering. Imbalance is created when teachers give too much attention to the contributions of certain social sciences and omit the important contributions of the others. A good program reflects the persistent factors and problems that characterize our times; and the content, built around areas of concern such as mobility, changes in family life, social responsibility, individual responsibility, population growth, civil rights, human rights, and other current happenings, can be identified in a number of generalizations in different disciplines.

For example, while traditional geography was centered in the location and names of places and things, and the identification of land masses and types, modern geography draws content from both physical geography and cultural geography, which is concerned with the arrangement of man in space and his relationship to his physical surroundings. In history, newer interpretations combine chronology, sequence, and change, attempting to relate space and time, man's struggle for freedom and human dignity, the historical past as it influences the present, preparation for social and political life, and the tempo and universality of change.

Political science is not only a study of government and the theory and practice of man's efforts to organize and control the power needed to formulate public policy and administer public services, but it is also concerned with the public law, politics, public administration, executive branches of government from the local to the national level, comparative governments, and international relations which include economic policies, ideologies, diplomacy, international laws, and cooperative international organizations. Within the framework of political science are also a large group of generalizations that relate primarily to democracy, including (49):

1. Democracy implies a way of life as well as a form of government.
2. Democracy is based on certain fundamental assumptions, among which are the integrity of man, the dignity of the individual, equality of opportunity, man's rationality, man's morality, man's practicality, and man's ability to govern himself and to solve his problems cooperatively.
3. Man develops his fullest potential in a climate of freedom. Much of civilization's advance can be traced to man's search for a larger measure of freedom. For the truly civilized man, no amount of material wealth can ever compensate for the lack of freedom. Since freedom allows individuals to develop their creative talents, a society benefits when its individual members are relatively free.
4. Human beings are creatures of self-interest. For democracy to function, self-interest cannot be the dominating force. Rather, it must be curbed in favor of public interest.
5. A chief end of democracy is the preservation and extension of human freedoms. Freedom is unworkable unless balanced by a corresponding responsibility. The line of advance in freedom appears to run from legal freedom to political freedom, and from political freedom to genuine economic and social freedom.
6. Civil liberty—freedom of thought, speech, press, worship, petition, and association—constitutes the central citadel of human freedom. With it, all other kinds of freedom become possible; without it, none of them can have any reality.
7. Basic to democracy is belief in progress. A free society is hospitable to new ideas and to change and encourages the unfettered search for truth. Peaceful action rather than violence is one of its hallmarks.
8. Certain factors are necessary for democracy to succeed. These include (a) an educated citizenry, (b) a common concern for human freedom, (c) communication and mobility, (d) a degree of economic security, (e) a spirit of compromise and mutual trust, (f) respect for the rights of minority groups and the loyal opposition, (g) moral and spiritual values, (h) participation by the citizen in government at all levels.
9. Opportunity sufficient to allow every individual voluntarily to choose the division of labor in which he will perform is a concept that has flourished under democratic philosophy and practice and the capitalistic system.

From the study of economics and the knowledge that economists have contributed to the social studies, we have knowledge about analyzing data, issues, and public policies connected with the production, distribution, and the consumption of wealth and income. Economic theories operate within these frameworks whether they originate in democratic, socialist, fascist, or communist countries, and economic theories are methods rather than doctrines.

Anthropology is concerned both with the evolution of man and his present characteristics as a biological being. It is also concerned with man's various methods of organizing his group life and coping with his natural environment, so we can see that it also overlaps with newer concepts of geography.

Psychology is concerned with the description and understanding of patterns of behavior exhibited by individuals, and is the science of studying human behavior with the aim of understanding and predicting behavior. It includes forms of behavior such as growth and development, learning, feeling, thinking, behaving, perceiving, atypical behaviors, social behavior, personality development, and the psychological processes underlying behavior. The teacher needs to realize that psychology is closely allied to the social studies on one hand, and to the biological sciences on the other. Individual psychology also includes appraisal of personality characteristics and the nature of growth and development, as well as the measurement of individual differences in various facets of behavior. It is vitally concerned with the various patterns of influence that produce behaviors such as withdrawal, aggression, creativity, delinquency, and others. As we stated in Section III, social psychology is the bridge between sociology—which focuses attention on understanding large social settings and group structures—and psychology, which focuses attention primarily on understanding individual behavior and personality. Here also, we talked a great deal about sociology as a scientific study of the social systems men develop in their interactions with one another.

The main purpose of social studies instruction and content is to help individuals grasp social generalizations. By understanding some of the "big ideas" that influence the living habits of man, and by having students build their understandings of these gradually through many carefully planned and directed learning experiences, teachers can enhance children's learning through actual experiences, audio-visual materials, reading, and discussions. They combine procedures of instruction with organized, conscious effort to help students arrive at valid and significant conclusions, as they reduce the big generalizations and concepts to workable subdivisions that then become reference points for particular lessons or units of study.

Students do not learn by verbalizing a great mass of information without first understanding through problem solving situations in which they are helped to gather knowledge, see relationships, have understandings, acquire new ideas and extend old ones, and arrive at valid conclusions.

Children probably enjoy the variety of activities and content in the social studies when textbooks, dates, facts, names, and places are not the main vehicle for exploration. Modern children have many interests and much to contribute because they are bombarded with world news and current new knowledge and technology. Additionally, they are developing interests in such current events as the rise and fall of the stock market (economics), the coup d'etat of foreign governments and the war in Vietnam (political science), home and family living (sociology), and the effect of cultures and customs on the attitudes of men (anthropology).

The advantage of having groups of large generalizations from which to create the "stuff" of content is that in breaking these down into smaller, workable units the teacher and his students can use what is of immediate concern and interest to develop understanding about the generalizations that lead to more global concepts. These can be used again and again with different content, current events, or problems to reinforce the same generalizations and concepts.

If a teacher of elementary schoolchildren, or secondary schoolchildren for that matter, finds that they are disinterested in social studies, he should take a good look at himself and his treatment of content. When a lull in interest appears, he should ask himself:

1. Are the children being bored by content that is restricted by too many human experiences? by the textbook? by too few field experiences? by too much lecturing and too little participation?
2. Am I teaching content and concepts that are inappropriate for these children's interests, concerns, and abilities?
3. Am I overlooking opportunities to capitalize upon the students' own backgrounds and cultures?
4. Am I killing interest by stressing "right" and "wrong" answers rather than placing emphasis on inquiry, relationships, and generalizations that have meaning to the children?
5. Am I working undemocratically with the students?
6. Do I show enthusiasm for reinforcing behaviors? for creating classroom situations that give children opportunities to discover new content and concepts for themselves?

Science

Since Sputnik, the average person has become more "science conscious" because, for the first time, he has perceived the significant social implications of scientific possibilism. With increasing awareness of science's potential influence upon civilization, elementary school teachers are attempting to improve classroom teaching of science. In this, they are also being aided by professional scientists from many specialized fields. The problem of the teacher is to provide orientation to the social implications of science without negating it as a discipline.

Not only the content of science has changed, but methods of teaching and learning and, particularly, the teacher's role have changed. The change in the teacher's view of his role is the key to involving children in firsthand experiences in which they make series of "discoveries" and teachers ask questions to intensify a child's interest and involvement in the process.

Thier (50) analyzes four levels of involvement and outlines the progression that should result in better science experiences for children. The first, or minimal involvement, is reading a book about science. This involvement is verbal and abstract, and a child's accomplishments are completely dependent upon his ability to read what is written and the author's choice of language and illustrations.

The second level, according to Thier, is a slightly higher degree of involvement in which a child takes part in classroom discussions about science. This is, of course, limited to verbal expressions and, while it does encourage dialogue between students and teachers, it can confuse children because the operation is still on a verbal-abstract level and the child is not really involved. A third level, which is slightly higher, is when either the teacher or the children do an experiment or a demonstration using "systems of objects," or some natural phenomena. Their investigation points out that the involvement of the "doers" will always be greater than the involvement of the "watchers" and that the problems of visibility and technique sometimes make part of the group unaware of what is really going on.

The highest degree of involvement for children in any science program is a process whereby each child has before him the system of objects he chooses or which have been chosen from the environment for him. He observes them, studies what happens to them, records in pictures or in writing or in discussion his observations about them, and directly experiences the phenomena himself. Because the observations and the involvement are his own personal reactions, they can be neither right nor wrong; sometimes the teacher only has to look at the way a child has sorted objects to see what his criteria have been. Often the child cannot verbalize his understanding and does not need to because, if we take the work of Piaget that was discussed earlier and apply it to science, some of the developmental learnings and behaviors may not be evident in verbalization for many years.

"Ideally," states Thier (50), "the science program should include a mixture of all four degrees of involvement. The reading about science, discussion, and demonstration should, however, be used only to foster the development of situations in which children can explore the natural environment through the individualized direct laboratory approach de-

Curriculum is

- Helping children to sample and process their own learning experiences.
- Providing constantly expanding experiences and opportunities to understand oneself and others.
- Dealing with interacting forces created by each child, the times, and knowledge.

(Photo by Mr. Mazon, New Haven, Connecticut, Public Schools.)

scribed as level four. . . . The adoption of this philosophy of science teaching makes impossible the separation of process goals from content goals, or either one from concept development."

To watch a group of eight-year-olds make observations about the habits of their own mealworm in an individual shallow box or about a thin slice of onion under microscopes used by individuals or shared by a pair of students is to observe children caught up at one time in content, process, and concept development. There are groups at work on such programs now; one of these is the Science Curriculum Improvement Study which develops a concept of science education that is based on communicating scientific literacy, the structure of science, the maturity of students, the pupil's past experiences and preconceptions about science, and a drastically changed role for teachers. Individual lessons are determined by use of the discovery method which includes concept development and the needs of students. The *discovery method* (51) involves new roles for both the learner and the teacher, in fact, and cannot be used by teachers who see their roles as either dispensers of facts or masters of drill and grill. The teacher spends a great deal of time listening, observing, questioning to encourage children to experiment or think further, and accepting children's answers as evidence of *their* understandings and observations (52).

Blackwood (53) gives this working definition of science to be of help in giving clues as to what may properly be included in the study of science. *Science is man's relentless search for verifiable patterns, concepts, descriptions, or explanations of phenomena in the universe.*

Generally speaking, a good way to think about the teaching of science is to involve children in day-by-day experience in behaving as do scientists at work. The following list of "clue words" (54) suggests a rich array of possibilities for teacher–pupil choice:

CLUE WORDS

Knowing		Applying	
Observes	Accumulates	Arranges	Compares
Identifies	Counts	Distinguishes	Concludes
Describes	Looks	Organizes	Experiments
Gathers	Sees	Estimates	Controls
		Equals	Ponders
Manipulating		Sorts	Groups
Measures	Demonstrates	Plans	Decides
Selects	Balances		
instruments	Weighs	*Creating*	
Computes		Hypothesizes	Selects data
		Induces	Designs
Applying		Deduces	experiments
Classifies	Defines	Speculates	Reflects
Assigns	Associates	Analyzes	Proposes

CLUE WORDS

Creating		*Evaluating*	
Criticizes	Appreciates	Pools data	Criticizes
Conceives	Infers	Recognizes	Transposes
Invents	Abstracts	errors	Generalizes
Guesses	Synthesizes	Equates	Controls
Comprehends	Formulates	Distinguishes	variables
Doubts	Interrelates		
Incubates	Generalizes	*Communicating*	
Predicts	Forecasts	Tabulates	Debates
Estimates	Extrapolates	Graphs	Argues
Explains	Interpolates	Writes	Describes
		Speaks	Demonstrates
Evaluating		Reports	Compares
Ponders	Questions	Explains	Questions
Rejects	Doubts	Teaches	Instructs
Accepts	Verifies	Informs	Plots
Believes	Decides	Charts	Draws
Disbelieves	Interprets	Reads	

Blackwood also suggests that if the answer to most of the following questions is yes, it is probable that the science experiences the teacher fosters are making a positive contribution to the science education of the children involved in it:

1. Did the activity involve the children in describing or explaining some phenomenon?
2. Did the children collect original data from which to draw conclusions?
3. Did the children organize and communicate about the data in useful ways?
4. Did the children have opportunities to speculate and predict?
5. Did the experience relate clearly to development of a major science concept?
6. Did some of the questions raised provide stimulation for further study?

The environment and experiences of children are good sources of science content because most children have natural curiosities about what they see, hear, touch, taste, and smell in their everyday life. They constantly ask questions and often reason out the answers with a minimum amount of guidance from the teacher.

An example of one teacher's development of the social implications of science occurred in a group of eleven-year-olds who were interested in the *how* and *why* of the Apollo Project. Their questions included these:

How does the spacecraft get to the moon? Why does man want to go to the moon? In exploring some of the dimensions of these questions, the children discovered new knowledge that has resulted from man's study of space and that he has been able to put to use as a result of space study:

1. Hydrazine, a drug that shows promise in the treatment of mental illness and tuberculosis, has been developed from a liquid fuel propellant.
2. Pyroceram, now being used in kitchenware, is a material used in the nose cone of a space capsule to withstand the extremes of cold and heat of outer space.
3. Microminiaturization, which is the use of small electrical and mechanical parts such as the transistor in radios and hearing aids.
4. Weather satellites, for more accurate forecasting of weather.
5. Worldwide television possibilities due to the launching of communication satellites.
6. People are learning new skills and new knowledge for new jobs that are needed in space study and space exploration.
7. Space treaties, which call for the cooperation and understanding of all nations.

The modern elementary school teacher believes that if science content can be handled in such a way that children are intimately involved in making their own observations and discoveries, they will retain and transfer functional scientific concepts to new experiences and situations. It is really the classroom teacher—not expensive materials and equipment—who is the key to a good, modern science program.

The real question for the professional teacher is not "Which method shall I use?" but rather, "What is my philosophy about meeting the needs of children and society through science, and in what ways shall I carry out that philosophy?"

Mathematics

Teachers of today's elementary schoolchildren find themselves in the midst of educational revolutions, and as part of these reformations mathematics has been undergoing considerable revision and important new emphases. New emphases include helping each child to understand the structure of mathematics, its laws and principles, its sequence and order, and the way in which mathematics as a tool contributes to logical thinking and problem solving of nonmathematical, as well as mathematical, problems; in other words, to the *kind* of thinking that one is able to do.

As in the field of science education, not only the method of learning and the subject matter content have been overhauled and updated, but the role of the teacher in a modern mathematics program is vastly different. Again, the key to thinking about and designing a modern elementary school mathematics program is really the *involvement of children* with stress on an atmosphere of informality and freedom to develop ideas, possibilities, and personal discoveries about mathematics. Formerly, goals of mathematics education were mainly two: (1) to teach computational skills for utilitarian purposes in life such as bookkeeping, shopping, balancing checkbooks, figuring interest rates, and the like; and (2) to serve as a basis for some professions requiring mathematical background.

New directions in elementary school mathematics are several. A U.S. Department of Health, Education, and Welfare publication (55) states that the following elements of newness have been added to the older goals:

1. To help each child understand the structure of mathematics, its laws and principles, its sequence and order, and the way in which mathematics as a system expands to meet new needs.
2. To help each child prepare for the next steps in mathematical learning which are appropriate for him in terms of his potential and his future educational requirements

In the statement of these objectives, we see incorporated also some of the newer information about learning and concept development. For example, perceptual psychology studies indicate relationships between the way individuals act and the way they perceive themselves and the world: "If his perceptions are extensive, rich, and highly available when he needs them, then he will be likely to behave in effective, efficient, 'intelligent' ways" (56). From the point of view of the perceptual psychologist, intelligent behavior can be developed because it is possible to modify, change, and shape it according to the quality of an individual's perceptions. Children perceive what seems appropriate to them in response to a need, in relation to their own goals and values, and when threat is part of the learning environment, perception is blocked or stymied.

The challenge to teachers is to be able to devise challenging, unique situations in which the learner will be involved and which he will approach with the idea that he will succeed. This is a different conception than that which formerly placed importance on *what children knew* and *what they did not know.* The emphasis now is on *what children can learn* about certain concepts as they progress through the elementary school years and on finding out which methods of involvement are the most fruitful. For example, Patrick Suppes, director of Stanford University's Institute for Mathematical Studies in the Social Sciences and a professor of philosophy and statistics, has been involved since about 1956 in experimental projects in modern elementary school mathematics; his programs in California have included thousands of boys and girls aged six to eleven. One of his projects was a math course for first graders using concepts such as: "A set is a collection of objects" and "Zero is the number of objects in the empty set."

Suppes and others have demonstrated that young children learn better when they start with concepts like these because *sets* are more concrete than numbers and because putting together sets of actual objects is a more *concrete* operation than adding numbers. Since everything in mathematics can be developed from concepts of "sets" and "operations upon sets," they feel that this is the most logical and productive place to begin mathematics education. Robert Davis, director of the Madison Project which has been centered jointly at Syracuse University and St. Louis Webster College, has worked to introduce algebra and coordinate geometry in elementary schools beginning as early as the second grade. Many teachers have worked with mathematicians and scientists to develop special projects that relate some aspects of mathematics *and* science. One of these programs is the Elementary School Science Project developed at the University of California (57). Another useful resource was developed by a pioneer in the field, W. W. Sawyer, whose booklet, *Math Patterns in Science* (58), was the basis for some of the programs in which many teachers have participated.

As children meet teachers during their elementary school years (and later), they are apt to meet many who perceive mathematics differently. Some view mathematics, as they have experienced it, as a "social process" with a utilitarian social purpose; others believe that mathematics is a matter of memorizing the rules and making computations. Many teachers disliked math thoroughly and communicate this dislike to their students. But fortunate is the child whose teacher sees mathematics as a process of discovering *how* and *why* things work as they do in the world of mathematics, and who recognizes that because of this involvement in the discovery process at an early age his students may be grasping ideas and seeing new possibilities that have not occurred to him.

It is true that quantitative thinking occurs daily in such activities as making purchases at the store, dialing telephone numbers, measuring, averaging, and weighing objects. It is also true that children have many opportunities to develop quantitative concepts naturally in everyday life, and from their immediate environments and interest. But too many teachers teach only what some mathematicians refer to as "grocery store mathematics" and the question of what to include in the curriculum is left to incidental number and number-operation experiences. With a planned program that involves both children's everyday experiences and their teacher's knowledge of the concepts and generalizations of mathematics upon which can be built a solid and defensible program, mathematics can hold new excitement for childern and their teachers.

For one thing, teachers who have recent training in newer mathematics programs know that the principles involved in the commutative, associative, and distributive laws of mathematics are fundamental, and that through helping children understand and apply these principles they are not only teaching the "skills" and "facts," but they are also developing concepts about *the nature of operations, the beauty of mathematical designs and progressions, the possible flexibilities of mathematics, and understandings basic to the algorithms or forms of mathematics.*

Another significant point for teachers to remember is that practice in developing specific skills is necessary in a variety of situations and that repetitive practice is necessary only after children understand the reasons for needing and using the skills. To introduce new skills before children are ready to understand them as a natural progression of their own mathematical needs and understandings is to discourage children from making their own discoveries. To discourage children from becoming involved in making their own discoveries about how and why a rule works actually has the effect of blocking children from eventually using rules, or algorithms, automatically in varieties of situations they will encounter.

Children vary in their needs for repetitive practice in skill development in mathematics just as they do in word recognition, spelling, or science activities. Some need to meet the same problem in a variety of situations while others need to meet it in only one or a few. No really professional teacher can defend, on any grounds whatsoever, the same drill and grill for every child; nor can he justify the same set of experiences for every child with the expectation that there will be the same results or personal discoveries. Returning to the idea of the "curriculum of hidden experiences," each one of us interprets differently what he sees, hears, or experiences depending upon our own background of associations, and therefore, no teacher can be certain that what *he thinks he has taught* has been learned.

In elementary school classrooms, there must be varieties of manipulative materials within easy reach of every child—blocks, marbles, buttons, dominoes, balancing boards, number lines, bead frames, number puzzles and games, counting frames and boxes, direction finders, and the like (59)—so that there are always available individual and group resources for making investigations and discoveries independent of teacher direction.

When resources and opportunities for making personal investigations are close at hand and can be used by each child in relation to his own readiness and capabilities and when teachers are able to combine their knowledge of individual children's learning styles and needs with the significant strands of mathematical content, mathematics will not only become the tool for thinking that will help children enormously but it will also be revealed in its true perspectives. Many groups have been working to identify the significant strands which run through mathematics and are applicable to elementary school education. A typical list of *strands* may look something like this one from the Summary Reports of a California State Department of Education conference (60):

1. Number, structures, operation
2. Number systems and numeration
3. Geometry and measurement
4. Sets
5. The mathematical sentence
6. Logic
7. Graphs and functions
8. Applications of mathematics

In a list such as this one, we see clearly that *practicality* and *applications* are not omitted, but that emphasis is placed also upon the content and structure of mathematics.

The Revolution in School Mathematics: A Challenge for Administrators and Teachers, published by the National Council of Teachers of Mathematics (61), is a good resource for teachers and administrators because it typifies, once more, the cooperation of groups such as this one with groups such as the National Science Foundation and shows efforts to interweave understandings, content, and concepts. In this report, G. Baley Price states that math research, automation, and computing machines have brought about the revolution in mathematics teaching. "Research," he says, "created more knowledge about mathematics in the twentieth century than in all the rest of history; automation created the necessity for solving complicated design and development problems; computing machines made rapid and reliable computation possible not only for problems which could be solved, however tediously, by traditional means, but also for problems which had been completely insoluble."

The teacher's philosophy will help him answer the critical questions of technique and evaluation and understand the conflicting issues that he will face in his teaching career. Certainly the status quo in mathematics, as in other content areas, is not adequate; "grocery store mathematics" is not accurate or defensible for the education of today's boys and girls and teachers can no longer teach mathematics "incidentally" if there *happens* to be a situation where some mathematics might be introduced. Beginning and experienced teachers should be able to:

1. Understand the importance of the basic strands of mathematics.
2. Examine present elementary school mathematics programs critically to see whether they incorporate both these and the best possible kinds of experiences for children.
3. Try experimental programs and adapt them to the individual needs of students in their classes or reject them as educationally indefensible.
4. Combine elements of various programs and content with knowledge about individuals in classes.
5. Incorporate elements of newer programs into traditional ones even though they enter a school system where *tradition* rules.

6. Work for and participate in in-service programs to build background in mathematics and to improve teaching techniques and methods.
7. Develop evaluative criteria that eliminate the exclusive use of grades and tests as marks of mathematical understanding and achievement.
8. Grow in evaluating children on the basis of learning styles and behaviors so that they are better able to guide children and to prescribe "next steps" on the bases of individual analyses.

Health and Physical Education

Earlier in this book, we devoted considerable space to the importance of a good program of health and physical education as part of a total elementary school program. Parallel to the philosophy of the Greeks, Americans believe that a society gains strength through the physical and mental development of its citizens; but older programs lumped health and physical education together as though they were one and the same, often to the detriment of both.

Children enjoy physical education activities, need outdoor exercise during every school day whenever possible, and benefit from many exercises provided by games of noncompetitive nature as well as the healthy competition of intraclass and intramural sports. We have not discussed the importance and the significance of *play activities* in children's lives because we wish to give it special emphasis here. Children are, by their very nature, active and fun loving. By choice they will play games such as hopscotch, tag, kite flying, and imaginary drag racing in good weather and enjoy skating, sledding, fox-and-geese, or building snow men when there is snow and ice. Bike riding and roller skating are favorites, too, as are jumping rope, swinging, and sliding. The point we want to make here is that modern children's lives are often so routinized and supervised that there is little room for making choices. Individually and in groups, they will almost invariably choose healthy and personally satisfying activities when provided with a wide range of possibilities.

In addition, of course, teachers should consider the following guidelines for planning enjoyable and purposeful activities:

1. Teachers can develop a "game file" which includes suggested activities for developing specific physical skills appropriate for the age group.
2. Teachers should modify physical education programs so that they will fit the needs of children in each group, e.g., children who are physically immature, who have various handicaps, or who have excessive need for physical activity and large muscle exercise.
3. School staffs and each individual teacher need to give careful attention to correlating health and physical education with other subjects in both indoor and outdoor activities.

4. School staff members should place emphasis on developing qualities such as team work, fair play, personal health and cleanliness habits, individual responsibility, self-direction, and self-control.
5. Each teacher should create situations for children to share games and sports with others of different age levels.
6. Parents and children can be encouraged to share outdoor activities.
7. Teachers and children can plan jointly for alternating activities such as rhythmic movement, calisthenics, relays, large and small group games, and individual activities for sharing and rotating available playground equipment.
8. Teachers should see that activities such as running, walking, jumping, skipping, dancing, hopping, and other play activities are included in children's balanced programs of recreation.

Health and physical education are frequently mentioned together and are presented as one unit in most curriculum guides, but they are actually two separate areas of the curriculum. They are allied in that they have some common goals, but "each field can be distinguished from the other in behavioral objectives, content, learning activities, and procedures" (62). In some cases, scheduling them as one unit within one block of time has been detrimental to each one, for neither gets its full share of time or attention. Sometimes health education receives the emphasis because the teacher enjoys teaching it more than he does physical education; at other times physical education receives the major emphasis for the same reason. Actually, one of the reasons that health education and physical education have often been lumped together has been an assumption about staffing—that a person certified for physical education is also qualified to teach health education. This is not necessarily true, for the person may be neither qualified nor motivated to teach health education. In addition, to assign the important area of health education to a person who is already overburdened with other assignments is unreasonable.

Sliepcevich (63) has pointed out that in view of the multidisciplinary nature of health instruction, the enormity of the task of keeping up to date with the voluminous amount of new and changing scientific information, the needed skill in the use of a variety of teaching methods, and the need for knowledge of the location and use of a wealth of materials and other resources, a health education specialist really has a full-time occupation. And Smith (62) also points out that in many school systems where there are no organized health education programs, there is a tendency to develop fragmented programs.

Included in health education at the secondary level for some time now in most school systems have been alcohol education, smoking education, drug abuse education, safety education, venereal disease education, and sex education; and these have begun to seep down into elementary schools as parents and educators have realized that at middle and upper school levels such education may be "too little too late."

In a broad interpretation of health education, new curriculum developments during the past few years have emanated from local and state efforts. For example, the Denver Public Schools have developed a health education curriculum from findings of their studies about the detailed health interests of youngsters at different age levels. Their curriculum guidelines, *Health Interests of Children* (64) encourage teachers to use children's needs, interests, and questions as the bases for instruction and also provide stimulation for next steps in health education curriculum development.

Another major contribution is contained in the five-year *School Health Education Evaluation Study of the Los Angeles Area* (65). This study created greater willingness and desire for teachers and school administrators to put health education with all of its extensions at the center of curriculum innovation. It also recommended evaluation guidelines and gave a curriculum framework for others working elsewhere.

Goodlad (66) warned of the dilemmas education faces in curriculum reform movements in health education, physical education, and other curriculum content areas as teachers seek out fundamental concepts, keep up with and understand new facts as they develop at an ever-increasing rate, select from among facts and information those necessary for the education of children, and put them in the units where they logically belong: "The selection of the most significant bits of content no longer is difficult; it is impossible. Consequently teachers and pupils must seek out those fundamental concepts, principles, and methods that appear to be most useful for ordering and interpreting man's inquiries."

The scope of interest in health education studies can also be interpreted by the national interest that has been focused upon the conceptual approach to teaching health. One of these was completed by the Health Education Division, Curriculum Commission, American Association for Health, Physical Education, and Recreation (NEA). This group followed a plan of action to determine basic health concepts related to crucial health problems of school-age youngsters. The publication, *Health Concepts: Guides for Health Instruction* (67), provides a valuable guide and structure for local and state curriculum development efforts.

In fact, Ole Sand (68) describes its basic document as the most thorough analysis yet made of the field. He states, "It [the document] makes an important milestone in the progress and development of health education and is, therefore, of great interest to everyone concerned with curriculum and instruction."

It describes health as a "quality of life involving dynamic interaction and interdependence among the individual's physical well-being, his mental and emotional reactions, and the social complex of his existence." This is the concept that appears at the highest level of the conceptual structure. This definition of health, as a broad concept, includes physical, mental, and social dimensions which are typical of all of its generalized concepts.

The next level of the conceptual model focuses on three key concepts which characterize the processes underlying health and serve as unifying strands of the health curriculum. They are (69)

1. *Growing and Developing*—a dynamic life process by which the individual is in some ways like all other individuals, in some ways like some other individuals, and in some ways like no other individual.
2. *Interacting*—an ongoing process in which the individual is affected by and in turn affects certain biological, social, psychological, economic, cultural, and physical forces in the environment.
3. *Decision Making*—a process unique to man of consciously deciding whether or not to take an action or of choosing one alternative rather than another.

The following ten concepts serve at the next level as the major elements around which curriculum for health education is to be designed, as well as the scope of health education:

1. Growth and development influence and are influenced by the structure and functioning of the individual.
2. Growing and developing follow a predictable sequence, yet are unique for each individual.
3. Protection and promotion of health is an individual, community, and international responsibility.
4. The potential for hazards and accidents exists, whatever the environment.
5. There are reciprocal relationships involving man, disease, and the environment.
6. The family serves to perpetuate man and to fulfill certain health needs.
7. Personal health practices are affected by a complexity of forces, often conflicting.
8. Utilization of health information, products, and services is guided by values and perceptions.
9. Use of substances that modify mood and behavior arises from a variety of motivations.
10. Food selection and eating patterns are determined by physical, social, mental, economic, and cultural factors.

Influences in Curriculum Change (70) states that the "long-range goals for each of the ten concepts have been derived from the corresponding concept and subconcepts. They serve as general guides for the desired outcome of a sequential program in health education from kindergarten through grade twelve." It also says that both these goals and a group of more specific behavioral objectives can be stated in terms of three domains:

1. *The cognitive behaviors,* which include behaviors that pertain to "knowledge," "intellectual abilities," or "intellectual skills."
2. *The effective behaviors,* which refer to objectives that stress "a feeling tone," "an emotion," or a "degree of acceptance or rejection."
3. *Specific and operational objectives,* which are developed for each concept.

There are four levels of progression organized vertically so that the educational levels of the behavioral objectives and the content reflect the content and one another. They are also arranged horizontally so that the sequence of objectives at a given level also becomes apparent and thus the behavioral objectives represent the priority in desired competencies (71).

In the separation of *health education* and *physical education,* the emphasis in *physical education programs* has come to be stress on perceptual-motor training, physical education for the mentally retarded, and movement exploration. This stress has developed because of the significance of motor experiences in developing human intelligence and personality and in the preservation and extension of man's various cultures. Most educators believe that physical education is moving toward a healthy combination of emphases on participation, socialization, and physical fitness with increasing understanding of the interrelationships among man, his environment, and his movements.

The effects of early motor training for mentally retarded children have been forerunners of more research for children in regular preschool, kindergarten, and primary levels according to Rapp (72). He also says that it is

generally agreed that children grow and develop neurologically in a definite recognizable sequential pattern. Most of our instruments used to assess intellectual development at infancy and in young children are based on developmental inventories which sample the neuromotor areas of development and the early perceptive abilities of the child. Each state of neuromotor development serves as a base for further development. As the child explores the relationship of his perceptions—auditory, visual, tactile, and kinesthetic—a coordinated development takes place in his neuromotor system. The awareness, skills, and information are carried over from one developmental level to another and are further developed and utilized in the next stage of development. When there is an omission or an interruption in development, the next level of neuromotor organization will be affected. There is some evidence that many of the learning problems in children can be traced to this developmental omission or interruption. . . . The child's self-image is very important, for it determines how he interacts with others. His ability to perform common skills—his range of movement and body control—his body figure—all affect his confidence and his willingness to attempt new activities. Self-image is related to success and success is necessary for continued motivation, and therefore, must be built into the activity. Planned achievement should be one of our teaching techniques in working with all young children.

Very dramatic results have also been reported by Oliver and Corder (73) who have worked with mentally retarded boys. Through introducing systematic programs of physical education, the boys in the experimental groups in both of their studies improved significantly in emotional stability, medical evaluation, personality adjustment, and intellectual development as they improved in various physical aspects and tasks. A number of studies show that as children become educated physically, their physical, mental, and social competencies improve.

All of the recent studies about new emphases in physical education, with specialized stress on perceptual-motor training and movement exploration, seem to point toward the conclusion that training in motor experiences advance and enrich human intelligence, development of personality, and preservation of extension of various cultures (74).

Art Education

As child study has led educators to grow in understanding the cognitive development of children, as views have changed from seeing children as "little adults" to seeing them as developing organisms with needs and feelings of their own, and as psychologists have learned that a person grows "from the inside *out* rather than from the outside *in*," there have been corresponding changes in art education and in artistic learning, generally.

Emerging views during the early part of the twentieth century began to see "art activities" for their potential in releasing children's imagination and creativity, as well as mediums of nonverbal expression which provided another means of understanding more about children's emotions and talents. They also began to see that art education was a way to involve children in active, rather than passive, school experiences. But the teaching of art during this period can probably best be described as laissez-faire, because the teacher was a dispenser of art media with which children were to experiment and was to assume a passive motivational role.

Newer conceptions of art education give the teacher a more important and active role and are not limited to the *production* of an artistic piece. They also include, according to Eisner (75), "an awareness of the qualities of great works of art," "an understanding of the criteria that can be employed to appraise these works," and "respect for and appreciation of the culture out of which the work has emerged." He calls these areas, or aspects, of a modern art curriculum *the productive, the critical,* and *the historical aspects of art education.* These give the teacher an important responsibility for instruction in art and change curriculum emphases from art activities to *art education.*

As teachers' philosophies of education grow to include new views of learning, new views of the roles of teachers, and new views about the function of instruction, they are better able to incorporate the vast, untapped

As child study has led educators to grow in understanding the cognitive development of children, as views have changed from seeing children as "little adults" to seeing them as developing organisms with needs and feelings of their own, and as psychologists have learned that a person grows from the "inside out" rather than from the "outside in," there have been corresponding changes in art education and in artistic learning generally.

(Photo courtesy of Scandinavian Airlines System.)

potential available to them through the use of professional and semiprofessional artists and craftsmen who are not professional educators.

Remember the lay-professional projects developed in New City and
mentioned earlier? Like many other cities and areas, New City had a fine
university with an outstanding art department and art galleries; they
also had active arts groups and numerous artists and craftsmen. Typical
of so many large and small school systems, they had too few art teachers
who reached each group of children too seldom, and many of the regular
classroom teachers had had little or no training in art education. In the
initial phase of the program, the art teachers, selected classroom teachers,
and members of the curriculum department worked closely with a group
of professional and semiprofessional artists who formed a Visual Arts for
School Programs group. The stated purpose was to use artists with teachers
in elementary school classrooms to enrich the art curriculum through
various modes of artistic expression and through introductory experiences
in the history of art. Early exposure to art history and appreciation, teachers and volunteers agreed, would not only update the city's very inadequate programs, but would have three main purposes:

1. To heighten the student's perceptions of art in traditional forms and
   in the world around them.
2. To supplement the student's knowledge and interest in history and
   various cultures by making art more visual and thus more vital.
3. To make students aware of art as both vocation and avocation.

One phase of the program consisted of a series of slide lecture-discus-
sions for each fourth, fifth, and sixth grade in the city. Initially there were
three of these dealing with the development and changes in American
art forms from 1600 to the end of the colonial period, the Revolutionary
period, and the eighteenth and nineteenth centuries. Later, lecture-dis-
cussions were developed in architecture, twentieth-century art, pop art,
and sculpture. In advance of scheduled appearances by volunteers from
the Visual Arts group, teachers and volunteers developed suggested activity lists, word lists, and bibliographies which were circulated to each
classroom previous to the classroom sessions. "Art Goes to School" became
a very much praised and highly successful effort of school and community;
professional and semiprofessional artists who were, in addition to their
vocations and avocations, also often busy mothers and father, brought to
New City boys and girls valuable art education for which teachers agreed
they had neither the time nor the talent.

Earlier we discussed the importance of language as a cognitive tool,
as a means of sharing meanings and of communicating with one another.
Eisner (75) states that since language is, in part, "a window through which
we see the world" and that there are different languages such as "the
languages of poetry, biology, visual art, dance, and mathematics, for

example." He also says that in the "teaching of art it appears defensible and aesthetically relevant to enable the student to acquire linguistic tools through which to view the work. Terms such as value, intensity, composition, contour, volume, foreground, and the like stand for qualities to be perceived." While agreeing that these terms in no way are adequate to describe the qualities one finds in art, he nevertheless says that they do serve as reminders of what to "look for," and that linguistic tools encompass not only concepts but also "generalizations about the very nature of art."

Surely with the increasing amount of leisure time that citizens of today and tomorrow are having and will have, every teacher owes it to himself and his students to extend his own knowledge of art, of painters, sculptors, designers, various media and resources, and architects, and to participate himself in various art appreciation and production activities. It is this teacher who will either provide these experiences himself for his students or who will insist that his students have them in their curriculum, and it is this teacher who, because his own creative abilities and knowledge have been unleashed, will help others develop theirs.

Music Education

America is still a young nation in comparison with other, older world cultures. It is still in the process of adding aesthetic richness to the quality of its existence and building a fine arts culture of its own. We have mentioned the sharply increased concern and interest in the arts, and the philosophical foundations necessary in the fine arts if they are to make the kinds of contributions to society and to this society's culture, in particular, which are needed and wanted. The arts have never been held in higher regard in America than they are today, and as our society becomes more concerned with the *qualitative* aspects of living, they will continue to take on more significance.

Generally, efforts to extend and improve music education are centered on *improving musical understanding and appreciation* rather than the older emphases of improving each child's musical skill and techniques. As in other curriculum improvement efforts, music curriculum reform holds that understanding the nature and structure of music is what is of real importance. Music educators agree that the skills of execution do not necessarily assure musical understanding and that a skills-and-technique oriented curriculum is too specialized to be relevant to all students. Just as art education and other areas of the curriculum have swung their emphasis from the mere manipulation of materials without concern for insight into the nature of the subject, so music education has changed its attitudes about *performance* as the only desired end product of instruction in music. Old assumptions about the efficacy of performance in developing musical sensitivity are being seriously questioned, and old attitudes of unconcern about the classroom teaching of music are being re-examined (76).

One major contribution to the field of modern music education illustrates the shifting interest of MENC (Music Educators National Conference) and is typical of efforts to define essential musical skills, understandings, and attitudes which should be a part of the general education of every individual—*Music in General Education* (77). This is not a curriculum guide nor is it a curriculum, but it does give specific kinds of examples of the experiences that contribute to each child's developing understanding, appreciation, and competence in music. Raising each child's sensitivity level is really the generalized goal of most of the newer music education programs today. In this publication, performance groups are not eliminated but are seen as one of the ways to help each person who is able to perform in groups or individually raise his own sensitivity level.

A few experimental programs at the elementary school level will serve to illustrate some of the avant garde thinking and action that is taking place around the country:

1. The Juilliard School of Music, believing that the quality of music that children study affects the quality of the musical experiences they have and that present material used in elementary schools is often of questionable quality, has attempted to collect music of high quality from each period of history and arrange it appropriately for children from kindergarten through sixth grade. Included in the collection are works from Medieval and Renaissance periods as well as works especially commissioned by contemporary composers. There are songs and instrumental selections; one of the contemporary commissioned pieces, as an example, is written for an elementary school band and is accompanied by taped electronic sounds of very experimental nature. These materials are being tested in selected school systems for appropriateness and complexity (78).
2. A project at the University of Illinois attempted to
    a. Identify the behaviors which go into perceptive listening to music.
    b. Use the theory of expectation postulated by Leonard B. Meyer in *Emotion and Meaning in Music* (79) as a means of structuring listening responses.
    c. Try four different approaches to teaching listening in the fifth grade.

    The list of elements that were considered essential for perceptive listening include: recognizing imitation, rhythmic motives, thematic use of melody, dissonance and consonance, the major forms, and other listening responses.

    Using music from the classical period, four approaches were devised for experimental purposes: (1) Meyer's theory of expectation with stress on form, (2) general textbook statements with stress on factual knowledge, (3) a textbook approach with stress on aural skills, and (4) textbook approach with stress on keyboard experiences.

When children were tested it was learned that none of the four approaches had an advantage over any other one, and the general conclusion was that the approach itself was not as important as a higher level of musicianship for classroom teachers and for music specialists with emphasis on *teaching listening* (80).

Obviously, once again, the classroom teacher cannot be all things to all people; nor will there ever be enough qualified music specialists to do a thoroughly professional job for every child in every classroom. The average classroom teacher can, and must, improve his knowledge and sensitivity to music and to the other fine arts so that he is in a position to provide, through the use of professional and semiprofessional musicians who are not necessarily certified teachers, appropriate musical experiences for children.

The authors believe that sensitivity training in music, art, dance, and other fine arts is so important that schools in general, and individual teachers in particular, should be willing to bring to bear the talents of every qualified educator together with varieties of talented professional and semiprofessional artists who are not certified teachers but who have a great wealth of talent and insight to bring to boys and girls during their formative years. There are many exemplary and experimental programs throughout the country to indicate that this is beginning to happen, and we feel that this is a thoroughly defensible and practical way to ensure for today's children a share of aesthetic sensitivity which is going to become more and more central and necessary to the education of tomorrow's citizens.

Looking at Future Curriculum Design

In the examples of curriculum emphases and content that we have discussed here and elsewhere in this book, we have tried to show the shape of outstanding present-day curriculum trends and forces that augur future curriculum designs. Future elementary school curriculum will give almost equal weight to three main characteristics, we believe. In order to meet the needs of children and the needs of changing times, every child must be provided with opportunities for

Growth in personal development and self-understanding.
Growth in intellectual and aesthetic sensitivities.
Current knowledge and organized curriculum content.

As concepts of curriculum organization have changed from emphasis on prepackaged, drill-and-grill varieties to be *received* by children and *administered* by teachers to healthy emphasis on combinations of self-direction, self-selection, and organized subject matter content, the professional teacher has an enormous challenge in being able to design appropriate curriculum experiences for each individual child. Group teaching does not mean the same experience for every child, nor does individualization omit the significant contribution to be made by some group learning; rather, new curriculum requirements include healthy combinations of working alone and in large and small groups, having opportunities to use new media for content and skill acquisition, and having available to each child teachers who are thoroughly knowledgeable in the psychological, sociological, and philosophical forces at work in their own and children's lives.

Professional teachers will be helped continuously by new content and organizational input, but the present trend to provide curriculum outlines composed of generalizations, concepts, and facts from which individual teachers and students select alternative units and sequences is a healthy one. As knowledge and facts change (and we have said before that nothing is so certain as change), teachers can make the necessary and corresponding changes in curriculum. As larger spectrums of content are available, teachers must develop alternative paths that depend upon each child and his needs and interests.

The teacher of the future will have at his fingertips many more possibilities for helping children locate and use alternative routes to personal and intellectual development. There will be new media as yet undreamed of, and the knowledgeable teacher, with the help of a wide array of technologists and other professional specialists, will be able to accomplish what has never yet been accomplished in education, the *real* education best tailored to every individual's personality and potential. *Continuous progress* for each child at all times can become a reality, and no child need ever be alienated, unskilled, unloved, unwanted, or uneducable. Teachers who are well trained and who know children best will be the ones who design individual programs, ensure continuous progress, are responsible for a child's successes rather than his failures and retardations, keep up to date on children's learning experiences and needs, understand children emotionally and socially, and provide the wherewithal for intellectual stimulation and accomplishment based on individual assessments.

The school of the future can provide a much more complete spectrum of learning opportunities and a much better diagnosis of learner's needs and motivations. With these greater assets we may be able to match learners and opportunities as well as to achieve in practice a wonderful bit of Goethe's philosophy: *If you treat an individual as he is, he will stay as he is; if you treat him as he ought to be and could be, he will become what he ought to be and could be* (81).

Educational possibilities have never been so challenging. There are many psychological, sociological, and philosophical hypotheses waiting for better teachers and better teaching now!

References

30. Daley, Leo Charles, *Philosophy of Education*. New York: Monarch Press, 1966.
31. Lindsey, Margaret, "Preservice Training for Creativity in Teaching," *Creativity in Teaching*. Edited by Alice Miel. Belmont, Calif.: Wadsworth Publishing Company, Inc., 1961.
32. Torrance, E. P., "Education and Creativity," *Creativity: Progress and Potential*. Edited by C. W. Taylor. New York: McGraw-Hill Book Company, 1964.
33. Gallagher, James J., *Teaching the Gifted Child*. Boston: Allyn and Bacon, Inc., 1964.
34. Bish, Charles E., in the preface of *Productive Thinking in Education*. Edited by Ascher and Bish. The National Education Association and the Carnegie Corporation of New York, 1965. (NEA Library of Congress Catalog No. 65-25621.)
35. Cremin, Lawrence A., *The Genius of American Education*. Pittsburgh: University of Pittsburgh Press, 1965.
36. Daley, Leo Charles, *Philosophy of Education*. New York: Monarch Press, 1966.
37. Gordon, Ira J., Chairman and Editor, *Theories of Instruction*. Washington, D.C.: Association for Supervision and Curriculum Development, 1968.
38. Frances, W. Nelson, "Revolution in Grammar," *Readings in Applied English Linguistics*. Edited by Harold B. Allen. New York: Appleton-Century-Crofts, 1958.
39. Witty, Paul, and Paul Kinsella, "Televiewing: Some Observations from Studies 1949–1962," *Elementary English*, Vol. XXXIX, December, 1962.
40. Nichols, Ralph T., and Leonard A. Stevens, *Are You Listening?* New York: McGraw-Hill Book Company, 1957.
41. Canfield, G. Robert, "How Useful Are Lessons in Listening?" *Elementary School Journal*, December, 1961.
42. Trivette, Sue E., "The Effect of Training in Listening for Specific Purposes," *Journal of Educational Research*, March, 1961.
43. Noell, Doris L., "A Comparative Study of the Relationship between the Quality of Children's Language Usage and the Quality and Type of Language Used in the Home," *Journal of Educational Research*, November, 1953.
44. Smith, Henry Lee, Jr., "Linguistic Science and the Teaching of English," in *Inglis Lectures—1954*. Cambridge, Mass.: Harvard University Press, 1958.

45. Strickland, Ruth G., *The Language of Elementary School Children: Its Relationship to the Language of Reading Textbooks and the Quality of Reading of Selected Children.* Bulletin of the School of Education, Vol. 38, No. 4, Bloomington, Indiana University, 1962.

46. Loban, Walter D., *The Language of Elementary School Children.* Research Report No. I, Champaign, Ill., National Council of Teachers of English, 1963.

47. Mackintosh, Helen K., Editor of *Children and Oral Language* (a joint statement of Association for Childhood Education International, Association for Supervision and Curriculum Development, International Reading Association, and the National Council of Teachers of English). Washington, D.C.: U.S. Office of Education, 1964.

48. Calitrini, Charles J., "The Nature and Values of Culturally Different Youth," *Improving English Skills of Culturally Different Youth.* Washington, D.C.: U.S. Office of Education, 1964.

49. *Generalizations from the Social Sciences.* From the Report of the State Central Committee on Social Studies to the California State Curriculum Commission. Sacramento: California State Department of Education, 1961.

50. Thier, Herbert D., "The Involvement of Children in the Science Program," *Science and Children,* Vol. 2, February, 1965.

51. Atkin, J. M., and R. Karpus, "Discovery or Invention?" *The Science Teacher,* September, 1942.

52. Karpus, R., "Science in the Elementary School," *Science Curriculum Improvement Study Newsletter.* Berkeley: University of California, January, 1966.

53. Blackwood, Paul E., "Science Teaching in the Elementary School," *Elementary Education.* Edited by Maurie Hillson. New York: The Free Press, 1967.

54. Based on an unpublished committee report of the American Association for the Advancement of Science, Conference on Science for the Elementary and Junior High School, Cornell University, Ithaca, N.Y. Quoted in Blackwood (ref. 53), p. 139.

55. Deans, Edwina, *Elementary School Mathematics: New Directions.* Washington, D.C.: U.S. Office of Education, 1963.

56. Combs, Arthur W., "New Ideas About Personality Theory and Its Implications for Curriculum Development," *Learning More About Learning.* Washington, D.C.: Association for Supervision and Curriculum Development, 1959.

57. Ispen, D. C., *Coordinates—An Introduction to the Use of Graphs and Equations to Describe Physical Behavior.* Berkeley: University of California, 1960. A monograph.

58. Sawyer, W. W., *Math Patterns in Science.* Columbus, Ohio: American Education Publications, Education Center, 1960.

59. Wright, Betty Atwell, *Who's Too Young for Mathematics?* Doylestown, Pa.: Bucks County Office of Education, 1962.

60. California State Department of Education, *Looking Ahead in Mathematics* and *Reports on Regional Conferences on Improving Mathematics Instruction in Elementary Schools.* Sacramento, Calif., The Department, 1961.

61. National Council of Teachers of Mathematics, *The Revolution in School*

Mathematics: A Challenge for Administrators and Teachers. Washington, D.C.: The National Council of Teachers of Mathematics, 1961.

62. Smith, Lester V., "Changes in Health Education and Physical Education," *Influences in Curriculum Change.* Washington, D.C.: Association for Supervision and Curriculum Development, 1968.

63. Sliepcevich, Elena M., "The Responsibility of the Physical Educator for Health Instruction," *Journal of Health, Physical Education, and Recreation,* January, 1964.

64. Denver Public Schools, *Health Interests of Children.* Rev. Ed. Denver, Col.: Board of Education, 1954.

65. Johns, Edward B., "School Health Education Evaluative Study, Los Angeles Area: An Example of a Modern Evaluation Plan," *Journal of School Health,* January, 1962.

66. Goodlad, John I., *Some Propositions in Search of Schools.* Washington, D.C.: National Education Association, 1962.

67. American Association for Health, Physical Education, and Recreation, *Health Concepts: Guides for Health Instruction.* Washington, D.C.: The American Association for Health, Education, and Recreation, 1967.

68. Sand, Ole, "Foreword," *Health Education: A Conceptual Approach to Curriculum Design.* School Health Study, St. Paul, Minn.: 3M Education Press, 1967.

69. Edited version of a presentation made by Anne E. Nolte, Associate Director, School Health Education Study at the Fourth National Curriculum Conference, "Curriculum Designing for the Future," ASCD, New York, December, 1966.

70. Unruh, G. G., and Leeper, P. R. (eds.), *Influences in Curriculum Change.* Washington, D.C.: Association for Supervision and Curriculum Development, 1968.

71. Information here is adapted from the book, *Health Education: A Conceptual Approach to Curriculum Design.* St. Paul, Minn.: 3M Education Press, 1967 (School Health Education Study).

72. Rapp, William E., Consultant in Physical Education and Recreation, The Joseph P. Kennedy, Jr., Foundation, in a presentation at the ASCD Fourth National Curriculum Conference, New York, December 2, 1966.

73. Reported in Frank Hayden's *Physical Fitness for the Mentally Retarded.* Toronto, Canada: Metropolitan Toronto Association for Retarded Children, 1964.

74. Allenbaugh, Naomi, "Learning About Movement," *NEA Journal,* March, 1967.

75. Eisner, Elliot W., "Knowledge, Knowing, and the Visual Arts," *Harvard Educational Review,* Spring, 1963.

76. Reimer, Bennett, "New Curriculum Developments in Music Education," *Influences in Curriculum Change.* Washington, D.C.: Association for Supervision and Curriculum Development, 1968.

77. Ernst, Karl D., and Charles Gray (eds.), *Music in General Education.* Washington, D.C.: Music Educators National Conference and the National Education Association, 1965.

78. Juilliard School of Music, *An Enlarged Music Repertory from Kindergarten Through Grade Six.* New York: Juilliard School of Music.

79. Meyer, Leonard B., *Emotion and Meaning in Music*. Chicago: University of Chicago Press, 1956.
80. University of Illinois, "Development and Trial in Public Schools of a Three-Year Program in Music Education Based upon the Theory of Expectation," Urbana, Ill.: University of Illinois, 1962.
81. Alexander, William M., "Shaping Curriculum: Blueprint for a New School," *Influences in Curriculum Change*. Washington, D.C.: Association for Supervision and Curriculum Development, 1968.

INDEX